The News That Didn't Make the News—and Why

The 1995 Project Censored Yearbook

CARL JENSEN & PROJECT CENSORED

INTRODUCTION BY MICHAEL CRICHTON

CARTOONS BY TOM TOMORROW

FOUR WALLS EIGHT WINDOWS

NEW YORK/LONDON

Copyright © 1995 by Carl Jensen.
Introduction © 1995 by Michael Crichton.

A FOUR WALLS EIGHT WINDOWS FIRST EDITION

Censored: the news that didn't make the news and why
ISSN 1074-5998

10 9 8 7 6 5 4 3 2 1

FOUR WALLS EIGHT WINDOWS
39 West 14th Street, #503
New York, New York, 10011

Designed by Cindy LaBreacht

To my Wife
Sandra Scott Jensen
who has given up much
so that Project Censored
could grow

Table of Contents

"Whatever is covered up
will be uncovered
and every secret will
be made known."
—Luke 12:2

PREFACE

Raking Muck, Raising Hell

CENSORED! The News That Didn't Make The News—And Why is published annually in response to a growing national demand for news and information not published nor broadcast by the mainstream media in America.

Originally self-published by Project Censored as a spiral bound resource book, the 1995 Project Censored Yearbook is published by Four Walls Eight Windows of New York. As in the five previous Yearbooks (1990-1994), *CENSORED!* features the top 25 *Censored* stories of the year, background information about Project Censored, comments about the top 25 stories by the original authors and others, brief synopses of each of the stories, and a chapter on the top "junk food news" stories, with comments by the news ombudsmen who selected them.

This edition also includes a special introduction, titled "Mediasaurus," by Michael Crichton; a déjà vu chapter of previously censored stories that finally have been "discovered" by the mainstream media; an updated eclectic chronology of censorship since 605 BC which attempts to put the whole issue into historical context; and an annually updated censored resource guide to alternative media organizations, electronic and print alternative media, and selected mainstream media sources.

The Alternative Writer's Market, which was introduced in the 1994 Yearbook, has been updated and expanded. It provides brief information about publications that are open to the work of alternative journalists.

In response to an increasing number of nominations of books which failed to attract the attention of major publishers, let alone the chain booksellers, we have added a new chapter to CENSORED! this year. Chapter 3, Censored Books, provides a modest, but intriguing, insight into some of the books nominated by alternative publishers and others. We hope you enjoy this addition.

Also, as before, this edition contains complete reprints of the original top 10 Censored articles wherever possible. You'll be able to review the brief synopsis of the story, see what the author has to say about the subject, and then read the original article in its entirety.

The synopses are originally written by Project Censored researchers participating in a seminar in news media censorship offered by the Communication Studies Department at Sonoma State University, a member of the California State University system. They are then edited for style and clarity. The synopses are not meant to replace the original articles upon which they are based, but rather to briefly summarize the major thrust of a much longer article or, in some cases, a brochure or book.

CENSORED! The News That Didn't Make The News—And Why is another effort by Project Censored to provide information on important issues the public should know about. I hope you will learn more about issues that touch your life, your community and, in a larger context, the global village of which we are all citizens.

I also hope that it will disturb you to discover that all this information was available to the press and that you will wonder why your local and national news media haven't already told you about these subjects.

I would like to invite you to become a news muckraker by joining Project Censored as a scout or source for stories that deserve more attention from the mainstream media. Please see the postscript for information on how to nominate stories for the "Best Censored News Stories of 1995."

Project Censored is flattered when we are referred to as a muckraking organization with goals similar to those who gave birth to the Golden Age of Muckraking from 1902 to 1912. However, we hasten to point out that the true muckrakers are the individual journalists who are responsible for the articles cited as censored stories. Project Censored is better compared to the irritating grain of sand in an oyster.

Our role is to stimulate journalists, editors, producers, and publishers to support more muckraking investigative journalism. Unfortunately, despite a slight blip in the aftermath of Watergate, journalism has failed to fulfill its watchdog role as exemplified during the Golden Age of Muckraking.

Indeed, while the United States is without equal in terms of communications technology, it would appear that it has suffered a massive breakdown when it comes to communications content. While we may have a free press and the most sophisticated communications system in the world, unfortunately a free press and high technology do not guarantee a well-informed society.

As a society, we are exposed to more information now than ever before in history. Thanks to recent advances in communications technology followed by the current explosion in computer sciences, the average citizen today is exposed to more information, at a greater speed, from throughout the world, than was available to our country's leaders not too many years ago. CNN viewers in Keokuk, Iowa, were probably more quickly informed of what was happening during the events in Haiti than the President of the United States was of events in Vietnam during that conflict.

Like the horse and buggy, the agricultural and industrial ages are far behind us; we are hurtling headlong into the information age. All indicators support this thesis—from the diversity of information sources to the sophistication of communications technology to the amount of time people spend with the media.

But the problem is not with the quantity of information available in our society, which sometimes seems to reach an overload level, but rather with the quality of that information.

For example, when something starts to go wrong in your personal life, there generally are some warning signals that alert you to the problem. If you are a rational person, you normally act upon that information in an effort to solve the problem.

So too, it is with a society. When a problem arises, there should be a warning signal—information—that alerts citizens that something is wrong which needs attention and resolution. An aware and informed populace could then influence its leaders to act upon that information in an effort to solve the problem. This, unfortunately, is not the case in the United States.

I suspect there are few people who do not believe that the United States has serious problems that need to be resolved if we are to succeed and survive in the future. Yet, how many of us are fully aware of the scope of these problems and how many of us have all the information we need to deal with them?

Despite the quantity of news and information being disseminated around the clock, you and some 250 million other Americans are not being told everything you have a need and right to know. And, without full information about the affairs of our society, we cannot function as good citizens.

It is not realistic to expect anything to change, in America or in your community, until enough people lean out their windows and shout: "I'm mad as hell and I'm not going to take it any more!"

But, for that to happen, we need someone out there raking muck and raising hell. This of course should be the role of a free press—but the media are selling us short. Instead they have become the willing tools of the propagandists that Jacques Ellul warned us about in *Propaganda: The Formation of Men's Attitudes*, in 1965—propagandists so skilled we are not even aware of being manipulated.

The point is that our primary sources of news and information are increasingly being controlled by a very small group of men—supporting the thesis that an elite group has gained control over the information industry in the United States. As media scholar Ben Bagdikian points out in the latest edition (1992) of *The Media Monopoly*, his classic critique of corporate media control, fewer than 20 corporations now control most of the nation's mass media.

The next step in the information control process in America is to use this control to effectively exploit our minds. This, also, it seems, has been accomplished. The mind manipulators are well aware of the first principle of successful mind control—repetition.

To be successful, as Jacques Ellul wrote, propaganda must be continuous and lasting—continuous in that it must not leave any gaps, but must fill the citizen's whole day and all his days; lasting in that it must function over a long period of time.

Today's information industry learned this lesson well from Adolph Hitler who so successfully used propaganda in his quest for power. More than a half century ago Hitler said the masses take a long time to understand and remember, thus it is necessary to repeat the message time and time and time again—the public must be conditioned to accept the claims that are made...no matter how outrageous or false those claims might be.

We, as a society, appear to have been well-conditioned to accept any number of claims regardless of how detrimental they may be to our environment or to our own well-being.

The Madison Avenue propagandists use the same techniques to sell us products and services we don't need and often can't afford. Repetition is also the key to success on Madison Avenue. Propaganda tends to make an individual live in a separate world, a world lacking outside points of reference. You must not be allowed time for meditation or reflection in which to see or define yourself as might occur when the propaganda is not continuous. For if propaganda is not continuous, you might have a moment or two when you can emerge from its grip and realize you have been manipulated.

Finally, to assure complete compliance with the propagandistic techniques, to close the information control loop, to prevent you from finding external points of reference which might cause you to question the propagandists' messages, the information industry insulates you by censoring anything contradictory, any dissonant messages that might come in from the outside.

Since 1976, I have been conducting a national media research project which seeks to locate and publicize those dissonant messages, messages the media elite don't want the rest of us to know about.

PROJECT CENSORED LAUNCHED

Concerned about increasing social problems and apparent public apathy, I launched a national research effort in 1976, called Project Censored, to explore whether there really is a systematic omission of certain issues in our national news media. My concern was specifically stimulated by personal bewilderment over how the American people could elect Richard Nixon by a landslide more than four months *after* Watergate, one of the most sensational political crimes of the century. (For an insight into how the mass media failed the electorate in that election, see the 1972 Watergate reference in Chapter 6, "An Eclectic Chronology of Censorship from 605 B.C. to 1995.")

Project Censored is now an internationally renowned media research project in its 19th year. By exploring and publicizing stories of national importance on issues that have been overlooked or under-reported by the mainstream news media, the project seeks to stimulate journalists and editors to provide more mass media coverage of those issues. It also hopes to encourage the general public to seek out and demand more information on significant issues.

Since its start, the research effort has generated queries for more information about the project as well as about individual stories from journalists, scholars, and concerned people throughout the world. It has been described as a tip sheet for investigative television programs like "60 Minutes" and "20/20," as a distant early warning system for society's problems, and even as a "moral force" in American media, as cited by media columnist David Armstrong in the *Washington Journalism Review*, July 1983. The National Association for Education in Journalism and Mass Communication cited the project for "providing a new model for media criticism for journalism education."

Concerned with the increasing attempts at censorship in our public schools and on college campuses since the Supreme Court's 1988 *Hazelwood* decision, Project Censored conducts a national educational outreach program specifically developed for journalism teachers, advisors, and students. The objective of this program is to offer stimulating resource materials to student journalists in an effort to broaden discussion, understanding, and response to the threat of news media self-censorship.

In response to the many tips and suggestions the Project receives concerning issues that might well be of interest to investigative journalists, we developed a "CENSORED TIPS" program. As news tips are received, they are summarized and sent out to media and journalism organizations who have the resources to investigate them. Some of the "tips" sent out in 1994 included information about a giant utility that attempted to blackmail the public, a university laboratory leaking radiation into the air, a super-secret U.S. foreign intelligence court with a perfect record, the secretive but influential Business Roundtable lobby, and the little-known 71-year-old Rosewood racial massacre.

Project Censored Canada was launched in 1994 with the support and counsel of Project Censored. The Canadian Association of Journalists, located in Ottawa, Ontario, and the communication department at Simon Fraser University, in Burnaby, British Columbia, jointly initiated Project Censored Canada. The project explores issues and events that do not receive the coverage they deserve in the Canadian media.

The Canadian effort originated with Bill Doskoch, a journalist with the *Leader-Post*, in Regina, Saskatchewan, and is coordinated by Dr. Bob Hackett, associate professor, and Don Gutstein, lecturer, both with the Department of Communication at Simon Fraser University.

Another Project Censored-inspired effort is Bay Area Censored, a regional project sponsored by the Media Alliance, an association of more than 3,000 San Francisco Bay Area media professionals. It has successfully explored and exposed scores of undercovered stories in the Bay Area and will conduct its fifth research effort in 1995.

THE CENSORED RESEARCH PROCESS

Researchers who participate in the censorship seminar (taught each fall semester at Sonoma State University, in Rohnert Park, California) have reviewed thousands of stories over the past 19 years that many Americans have not seen or heard about—but should have. The stories are nominated annually by journalists, scholars, librarians, and the general public from across the United States and abroad.

From the hundreds of articles submitted each year, the seminar researchers select the top 25 stories according to a number of criteria including the amount of coverage the story received, the national or international importance of the issue, the reliability of the source, and the potential impact the story may have. Next, the top 25 *Censored* stories are submitted in synopsis form to a panel of judges who select the top ten stories of the year.

Some of the judges who have participated in the project in the past include Hodding Carter, Shirley Chisholm, John Kenneth Galbraith, Charlayne Hunter-Gault, James J. Kilpatrick, Robert MacNeil, Mary McGrory, John McLaughlin, Jessica Mitford, Bill Moyers, George Seldes, Susan Sontag, Alvin Toffler, and Mike Wallace. This year's judges are cited later in the acknowledgments.

Before examining why some issues are overlooked—what we call "censored"—and why other issues are over-covered—what we call "junk food news"—we must define what we mean by censored.

WHAT IS CENSORSHIP?

Censorship has a long and scurrilous history which started at least two millennia before the invention of the printing press, as noted in the chronology found in Chapter 6.

A brief review of definitions offered by more traditional sources provides an insight into the problems surrounding the censorship issue. The definitions seem to be as varied and numerous as there are scholars, politicians, and lexicographers eager to address the subject.

When I started Project Censored in 1976, I developed an alternative definition of censorship. Rather than starting with the source of censorship as traditionally defined—with the obligation of an elite to protect the masses (the classic "we know what's best for the people and they're better off without this information" syndrome)—my definition starts at the other end—with the failure of information to reach the people.

Expanding on this foundation, following is our alternative definition of censorship as originally offered in 1976:

First, we assume that real and meaningful public involvement in societal decisions is possible only if a wide array of ideas are allowed to compete daily in the media marketplace for public awareness, acceptance, and understanding.

Next, we realize that the mass media, particularly the network TV evening news programs, are the public's primary sources of information for what is happening in the world.

If, however, the public does not receive all the information it needs to make informed decisions, then some form of news blackout is taking place.

In brief, then, for the purposes of this project, censorship is defined as the suppression of information, whether purposeful or not, by any method—including bias, omission, under-reporting, or self-censorship—which prevents the public from fully knowing what is happening in the world.

WHY ARE SOME ISSUES OVERLOOKED?

One of the questions often asked of Project Censored is why doesn't the press cover the issues raised by the research. The failure of the news media to cover critical and sometimes controversial issues consistently and com-

prehensively is not, as some say, a conspiracy on the part of the media elite. News is too diverse, fast-breaking, and unpredictable to be controlled by some sinister conservative Eastern establishment media cabal.

However, there are a variety of factors operating that, when combined, lead to the systematic failure of the news media to fully inform the public. While it is not an overt form of censorship, such as the kind we observe in some other societies, it is nonetheless real and often equally dangerous.

The traditional explanations, or excuses, for censorship are plentiful. Sometimes a source for a story isn't considered to be reliable; other times the story doesn't have an easily identifiable "beginning, middle, and end;" some stories are considered to be "too complex" for the general public; on occasion stories are ignored because they haven't been "blessed" by *The New York Times* or *The Washington Post*. (Reporters and editors at most of the other 1650 daily newspapers know their news judgment isn't going to be challenged when they produce and publish fashionable "follow-the-leader" stories, a practice which leads to the "pack" or "herd" phenomenon in journalism.)

Another major factor contributing to media self-censorship is that the story is considered potentially libelous. There is no question that long and costly jury trials, and sometimes multi-million-dollar judgments against the media, have produced a massive chilling effect on the press and replaced copy editors with copy attorneys.

Nonetheless, the bottom line explanation for much of the censorship that occurs in the mainstream media is the media's own bottom line. Corporate media executives perceive their primary, and often sole, responsibility to be the need to maximize profits, not, as some would have it, to

inform the public. Many of the stories cited by Project Censored are not in the best financial interests of publishers, owners, stockholders, or advertisers. Equally important, investigative journalism is more expensive than the "public stenography" school of journalism. And, of course, there is always the "don't rock the boat" mentality which pervades corporate media boardrooms and filters on down to the newsroom.

Real news is not repetitive, sensationalistic coverage of events such as the O.J. Simpson trial, or Michael Jackson's wedding to Lisa Marie Presley, or the baseball strike, or the sexual dalliances of Diana and Charles, or the truly unforgettable introduction of the Wonder Bra! These are examples of what I call "Junk Food News" as described in Chapter 5.

By contrast, real news is objective and reliable information about important events that affect the lives and well-being of the public. The widespread dissemination of such information helps people become better informed, and a better informed public can elect politicians who are more responsive to its needs.

WOULD IT MAKE ANY DIFFERENCE?

Finally, there is yet another question that is often asked about the project. Would it really make any difference if the press were to provide more coverage of the kinds of stories cited by Project Censored?

The answer is very simple: yes. But first, we must address the issue of public apathy. Critics of Project Censored say that the media give the public what it wants, i.e. "junk food news," because people are not interested in reading about the issues raised by Project Censored. We counter this by suggesting that the public is not given the opportunity to read those stories in the mainstream media and thus, unfortunately, will read or watch what the mass media do offer. At the height of the O.J. Simpson affair in 1994, the media delighted in reporting poll after poll that revealed that most American's were closely following the case. In truth, what other choice did the American readers and viewers have?

We suggest that it is the media's responsibility, as watchdogs of society with the unique protection of the First Amendment, to explore, compile, and present information that people should be aware of in a way that will attract their attention and be relevant to their everyday lives. And, when the media do this, people will read and respond to the issues raised. There is, indeed, a genuine desire on the part of the public to know more about issues that truly affect them. Your interest in this book confirms that.

But then, the question remains, would it make any difference if people were better informed?

Hunger in Africa was consistently nominated as a "censored" subject during the early 1980s. When I would ask journalists why they did not cover the tragedy unfolding there, they would say: "It is not news," or, "Everyone already knows about starving Africans," or "Nothing can be done about it anyway."

Early in 1984, an ABC-TV News correspondent in Rome came upon information that led him to believe that millions of lives were being threatened by drought and famine in Africa. He asked the home office in New York for permission to take his crew to Africa to get the story. The answer, based on costs, was no.

Later, a BBC television crew traveling through Ethiopia, captured the stark reality of children starving to death. People throughout the world saw the coverage and responded. Overnight, it sparked a world-wide reaction that reportedly saved the lives of seven million Ethiopians. Indeed, the media can make a difference.

The press has the power to stimulate people to clean up the environment; to prevent nuclear proliferation; to force corrupt politicians out of office; to reduce poverty; to provide quality health care for all people; to create a truly equitable society; and, as we have seen, to literally save the lives of millions of human beings.

And this is why we must look to, prod, and support a free, open, and aggressive press. We have a constitutionally guaranteed free press in the United States and we have the best communications technology in the world. Now let us seek a more responsible and responsive press—a press that truly earns its First Amendment rights. Indeed, a press not afraid to do a little muckraking. Then, and only then, will we all have the information we need to build a more enlightened and responsive society.

—Carl Jensen
Cotati, California

Acknowledgments

The first acknowledgment must go to all our *Censored* colleagues who contribute to the success of Project Censored by sending us stories as nominations. We receive some 700 nominations annually from journalists, educators, librarians, and many others who are concerned with the public's right to know. We truly are grateful to all of you who bring those stories to our attention.

Another group critical to the success of the project are the Sonoma State University students who participate as *Censored* researchers in the annual Project Censored seminar. It is their responsibility to analyze the hundreds of nominations received in order to determine whether they qualify as censored stories of the year. Following are the SSU students who evaluated the *Censored* nominations of 1994:

PROJECT CENSORED RESEARCHERS OF 1994

William Beaubien, Stephen Beckner, Jennifer Burns,
Paul Giusto, Lisa Golding, Billy Hawes,
Susan Kashack, Kate Kauffman, Dave Lake, Marilyn Leon,
Jessica Nystrom, Scott Oehlerking, Lori Stone, Dan Tomerlin

Many other groups and individuals contribute to the success of Project Censored, not the least of which are the publications, mostly from the alternative media, that publicize the annual results and the many radio and television news and talk show hosts who discuss the *Censored* stories each year.

A special thanks goes to our colleagues at the Media Alliance in San Francisco, who are now into their fifth year of Bay Area Censored, and to

Bill Doskoch, of the Canadian Association of Journalists, and Bob Hackett and Don Gutstein, of Simon Fraser University, who launched Project Censored Canada in 1994.

We also wish to acknowledge the support we receive from Sonoma State University including its president, Ruben Armiñana; Alan Murray, Director of Entrepreneurial Services; Mark Resmer, Associate Vice President for Information Technology; and Brian Wilson, a systems specialist with the Computer and Information Science Department, who has wrought miracles in getting our system up and running.

There are five organizations that deserve special recognition. The interest, encouragement, and financial support from the C.S. Fund, of Freestone, California; Anita Roddick and the Body Shop Foundation, of England; The John D. and Catherine T. MacArthur Foundation, of Chicago; The Angelina Fund, of New York; and the Threshold Foundation, of San Francisco, contribute significantly to the successful outreach of Project Censored.

Also, if it were not for support from these foundations, we would not have an assistant director, Mark Lowenthal, who helps me run the Project, nor a research associate, Amy S. Cohen, working with us. Among many other activities, they are responsible for responding to the thousands of letters and phone calls we receive from people throughout the country and abroad each year. Amy is in charge of the *Censored* outreach program which is designed to serve journalism professors and students across the country and she also compiled and updated this year's resource guide and Alternative Writer's Market. I'm also grateful to both Mark and Amy for the time they spent reviewing and editing this manuscript. Tina Duccini, majoring in rhetoric and political science at the University of California, Berkeley, also joined us as a research associate this year and has made a significant contribution to the impact of the Project.

I am indebted to Dan Simon, John Oakes and their colleagues at Four Walls Eight Windows, in New York, for having the faith and fortitude to take on a subject that the conglomerate publishers rejected. For the same reasons, I appreciate the support and help of my literary agent, Michael Larson.

I want to especially thank my wife, Sandra Scott Jensen, for the many hours she spent reviewing early versions of this document and for all the support and encouragement she has given me and Project Censored since its start in 1976. Once again we observed a *Censored* Thanksgiving, Christmas, and New Year's Day.

MICHAEL CRICHTON—"MEDIASAURUS"

I am also indebted to Michael Crichton, the best-selling author, screenwriter, and television producer, for permitting us to reprint a provocative talk he presented at the National Press Club in Washington, D.C. Crichton laments the quality of today's news media, characterizing it, as we have, as "junk food journalism." He calls for a "sensitive, informed, and responsive media" if we are going to accomplish the social changes needed in our society.

TOM TOMORROW—THE CARTOONIST

Tom Tomorrow's comic strip, "This Modern World," appears in more than 75 newspapers across the country. He now has two critically acclaimed, and publicly adored books—*Greetings From This Modern World* and *Tune In Tomorrow*—available from St. Martin's Press. To communicate with Tom, write him at POB 170515, San Francisco, CA 94117, or, by E-mail: tomorrow@well.com.

PROJECT CENSORED JUDGES OF 1994

One of the most difficult challenges of Project Censored is to select the "Ten Best Censored" stories from among the 25 top nominations. This responsibility falls on our distinguished national panel of judges who volunteer their efforts. Perhaps one of the greatest tributes to the project is that some of our judges, identified with asterisks, have participated in Project Censored every year since selecting the first group of *Censored* stories in 1976. (Ben Bagdikian sequestered himself in the years he also was a *Censored* author.) We are deeply indebted to the following judges who selected the top ten *Censored* stories of 1994.

DR. DONNA ALLEN, founding editor of *Media Report to Women*

BEN BAGDIKIAN,* professor emeritus, Graduate School of Journalism, UC-Berkeley

RICHARD BARNET, senior fellow, Institute for Policy Studies

NOAM CHOMSKY,* professor, Linguistics and Philosophy, Massachusetts Institute of Technology

SUSAN FALUDI, journalist/author

DR. GEORGE GERBNER, professor of communication and dean emeritus, Annenberg School of Communications, University of Pennsylvania

EDWARD S. HERMAN, professor emeritus of finance, Wharton School, University of Pennsylvania

SUT JHALLY, professor of communications, and executive director, The Media Education Foundation, University of Massachusetts

NICHOLAS JOHNSON,* professor, College of Law, University of Iowa

RHODA H. KARPATKIN, president, Consumers Union, nonprofit publisher of Consumer Reports

CHARLES L. KLOTZER, editor and publisher, St. Louis Journalism Review

JUDITH KRUG, director, Office for Intellectual Freedom, American Library Association

FRANCES MOORE LAPPÉ, co-founder and co-director, Center for Living Democracy

WILLIAM LUTZ, professor, English, Rutgers University

JULIANNE MALVEAUX, Ph.D., economist and columnist, King Features and Pacifica radio

JACK L. NELSON,* professor, Graduate School of Education, Rutgers University

MICHAEL PARENTI, political analyst, author, and lecturer

HERBERT I. SCHILLER, professor emeritus of communication, University of California, San Diego

SHEILA RABB WEIDENFELD,* president, D.C. Productions, Ltd.

INTRODUCTION

"MEDIASAURUS" by Michael Crichton

I am the author of a novel about dinosaurs, a novel about U.S.-Japanese trade relations, and a novel about sexual harassment—what some people have called my dinosaur trilogy.

But I want to focus on another dinosaur, one that may be on the road to extinction. I am referring to the American media. And I use the term extinction literally. To my mind, it is likely that what we now understand as the mass media will be gone within ten years. Vanished, without a trace.

There has been evidence of impending extinction for a long time. We all know statistics about the decline in newspaper readers and network television viewers. The polls show increasingly negative public attitudes toward the press—and with good reason. A generation ago, Paddy Chayefsky's "Network" looked like an outrageous farce. Today, when Geraldo Rivera bares his buttocks, when *The New York Times* misquotes Barbie, the doll, and NBC fakes news footage of Chevy trucks, *Network* looks like a documentary.

According to recent polls, large segments of the American population think the media are attentive to trivia, and indifferent to what really matters. They also believe that the media do not report the country's problems, but instead is a part of them. Increasingly, people perceive no difference between the narcissistic self-serving reporters asking questions, and the narcissistic self-serving politicians who evade them.

And I am troubled by the media's response to these criticisms. We hear the old professional line: "Sure, we've got some problems, we could do our job better." Or the time-honored: "We've always been disliked because we're the bearer of bad news; it comes with the territory; I'll start to worry when the press is liked." Or after a major disaster like the NBC news fiasco, we hear "This is a time for reflection."

So for a moment, let's set aside the usual bromides about the press. Let's take it as given that the bearer of bad news is often executed; that all human beings have an appetite for gossip and scandal; that the media must attract an audience; that bias is in the eye of the reader as much as in the pen or sound-bite of the reporter.

And let's talk instead about quality.

The media are an industry and their product is information. And along with many other American industries, the American media produce a product of very poor quality. Its information is not reliable, it has too much chrome and glitz, its doors rattle, it breaks down almost immediately, and it's sold without warranty. It's flashy but it's basically junk. So people have begun to stop buying it.

Poor product quality results in part from the American educational system, which graduates workers too poorly-educated to generate high quality information. In part, it is a problem of nearsighted management that encourages profits at the expense of quality. In part, it is a failure to respond to changing technology. And in large part, it is a failure to recognize the changing needs of the audience.

In recent decades many American companies have undergone a painful restructuring to produce high quality products. We all know what this requires. Flattening the corporate hierarchy. Moving critical information from the bottom up instead of the top down. Empowering workers. Changing the system, not just the focus of the corporation. And relentlessly driving toward a quality product. Because improved quality demands a change in the corporate culture. A radical change.

Generally speaking, the American media have remained aloof from this process. There have been some positive innovations, like CNN and C-SPAN. But the news on television and in newspapers is generally perceived as less accurate, less objective, less informed than it was a decade ago. Because instead of focusing on quality, the media have tried to be lively or engaging—selling the sizzle, not the steak; the talk-show host, not the guest; the format, not the subject. And in doing so it has abandoned its audience.

Who will be the GM or IBM of the nineties? The next great American institution to find itself obsolete and outdated, while obstinately refusing to change? I suspect one answer would be, *The New York Times* and the commercial networks. Other institutions have been pushed to improve their quality. Ford now makes a better car than it has any time in my life; we can thank Toyota and Nissan for that. But who will push *The New York Times*?

The answer, I think, is technology. The media have always been driven by technology, but it's surprising how many of its attitudes and how much of its terminology are very old. Stereotype and cliché are eighteenth century printers' terms, referring to metal type. The inverted pyramid story structure was a response to the newly-invented telegraph; reporters were not sure they could get the whole story in before the telegraph broke down, and so began to put the most important information first. The first image broadcast on television was a dollar sign, setting the tone for the future of that medium.

But the modern thrust of technology is radically different, because it is changing the very concept of information in our society.

Information today is vitally important. We live by it. We are an information society. For the first time in our history, by the year 2000, 50 percent of all American jobs will require at least one year of college. In this environment, news isn't entertainment. It's a necessity. We need it—and we need it to be of high quality: comprehensive and factually accurate.

More and more, people understand that they pay for information. Online databases charge by the minute. As the link between payment and information becomes more explicit, consumers will naturally want better information. They'll demand it, and they'll be willing to pay for it. There is going to be—I would argue, there already is—a market for extremely high quality information, what quality experts would call six-sigma information.

Yet none of the traditional media has begun to address this need. (The trendsetter for benchmarking American quality was always Motorola, and until 1989 Motorola was talking about three-sigma quality, three bad parts in a thousand. Six-sigma is three bad parts per million. It's a quantum leap, previously incomprehensible for American quality, although the Japanese have been doing it for years. But such rigor is unknown in the media.)

In my own case, when I add up what I spend for newspapers, magazines, books, databases, cable services, and so on, I find I spend about as much for information—food for thought—as I do for food. I may not be typical, but I'm hardly unique. But I don't pay all this money because I think I'm getting good information. I pay to find out what Ken Kesey used to call "the current fantasy"—what is being written and bruited about.

But what if somebody offered a service with high-quality information? A service where all the facts were true, the quotes weren't piped, the statistics were presented by someone who knew something about statistics?

What would that be worth? A lot. Because good information has value. The notion that it's filler between the ads is an outdated idea.

There is a second and related trend. I want direct access to information of interest to me, and increasingly I expect to get it. This is a long-standing trend in many technologies. When I was a child, telephones had no dials. You picked up the phone and asked an operator to place your call. Now, if you've ever had the experience of being somewhere where your call was placed for you, you know how exasperating that is. It's faster and more efficient to dial it yourself.

Today's media equivalent of the old telephone operator is Dan Rather, or the front page editor, or the reporter who prunes the facts in order to be lively and vivid. Increasingly, I want to remove those filters, and in some cases I already can. When I read that Ross Perot appeared before a Congressional committee, I am no longer solely dependent on the lively and vivid account in *The New York Times*, which talks about Perot's folksy homilies and a lot of other flashy chrome trim that I am not interested in. I can turn on C-SPAN and watch the hearing myself. In the process, I can also see how accurate the *Times* account was. And that's likely to change my perception of the *Times*, as indeed it has. Because the *Times* seems to have a problem with Ross Perot. It reminds me of the story told about Hearst, who remarked upon seeing an old adversary on the street, "I don't know why he hates me, I never did him a favor."

But my ability to view C-SPAN brings us to the third trend: the coming end of the media's information monopoly. For 200 years, since the inception of our nation—the American Revolution was the first war fought in part through public opinion in the newspapers, and Ben Franklin the first media-savvy lobbyist to employ techniques of disinformation—for 200 years, the media have been able to behave in a basically monopolistic way. The media have treated information the way John D. Rockefeller treated oil—as a commodity, in which the distribution network, rather than product quality, is of primary importance. But once people can get the raw data themselves, that monopoly ends. And that means big changes, soon.

Once Al Gore gets the fiber optic highways in place, and the information capacity of the country is where it ought to be, then I will be able, for example, to view any public meeting of Congress on tape. And I will have artificial intelligence agents roaming the databases, downloading stuff I am interested in, and assembling for me a front page, or a nightly news show, that addresses my interests. I'll have the twelve top stories that I want; I'll have short summaries available, and I can double click for more detail. How will Peter Jennings or MacNeil-Lehrer or a newspaper compete with that?

So the media institutions will have to change. Of course, I still don't know what I don't know, which means broad based overviews or interpretive sources will have value. But only if these sources engage in genuinely high-quality interpretive work, or genuinely high-quality investigative work. At the moment, neither occurs very often.

On the contrary, superficiality is the norm, and everybody in the world knows it. When Barry Lopez went to a remote Eskimo village in 1986, one of the residents asked him how long he was staying. Before he could answer, another Eskimo said: "One day—newspaper story. Two days—magazine story. Five days—book." Even in the Canadian Northwest, the audience is way ahead of the press.

Moving closer to home, let's consider some questions that journalists have asked public figures. I invite you to guess the answers:

Mr. Kantor, are you a protectionist?

Mr. Christopher, do you think your Mideast trip was a waste of time?

Mr. Aspin, do you think we'll really see homosexuals accepted in the military?

Mr. Gergen, did the White House treatment of Lani Guinier hurt the administration?

Mr. Reich, do you think Clinton's stimulus package will do enough to create jobs?

There are two points to be made here. The first is that the structure of the questions dictates the answer, because no one is going to say he's a protectionist, or a time waster, or that he's promoting policies that will fail.

But the more important point is that such questions assume a simplified, either/or version of reality to which no one really subscribes. In the real world, no one is "a protectionist." Because in the real world, there is no such thing as a free market. Haven't you noticed how free market advocates want tenure?

So what we really want to know from Mr. Kantor is not some general characterization of his approach, because that characterization is too simplistic to be useful. What we want to know is his thinking on specific trade issues. Even to say, "What's your approach to Japan?" is too simplistic, because it is highly unlikely that Mr. Kantor thinks the same way about semiconductors, automobile parts, rice, and flat panel displays. No simple answer will satisfy the complex questions he faces. And no one imagines it does—except the press.

This is one reason why so many people who regularly interact with the press come to view it as an anomaly. They go about their daily work, which is specific and complex, and then they meet with the press, where interactions are general and oversimplified.

Why? One answer is that it's easy for the press to behave this way. You don't have to be knowledgeable about trade to ask Mickey Kantor if he is a protectionist. In fact you don't have to know much to ask any question that takes the general form of: "Are we doing enough?" Or "Are we going too fast or too slow?" Or "Is it fair?" Or "Is it really the best way to go about it?" I would argue this whole journalistic procedure is a way to conceal institutional incompetence.

Consider the following: I don't know much about the military. I don't follow it. Someone says to me, "Okay, Crichton, you're doing an interview with Les Aspin. You have two hours to prepare questions." What am I going to ask? Well, let's see. I know he's been in the hospital for some reason. I'll inquire about his health, but I don't want to be obvious, so I'll frame it as a national security issue. Are you really fit to do the job? Then I'll ask him something about base closings: are there too many? Is it happening too fast? Is the process fair? Then I'll ask him about defense conversion. Are we doing enough for unemployed engineers? Then let's see, waste in procurements. Wasn't there a $600 toilet seat? I know it was a few years ago, but it's always good for a few minutes. Then the Soviet Union, should we be downsizing so fast with all the uncertainty in the world? Then I'll ask him about gays in the military. Was Clinton's approach wise? Is this really the best way to go about it? And that should do it.

Unfortunately, that's also the standard Les Aspin interview. But I don't know anything about the military. Still, I managed to do the interview, because the questions are structurally very general.

This generality creates a fundamental asymmetry between subject and journalist—and ultimately, between journalist and audience. Les Aspin has to know much more detail, has to address very specific pressures, to carry out his job. But I can frame very general questions and get away with doing mine. How do I justify my position? Well, I can tell myself that I'm too busy to do better, because news rushes onward. But that's not really satisfactory. Better to say the American people don't want details, they just want "the basics." In other words I can blame my own shoddy behavior on the audience. And if I hear the audience criticizing me, I can say I'm being blamed as the bearer of bad news. Instead of what is really going on—which is that my customers are telling me that my product is poorly researched, and often either uninteresting or irrelevant. It's junk-food journalism. Empty calories.

The media's tendency to be general instead of specific has many unhappy consequences. It is inherently superficial. It is also inherently speculative, because it focuses on attitudes—what a person thinks—and not what they do. But what a person thinks is far less important than what they do—because the two are often contradictory.

The tendency to characterize a person's beliefs—instead of focusing on their actions—is one of the true abuses of the power of the media. Look how quickly Kimba Woods was transformed from respected jurist to Playboy bunny. Just as I went from author to racist Japan-basher. In my case, what was striking was how many journalists applied the Japan-bashing label, without appearing to have read my book. The hazards of this practice became clear when the Columbia Journalism Review reported that the term "Japan-bashing" was invented by an American public relations flack at the Japan Economic Institute, a Japanese lobbying organization. The term was promoted as a way to stifle debate, including legitimate debate, on relations with Japan. The man who coined the phrase said, "Anyone who uses that term is my intellectual dupe."

Worse still, characterization lies at the heart of the impulse to polarize every issue—what we might call the Crossfire Syndrome.

We are all assumed, these days, to reside at one extreme of the opinion spectrum, or another. We are pro-abortion or anti-abortion. We are free traders or protectionist. We are pro-private sector or pro-big government. We are feminists or chauvinists. But in the real world, few of us hold these extreme views. There is instead a spectrum of opinion.

The extreme positions of the "Crossfire" Syndrome require extreme simplification—framing the debate in terms which ignore the real issues. For example, when I watch "Crossfire," or "Nightline", or "MacNeil-Lehrer," I often think, wait a minute. The real issue isn't term limits; it's campaign finance reform. The real issue isn't whether a gasoline tax is regressive, it's national security—whether we'd prefer to go back to war in the Gulf instead of reducing oil consumption by taxing it more heavily, as every other nation does. The real issue isn't whether the U.S. should have an industrial policy, it is whether the one we have—because no policy is a policy—serves us well. The issue isn't whether Mickey Kantor is a protectionist, it's how the U.S. should respond to its foreign competitors.

This polarization of the issues has contributed greatly to our national paralysis because it posits false choices which stifle debate that is essential for change to occur. It is ironic that this should happen in a time of great social upheaval, when our society needs more than ever to be able to experiment with different viewpoints. But in the media world, a previously-established idea, like a previously-elected politician, enjoys a tremendous advantage over any challenger.

Hence the familiar ideas continue to be repeated, long past their demonstrable validity. More than two decades after right-brain, left-brain thinking was discredited in scientific circles, those metaphors are still casually repeated in the media. After thirty years of government effort to banish racism, persistent racial inequality suggests the need for fresh perspectives; those perspectives are rarely heard. And more than three decades after the women's movement began amid media ridicule, the men's movement finds itself ridiculed in exactly the same way—often by leading feminists, who appear to have learned little from their own ordeals.

This leads me to the final consequence of generalization: it caricatures our opponents, as well as the issues. There has been a great decline in civility in this country. We have lost the perception that reasonable persons of good will may hold opposing views. Simultaneously, we have lost the ability to address reasoned arguments—to forsake ad hominem characterization, and instead address another person's arguments. Which is a tragedy, because debate is interesting. It's a form of exploration. But personal attack is merely unpleasant and intimidating. Paradoxically, this decline in civility and good humor, which the press appears to believe is necessary to "get the story," reduces the intensity of our national discourse. Watching British parliamentary debates, I notice the tradition of saying "the right honorable gentleman" or "my distinguished friend" before hurling an insult does something interesting to the entire process. A civil tone permits more bluntness.

So I hope that this era of polarized, junk-food journalism will soon come to an end. For too long the media have accepted the immortal advice of Yogi Berra, who said: "When you come to a fork in the road, take it." But business as usual doesn't serve the audience any more. And although technology will soon precipitate enormous changes in the media, we face a more immediate problem: a period of major social change. We are going to need a sensitive, informed, and responsive media to accomplish these changes.

And that's the way it is.

"As we move toward Endgame,
consider this. We live in a country
that has never made a movie about
Leonardo da Vinci and has produced
three about Joey Buttafuoco."
—Pete Hamill

CHAPTER 1

U.S. Censorship in 1994

While 1994 might not have been the worst of times for journalism, it surely was not one of the best.

The First Amendment was ignored, trashed, or criticized on almost every front: the Sacramento, California, chapter of the American Family Association intimidated 16 Burger King franchisees into removing the distribution boxes of the alternative *Sacramento News & Review*; the Board of Education in Kenai, Alaska, removed the *Utne Reader* from the magazine racks of the Nikiski Junior-Senior High School Library after some parents complained about it; the Neosho County Commission in Kansas approved a resolution banning nude dancing in the county; the Kyrene Elementary School District Governing Board, in Arizona, removed *The Complete Fairy Tales of the Brothers Grimm* from the reading list for fourth and fifth graders; and the final frontier for freedom of expression, cyberspace, succumbed to censorship by companies which control the computer networks: in June, America Online shut down several feminist discussion forums, saying the subject matter might be inappropriate for young girls.

After years of teasing the public with junk food news about the Royal Family, Joey Buttafuoco and Amy Fisher, Jim and Tammy Faye, Ivana and The Trump, Michael Jackson, and the Bobbitts, the mainstream media completed the tabloidization process with the O.J. Simpson case. (See Chapter 5 for a complete analysis of the Junk Food News syndrome.)

Political correctness reached new peaks when principal cellist Anne Conrad-Antoville quit the Eureka, California, Symphony Orchestra to protest the killing of wolves in *Peter and the Wolf*. Indeed, some PC observers suggest that the PC pendulum has swung to the extreme and is now heading back.

The media and the nation celebrated a day of mourning for Richard Nixon who trampled on the rights of individuals, defiled the First Amendment, built a political career on vilifying the press, and was the only president who ever had to resign from office. Trudy Lieberman, a contributing editor of *Columbia Journalism Review*, warned that consumer reporting, a tradition that started with the muckrakers, is on the wane.

The Committee to Protect Journalists reported that ten journalists have been killed in the United States since 1981, but their deaths have been ignored because the victims were immigrants. Altogether, 115 journalists were killed throughout the world in 1994—more than half of them in Rwanda and Algeria—according to the International Federation of Journalists.

Television news magazines, ranging from the respected "60 Minutes" and "20/20" to the less reputable "A Current Affair" and "Hard Copy," proliferated by quantum leaps during the year and soon overshadowed the nightly newscasts as the primary business of news divisions. And while most observers agree they're a glut on the market, with ratings starting to suffer, the networks resist giving them up since they're profitable, costing

THIS MODERN WORLD by TOM TOMORROW

IN OUR BOTTOM-LINE SOCIETY, SOCIAL REFORM IS OFTEN LAMBASTED AS *UNPROFITABLE*.

PERHAPS SOMETHING SHOULD BE DONE ABOUT OUR COUNTRY'S SHAMEFULLY HIGH NUMBER OF MALNOURISHED CHILDREN.

DON'T BE ABSURD! THAT WOULD COST MONEY!

PORK-BARREL MILITARY SPENDING IS APPARENTLY *IMMUNE* TO SUCH CRITICISM HOWEVER... FOR INSTANCE, CONSERVATIVES CERTAINLY DON'T OBJECT TO SPENDING $4.5 BILLION ON AN AIRCRAFT CARRIER THE PENTAGON ADMITS IS *UNNECESSARY*...

BUT THAT'S *DIFFERENT!* IT WILL CREATE *JOBS!*

HMM...SO THE POST-COLD-WAR MILITARY BUDGET CAN BE JUSTIFIED...AS A *WORKFARE PROGRAM?*

only about half as much to produce as entertainment programming.

The 1994 political campaigns established new levels of political slime and mudslinging, leaving an electorate angry, cynical, and, perhaps even worse, apathetic to the democratic process. Exit polls conducted for the Times Mirror Center for People and the Press, revealed that voters were disgusted by media campaign reporting with 59 percent giving the press a grade of C or below for its coverage. All the ballots weren't even tallied before the *Washington Post* reported a "dump Clinton" media frenzy with the president being labeled a lame duck.

As it turned out, the public was not deceived by the political sleaze-meisters and the media's trend toward sensationalism. The Freedom Forum's First Amendment Center reported that the public lumps politicians and journalists together as untrustworthy, power hungry, and out of touch with what the public wants.

The Center's study revealed that 79 percent of the people surveyed agreed that news media managers were more interested in increased circulation and profits than in telling the public what it needs to know; 70 percent agreed that the country is governed "by a handful of powerful politicians, journalists, and businesses" and that the public can do little or nothing to change things; 57 percent said journalists are no more honest than the politicians they criticize; and 53 percent said journalists are more interested in wielding power than in what is good for the country.

Not surprisingly, a semi-annual report by the Audit Bureau of Circulation showed a declining circulation for 20 of the 25 largest newspapers in the United States.

While the media were focusing on the bottom line and the politicians were slinging mud at one another, many Americans were hurting, many Americans were hungry, many Americans were homeless, many Americans were ill, and many Americans were frightened. And statistics revealed that some of their fears were well-founded.

The U.S. Census Bureau reported in early October that 1.3 million Americans fell below the poverty line in 1993; 39.3 million Americans, 15.1 percent of the population, lived in poverty, the highest rate in a decade; Americans without health insurance rose to 39.7 million, 15.3 percent of the population; and the wealthiest 20 percent of Americans earned nearly 50 percent of all household income—the highest disparity ever recorded.

On November 15, the Children's Defense Fund reported that while the nation was getting richer, its children were getting poorer. The nation now has more child poverty than at any time since 1964 and more child poverty than virtually all other developed nations. The Justice Department reported in late October that violent crimes, such as assaults and robberies, rose 5.6 percent in 1993 to 10.9 million; the total number of personal and household crimes rose 1.7 percent to about 43.6 million.

For the first time in history, the nation's state and federal prison population topped one million, hitting 1,012,851 prisoners at the end of June. The U.S. incarceration rate is second only to Russia's.

By the end of 1994, the 103rd Congress adjourned without passing health care reform, campaign finance reform, lobbying and gift rule reform, and welfare reform. At the same time, the national media looked forward to giving the public everything it needs to know about the O.J. Simpson trial—the latest "Crime of the Century."

Following are additional insights into other media issues of 1994.

1994 MEDIA YEAR IN REVIEW

THE BASEBALL STRIKE—The Great Baseball Strike of '94, heralded with a *Time* "STEE-RIKE!" cover, started on August 12 and continued through the end of the year. In addition to the grief it brought diehard baseball fans, it provided an interesting insight into the media's priorities when faced with a glitch in their normally smooth-running schedule.

For example, our annual Junk Food News effort evolved from criticism of Project Censored by news editors and directors that the real issue isn't censorship but rather a difference of opinion as to what information is important to publish or broadcast.

Editors point out that there is a finite amount of time and space for news in the press and on television and that it's their responsibility to determine which stories are more critical for the public to know. Since this seemed like a reasonable thesis, it would follow that when a major void occurs in the news supply channel, editors would be eager to fill it with other important information critical to the public's need to know.

It was with great anticipation that I watched how the media would replace all the time and space normally devoted to covering baseball. Following are some of the ways the media filled the void.

First, the baseball season did *not* end just because of a strike. Indeed, it continued on a daily basis as newspapers across the country, including the *New York Daily News*, the *Miami Herald*, the *Chicago Sun-Times*, and the *San Francisco Chronicle*, reported box scores, player statistics and trades, and stories of games that were never played except on a computer program called "Pursue the Pennant V.5."

Other newspapers eschewed computer fiction to take the historic approach of reliving games from earlier years. The *New York Post* provided its readers with a series titled "The Greatest Games In New York Baseball History." When the world series was supposed to start, the *San Francisco Examiner* reprinted original staff stories and photos about historic series games and *USA Today* reprised seven of the most memorable world series games.

One baseball columnist, frustrated by not having baseball teams to rank, instead filled a column by ranking baseball's best movies. He cited "Pride of the Yankees" as number one because of its "good story and acting."

Not to be outdone by its competition, some radio and television stations filled their "baseball" time with coverage of minor league Class A, AA, or AAA games when available. On October 25, NBC's news magazine, "Dateline NBC," launched a three-part computer simulation of the 1994 world series.

An 18-hour baseball fix was provided in mid-September by Ken Burns' nine-part series, titled "Baseball," on PBS Television.

Not all media filled their baseball space with fictionalized or historic games. Some, including the *Detroit Free Press*, decided to save money by simply reducing the number of sports pages. Dave Robinson, *Free Press* deputy managing editor for sports, told *Editor & Publisher* (9/3/94), "The space budget this year was way over because of the Olympics, the World Cup, and so on, so we were going to have to pay back a little every day anyway."

New York Daily News sports editor Kevin Whitmer defended use of fantasy computer games, saying, "It's just something to get people through a time when they don't have baseball."

However, Everette Dennis, executive director of the Freedom Forum Center for Media Studies, did not perceive it to be quite so innocent. Dennis told *USA Today* (9/12/94) that computer baseball is a sign of "the bankruptcy of sports journalism." Newspapers are "slavishly wedded to these professional teams." And without daily games, "they don't have anything else to write about."

In a decision befitting its austere image, *The New York Times* said it would pass on the gimmicks and limit its coverage to strike news.

In a fitting climax to a fictionalized baseball season, the avid baseball fan was given the opportunity of paying $29.95 for an "Official 1994 World Series" baseball. The distributor, Centennial Sports, said it was "guaranteed genuine," made by Rawlings, and an "official collector's item."

Given the resourceful manner in which the media were able to fill the void left by the strike, plus the added coverage of reporting the strike, it is quite possible there was as much media space and time devoted to baseball in 1994 as there would have been had the games been played. In any event, news ombudsmen ranked The Great Baseball Strike of '94 as the #20 Junk Food News story of the year.

MEDIA MERGER MANIA—While 1994 paled in comparison to 1993 when it came to major media mergers, there were enough to stimulate some financial wizards to speculate whether the '90s could reprise the '80s as another decade of greed.

The largest newspaper deal of the year saw the *Chicago Sun-Times*, one of the nation's biggest newspapers, sold to Hollinger Inc., a Canadian publishing company, for $180 million on February 28. The agreement included 60 weekly and biweekly suburban papers.

In May, Rupert Murdoch shook up CBS-TV when he persuaded New World Communications Group to align 12 of its television stations with Murdoch's Fox network in return for a $500 million investment. Eight local CBS affiliates were included in the deal. An added sweetener for New World, was that Murdoch had already paid the National Football League $1.58 billion to move its Sunday afternoon games from CBS to Fox.

In early June, Cox Enterprises, the nation's sixth largest cable company, announced it would pay the Times Mirror Company $2.3 billion for its cable TV unit and would create Cox Cable, the nation's third largest cable operator. TM would retain 20 percent of the new cable company.

Bell Atlantic and Nynex, both regional phone giants, announced on June 30 that they would pool their assets to form a new joint venture combining their cellular phone operations.

On July 11, Viacom announced final victory in its long battle with QVC to take over Paramount Communications Inc., in a cash and stock deal estimated at about $10 billion. Earlier, Blockbuster Entertainment had invested $1.25 billion in Viacom to give it the cash it needed to complete the Paramount acquisition.

In a deal similar to the Bell Atlantic/Nynex one, US West and Airtouch Communications announced on July 15 that they would merge their cellular phone businesses to form a new joint venture.

The merger flop of the year was announced on February 23 when Bell Atlantic and Tele-Communications Inc. called off what would have been the largest merger in U.S. history. The proposed $33 billion merger, which had been announced in 1993, would have joined Bell's telephone business with cable operations of TCI and Liberty Media Corp.

On April 5, Southwestern Bell Corp. and Cox Cable Communications agreed to end plans for a $4.9 billion cable television partnership. Cox went on to form a new partnership with the Times Mirror Co. as noted above.

In mid-July, one of the most highly publicized media mergers of the year ended abruptly when CBS dropped its offer for QVC, the home shopping channel operator.

As 1994 came to an end, there were still many unrequited and unresolved relationships: Wall Street speculation had it that the three big television networks, ABC, CBS, and NBC, were still receiving suitors with Ted Turner as one of the most ardent; Time Warner, the result of the blockbuster media merger of 1989, still not comfortable with its new image, was said to be considering restructuring itself once again; NBC filed a petition with the FCC asking it to rule on the level of foreign ownership of the Fox network; media entrepreneur and founder of Channel One, Chris Whittle, having seen much of his Whittle Communications empire collapse, concentrated on keeping the Edison Project, a for-profit venture to manage public schools, afloat; and *The New York Times*, having finally read the handwriting on the screen, admitted it was too dependent on newspapers and planned to spend $1 billion to buy TV stations and cable networks.

INFORMATION HIGHWAY TRAFFIC REPORT—Last year we reported that the map had been drawn for the Information Superhighway and progress was being made. But, as 1994 ended, we find that the access road isn't even under construction yet. While the Congressional telecommunications bill, H.R. 3636, designed to form a national telecommunications policy, passed the House with an overwhelming majority in June, a parallel bill in the Senate bogged down and will not come up for a vote until sometime in 1995. Meanwhile, a national survey by *Macworld* revealed that consumers and the telecommunications industry don't agree on where the Information Superhighway, or IH as some refer to it, should go. While consumers are interested in the IH for information access, community involvement, self improvement, and communication, the industry executives see the IH filled bumper to bumper with advertising, entertainment, shopping, and gambling. Care to bet on who is going to win?

CENSORSHIP ON CAMPUS—The 1993-94 report on public school censorship by the People for the American Way revealed that the religious right increased its attack on library books, testing materials, sex-education courses, and education reform. Arthur J. Kropp, president of People for the American Way, said objections from the religious right amounted to 22 percent of 462 censorship attempts in 46 states, with another 14 percent using religious right "buzzwords and arguments." Not surprisingly, speakers at the 1994 National Education Association's convention in Seattle reported that curriculum challenges by religious conservatives are having a chilling effect on teachers. As a result teachers are starting to censor themselves by thinking twice before asking children to write in journals, use their imagination, or study people from other cultures.

THIS MODERN WORLD by TOM TOMORROW

Confirming the problems at public schools, a report by the Freedom Forum, presented at the Annual Convention of Newspaper Publishers, revealed that high school newspapers are losing their financial support while school administrators, relying on the Supreme Court's *Hazelwood* decision, increasingly censor their contents. Speakers suggested that high school newspapers are dying a slow death and that censorship might be the greatest threat to them.

MISCELLANEOUS MEDIA GAFFES OF 1994—Symptoms of an ailing institution:

Time magazine apologized for publishing a staged photo essay on child prostitution in Moscow; *USA Today* followed suit and apologized for publishing a staged photo of gang members brandishing guns; Rick Kaplan, executive producer of ABC's "World News Tonight," told news correspondent Cokie Roberts to put on a coat for a faked outdoor shot at Capitol Hill; CBS News admitted that an earlier report on Haitian President Jean-Bertrand Aristide as someone in need of "psychiatric treatment" was "flat out wrong;" the *Los Angeles Times* disciplined a photographer for faking a photo of a weary firefighter dousing himself with water from a swimming pool during a Southern California fire.

Reviewing new congressional cable TV regulations, the chief operating officer of TCI Cable Management Corp. told his top managers, "The best news of all is now we can blame the charges on regulation and the government. Let's take advantage of it;" *New York Newsday* ran a front-page composite photo of Tonya Harding and Nancy Kerrigan skating together,

which didn't happen; reporters from *The New York Times, San Jose Mercury News*, and *Detroit Free Press* were caught breaking into Tonya Harding's private electronic mailbox during the Winter Olympics in Norway.

Diane Sawyer, ABC's reported seven-million-dollar newswoman, reprised Charlie Manson's Tate-La Bianca murders in her "Turning Point" interview with "Charlie's Girls;" the executive editor of the Alameda Newspaper Group in California banned photos of snakes saying readers do not want to see such photos with their breakfast; *Newsweek* admitted running a "false and irresponsible" article accusing Hillary Rodham Clinton of profiting from a sweetheart deal in cattle futures; *Sports Illustrated*, known for its near-nude women in its swimsuit issue, refused to publish an Adidas ad featuring a nude male soccer team whose private parts were all completely concealed.

A Texas radio station's promotional announcement that it had hidden money in Fort Worth's library encouraged hundreds of listeners to storm the building, tear out pages, and toss books on the floor; three days after publishing a reader-friendly graphic exposé of auto leasing "fine print," *USA Today* disowned the piece, saying it did not meet *USA Today's* "standards for fairness and objectivity" and used "inappropriate commentary." The communications industry has donated $50 million to national political campaigns since 1984—with nearly $4 million going to current members of the House Energy and Commerce Committee which regulates communications businesses.

Watch for all the tennis news that fits since *The New York Times* signed a three-year contract with the United States Tennis Association to become an official sponsor of the U.S. Open Championship starting in 1994; some of ABC's highest paid correspondents, including David Brinkley, Sam Donaldson, and Cokie Roberts loudly protested a new network policy that bars them from getting paid for speaking to corporations and trade associations; checkbook journalism reaches new heights as media offer O.J. Simpson witnesses hundreds of thousands of dollars for exclusive interviews.

While the media did not forget to celebrate Barbie's 35th birthday, it did manage to overlook the 30th anniversary of the fabricated Gulf of Tonkin crisis which paved the way for the Vietnam War; the *Washington Post* ran a series of editorials supporting the GATT trade agreement without telling readers that GATT would provide a $2 billion windfall for three companies, including the *Washington Post*; a federal district judge ruled that CNN was in contempt of court when it broadcast taped telephone calls made from jail by Gen. Manuel Noriega in defiance of a court order not to.

In June, newspapers pulled Doonesbury comic strips that suggested the

Catholic Church once sanctioned same-sex weddings and on the day before the November election, the Universal Press Syndicate sent out a replacement strip toning down Garry Trudeau's comments about Florida gubernatorial candidate Jeb Bush; the Fox Network denied there was a problem even though Canada, Denmark, Norway, and Sweden all censored its "Mighty Morphin Power Rangers" children's program because of its violence; "60 Minutes" correspondent Mike Wallace and his producer were reprimanded by CBS News for secretly taping an interview with a freelance writer without her permission; and finally, for shame to the Walt Disney Company for its 60-second TV commercials that appear to be objective movie reviews of Disney films—cited as one of the top 10 worst ads of 1994 according to the Center for Science in the Public Interest.

THE TOP TEN MEDIA HEROES OF 1994

Before leaving this downbeat albeit realistic review of the media's performance in 1994, we want to acknowledge that there are many socially responsible journalists and some fearless publishers. Don Hazen, executive director of the San Francisco-based Institute for Alternative Journalism (IAJ), and Christina Triano, IAJ program director, remind us that it is important to honor and support those individuals and organizations that are devoted to keeping critical and truthful information alive and well in the body politic. They sent along the following selection of "Ten Media Heroes" of 1994 who are "working to make independent voices heard and to tell stories shut out by the mainstream media."

1. FAIRNESS AND ACCURACY IN REPORTING (FAIR)—In its detailed study, "Rush Limbaugh's Reign of Error," the New York-based media watch group documented hundreds of careless inaccuracies and bold-faced lies from Limbaugh's programs and books.

2. THE PUBLIC MEDIA CENTER (PMC)—This San Francisco-based nonprofit advertising agency created a brilliant non-partisan educational campaign that thwarted Phillip Morris's $30 million misinformation attempt to supplant strict, local smoking restrictions with a much looser statewide law in California.

3. THE INSTITUTE FOR GLOBAL COMMUNICATIONS (IGC)— The IGC networks—PeaceNet, EcoNet, LaborNet, and ConflictNet—along with its conferences, Internet Gopher, and a diverse and active membership, provide an outlet for a wealth of information overlooked or blocked out by the mainstream media.

4. GARY DELGADO: ORGANIZER/ACTIVIST—Founder of the Center for Third World Organizing and the Applied Research Center, Gary Delgado has both the vision and the sense to take on critical issues in ways that make progress possible.

5. THE HAITI TRUTH TEAM—The relentless efforts of the "truth team"—including the Haitian Information Bureau, an alternative news agency which operated at great risk out of Port-au-Prince; the Washington, DC-based Haiti Information Project; and the progressive, New York-based PR firm, New Channels Communications—armed with accurate information and true grit, exposed the fabricated CIA disinformation campaign against Jean-Bertrand Aristide.

6. DAVID BARSAMIAN AND ALTERNATIVE RADIO—Using a do-it-yourself approach to the airwaves, David Barsamian's one-man operation is responsible for *Alternative Radio*, a one-hour weekly public affairs program broadcast on more than 100 stations in the U.S., Canada, and throughout the world, which presents views and perspectives either ignored or distorted by the corporate-owned media.

7. SALIM MUWAKKIL: JOURNALIST—Year after year, journalist Muwakkil's regular reporting in *In These Times* has consistently provided the most intelligent and insightful coverage of the African-American community—from the inside—found anywhere in the media.

8. LAURA FLANDERS/JANINE JACKSON AND COUNTERSPIN—Co-hosts of the weekly *CounterSpin*, the radio show of Fairness and Accuracy in Reporting, Flanders and Jackson crank out substantive media critiques—and find the humor in the sometimes harrowing world of the mainstream news.

9. JOHN SCHWARTZ, FOUNDER AND PRESIDENT OF THE 90s CHANNEL—As president of the Boulder-based 90s Channel, telecommunications expert and media activist John Schwartz operates full-time cable channels for more than half a million viewers as an alternative to the pay-per-view and home-shopping-dominated vision of cable TV giants like TCI.

10. ARTISTS FOR A HATE FREE AMERICA (AHFA)—With the support of the music and entertainment community, the Portland-based AHFA raises awareness, and funds, in support of groups fighting bigotry, violence, racism, and censorship across the nation.

(Ten Media Heroes was excerpted with permission from Don Hazen and the AlterNet News Service.)

"I think if the people
of this country
can be reached with the truth,
their judgment will be
in favor of the many,
as against the privileged few."
—Eleanor Roosevelt

CHAPTER 2

The Top 25 Censored News Stories of 1994

In this chapter we provide a detailed analysis of each of the top 25 *Censored* stories of 1994. In each case we start with the publication source and author of the original article (or articles). A brief synopsis by the Sonoma State University *Censored* researcher of the nominated article follows. We conclude with comments about the issue and article, in most cases by the author of the original source article. An asterisk (*) after an article title indicates it is reprinted in Appendix C, "*Censored* Reprints." Following the top 25 stories is a comparison of our top ten *Censored* stories with the top ten *biggest* stories cited by the Associated Press; a brief description of the subjects and categories of *Censored* stories of 1994; and comments about this year's nominations by some of our *Censored* judges.

1

The Deadly Secrets of the Occupational Safety Agency

Source:
HEALTH LETTER
Date: March 1994
Title: "Unfinished Business:
Occupational Safety Agency
Keeps 170,000 Exposed Workers
in the Dark About Risks
Incurred on Job"*
Authors: Peter Lurie, Sidney Wolfe,
Susan Goodwin

SYNOPSIS: In the early 1980s, the National Institute for Occupational Safety and Health (NIOSH) completed 69 epidemiological studies that revealed that 240,450 American workers were exposed to hazardous materials at 258 worksites.

Many of the affected workers were unaware that they were being exposed to hazardous substances (such as asbestos, silica and uranium) that were determined in those studies to increase the risk of cancer and other serious diseases.

In 1983, NIOSH and the Health and Human Services Department's Centers for Disease Control and Prevention (CDC) concluded that NIOSH had a duty to inform workers of exposure "particularly when NIOSH is the exclusive holder of information and when there is clear evidence of a cause and effect relationship between exposure and health risk." Obviously, workers who learned they were at risk could undergo screening that could lead to earlier detection of cancer.

Nonetheless, despite the 1983 recommendations of its own scientific and ethical experts to notify exposed workers, the Reagan administration refused to fund a $4

THIS MODERN WORLD by TOM TOMORROW

OVER THE LAST FEW YEARS, FAR RIGHT EXTREMISTS HAVE WON LOCAL ELECTIONS ACROSS THE COUNTRY BY ORGANIZING AROUND SUCH ISSUES AS *FAMILY VALUES* AND *SCHOOL PRAYER*...

WE'VE GOT TO STOP TH' *LIBERALS!* THEY WANT TO *OUTLAW RELIGION* --AND FORCE US ALL TO BECOME *HOMOSEXUALS!*

REVEREND FALWELL TOLD US!

POLLING PLACE

IT HAS BEEN EASY FOR THEM TO HAVE A DISPROPORTIONATE IMPACT WHEN SO MANY OTHER AMERICANS *DON'T* VOTE-- APPARENTLY PREFERRING TO REMAIN POLITICALLY *ABSTINENT* THAN TO CHOOSE THE LESSER OF TWO ELECTION-DAY *EVILS*...

AAAH--WHAT DIFFERENCE DO *ELECTIONS* MAKE, ANYWAY? ÷BURP÷

--*HUFFINGTON* & *NORTH LOSE BY NARROW MARGINS*--

--*GOP SWEEP*--

--SINGLE-PAYER DEFEATED IN CALIFORNIA--

--*PROP 107 PASSES*--

--*GINGRICH TRIUMPHANT*--

BEER

million pilot notification program and opposed legislation that would have required such notification.

As a result, by 1994, fewer than 30 percent of the workers, covered by only a handful of studies, have been notified. The Public Citizen's Health Research Group learned that NIOSH has individually notified a maximum of only 71,180 (29.6%) of the original 240,450 workers, leaving 169,270, more than 60%, still in the dark about health risks from on-the-job exposure.

Follow-up studies done on workers who had been warned about the risks provide evidence that notification is both feasible and potentially lifesaving. Unfortunately, the majority of the workers identified in the original studies as being exposed to carcinogens and other hazards at massive levels continue to be victims—this time of an unethical coverup that has characterized the federal response to date.

While Public Citizen's Health Research Group wrote to President Clinton on February 2, 1994, urging him to immediately reverse Reagan-Bush policies and order acceleration of the notification program, broader media exposure of this issue would no doubt stimulate a faster response. It has been estimated that notification of each individual worker would cost from $150 to $300. Nonetheless, more than 169,000 workers across the U.S. still have not been informed about their deadly exposure to cancer-causing agents despite 10 years of effort on the part of watchdog groups.

**SSU Censored Researcher:
Susan Kashack**

COMMENTS: Co-author Sidney Wolfe felt there was little effective national coverage of the study by the National Institute for Occupational Safety and Health (NIOSH). "The bulk of the cov-

erage was local," Wolfe said, "including several of the radio stations and newspapers in cities or states where the plants were located." The few national stories that appeared did not indicate which plants and therefore which workers were affected.

Wolfe said the general public would benefit from wider coverage of the study since they would know "whether they, their relatives or acquaintances worked at any of these plants and would now know what types of tests, if any, to be asking their doctors to do or what symptoms to look for to detect disease at an earlier and hence more treatable stage." National coverage of the subject is necessary, Wolfe added, since many of the 170,000 people involved may not still live near the plant, and/or may have worked there many years ago.

Wolfe noted that it is interesting that this story is coming out while revelations are being made about subjects in radiation experiments who had not known of their exposures (as cited in *Censored* story #6). The *Health Letter* story emphasizes that unethical, government-funded research continues today, Wolfe said.

The primary beneficiary of the limited coverage given the issue would be NIOSH, Wolfe said, since there would be limited pressure brought on the organization to increase the snail's pace at which it is notifying workers. Also benefiting from the lack of coverage would be the plant operators who "certainly do not have an interest in workers knowing that they may have sustained injuries as they may file suit against the company. Earlier government concerns about companies incurring legal liability thwarted more funding for this government worker notification project."

Wolfe pointed out that the NIOSH information "was gathered with taxpayer money and the public has a right to know the information. Because NIOSH has taken so long to individually notify people, our hope was to release the list of plants so that the affected people could go to the government and get the information themselves. In our view," Wolfe concluded, "NIOSH's notification efforts to date remain inadequate."

2 CENSORED

Powerful Group of Ultra-Conservatives Has Secret Plans for Your Future

Source:
IN THESE TIMES
Date: 8/8/94
Title: "Right-Wing Confidential"*
Author: Joel Bleifuss

SYNOPSIS: Observers of the nation's political scene, who wonder why the United States took a sharp right turn in 1994, should know about the Council for National Policy (CNP). In May 1981, under a tent in the backyard of political strategist Richard Viguerie's suburban Virginia home, 160 new-right political leaders celebrated their political fortunes and the election of President Ronald Reagan the previous November.

This elite group of administration officials, congressmen, industrialists, and conservative Christians— including Interior Secretary James Watt, Office of Management and Budget Director David Stockman, Phyllis Schlafly, Joseph Coors, Sen. John East (R-NC), Sen. Orrin Hatch (R-UT), and Paul Weyrich, founding president of the Heritage Foundation, a right-wing think tank—launched a political federation to coordinate their own political agenda.

Weyrich, reportedly the single most important person of CNP, once proposed that the Republicans include a plank in their 1988 platform that AIDS be controlled by "reintroducing and enforcing anti-sodomy laws." And CNP's R.J. Rushdoony, a leader of the Christian Reconstruction movement, argues that right-thinking Christians should take "dominion" over the United States and do away with the "heresy" that is democracy.

After the public inauguration of the group, the CNP went underground. As investigative journalist Joel Bleifuss notes, "we do not know much about the CNP's actions or agenda," but we do know that the radical right is on the ascendant within the Republican Party and has taken over state GOP organizations in Texas, California, Minnesota, Hawaii, Iowa, Nevada, Arizona, Idaho, and Virginia.

Russ Bellant, author of *The Coors Connection*, said the meetings of this little-known organization are often a spring-board for radical-right campaigns and long-term planning. "But these efforts will seldom be traced to the CNP." The group meets quarterly behind closed doors and is so secretive that the group's Washington office will neither confirm nor deny where, or even if, the group meets.

While the roster of the 500 members of the organization is confidential, it is known to include Jerry Falwell, of the Liberty Alliance; Oliver North, CNP executive committee member; Sen. Don Nickles (R-OK); Sen. Trent Lott (R-MS); Sen. Jesse Helms (R-NC); Rep. Bob Dornan (R-CA); Brent Bozell III, of the Media Research Center; Iran-contra figure Gen. John Singlaub; Richard Shoff, former leader of the Ku Klux Klan in Indiana; Republican pollster Richard Wirthlin; Robert Weiner, head of Maranatha, a Christian cult; Howard Phillips of the Conservative Caucus; Linda Bean Folkers of the L.L. Bean Co.; televangelist John Ankerberg; Bob Jones III, president of the Bob Jones University; and former attorney general Edwin Meese, CNP president in 1994.

To emphasize the secret nature of their meetings, CNP Executive Director Morton C. Blackwell wrote a memorandum to members attending a meeting in St. Louis in 1993 instructing them that all remarks made at the conference were to be strictly private. "The media should not know when or where we meet or who takes part in our programs, before or after a meeting."

And, with the exception of the alternative press, the Council for National Policy has managed to escape the attention of the media.

SSU Censored Researcher:
Paul Giusto

COMMENTS: "No mass media outlet has ever investigated the doings of the Council for National Policy (CNP)," according to investigative author Joel Bleifuss. Bleifuss charged that the media's failure to investigate the CNP, a secretive political networking organization that includes every political figure of the far right, "is a major oversight, given the ascendancy of the Christian right, partic-

ularly the Christian Coalition under the guidance of Ralph Reed.

"The CNP is not powerful in and of itself," Bleifuss added, "its importance comes from the role it plays as the ideological tent under which far-right activists confer with the wealthy men and women who fund their activities. Policy discussions and strategic brain-storming both take place at the secretive CNP gatherings. The general public would benefit from a greater understanding of how the far-right functions in the U.S. and what plans it has for our future."

Bleifuss suggests that Ralph Reed and his ideological compatriots benefit from the lack of media attention given the CNP. "Unfortunately," Bleifuss added, "the mass media have been too willing to swallow the public relations line that Reed et al are merely players in a pluralistic democracy. This claim is baldly refuted by the collection of authoritarian extremists who rally under the CNP banner."

3 **CENSORED**

The Secret Pentagon Plan to Subsidize Defense Contractor Mergers

Source:
NEWSDAY
Date: 7/28/94
Title: "Flak for Defense Merger"*
Author: Patrick J. Sloyan

SYNOPSIS: The Pentagon is secretly funneling taxpayer dollars to giant military contractors to help them grow even larger. This extraordinary Pentagon ploy to pay defense contractors billions of dollars to underwrite expenses connected with acquisitions and mergers was approved without any announcement in 1993; it was not discovered until July 1994.

According to Deputy Defense Secretary John Deutch, the unprecedented payment plan will save taxpayers money. Deutch said the mergers would help reduce overhead charges by defense contractors as the industry becomes smaller. Members of the House Armed Services Investigations Subcommittee rejected Deutch's explanation saying the policy was a potential windfall for defense contractors and an incentive for hostile corporate takeovers ... with taxpayers picking up the bill.

David Cooper, of the General Accounting Office, said that while no specific savings could be seen, the new policy could involve "several billions of dollars" in payments to defense contractors for post-merger restructuring costs that have yet to be defined.

Norman Augustine, chairman of Martin Marietta, a giant billion-dollar defense contractor, supported the plan, arguing that the federal government would reap lower costs from defense mergers over the long term. Under the plan, Augustine's company would get $270 million from the Pentagon to cover expenses related to the purchase of a subsidiary from General Electric. Martin Marietta already quietly received a $60 million payment from the Pentagon to buy a General Dynamics subsidiary.

It was Martin Marietta's Augustine who originally persuaded Defense Secretary William Perry and Deutch to approve the money-for-merger plan. Both Perry and Deutch were on the Martin Marietta payroll before joining the Clinton administration.

The administration's payment plan was challenged as illegal and unnecessary by Brookings Institute expert Lawrence Korb, senior Pentagon official during the Bush administration, who said "Taxpayer subsidization is not necessary to promote acquisitions and mergers."

SSU Censored Researcher:
Will Beaubien

COMMENTS: Journalist Patrick Sloyan pointed out that his story had been distributed by the Los Angeles Times-Washington Post News Service but that the problem for him was not the lack of exposure.

"The real problem is the decline in enterprise reporting by the Establishment Press," Sloyan said. "Too much is made of reporting handouts by government public relations people." Sloyan added that his article was part of a series examining top Clinton Pentagon appointees and their close ties and fortunes made from the defense industry.

In late December 1994, *The Wall Street Journal* reported that a $10 billion mega-merger between defense giants Lockheed Corporation and Martin Marietta was approved by the Federal Trade Commission staff. Should the merger go through, the new company, to be called Lockheed Martin Corporation, would be the nation's largest defense contractor with 170,000 employees and $23 billion in annual sales.

4 CENSORED

Poisoning Ourselves with Toxic Incinerators

Source:
GOVERNMENT ACCOUNTABILITY PROJECT
Date: September 1994
Title: "Poisoning Ourselves: The Impact of Incineration on Food and Human Health, An Executive Summary"*
Author: Mick G. Harrison, Esq.

SYNOPSIS: By the latter part of the 1980s, the U.S. Environmental Protection Agency (EPA) understood two very important facts that should have fundamentally altered the nation's waste disposal policy.

First, government officials knew that incineration produced dioxin as a byproduct. Dioxin is one of the most potent, toxic, and carcinogenic chemicals known to science. Second, EPA scientists knew that dioxin accumulates through the food chain much like the banned pesticide DDT accumulates in the environment. Dioxin is a persistent substance that easily stores and remains in the tissues of plants and animals. EPA officials also admit that the EPA has no standards to address the immense risks posed by food chain contamination from incinerators emitting dioxin.

Despite this information, incineration has rapidly proliferated throughout the country as the "profitable answer" for disposal of the nation's stockpile of toxic waste and garbage. In fact, incineration does not destroy the waste, it transforms it. Dioxin, lead, mercury, PCBs and other air emissions from incinerator smokestacks cannot be adequately contained even with the most advanced equipment. These poisons are widely dispersed, and like acid rain, result in uncontrolled pollution of the surrounding water, soil, and farmland.

The dangers of these bio-cumulative chemicals multiply dramatically as they are absorbed up through the food chain, from soil and water to plant and animal life to humans. In the case of dioxin, it takes seven years for your body to eliminate half of the dioxin in your system. Unfortunately, rather than acting on the information it has, EPA has purposefully avoided even documenting the cumulative effects of hazardous and solid waste incineration. Flaws in the EPA-industry perspective, cited by the Government Accountability Project (GAP) which has been investigating the problem, include: 1) failure to acknowledge that our current national cancer rate is largely the result of environmental exposures to industry pollutants, and 2) the use of risk assessment methods, that when corrected for error and non-conservative assumptions, warrants far higher projections of risk than those reported by EPA and industry.

The most recent EPA waste combustion strategy fails to overcome the problems since: 1) it is not being applied to incinerators used in Superfund cleanups (more than 1,000 communities have a waste cleanup problem that may warrant Superfund action); 2) it is not being applied to the dioxin waste incinerator in Jacksonville, Arkansas, despite gross evidence of failure to meet standards and rulings in federal court; 3) it is not being used to require timely and strict compliance with *current* standards (the infamous WTI incinerator in East Liverpool, Ohio, and the LWD incinerator in Calvert City, Kentucky, are prime examples of non-compliance problems); and 4) it is only sporadically applied at commercial hazardous waste incinerators.

The problem is well known to the regulators, yet no preventative action is being taken in communities where unnecessary hazardous waste incinerators saturate the air and food supply with dioxin, lead, mercury, cadmium, and other persistent toxins.

GAP charges: "Our national policy of promoting incineration and other combustion methods of waste disposal is poisoning us."

SSU Censored Researcher:
Lisa Golding

COMMENTS: The author of this report, Mick Harrison, was director of the EPA Watch Program of the Government Accountability Project (GAP) when the study was conducted; he is now director of GreenLaw, an environmental protection organization. Harrison said the issue received minimal media coverage *per se* in 1994. "There was no national television coverage and no national newsweekly coverage of the subject," he noted. "There was some coverage on the periphery, including limited coverage by *The New York Times*, of two specific incinerator cases in which the author and GAP are involved: the WTI hazardous

waste incinerator controversy in East Liverpool, Ohio, and the Vertac Superfund site EPA incinerator in Jacksonville, Arkansas."

The author suggests that the public would benefit directly from greater exposure of the issue because "increased public awareness that incinerators and other pollution sources are causing mass contamination of food could lead directly to legislative and agency actions to dramatically reduce the number of cancer deaths and other environmental illnesses in the U.S. (and abroad), including breast cancer, and appropriate allocation of resources.

"Those who benefit from the lack of media coverage given the nominated subject are primarily the large corporations, and those who own and control them, involved in waste incineration and those that emit environmentally persistent chemical poisons into

THIS MODERN WORLD by TOM TOMORROW

NEWS REPORTS ON THE FINANCIAL MARKETS OFTEN SEEM AS IF THEY ARE BEING BROADCAST IN A FOREIGN LANGUAGE-- OR, PERHAPS MORE ACCURATELY, IN SOME *SECRET CODE*...

--ON WALL STREET TODAY...THE *BLUE CAT* WAITED NERVOUSLY BY THE *LARGE DOOR* IN THE *RAIN*.

NOW THIS...

LATELY THESE REPORTS HAVE BEEN PARTICULARLY SURREAL...BLAMING THE RECENT STOCK MARKET TURMOIL ON A *STRONG ECONOMY* & LOWER *UNEMPLOYMENT RATES*...

--CONDITIONS WHICH MANY AMERICANS MAY HAVE NAIVELY CONSIDERED *DESIRABLE*...

the air (or water and soil) such as power plants, cement plants, asphalt plants, chemical plants, steel plants, paint and solvent companies and certain manufacturing operations. Indirectly, politicians who receive substantial financial support from such corporations and individuals also benefit from the lack of coverage."

Harrison said that there had been some recent coverage on new EPA limits on dioxin risk assessments, but pointed out that this coverage did not focus on the central issue, an aspect of censorship that is often overlooked.

"The central issue of the article was the dire risks posed to human health and the environment by the *cumulative* impacts of atmospheric transport and deposition of chemical poisons such as dioxin, mercury and PCBs emitted from multiple waste incinerators and other air pollution sources over time. This

cumulative impact results in contamination of food sources and tens of thousands, if not millions, of cases of (preventable) cancers and other serious illnesses. Instead, the limited coverage that occurred focused on controversies over individual waste facilities and on EPA actions in response to public pressure. This had the effect of distracting public attention from the issue of cumulative impacts and gave the impression that the government was responding appropriately.

"The key point was ignored—that the bulk of our current catastrophic number of cancer cases (and several other serious non-cancer illnesses) are preventable if we simply acknowledge the combined national impact of multiple air pollution sources, and stop being distracted by the traditional EPA and industry approach which focuses public attention erroneously only on individual facilities

and the fraction of emitted chemical poisons from a single facility deposited in close proximity in the local community. This EPA/industry now-you-see-it now-you-don't approach to environmental assessment and analysis, a scientific slight of hand at best, leaves unaccounted for all the chemical poisons that are traded via the atmosphere from one community to another, and assumes these poisons fall harmlessly between food producing areas."

Harrison acknowledged that the EPA recently has been moving to regulate previously unregulated dioxin sources such as medical waste incinerators and to add dioxin limits for hazardous waste incinerators. "However," he said, "there has yet to be a public acknowledgment of the importance of food chain contamination from air pollution sources and the potential addressing such sources aggressively has for dramatically lowering current rates of cancer and other illnesses."

Harrison concluded that the "communication gap has largely resulted from the failure of the media to take this particular bull by the horns."

On December 16, 1994, at an EPA hearing to collect public comment, Arnold Den, senior EPA advisor in San Francisco, confirmed Harrison's concerns, saying, "90 percent of dioxin exposure is through the food chain route."

5 CENSORED

Clinton Administration Retreats on Ozone Crisis

Source:
IN THESE TIMES
Date: 1/24/94
Title: "Full of holes: Clinton's retreat on the ozone crisis"*
Author: David Moberg

SYNOPSIS: Since the United States banned chlorofluorocarbon (CFC) aerosols in the late '70s, increasing evidence has revealed that both the destruction of the ozone layer and the resulting dangers to human health and the ecosystem are far more serious than scientists had first recognized.

The ozone hole over Antarctica has continued to grow every year since its discovery in 1985 and damage to the ozone layer over heavily populated areas of the Northern Hemisphere also has been increasing rapidly. Scientists recorded all-time low levels of ozone over the United States in 1993.

The ultraviolet rays that penetrate a weakened ozone layer have been linked to increased cataracts, skin cancer, genetic damage and infectious diseases among humans—as well as reduced plant growth. Meanwhile, the Clinton administration has been moving backward on protecting the stratospheric ozone layer. This ominous precedent will encourage other industrial countries to stall on their own CFC phase-outs and puts the administration in a far weaker position to argue for an accelerated phase-out of CFCs in the developing countries where CFC production is soaring.

Du Pont, the giant chemical firm which developed the first industrial CFC, had planned to halt CFC production at the end of 1994. Yet, in late 1993, EPA *asked Du Pont to keep making CFCs until 1996.* The EPA defended its decision as a "consumer protection" measure that will make it easier for car owners to recharge their old air conditioners which use CFCs as a cooling agent.

Ozone-safe, environmentally sound cooling technologies are already available however. The Colorado-based Climatran Corp. already has produced 400 "heat-exchanger" systems currently in use in city buses in Denver and Salt Lake City. The federal Department of Transportation has found the system to use 90 percent less energy than conventional air conditioners and cost one eighth as much to maintain—for virtually the same initial purchase cost.

After two frustrating years for the manufacturer and under threat of a lawsuit, the EPA finally approved the technology last fall.

Additionally, an East German refrigerator company, in cooperation with Greenpeace, has begun manufacturing an ozone-safe refrigerator that utilizes a "Greenfreeze" technology. The consumer response has been so great that bigger companies have begun producing "Greenfreeze" models. But no U.S. company—including Whirlpool, which makes a European "Greenfreeze" model —offers this alternative in the U.S.

Bill Walsh, coordinator of Greenpeace's U.S. atmosphere and energy campaign, charges that Clinton's policies "reward companies that drag their feet," such as the auto companies, and fail to encourage sound alternatives.

Unfortunately, the old revolving-door way of doing business remains intact at the EPA. Robert Sussman, the deputy administrator who requested that Du Pont keep manufacturing CFCs, previously worked at a law firm that represented the Chemical Manufacturers Association.

SSU Censored Researcher: Dan Tomerlin

COMMENTS: Author David Moberg said the ozone crisis issue did not receive sufficient exposure in the mass media in 1994. "There were announcements of some changes in policy, but given the earlier high profile of the ozone crisis, recent developments were underplayed."

The general public would benefit from knowing more about the ozone crisis by becoming more aware of the health dangers of chlorofluorocarbons and some of the alternatives being promoted. Further, Moberg said, they would become aware of a wide range of safer alternatives that deserve and need research and development support.

Groups that benefit from the limited coverage given the issue, according to Moberg, include the chemical industry, the auto industry, and other major manufacturers, including makers of appliances.

1947 AEC Memo Reveals Why Human Radiation Experiments Were Censored

Sources:
SECRECY & GOVERNMENT BULLETIN
Date: March 1994

Title: "Protecting Government Against the Public"*
Author: Steven Aftergood

COLUMBIA JOURNALISM REVIEW
Date: March/April 1994
Title: "The Radiation Story No One Would Touch"*
Author: Geoffrey Sea

SYNOPSIS: As the secrecy ban is finally lifted, the unethical, immoral, and illegal Cold War radiation experiments on unsuspecting humans by the Department of Defense are illuminated by a most remarkable document that has emerged virtually unnoticed.

Dated April 17, 1947, an Atomic Energy Commission (AEC) memorandum, stamped SECRET and addressed to the attention of a Dr. Fidler, at the AEC in Oak Ridge, Tennessee, reads in part as follows: "*Subject: MEDICAL EXPERIMENTS ON HUMANS*

"*1. It is desired that no document be released which refers to experiments with humans and might have adverse effect on public opinion or result in legal suits. Documents covering such work field should be classified 'secret'.*"

The memorandum was issued over the name of O.G. Haywood, Jr., Colonel, Corps of Engineers. Apparently it was effective, for it was not until November 15, 1993, when *The Albuquerque Tribune* (circulation: 35,000) broke the story which was then catapulted into the national headlines by the forthright admissions and initiatives of Secretary of Energy Hazel O'Leary. Eileen Welsome's three-part investigative series for the *Tribune* later won her a Pulitzer Prize.

Ironically, as Geoffrey Sea, author and radiological health physicist, points out, documentation of the inhumane program was massive, solid, and publicly available, as early as 1986. But the major news media were not interested; it was only after the disclosures by a small daily newspaper and Secretary O'Leary—with all the victims dead and most of the perpetrators retired—that the news media put it on the national agenda.

Even now, as new revelations about the enormous scope of the horrifying experiments are discovered, there is little if any mention of the AEC memorandum which has been described by America's security classification expert, Steven Aftergood, as "One of the more remarkable documents to emerge" from the Energy Department's new openness initiative—the 1947 Atomic Energy Commission memorandum on the classification of human radiation experiments.

As Aftergood points out, the memorandum identifies the true enemy—"public opinion." And the

means used to defeat the enemy—"classification." "The practice of classifying information in order to prevent embarrassment to an agency has long been prohibited," Aftergood said. "And yet it is commonplace. The AEC memo itself was classified Secret (meaning it supposedly 'could be expected to cause serious damage to the national security')."

Classification of the AEC memo, which was obtained by Rep. John Dingell's subcommittee on oversight, was finally canceled by the authority of the Department of Energy, on February 22, 1994.

SSU Censored Researcher:
Jessica Nystrom

COMMENTS: While Steven Aftergood published the 1947 AEC memo on the front page of his nationally-distributed *Secrecy & Government Bulletin* in March 1994, the *Washington Post* did not report the same memorandum until December 15. Referring to the memo, the *Post* guilefully said that "newly uncovered government documents have revealed" that "government officials deliberately withheld information about the tests from individuals participating in them and from the general public in order to avoid lawsuits and negative public reaction."

Noting that the story of human radiation experiments has justifiably received a flood of media coverage recently, Aftergood pointed out, "the role of the classification system in facilitating and concealing such experiments did not receive the attention it deserves."

Aftergood charged, "The government's ability to withhold information from the public in order to prevent 'adverse effects on public opinion,' or lawsuits, is about as frightening as some of the secret experiments themselves.

"The willful abuse of classification authority that is described so explicitly in the 1947 Atomic Energy Commission memorandum is what lifts the human experimentation story out of its historical context and makes it an urgent contemporary issue. As long as there are no effective constraints on the government secrecy system, the same kinds of abuses that occurred in the past could continue to take place today."

Aftergood said the "lack of sustained attention to the workings of government secrecy naturally makes it more difficult to change ingrained bureaucratic habits." Noting how the cold war secrecy system has proven to be amazingly resilient, Aftergood said that classification activity has actually increased since the end of the cold war. Aftergood added that the Advisory Committee on Human Radiation Experiments, expected to complete its work in the spring of 1995, will address the all-important question: "Could similar hazardous experiments be secretly conducted today?"

Geoffrey Sea, author of the *Columbia Journalism Review* article analyzing the history of the radiation story, has testified before the Advisory Committee several times and is actively involved in helping victims achieve some measure of justice. Sea has worked as a radiation specialist for a law firm which filed two class action lawsuits on behalf of the victims; he is a founding member of the Task Force on Radiation and Human Rights; he also directs the Tides Foundation's Atomic Reclamation and Conversion Project; and he is writing a book about radiation experiments, *Eyes Only: A Subject's Story.*

Sea points out that while the media did have access to the radiation story much earlier (most of the clinical radiation experiments were published in major medical journals or publicly available government reports), they chose to ignore it for decades as his article detailed. In the following, Sea updates the story with an account of developments since the 1993 announcement by Secretary of Energy Hazel O'Leary which instigated the initial press coverage.

"After a flurry of media attention following O'Leary's 'revelations,' the mass media apparently considered that the story had run its course. In February of 1994, just when the truly revelatory documents began to be released and the full picture began to emerge of government-planned injuries to millions of Americans, the radiation experiment story was knocked off the front page—and out altogether—by an orgy of sensationalistic journalism focused on injuries to John Wayne Bobbitt's penis, Nancy Kerrigan's knees, and the feelings of two murderous brothers named Menendez.

"As if this wasn't enough, *The New York Times* then took a cue from the trashy coverage of these stories and decided to give a new spin to the radiation experiments: the victimizers as victims. On two consecutive days in March, *The Times* ran articles about the Vanderbilt and Cincinnati experiments suggesting that in both cases the scientists were 'sharing the anguish' felt by surviving subjects and families. Citing university contentions that 'scientists did nothing wrong,' *The Times* equated 'the searing experience' of the real experimental victims with that of the scientists and universities involved. The perpetrators, in their turn, took their cue from *The Times* and began bemoaning *their* victimization.

"Rather than receive O'Leary's disclosures as an opening—then to be followed through all the developing intricacies as one would a Watergate or a Whitewater—the media's approach to O'Leary was wham, bam, thank you ma'am. Everyone carried the news of O'Leary's call for the victims to be compensated. But then the issue was dropped as if it would just happen of its own accord. No one has even begun to explore the complications—technical, political and budgetary—of what real compensation would entail. Nor has anyone honestly stated what is, in Washington, a poorly guarded secret: that unless the victims take their claims to court, they won't get squat from the government that betrayed them.

"The Department of Energy's toll-free experiment hotline was publicized with great fanfare. But no one has bothered to ask what will happen to the massive list of callers. The answer? Nothing. It seems the hotline was established to create the appearance of government action and concern. There is actually not a single government plan for systematically identifying and helping the victims of the radiation experiments.

"Other substantive issues have gone wholly neglected by the media. We have heard a lot about the eighteen plutonium injectees, but nothing at all about the hundreds of people who were injected with uranium and at least a dozen other radionuclides; a lot about the schoolchildren who were fed radioactive iron and calcium in Massachusetts, but nothing about the larger number of similar children who were fed radioactive iron in Tennessee; a lot about the people who were exposed to radiation as part of an experiment, but nothing about the people who, once exposed, then became guinea pigs for the development of experimental drugs and radiation 'treatments.'

"In the mid-1950's, when radioactive strontium and iodine from fallout were discovered at dangerous levels in human breast milk, the atomic establishment decided, in the interest of 'national security,' that it would be better to stop breast-feeding than to stop nuclear testing. With its true motivations kept secret, the 'scientific' campaign against breast-feeding was thereby launched—perhaps the largest human experiment ever conducted on the planet. But we haven't heard about it from the mass media—and won't—unless O'Leary decides to hold another press conference.

"O'Leary will not likely be holding any more such press conferences. It is clear that she was strongly chastened by the White House, both for committing the Administration to the budgetary black hole of victim compensation, and for exposing the government to unspecifiable liability through the admission of wrongdoing. By the time she was called before a Senate committee and asked if the radiation experiments had been unethical, O'Leary claimed incompetence in the rendering of moral judgment and referred the question to her agency's lawyer. When people start referring ethical questions to lawyers, you know the fix is in. But you won't read about *that* in *The New York Times*.

"In fact, no one wants to be the one to render moral judgment. Not O'Leary, not the President's Advisory Committee (members have already said that they are not interested in 'laying blame'), certainly not the White House, nor the new Republican Congress. The media won't lay any blame—it's just not what professional journalists do nowadays (they might get sued). And so we find ourselves in a curious situation. Crimes against Humanity, committed on a massive scale, without any criminals!

"Perhaps the biggest failing of the media's coverage of this issue has been the abject inability to grasp the institutionalized, programmatic character of the unethical experimentation. Stories continue to portray single experiments or governmental decisions as if each were an aberration; a case of individual misdeed, lapse in judgment or failure in communication. Nowhere do we get the sense that, for decades, an organized group of doctors and policy makers at the nexus of the military-industrial-university establishment conspired to deceive and injure experimental subjects—often intentionally selected from the disempowered segments of our society—to further the planning of and production for war. This is the same crime for which physicians at Nuremberg were tried, convicted, and hung. 'Mistakes were made,' the media now seem to be saying *en masse*, 'now let's get on with less complicated news. This isn't Nuremberg. We don't hang people for atrocities anymore.'

"The cold war radiation experiments affected a far greater number of people than early reports indicated. Tens of thousands of people were the unwitting subjects of clinical experiments involving needless exposure to ionizing radiation, or dangerous radiation 'treatments.' Millions of people were exposed to fallout or other environmental contamination from intentional releases of radioactive material. Only a very small percentage of the affected population has so far been identified, so greater media exposure of the experiments would have an obvious and vital impact on the further identification of subjects. These subjects may be at greater risk of disease or reproductive damage, should be included in medical monitoring programs, and have legal rights to seek compensatory and punitive damages.

"In addition, the radiation experiment program has been a gross violation of universal ethical principles and the public trust. In the former Soviet Union, numerous perpetrators of the Chernobyl disaster are still serving out prison terms, and officials held responsible for the accident have been either voted or thrown out of office. In the United States, however, not a single criminal prosecution has been initiated, election swayed or resignation compelled in the cases of perpetrators who clearly and willfully planned a larger program of intentional harm.

"A startling fact about the experiments is that, despite the documentation of hundreds of cases of unethical conduct resulting in lasting damage to thousands of people, not a single physician or nurse, scientist or technician, policy maker or administrator has yet come forward to admit wrongdoing. Accurate and morally persuasive coverage might bring whistleblowers forward and might build the level of public indignation to the point where criminal proceedings are initiated and public officials held accountable on this issue.

"Finally, we are in jeopardy of losing the universal applicability of the Nuremberg Code. American physicians involved in the radiation experiments have already said that the Code applied to German war criminals, but not to them. In order to insure that unethical human experimentation does not happen again, all violations of the Code must be publicized, the violators punished, and the universality of ethical standards upheld.

"The physicians and scientists who implemented the human radiation experiment program clearly benefit from its limited media exposure—many of them continue to practice or hold office and enjoy high standing in their professional communities. Likewise the many universities, hospitals and corporations involved have not been held to account. The media and politicians in mid-sized cities like Nashville or Cincinnati often have very close ties to the local universities and companies that were involved in the experimentation. It is easy to pursue a story about atrocities—as long as they are distant in time and space. But the radiation atrocities happened close to home, and not long ago, often involving familiar physicians and public officials of some renown. The story has therefore been an uncomfortable one for editors, reporters, readers and viewers alike."

Finally, Sea points out that in a larger sense, the radiological and nuclear industries stand to lose a lot from greater coverage of this story since many of the most prominent experimenters were also central figures in establishing current radiation protection standards and practices. Sea concludes, "If it becomes common knowledge that many of these advisers and regulators were themselves guilty of unethical conduct in causing intentional harm to patients, then all radiation safety standards and practices would need to be reviewed."

60 Billion Pounds of Fish Wasted Annually

Source:
MOTHER JONES
Date: July/August 1994
Title: "Special Report: A Farewell To Fish?"*
Authors: Peter Steinhart, Hal Bernton, Brad Matsen, Ray Troll, and Deborah Cramer

SYNOPSIS: While the world's oceans are almost totally fished out and while millions of people starve, the world's fishing fleets waste about 60 billion pounds of fish and seafood every year—enough for 120 billion meals.

Once upon a time, on a good day in the 1960s, an Atlantic fisherman could harpoon 30 large swordfish. Today, such swordfish are hardly ever seen. And what has happened to swordfish has happened to hundreds of marine species in just the last 15 years. New England cod, haddock, and yellowtail flounder have declined 70 percent; South Atlantic grouper and snapper, 80 percent; Atlantic bluefin tuna, 90 percent. More than 200 separate salmon spawning runs have vanished from the Pacific Northwest. The United Nation's Food and Agriculture Organization determined in April 1994 that roughly 60 percent of the fish populations they monitor are fully exploited or depleted.

As large-scale fishing technologies have taken over the world's oceans, they have become less and less selective in their catch. Fish too small to be taken and species not legally fished are caught, and then thrown overboard to die. Often the catch is tossed overboard because it is too small or too large to be processed on the factory trawlers, which drag large, bag-like nets that scoop up both wanted and unwanted species.

Ironically, the federal government's efforts to manage the catch—such as limiting the seasons for different species of fish—has instead led to incredible waste, unsafe fishing practices, and economic chaos for the industry. Under the "derby system," the fishermen lack the time and financial incentives to try to avoid catching fish that aren't worth processing or are not legally in season. Last year, the Alaska fleet alone caught 4.2 billion pounds of fish, then dumped a staggering 763 million pounds—seven times more fish than is retained by the entire New England fishing fleet.

The human cost of the disappearing fish harvest is considerable. For many it means hunger, since in some countries more than half of the population's animal protein comes from the sea. Michael Sutton, of the World Wildlife Fund, says "Unlike rhinos, tigers, and bears, when you deplete fish populations, you're threatening the survival of humanity."

For many others, it means the end of a way of life. The collapse of the Newfoundland cod fishery put 40,000 people out of work; increased risks to the Alaska fleet led to the deaths of more than 165 fishermen off Alaska in the past six years.

And the problem is worldwide. For example, in the Philippines, as traditional fishing by net and spear yields smaller and smaller returns, divers stay down 150 to 200 feet for hours, breathing air pumped through hoses, in hopes of spearing a profitable catch. In some villages, paralysis and brain damage caused by submersion at such depths is now a common affliction.

Environmental author Peter Steinhart warns that by continuing to deplete the ocean's productivity, we risk hunger, poverty, dislocation, and war. The solution, he suggests, is a set of international agreements binding all nations to a common set of rules that will reduce the size of the world's fishing fleet, set new limits, and enforce them.

SSU Censored Researcher:
Dan Tomerlin

COMMENTS: Sarah Pollock, project editor at *Mother Jones*, said that the problem addressed in the "Farewell to Fish" special report—the serious decline of the world's fisheries—received a brief flurry of attention in the mainstream media in 1994, much of it after and in response to the *Mother Jones* coverage. However, she added, "the mainstream media continue to neglect what's happening in Alaska, where the spoils of one of the remaining great fisheries are being divided by competing and powerful interests."

Noting that fish are the last of the world's wild food, Pollock said, "Most people think the ocean is boundless, and few have any idea of the amount of *waste* involved in the annual fish harvest. If they knew how rapidly we're depleting the oceans, with little or no regard to a sustainable future, they would be up in arms to demand better controls on commercial fishing and elimination of waste."

While the short-term interests of some huge food conglomerates are served by the lack of media coverage, Pollock points out, "Sadly, in the long run, no one's interests will be served if we run out of fish."

Pollock also explained the efforts the publication made to bring greater attention to its report on the fish crisis. In addition to the 150 key press contacts who regularly receive advance copies of *Mother Jones*, they sent copies of the story to more than a hundred additional reporters who cover fisheries for major papers, magazines, and trade journals; they sent 50 advance copies to The Marine Fish Conservation Network in time for a focused lobbying effort; they worked closely with the Washington office of Fish Forever which distributed nearly 300 copies of the issue to members of the press, politicians, and activists; and supplied Gerry Studds (D-MA), chair of the Merchant Marine and Fisheries Committee, his aides, and members of the committee with copies of the issue.

On December 8, 1994, the Associated Press reported that the U.S. Commerce Department had closed three prime fishing grounds off New England, about 6,600 square miles of ocean, to virtually all commercial fishing. Rollie Schmitten, director of the department's National Marine Fisheries Service, said the action was taken in an effort to rebuild depleted stocks of cod, haddock and flounder. The closure will be in effect at least until March 12, 1995, when it might be extended. As noted above, the *Mother Jones* article pointed out that New England cod, haddock, and yellowtail flounder had declined 70 percent in the last 15 years.

The Return of Tuberculosis

Source:
WORLD WATCH
Date: July/August 1994
Title: "Why Don't We Stop
   Tuberculosis?"*
Author: Anne E. Platt

SYNOPSIS: Tuberculosis, thought to be a disease of the past, has surged back with a vengeance and now kills more people than any other infectious or communicable disease in the world—despite the fact that it is curable.

Today, the reemergence of tuberculosis, also called TB, threatens more people than AIDS, cholera, dengue fever, and other infectious diseases *combined*. In 1993, TB killed 2.7 million people around the world; it infected another 8.1 million people; and an estimated one-third of the world's population, or 1.7 billion people, were infected but had not yet developed the disease. In the United States, the U.S. Centers for Disease Control and Prevention reported 26,000 cases of TB in 1992, an increase of nearly percent from 1985.

Further, the current TB epidemic is expected to worsen, especially in the developing world, because of the lack of adequate health care, the evolution of multi-drug-resistant strains, and the emergence of AIDS, which compromises human immune systems and makes them more susceptible to infectious diseases. For a person with an immune system under severe stress—from HIV, diabetes, or chemotherapy for cancer, for example—the chances that the infection will develop into disease increase to as much as 10 percent in a single year.

A person who has active TB can spread the infection simply by coughing, sneezing, singing, or even talking, while another person has only to inhale the bacilli to become infected. If the infection is not detected and treated promptly, one person with active tuberculosis can infect an average of 10 to 14 people in one year and sometimes even more.

By the year 2,000, the global incidence of TB alone is expected to increase to 10.2 million cases per year, an increase of 36 percent over 1990's 7.5 million cases. And, overall, tuberculosis deaths are predicted to increase by one-sixth, to

3.5 million by the year 2000, killing 30 million people in this decade alone.

However, "this tragedy is totally unnecessary" according to Dr. Hiroshi Nakajima, Director-General of the World Health Organization. The medical knowledge to treat and cure TB exists and the costs are not prohibitive.

In 1993, the World Bank identified short-term TB treatment as one of the most cost-effective ways to reduce the global burden of the disease. In China, it costs only $13 for a supply of drugs to cure one person. In most developing countries, it costs less than $30 to save a life and prevent further transmission of the disease. In the U.S., it costs up to $10,000 to treat an active case of TB compared to $200,000 to treat an active TB infection that has become drug-resistant.

The growing TB epidemic is a classic case of a public health crisis that can be resolved inexpensively. However, governments and public health officials need to invest up front in prevention and early intervention. If they do so, early treatment could prevent nearly 12 million deaths worldwide in the next decade and save vast amounts of money.

**SSU Censored Researcher:
Jessica Nystrom**

COMMENTS: Author Anne E. Platt felt there was little coverage on the rise of tuberculosis outside the United States in 1994 and few substantive pieces on the global nature of the disease that put things into perspective. "During a year when health care reform was the number one issue on the domestic political agenda," Platt said, "there was surprisingly little coverage of the resurgence of tuberculosis. The majority of media attention was in a reactionary vein, i.e. it tended to create fear and misunderstandings rather than clarify the issue. When a crisis occurred or an outbreak was reported, media attention focused on that particular event, usually with limited reporting on underlying causes."

Many reports tended to feed off the public's fears that foreigners, immigrants, and outsiders were bringing TB back inside our country's borders. Here's a sample of some national headlines in 1994 that promoted xenophobia and played on people's fears:

'TB case sparks hunt on Indiana Univ. campus'—*Chicago Tribune*

'Reluctant TB patient hunted by police'—*San Francisco Chronicle*

'TB Increase Found in Immigrants' and 'TB an Unwelcome Hitchhiker With Immigrants'—*Los Angeles Times*

Platt notes that while the headlines don't tell the whole story, unfortunately, they are usually the focus of people's attention.

The immediate benefit of more coverage about TB would be educational, according to Platt. "There are many misconceptions and myths about how TB is spread, what causes the infection vs. the disease, and how to take care of it. With greater media attention, people would understand the disease and the need for vigilance. Knowledge is power to change and redirect policy. Again, by understanding that the poor, AIDS patients, and immigrants do not actually *cause* the spread of TB, but simply *increase the chances* that the infection will progress to the disease stage, the public can push for change. Legislatures and health care providers can then target underserved populations and high-risk groups.

"Wider exposure would also open up the health care debate to discussion and evaluation of prevention and targeted treatment, rather than cures and medical technology. Using TB as a case study for preventive and low-tech treatment, we could promote changes in how we treat other infectious diseases. Finally, wider exposure would show how TB is a greater threat in the developing world. The media could show how it is within our scope of choice to determine funding and aid to other parts of the world. Also, it is within our powers to influence and redirect international attention to the issue of TB and AIDS."

Platt feels there are several groups which benefit from the limited coverage given the subject. "1. The medical research community: With a limited pool of public research dollars, the research industry does not want health care providers to rely on low cost, low-tech treatment, because the industry would lose research funding. Cures are more profitable than prevention, so the industry wants to steer attention away from solutions that might hurt their business. 2. Medical care providers: The medical care community does not want to admit the failings or short-comings of the shift away from preventive care, health education, and low-tech solutions to their current focus on cures and high-tech intervention. Additionally, medical care providers have shifted care away from the poor and at-risk populations to the wealthier populations (who are at a lower risk of developing tuberculosis in the first place). There is more money to be made by treating drug-resistant strains of TB than treating the thousands of cases that require testing, screening, basic intervention, and low-cost pills spread out over six to eight months. 3. Ourselves: We have put too much faith in technological fixes. We dared to think we could control nature and wipe out TB."

Platt received several letters to the editor in response to her article in *World Watch*. One was from a public health worker in New Mexico who suggested the real question was "Why we *can't* control TB." Platt says she agrees that the infection is difficult to detect, difficult to treat, and that in developing countries there are still millions of people who have no access at all to modern health care. However, Platt says her question is why *don't* we stop TB? "My article examines the bureaucratic inertia; the public's lack of understanding and the myths that are perpetuated by the media; our fears of TB coming from immigrants, the poor, the mentally disabled, and AIDS patients; and our failure to fund and provide treatment in other countries, especially where the people are at greater risk from the co-infection of HIV and TB. It may be impossible to completely eradicate TB, but we can certainly do a better job of controlling it—especially in our global community."

Reinforcing Platt's thesis, the *San Francisco Chronicle* carried a wire service story on November 18, 1994, which warned that drug-resistant strains of tuberculosis are spreading rapidly because of improper use of existing drugs and the failure to develop new ones according to a new report by the World Health Organization.

The Pentagon's Mysterious HAARP Project

Source:
EARTH ISLAND JOURNAL
Date: Fall 1994
Title: "Project HAARP: The Military's Plan to Alter the Ionosphere"*
Authors: Clare Zickuhr and Gar Smith

SYNOPSIS: The Pentagon's mysterious HAARP project, now under construction at an isolated Air Force facility near Gakona, Alaska, marks the first step toward creating the world's most powerful "ionospheric heater." The High Frequency Active Auroral Research Project (HAARP), a joint effort of the Air Force and the Navy, is the latest in a series of little-known Department of Defense (DOD) "active ionospheric experiments."

Internal HAARP documents state: "From a DOD point of view, the most exciting and challenging" part of the experiment is "its potential to *control* ionospheric processes" for military objectives. Scientists envision using the system's powerful 2.8-10 megahertz (MHz) beam to burn "holes" in the ionosphere and "create an artificial lens" in the sky that could focus large bursts of electromagnetic energy "to higher altitudes ... than is presently possible." The minimum area to be heated would be 31 miles in diameter.

The initial $26 million, 320 kw HAARP project will employ 360 72-foot-tall antennas spread over four acres to direct an intense beam of focused electromagnetic energy upwards to strike the ionosphere. The next stage of the project would expand HAARP's power to 1.7 gigawatts (1.7 billion watts), making it the most powerful such transmitter on Earth.

For a project whose backers hail it as a major scientific feat, HAARP has remained extremely low-profile—almost unknown to most Alaskans, and the rest of the country. HAARP surfaced publicly in Alaska in the spring of 1993, when the Federal Aviation Administration (FAA) began advising commercial pilots on how to avoid the large amount of intentional (and some unintentional) electromagnetic radiation that HAARP would generate. Despite protests of FAA engineers and Alaska bush pilots, the final Environmental Impact Statement gave HAARP the green light.

While a November 1993 "HAARP Fact Sheet" released to the public by the Office of Naval Research stressed only the civilian and scientific aspects of the project, an earlier, 1990, Air Force-Navy document, acquired by *Earth Island Journal*, listed only military experiments for the HAARP project.

Scientists, environmentalists, and native people are concerned that HAARP's electronic transmitters could harm people, endanger wildlife, and trigger unforeseen environmental impacts.

Inupiat tribal advisor Charles Etok Edwardsen, Jr., wrote President Clinton on behalf of the Inupiat Community of the Arctic Slope and the Kasigluk Elders Conference expressing their concern with the prospect of altering the earth's neutral atmospheric properties.

HAARP also may violate the 1977 Environmental Modification Convention (ratified by the U.S. in 1979), which bans "military or any other hostile use of environmental modification techniques having widespread, long-lasting, or severe effects."

HAARP project manager John Heckscher, a scientist at the Air Force's Phillips Laboratory, has called concerns about the transmitter's impact unfounded. "It's not unreasonable to expect that something three times more powerful than anything that's previously been built might have unforeseen effects," Heckscher told *Microwave News*. "But that's why we do environmental impact statements."

SSU Censored Researcher:
Scott Oehlerking

COMMENTS: Co-author Gar Smith said that to his knowledge, "there has been absolutely no coverage of Project HAARP and its implications in the mainstream media. The only report that I am aware of was an exchange of letters in *Physics and Society* and an article in *Microwave News*. I had written an article on the Eastlund patents in *Earth Island Journal* in 1988, the same year that *OMNI* magazine ran an article on Eastlund's work. As far as I know, there has been no coverage of this story in the environmental press. Given the nature of the proposed experiment and the covert-defense-related implications of the project, I believe that Project HAARP deserves a full and thorough public debate."

Smith said the public should be aware of Project HAARP since, as taxpayers, they have already paid for the demonstration phase of the project and will be footing the bill for the costly, vastly expanded version of the ionospheric transmitter. "Perhaps of greater importance, is the possibility that HAARP may expose nearby human populations to health and safety hazards and—given the planet-wide nature of an experiment that would interact with the Earth's ionosphere and magnetic fields—potential risks to the entire planet. I believe the public should be entitled to determine the real purposes of HAARP, the possible risks, and the process by which this proposal was promoted."

The limited amount of coverage given the issue tends to benefit the Navy and Air Force scientists who are involved in Project HAARP and would rather conduct their research without undue interference. Also, says Smith, Pentagon strategic planners are clearly interested in the "secret agenda" behind the public face of HAARP—i.e. "triggering ionospheric processes that potentially could be exploited for DOD purposes." Smith added that the ARCO oil company and its subsidiaries are involved in the project to various degrees.

Gar Smith, co-author of the article and editor of *Earth Island Journal*, said that one of the biggest obstacles he had to overcome to get the article published was his own staff. "Both the assistant editor and managing editor insisted that the article should not be considered for publication because HAARP had 'no environmental impact' and the article, by its nature, was 'too jargony' to be understood by the average reader. This served to demonstrate a critical problem that stymies environmental criticism: without 'positive proof' of a harmful impact, some people argue, it is irresponsible to speculate on potential hazards. This, of course, is the technique that Rush

Limbaugh uses so effectively to dismiss claims of 'global warming.'

"Non-experts are not supposed to ask questions concerning rarefied scientific matters. As my managing editor put it, being concerned about the possible environmental impact of HAARP was tantamount to being concerned about the impacts of 'farting into the wind.' I consoled myself with the thought that, had more non-experts asked more questions about CFC gases, we might still have an intact ozone shield.

"I was struck by the argument of HAARP's scientists that heating the ionosphere and altering the region's electron densities should not be a matter of concern because the energy released by HAARP was 'insignificant' when compared to the energy pouring into the magnetosphere from the sun. This is another logical fallacy favored by Rush Limbaugh, who has argued that there is no reason to be alarmed by the release of man-made atmospheric gases because volcanoes release much *larger* volumes of similar vapors. This is something like advising jaywalking pedestrians that they needn't worry about being hit by motorcycles because, compared to being run down by a Sherman tank, the consequences would be 'insignificant.'

"When I attempted to obtain a Final Environmental Impact Statement (FEIS) from the regional EPA, I was told that I would have to go 'to Seattle or Alaska to see it.' Project HAARP officials were difficult to locate. It required two hours and a dozen misdirected calls to establish contact. Several attempts were made to obtain the FEIS from HAARP officials.

"The documents didn't arrive until after the article deadline had passed. In order to complete the article, I haunted the local libraries to educate myself about the Earth's geomagnetic fields, trolled a variety of scientific conferences on computer networks, and called a dozen scientists for comment.

"I was able to contact a number of correspondents in the U.S. (and one as far away as Australia) who were lay-experts in electromagnetic phenomenon. They provided useful commentary and suggestions.

"Lacking the FEIS, I was able to draw from my own clipping and document files and from an article on the PAVE PAWS radar that I had written for *New West* magazine many years ago. Library research suggested that the frequency and power range of the proposed HAARP transmitter would be comparable to the PAVE PAWS radar. Using this information, I was able to extrapolate a number of potential harmful effects that might be expected from the operation of the HAARP transmitter. When the FEIS finally arrived, I was pleased to see that these issues were, in fact, cited as problems that were expected to accompany the activation of Project HAARP.

"I sent drafts of the developing article to scientists at the American Federation of Scientists, Union of Concerned Scientists, NOAA, and the Institute for Energy and Environmental Research. I also sent copies of the article to leading environmental writers, including Dr. Steven Schneider, David Suzuki and Paul and Anne Ehrlich. Everyone contacted has expressed concern about the project but professed ignorance about the nature of ionospheric experiments.

"A copy of the magazine reached the desk of Ryan Ross of the Washington, DC-based Environmental News Service. I have spoken with Ross and shared information. Ross hopes to produce an article based on the *Journal*'s initial disclosures.

"At the same time copies of the articles were being sent to scientists for comment, I was engaged in a parallel campaign to get the attention of members of Congress. Copies of the article were faxed to Washington and copies of the magazine were sent in the mail. The hope was that a public debate might take place before an expected vote on full funding of the 1.7 billion-watt transmitter.

"Finally, in late November, I succeeded in reaching Lee Halterman, Rep. Ron Dellums' (D-CA) aide, at the House Armed Services Committee in Washington. After a flurry of faxes and a telephone conversation, I received a faxed copy of a letter sent by Rep. Dellums to the Pentagon's Deputy Under Secretary for Environmental Affairs requesting a halt to the planned 'test' of the HAARP demonstration transmitter on December 1."

The planned "test" of HAARP did not occur on December 1, nor was it known when the test might take place; it seems that no money had been budgeted for the test.

News Media Masks Spousal Violence in the "Language of Love"

Source:
USA TODAY
Date: 3/10/94
Title: "Crimes against women: Media part of problem for masking violence in the language of love"*
Author: Ann Jones

SYNOPSIS: A man guns down his former wife and her new boyfriend; reporters call it a "love triangle."

A man shoots and kills several co-workers, including a woman who refused to date him; the press reports a "tragedy of spurned love."

A man kidnaps his estranged wife, rapes her, accuses her of an imaginary affair, and chokes her to death; a reporter writes that he "made love to his wife," then strangled her when "overcome with jealous passion."

A New York City cop drags his ex-girlfriend out of police headquarters where she works, shoots her four times, killing her, then kills himself; the *New York Post* headlines it: "Tragedy of a Lovesick Cop."

Ann Jones, journalism professor and author of *Next Time, She'll be Dead: Battering and How to Stop It*, charges that the media are part of the problem by masking violence in the language of love. She says, "This slipshod reporting has real consequences in the lives of real men and women. It affirms a batterer's most common excuse for assault: 'I did it because I love you so much.'"

Noting that every 12 seconds in this country, some man batters his current or former wife or girlfriend, Jones says that battering is currently the leading cause of injury to American women, sending more than one million to doctors offices or emergency rooms every year for treatment.

According to Jones it also drives women into the streets with a reported 50 percent of homeless women and kids fleeing from male violence; it figures in one quarter of all suicide attempts by women, one half of all suicide attempts by black women; and, according to the American Medical Association, it also injures fetuses in utero: 37 percent of all obstetric patients are battered during pregnancy.

Yet, as Jones points out, battering, the most frequently committed crime in America, is conspicuously missing from the current national debate on crime. The press, she adds, could go a long way toward providing accurate information and setting a serious tone for public discussion of this issue. "Instead it often fails to cover crimes against women at all."

SSU Censored Researcher:
Paul Giusto

COMMENTS: "The problem is not simply that male violence against wives and girlfriends is underexposed," author Ann Jones charged. "We read the grim headlines all the time. The problem is, as I argued in my op-ed piece and at greater length in my book *Next Time She'll Be Dead*, that the coverage is so wrongheaded.

"This year the subject euphemistically called 'domestic violence' got a lot of inches and air time, thanks to the murder of Nicole Brown, or rather what the press likes to call 'the tragedy of O.J. Simpson.' That case was the *most* reported story on television; and both *Time* and *Newsweek* ran cover stories on 'domestic violence.' Unfortunately, most of the coverage was hopelessly outdated, focusing on individual psychology (Freudian masochism no less!), 'love' and jealousy, and the victim's personal life. This despite the fact that Nicole Brown's story provides a textbook example of how police, prosecutors, and judges routinely violate women's civil rights by denying them protection from assault by intimate partners— surely a newsworthy issue. You'd think that at least African-American reporters would recognize civil rights violations when they see them, but often they focused on 'the race card' and ignored the 'women's issue' altogether. (Once again the interests of women and the interests of African Americans were pitted against each other, as though sexism and racism do not go hand in hand.)

"The coverage was biased in the extreme, relying on the same old (mostly male) sources. Apart from *Ms.* magazine, none of the coverage I read or saw cited a single advocate for battered women or feminist authority on the subject—(God forbid they should talk to a feminist!).

"How is the public supposed to choose effective solutions if it doesn't know what's really going on? Model programs to combat 'domestic violence' are working effectively in Duluth, Minnesota, San Francisco and San Diego, California, Quincy, Massachusetts, and many other cities. But as long as the general public thinks of wife beating and murder as isolated crimes of passion—mere 'private' violence—they have no basis to devise or even recognize social policies that might be effective in ending violence. As things stand now, battering takes a huge economic toll in lost productivity and staggering costs of health care, law enforcement, social services, and so on. Evidence also suggests that the violence plaguing America's streets is learned first in violent homes. In my view, the press is obliged to let the general public know what all these isolated 'crimes of passion' add up to, how deeply this violence affects the quality of our society, and what some communities are doing to stop it."

Jones said that no one benefits from the lack of media coverage "because battering takes such a toll on the whole society, including the future generation. But insofar as battering intimidates women, it serves the interests of male dominance and all the macho boys who are still into that. Especially those in power. When we view lethal assault as romantic, men literally get away with murder. And so does the criminal justice system that refuses to hold them to account.

"This issue suffers particularly from our peculiarly American tendency to see everything in terms of personal psychology. The standard TV talk show on battering, for example, features a sobbing woman recounting the horrible things her husband or boyfriend did to her, followed by a psychologist explaining why the woman 'let' him do it. When have you seen a show—or an article—that asked police officers or judges or elected officials to describe what they do to stop violence against women, and how you can help? Wouldn't that be enlightening?"

11 CENSORED

The Treasury Department Ignores S&L Crimes

Source:
IN THESE TIMES
Dates: 5/30/94, 6/13/94
Titles: "The 21st FinCENtury" and "Crime of the FinCENtury"
Author: Joel Bleifuss

SYNOPSIS: The database of all financial databases is operated by the Financial Crimes Enforcement Network, a division of the Treasury Department, and is known as FinCEN for short. It was established in 1990 to help wage the war against drugs by tracking the flow of narcotics money. And law enforcement officials hail FinCEN as a technological breakthrough that makes it near impossible for criminals to hide illegal financial gains. So far, FinCEN has been successful in catching big-time drug dealers, helped finger Russian spy Aldrich Ames, and compiled evidence used to convict the Islamic extremists who bombed the World Trade Center. The agency now has a staff of 200, a budget of $20 million, and operates quietly out of its headquarters in Vienna ("Spook City"), Virginia.

FinCEN's stated mission is "to provide a government-wide, multi-source intelligence and analytical network to support law enforcement and regulatory agencies in the detection, investigation and prosecution of financial crimes." Its computer capabilities make it very difficult for criminals to hide their illegal gains through money laundering.

Given its stated mission, and exceptional track record, one could expect it would be used to track down the financial criminals who looted the S&Ls and laundered their ill-gotten gains. According to the *Stanford Law and Policy Review*, the final cost of the S&L crime could add up to $1.4 trillion when all the Resolution Trust Corporation and Federal Deposit Insurance Corporation accounts are settled.

However, the Treasury Department apparently has decided not to use FinCEN's extraordinary capabilities to track down the money laundered by the well-heeled S&L crooks—a crime Americans will be paying for into the next century. According to a report FinCEN filed with Congress, the agency has received no requests from Treasury to assist in the investigation of the S&L crimes since its founding in 1990.

Apologists argue that it would be a waste of time since much of the money is irretrievable anyway; that it was speculated away in real estate deals that later went bust, or that it was lost with the fall in oil prices, or eaten up by the high interest rates of the '80s, or frittered away by S&L execs living high on the hog. Non-apologists suspect some portion of those billions was hidden from federal authorities, laundered in offshore foreign banks by the directors and officers of the failed S&Ls, surreptitiously handed off to family members—in other words, stolen.

Finally, it must be noted that about 41 percent of the $84.2 billion in taxpayer bailouts from 1989 to 1993 will go to Texas thrifts. It also should be noted that Texans are well connected: from 1985 to 1988, the U.S. treasury secretary was Texan James Baker; from 1988 to 1992, the president was Texan George Bush; and since 1992, the treasury secretary has been Texan Lloyd Bentsen. Also worth noting is that both Bush and Bentsen have sons who got rich at the S&L trough.

The bottom line is that FinCEN has the technological capability to track the billions of dollars lost in the S&L looting but the Treasury Department has not yet asked it to do so.

SSU Censored Researcher: Will Beaubien

COMMENTS: Investigative author Joel Bleifuss claims that "FinCEN is unknown even to many lawmakers. Very little has been written about this secretive agency."

FinCEN's vast databases could be a powerful tool used to fight white-collar crime, Bleifuss points out, and particularly useful "to track down some of the billions of dollars that S&L crooks laundered in offshore banks. But," Bleifuss adds, "FinCEN has not used the databases that are at its disposal to track down this 'stolen' money. The general public, which is picking up the tab for S&L crimes, has a right to know why."

Bleifuss says that the primary beneficiaries of the limited coverage given FinCEN are the "politically connected S&L looters—particularly those from Texas—who have benefited from Texan Treasury Secretary Lloyd Bentsen's decision not to use FinCEN's crime fighting potential to track down the hidden billions." (Bentsen resigned his position effective 12/21/94.)

How Unocal Covered Up a Record-Breaking California Oil Spill

Source:
SANTA BARBARA NEWS-PRESS
Date: 9/25/94
Title: "Environment: Why not a three-strikes law for corporations?"
Author: Gary Hart

SYNOPSIS: In March 1994, the Unocal Corporation quietly pled guilty to three misdemeanor counts of spilling oil, agreed to clean up the spill, and to pay $1.5 million in criminal fines.

The "misdemeanor" spill—possibly the largest oil spill in California history—was far larger than the 1969 Santa Barbara Channel oil platform blowout that spilled 4.2 million gallons of crude oil. While the full scope of the Unocal spill can't be accurately determined, it is estimated to approach the size of the internationally infamous Exxon Valdez spill in Alaska.

Here's how an environmental disaster of this magnitude went unnoticed and uncovered by the media:

It started back in the early 1950s when Unocal started using a light oil to dilute heavy oil at their production facilities near Guadalupe. The blend of the two oils was easier to extract and speeded the growth of a network of pipelines criss-crossing Unocal's facilities. Over the years many of these pipelines began to leak with much of the lost oil entering the water table and an undetermined amount seeping into the ocean.

Although Unocal knew they were losing significant quantities of light oil, they ignored state laws by not reporting the spillage nor attempting to clean it up. When ocean spills were reported nearby, Unocal denied it could have originated from their facility.

For years, Unocal succeeded in warding off any discovery that there were, in fact, millions of gallons of oil in the water table slowly working their way to the ocean from all over the production field.

The full extent of the spill came

to light in 1992, when a Unocal employee tipped authorities that the facility was experiencing widespread loss of light oil in its pipelines; acting on the tip, the California Department of Fish and Game obtained a search warrant for inspection of the facility and found conclusive evidence of a corporate coverup.

Company records revealed the large quantities of oil lost from the pipelines and confirmed that no effective steps were taken to clean up the chronic spills. In fact, Unocal actively worked to hide the spills—when light oil would rise to the surface, the company would use heavy equipment to bulldoze over the oozing pools.

Possibly worst of all, Unocal's conspiracy of silence over several decades achieved much of its goal. The public probably will never know exactly how much oil escaped into the ocean since the facility was never monitored by authorities because no problems were ever reported by Unocal. Further, the state's case against Unocal was hindered from the beginning by a judge's ruling that the statute of limitations had been exceeded with regard to much of the leakage—a direct result of Unocal's coverup.

Incidentally, Unocal also was the company responsible for the 1969 Santa Barbara oil spill disaster.

SSU Censored Researcher: Lori Stone

COMMENTS: The author, Gary Hart, a California state senator who retired in December 1994, felt that the issue of Unocal's coverup did not receive the exposure it deserved in the mass media last year. His article appeared in the local Santa Barbara newspaper and generated some letters to the editor and at best may have generated a story or two in the larger press.

"In this era of blame the government and criminal sloganeering, i.e. 'Three strikes and you're out,'" Hart believes this article "focuses upon an important issue: corporate irresponsibility and accountability." Hart says that the primary beneficiary of the limited coverage given the oil spill and the coverup is obviously Unocal.

13 CENSORED

The Nuclear Regulatory Commission's Dirty Secret

Source:
PUBLIC CITIZEN
Date: January/February 1994
Title: "What the Nuclear Regulatory Commission Won't Tell You: Aging Reactors, Poorly Trained Workers"
Authors: Matthew Freedman and Jim Riccio

SYNOPSIS: Secret internal industry documents obtained by *Public Citizen's* Critical Mass Energy Project reveal that America's nuclear reactors have more serious safety, training, and equipment problems than government regulators acknowledge.

The internal documents are plant evaluations performed by the Institute of Nuclear Power Operations (INPO), an Atlanta-based group founded by nuclear utilities in the wake of the 1979 accident at Three Mile Island. INPO routinely sends inspection teams to operating reactors, reviews significant operating problems and equipment malfunctions, and maintains data bases on nuclear power plant operation. The detailed reports are submitted to the Nuclear Regulatory Commission (NRC), where they are required reading for NRC inspectors. However, the NRC has not released the reports to the public nor has it been diligent in acting on reported problems.

A 1991 report by the General Accounting Office (GAO), the investigative arm of Congress, found 12 instances in the previous two years where "NRC decided not to issue its own information notice because INPO had already alerted the industry to a potential problem." The GAO concluded that "information that may be important to the public's under-standing of nuclear power operations is not publicly available."

Public Citizen's examination of the documents reveals long-standing deficiencies at nuclear reactors across the nation that could jeopardize public health and safety. The findings conflict with public assessments made by the NRC.

While the NRC is expected to use the INPO reports to improve conditions at the nuclear reactors, a comparison of the INPO and NRC documents by *Public Citizen* reveals that NRC regulators often recommend *reduced* oversight at reactors where INPO identified serious deficiencies. Altogether, NRC's reports only managed to report on about one-third of the total findings identified by INPO; the other two-thirds were either ignored or directly contradicted. Out of 55 findings at 34 reactors cited by INPO for deficient chemistry programs, NRC addressed only two.

The failure of NRC to report and correct deficiencies at the nation's nuclear reactors is a serious one; since current reactors are the first generation to operate for any substantial length of time (the oldest operating unit just turned 30 years old), much of the understanding of long-term aging problems remains incomplete and hypothetical.

Most importantly, the secret documents reported by *Public Citizen* reveal that the aging nuclear reactors are plagued by a variety of management and technical problems which reduce the margin of safety at operating reactors. And while the NRC has evidence of the problems, it is neither reporting nor admitting them.

SSU Censored Researcher: Kate Kauffman

COMMENTS: While the story was reported in most daily newspapers and carried on the Associated Press and Reuters wires, no major television networks nor newsweekly magazines carried it. The authors, Matthew Freedman and Jim Riccio, felt that the level of exposure was constrained by the paucity of reporters who cover nuclear energy and the tendency of many major newspapers to bury stories critical of the nuclear industry. *The New York Times* placed the story in the Metro Section while the *Boston Globe* put it on page 70.

Equally important, according to the authors, "There was no follow-up by any reporters, despite our urging them to investigate further the connections between the Nuclear Regulatory Commission (NRC) and the Institute of Nuclear Power Operations (INPO). Reporters are generally reactive on nuclear safety issues and rarely take any initiative to investigate nuclear regulation unless there is an accident or an imminent risk of dis-

aster. Our report raised many questions about the propriety of relations between NRC and INPO and asserted that NRC is misrepresenting the state of nuclear safety in public evaluations of specific reactors. No reporters attempted to explore the reasons for such misrepresentation, nor have they subsequently challenged other NRC public evaluations on the basis of our report's findings."

Noting that nuclear regulation is extremely complex and difficult for most citizens to understand, the authors also feel that the arcane nature of regulatory procedures do not facilitate a free exchange of information between regulators and the public. However, they add, "Government regulators, charged with overseeing the operation of the nation's commercial nuclear reactors, have a special duty to be open, honest and aggressive about safety problems. When agencies like the NRC find deficiencies at licensed facilities, the public has a right to know that their health and safety may be in danger.

"If regulators provide incomplete or incorrect information, then reporters have a responsibility to publicize the agency's failure to act in the public interest.

"Without timely and thorough media coverage of federal regulatory actions, citizens have no ability to know whether or not they are being adequately protected from risks which could endanger their families and communities."

The authors consider the primary beneficiaries of the limited coverage to include "the Nuclear Regulatory Commission and the commercial nuclear power industry, which includes reactor manufacturers, industry associations and electric utilities who own or operate nuclear facilities. In the absence of information to the contrary, the public will continue to trust the NRC and local utilities to ensure the safe and economical operation of nuclear reactors."

While the authors feel their investigative article issued a strong wake-up call to the nuclear industry and journalists, they doubt whether anyone was listening.

"Our article details the first comprehensive comparison of internal nuclear industry documents with public evaluations of reactor safety performed by the NRC. Our findings that wide disparities exist between what the industry knows and what NRC makes publicly available should have generated far more investigation into the INPO-NRC relationship. It also should make reporters increasingly skeptical about the NRC's willingness to be forthright about safety concerns and provide accurate information to the public.

"These results failed to materialize primarily because reporters tended to treat our report as a one-day flash in the pan, not a basis for undermining long-term confidence in the behavior of federal nuclear regulators.

"Since our initial release, there has been little, if any, further press attention given to the story."

Faulty Nuclear Fuel Rods Spell Potential Disasters

Source:
MOTHER JONES
Date: May/June 1994
Title: "Faulty Rods"
Author: Ashley Craddock

SYNOPSIS: The critical fuel rods in 108 of our nation's licensed nuclear power plants are failing in increasing numbers and the Nuclear Regulatory Commission (NRC) knows about it ... but is doing nothing.

Fuel rods, zirconium alloy tubes that contain the radioactive uranium in reactor cores, are the first level of protection against the release of deadly radioactive material. The coolant system is the second level of protection; the third and final level is the actual containment building.

The NRC has been warned about a faulty manufacturing process by the engineer who helped design it, but has done little to prevent potentially flawed fuel rod casings from being shipped to plants here and abroad. While the NRC sent a notice warning plant operators about fuel rod failures and specifically cited seven reactors where such failures had occurred, it didn't mention that two of those reactors were of the type susceptible to containment building failure.

For more than three years, Chris Hall, the mechanical engineer who blew the whistle on the faulty fuel rods, tried to tell the NRC that a manufacturing process used by his former employer, Teledyne Wah Chang Albany (TWCA), could explain the fuel rod failures. For his efforts, Hall, who helped design the process, was fired by TWCA.

TWCA's faulty fuel rods could be discovered in the manufacturing process if the company's quality control efforts were more rigorous. However TWCA quality assurance engineers usually test just one end of three random tubes out of each batch of approximately 120, (or 1.25 percent, given that each tube has two ends).

According to Dr. Michio Kaku, professor of nuclear physics at City University of New York, a major problem with the NRC is the agency's "hear no evil, see no evil" approach. In fact, a 1990 General Accounting Office (GAO) report concluded that this policy historically resulted in the installation of substandard and even counterfeit parts in nuclear reactors. The report said that after finding "problems with 12 utilities' quality assurance programs" (out of 13 inspected), the NRC simply concluded that substandard products were an industry-wide problem and, as such, weren't the fault of individual utilities. The GAO report blasted the NRC for "deferring its regulatory responsibility" at a time when "an increasing number of commercial-grade products" used in nuclear reactors were of questionable quality.

Equally disturbing, even if no meltdown occurs, failing fuel rods pose other potentially lethal hazards. A 1990 study by the Massachusetts Department of Public Health revealed that failed fuel rods at Boston Edison's Pilgrim plant regularly released radioactivity into the atmosphere between 1972 and 1979. The study also noted that the adult leukemia rate within a 10-mile radius of the plant was four times that of outlying areas.

Investigative journalist Ashley Craddock, a fellow at *Mother Jones*, described the public implications of the fuel rod issue: "The rods are a potential safety hazard to millions of people through the release of radioactive material into the environment. Some experts believe that corroded rods could exacerbate other system failures and contribute to a core meltdown, resulting in substantial fatalities and the contamination of food, air, and water."

SSU Censored Researcher:
Dan Tomerlin

COMMENTS: Author Ashley Craddock reports that the problem of potentially faulty nuclear fuel rods (the primary level of protection against radiation leakage) received zero attention in the mass media last year. Craddock feels it is "probably as a result of the subject matter's being fairly dense and scientific, combined with the fact that nuclear reactors are essentially out of fashion as story subjects—they aren't sexy."

However, Craddock points out, "If the mass media had picked up the story, the general public could demand that reactors be run at power levels that would put less stress on potentially flawed rods. Moreover, mass coverage would force the NRC to conduct more rigorous tests of the rods. More generally, it might galvanize the general public into putting more pressure on the NRC to responsibly administer the nation's nuclear plants."

While acknowledging that the NRC escapes criticism that might be leveled against it, Craddock charges that Teledyne is the real beneficiary of the lack of coverage.

"They hold a locked grip on the supply of zirconium tube hollows used to manufacture fuel rods for most GE-manufactured reactors. As long as no one questions the quality of their tubes, they can send out whatever they like, wherever they like, no matter what the potential dangers to the public."

Craddock notes that while "Faulty Rods" was sent to hundreds of print and broadcast media and nearly 200 reporters whose beats include monitoring nuclear power plants, the story was only picked up by Swiss television, local TV in Portland, the *Boston Phoenix* and the *L.A. Weekly*. Nonetheless, the story continues to develop and has helped precipitate renewed interest and investigation by additional government agencies, according to Craddock.

15 CENSORED

DARE Program Cover-up Continues

Sources:
QUILL
Date: May 1994
Title: "Editor's deadline changes to DARE piece stir trouble"
Author: Richard P. Cunningham

THE BOSTON GLOBE
Date: 9/29/94
Title: "US rejects unfavorable
    DARE study"
Author: Sean P. Murphy

USA TODAY
Date: 10/4/94
Title: "Study critical of DARE
    rejected"
Author: Dennis Cauchon

SYNOPSIS: The 23rd *Censored* story of 1993, titled "The Biggest Drug Bust of All," revealed that the nation's most popular school-based drug prevention program—Drug Abuse Resistance Education (DARE)—was a failure, and how the media failed to cover the story. The story is nominated again for 1994 for three reasons: 1) evidence that one of the nation's leading newspapers, *The Washington Post*, revised an article, without the author's permission, on behalf of the DARE program; 2) evidence that the U.S. Department of Justice covered up the program's failure by rejecting a study it commissioned that concluded that the DARE program doesn't work; and 3) continued failure of the news media to put the issue on the national agenda.

In November 1993, freelance writer James Bovard submitted an article to *The Washington Post* that criticized the DARE program for "turning children into informants on drug-using parents or friends." On Sunday, January 30, 1994, following discussions between *Post* editors and attorneys and DARE attorneys, the article appeared with significant changes ... without consulting or notifying the author of the changes. On February 4, the *Post* published a correction admitting an error due to an editing change not discussed with the author. The *Post* also reimbursed the family cited in the article for costs incurred in negotiating the correction. Commenting on DARE's influence, the attorney representing the family said, "To be able to control *The Washington Post* is awesome."

On September 29, 1994, *The Boston Globe* reported that the Justice Department had rejected its own study criticizing the DARE program. Justice paid the Research Triangle Institute (RTI) $300,000 for the two year-study that concluded that DARE's short-term effectiveness for reducing or preventing drug use behavior is small. DARE received about $750 million in government appropriations and private donations. RTI found that while DARE improved the students' knowledge of drugs and their social skills, it had no significant effect on their use of drugs. Despite the Justice Department's attempts to have RTI modify its findings, RTI decided to stick with its conclusions which were published in the *American Journal of Public*

Health (AJPH) on October 4, 1994.

Dennis Cauchon, the *USA Today* reporter who wrote the original story on DARE in 1993, reported that the DARE study passed rigorous scrutiny by academic experts before publication by AJPH. The *Journal's* Sabine Beisler said DARE "tried to interfere with the publication of this (article). They tried to intimidate us." In its conclusion, RTI wrote, "DARE's limited influence on adolescent drug use behaviors contrasts with the program's popularity and prevalence. An important implication is that DARE could be taking the place of other, more beneficial drug use curricula that adolescents could be receiving."

In rejecting the RTI study, Anne Voitt, Justice Department spokeswoman, said the study did not examine a big enough sample of students involved in DARE to properly judge it. Voitt also said that the DARE study is the first time the National Institute of Justice, the Justice Department's research branch, has rejected a study in recent years.

SSU Censored Researcher:
Jessica Nystrom

COMMENTS: Richard P. Cunningham, author of the *Quill* article, said that the "big news media have not written and broadcast enough about DARE. If they had, local newspapers would know that the program is controversial and would be saying so when DARE comes to their towns. That is not happening in my area: at least two school systems have admitted DARE, but I have never seen anything but positive feature stories about the program."

Cunningham also points out that if the media provided more coverage on the DARE program, "parents and taxpayers could ask better questions about the philosophy, the cost and the effectiveness of DARE." He concludes that "DARE must reap financial and propaganda benefits from not having to answer hard questions" about the program.

Sean P. Murphy, the *Boston Globe* journalist who reported in September that the Justice Department had rejected its own study criticizing the DARE program, agreed that the subject hadn't received sufficient coverage in the mass media. He pointed out that the public would benefit from additional exposure since there are million of dollars at stake ... as well as the future of children. The real beneficiary of the limited coverage, Murphy said, was the DARE program itself.

On Monday, December 12, 1994, the University of Michigan's Institute for Social Research released a major national study that revealed that the number of

American teens using illicit drugs increased for the third consecutive year. The study showed that marijuana use increased sharply in all age groups over the past two to three years and that use of LSD and powder and crack cocaine also increased, although not as sharply as marijuana.

Fallibility of the AIDS Test

Sources:
NEW YORK NATIVE
Dates: 8/15/94, 8/29/94
Titles: "Widow sues blood bank over misdiagnosis" and "Ohio woman awarded $100,000 after error in HIV antibody test"

LONDON SUNDAY TIMES
Date: 8/1/93
Title: "New doubts over Aids infection as HIV test declared invalid"
Author: Neville Hodgkinson

SYNOPSIS: In July 1994, the widow of a man who committed suicide sued an Augusta, Georgia, blood bank claiming an erroneous HIV-positive diagnosis drove her husband to kill himself.

In August 1994, a woman who had a hysterectomy after a blood test falsely indicated she had the "AIDS virus," was awarded $100,000 for the surgical procedure and emotional distress in a Court of Claims in Ohio.

Both cases, and other similar cases, were reported in the *New York Native*, a publication which covers gay and lesbian issues, but were not widely reported in the mainstream media.

The potential importance of the issue was noted by Phillip E. Johnson, University of California, Berkeley, law professor, who cited the immense damage the diagnosis of HIV-positive can do to a person, as well as the impact of product liability suits against test manufacturers. Johnson said that successful product liability lawsuits against the manufacturers of the HIV antibody tests could put the test makers out of business. He noted that the hysterectomy case appears to be just one of many in which faulty HIV antibody test results have injured people in such a way that they would have grounds to sue the test's manufacturer.

The problem of faulty HIV tests was front-page headline news in the *London Sunday Times* in August 1993, but did not make major news in the U.S. The *Sunday Times* reported: "The 'Aids test' is scientifically invalid and incapable of determining whether people are really infected with HIV, according to a new report by a team of

Australian scientists who have conducted the first extensive review of research surrounding the test.

"Doctors should think again about its use, say the authors. 'A positive HIV status has such profound implications that nobody should be required to bear this burden without solid guarantees of the verity of the test and its interpretation,' they conclude.

"The findings, likely to cause intense debate in the medical fraternity and anguish for many HIV-positive people, are contained in an article published by the respected science journal, *BioTechnology*. "Many people who appear to be infected with HIV, say the researchers, can be suffering from other conditions such as malaria or malnutrition that produce a positive result in the test. Even flu jabs can produce the same effect. As a result, predictions by the World Health Organisation (WHO) that millions are set to die because of being HIV-positive may be wildly inaccurate."

Law professor Johnson warns that "if the underlying science (of the HIV test) is ever called into question, as I think it is being called into question right now, then the possibility that a huge, massive harm has been done by bad science, is going to create a great reaction from the public."

SSU Censored Researcher: Jennifer Burns

COMMENTS: Responding for *New York Native*, Neenyah Ostrom said "One of the reasons this subject did not receive the exposure it should have is that most science reporters have grown used to quoting government press releases without questioning the facts contained in them. AIDS is frightening; a story that suggests that the 'AIDS test' doesn't work 100 percent of the time is even more frightening. And because the government scientists managing the AIDS epidemic don't want to frighten people, any reporter who questions the facts released by them is soon cut off from official sources of information (like scientists at NIH).

"Another unfortunate trend figures into the lack of exposure received by this story: many science writers have become quasi public health spokespeople. Rather than casting a critical eye on questionable information or data provided by public health officials, they assist their sources in molding public opinion."

Ostrom believes that the "amount of needless human suffering that arises from people receiving false positive HIV antibody test results would be reduced if the public knew the test is not 100 percent reliable. People have had all kinds of drastic reactions to being told they are HIV-positive: they've committed suicide, and murder; people have been arrested and convicted of crimes on the basis of positive HIV antibody tests; lives and livelihoods have been destroyed. If people understood that a positive test result might very possibly be a mistake, these drastic actions might decrease."

The most obvious beneficiaries of the lack of coverage given this story are the manufacturers of the HIV antibody test kits, both those already on the market and the impending home test kit, according to Ostrom. "But the people managing the epidemic for the government also benefit, because they can keep their message simple: 'Take the test.' If the public begins to doubt the 'AIDS test,' the story becomes more complicated and, therefore, more difficult to manage.

"A story that goes hand-in-hand with this story, and that has also received minimal coverage, is that there is a growing number of scientists who doubt that HIV is the sole cause of AIDS. These scientists have been called a threat to the public health for not toeing the official line on AIDS. If what we've reported about the unreliability of the HIV antibody test is true, the public may begin to suspect that much of what they've been told about AIDS is unreliable.

"One of the newest groups to suffer as a result of the censorship of this story is pregnant women. Pregnant women who test positive on the HIV antibody test are now being advised to take a very toxic drug, AZT, while they are pregnant, to prevent their babies from being infected in the womb. Now, only about 15 percent of babies born to HIV-positive women turn out to be HIV-positive anyway, but on the basis of a test that doesn't work very well, these women are being advised to take a very toxic—even carcinogenic—drug. Nobody knows what AZT does to a child exposed to it before birth. I think if these women knew how unreliable the HIV antibody test is, they would be less inclined to take AZT while they are pregnant."

Meanwhile, despite the potential problems, proposals to test all new hospital patients in the U.S. on a voluntary basis were being discussed as the year ended. In a report published in the *Journal of the American Medical Association* (JAMA), released 12/21/94, analysts said such a program could detect nearly 170,000 unrevealed infections among patients; it also could yield more than 30,000 "false positives."

17 CENSORED

Censoring Tomorrow's Journalists Today

Source:
FREEDOM FORUM
Date: February 1994
Title: DEATH BY CHEESE-
    BURGER: High School
    Journalism in the 1990s and
    Beyond
Authors: Alice Bonner and Judith
    Hines

SYNOPSIS: In 1988, the U.S. Supreme Court decided that the First Amendment did not apply to student journalists. In "Hazelwood School District vs. Kuhlmeier," the Court ruled that the principal of Hazelwood East High School, near St. Louis, did not violate the First Amendment rights of students by deleting two pages of the campus newspaper which contained material he found offensive. In what some considered an unconstitutional act, the Court gave school administrators the power to practice prior restraint over student newspapers.

Surprisingly, this unprecedented action generated little outrage among professional journalists, who might have been expected to spring to the defense of student journalists. In fact, many of the 1988 editorials commenting on *Hazelwood* in the professional press almost seemed to mock the students for their arrogance in believing they should be allowed to cover what was important to them. Comparing the principal to a newspaper publisher, they said young people might as well learn early that reporters and editors don't always get their way.

Not surprisingly, high school principals who want to control the student press seized upon *Hazelwood* as a justification for prior review or for restriction of subjects students can write about. The Student Press Law Center (SPLC), which monitors student press rights, has reported an increase in requests for assistance with censorship problems from high school journalists since *Hazelwood*. The student publications that call SPLC report censorship of articles, editorials, and advertisements considered controversial. Advisers report threats to their jobs if they refuse to follow school officials' orders to censor material.

The chilling effect of *Hazelwood* is also reflected in the quality of the student press. An in-depth analysis of high school journalism by The Freedom Forum, a non-partisan organization dedicated to a free press, found that 72 percent of 233 student newspapers were either "average" or "boring." The study also reported that of 270 high school newspaper advisors, 37 percent admitted that school principals had rejected newspaper articles or required changes.

In a foreword to the study, John Seigenthaler, chair of the Freedom Forum, warned of the threat of censorship to school newspapers. He also reproached the editors who rushed to endorse the press censorship in the *Hazelwood* decision in 1988 ... and who since have defended the Court's decision to crush high school press freedom. Seigenthaler also noted that the cases of outrageous censorship documented in the Freedom Forum's 182-page report are "horror stories—gripping to read, oppressive to think about, offensive to the First Amendment."

In describing how censorship can take hold quickly in a school, the report points out that "when students have been censored a number of times, they stop writing anything controversial, feeling that whatever they write either won't make it into print or will get them into trouble with school administrators."

Journalists already indoctrinated into accepting censorship at the high school level are well prepared to enter professional careers at publications more interested in maintaining the status quo than in muckraking. Perhaps this helps explain editors' reluctance to criticize and publicize the *Hazelwood* decision and its impact.

SSU Censored Researcher: Jennifer Burns

COMMENTS: Co-authors Alice Bonner and Judith Hines point out that while *Death By Cheeseburger* was not itself a "censored" publication, it tells the story of "the failure of high school journalism to live up to its high potential because of lack of funding, teacher preparation, equipment, school credit, and, yes, often overt censorship of the students' voices. The subject has received almost no exposure in the last 20 years, when 'Captive Voices,' the most recent in-depth study of the high school press was published. Both the good news of the writing, analytical, organizational and entrepreneurial skills students can gain from working on a high school newspaper, and the bad news about the weakness of scholastic journalism have received too little exposure."

The authors feel that if the subject were to receive more coverage, teachers and students might receive a better journalism education, and teenagers and adults would benefit from hearing and reading the voices of young people—too seldom heard from today, especially concerning issues that affect them directly.

Those who benefit from the limited media coverage given the issue include "school administrators and other adults who fear losing control—who have little faith in giving teenagers responsibility so they can prove they can act responsibly." And also those who have an investment in keeping things "the way we've always done it" in high school.

The Freedom Forum, seeking to increase the energy and support for high school journalism among educators, journalists, and especially young people, is distributing *Death By Cheeseburger* as widely as possible—offering a free copy to every high school and professional newspaper editor in the USA.

Nationwide Collusion between Drug Companies and Pharmacists

Source:
THE NEW YORK TIMES
Date: 7/29/94
Title: "Pharmacists Paid To Suggest Drugs"
Author: Gina Kolata

SYNOPSIS: Major drug companies have started to pay pharmacists to promote their drugs over those of their competitors.

In an investigative report in *The New York Times*, Gina Kolata explains how the process works at Medco, a company that buys drugs from manufacturers and sells them through pharmacies and mail orders to 38 million Americans: "When customers appear with prescriptions for high blood pressure medicine, for example, the pharmacist often advises them that they could receive another, similar drug for less money, under their Medco plan. Would it be O.K., the pharmacist might ask, if they called the doctor and had the prescription switched to the other drug?"

About 80 percent of the doctors say "no problem" when asked to approve the switch since they have no reason to doubt the good intentions of the pharmacists and because the new drugs often save the patient money. Studies also show that over a period of time, after repeated requests to switch the drug, doctors eventually start writing all prescriptions for that particular brand of medicine.

However, what the patient and doctor may not know is that Medco is owned by Merck, a major drug manufacturer, that the other drug is made by Merck, and that Merck will pay the pharmacist a cash commission for arranging the switch.

Merck pays rebates of six to ten percent of the wholesale price of each drug sold to pharmacists who dispense the company's line of generic drugs and also pays pharmacists $5 per prescription for increasing sales of the total line of drugs from Medco.

While Merck pioneered this new arrangement when it bought Medco last year, it is not alone. In May of 1994, SmithKline Beecham bought Diversified Pharmaceutical Services, which handles prescription drugs for 11 million people; in July, Eli Lilly said it would buy PCS Health Systems, which has enrolled 50 million Americans.

Some say there is nothing wrong with paying pharmacists for helping patients get the best drug at the best price. John Doorley, a Merck spokesman, said pharmacists would suggest a switch only if it would help a patient. However, other critics point out that pharmacists, who traditionally are ranked at the top of trusted professionals in opinion polls, are no longer disinterested parties once they start getting paid to recommend specific drugs.

"It's outrageous, it's manipulative and it's dishonest," said James Love, who follows the drug industry for the Center for the Study of Responsive Law.

Dr. Arthur Caplan, director of the Center for Medical Ethics at the University of Pennsylvania,

said, "Traditional medical ethics is being replaced by traditional business ethics." At the very least, he pointed out, any arrangements between pharmacists and drug companies should be explicitly disclosed to both doctors and customers.

Further, by adding an additional expense to drug distribution, the manufacturers are further increasing out-of-control health care costs which already are plaguing the American people. Sooner or later that additional cost is passed on to the consumer.

SSU Censored Researcher:
Susan Kashack

COMMENTS: Journalist Gina Kolata said the issue of medical kickbacks to pharmacists was largely ignored last year. She also pointed out that patients—and doctors—have a right to know that their pharmacist may no longer be as disinterested a party as before. "Although the pharmacist is widely viewed as an advocate for patients," Kolata added, "that role may be a relic of the past." The primary beneficiaries of the minimal coverage given this subject are the drug companies and pharmacists according to Kolata.

It should be noted that drug makers' kickbacks are not restricted to pharmacists. An editorial in *USA Today* (10/19/94) criticized drug makers for sometimes offering kickbacks to physicians who used their products.

19 CENSORED

Cesarean Sections Epidemic

Source:
HEALTH LETTER
Date: June 1994
Title: "Unnecessary Cesarean Sections: Curing a National Epidemic"
Author: Public Citizen Health Research Group

SYNOPSIS: While the U.S. cesarean (c) section rate, which skyrocketed during the 1980s, has plateaued and begun a very slow reversal, nearly one in four pregnant women still have a c-section. While often considered a routine procedure, the c-section is major surgery that involves entering the abdominal cavity and surgically modifying an organ. At times a c-section can be a life-saving intervention for both mother and child; however, at other times, it can do significant harm to mothers without providing additional benefits to infants when performed outside of certain well-defined medical situations.

There are only four indications for which a c-section is commonly performed. In order of frequency of diagnosis, these categories are 1) previous cesarean, 2) dystocia (abnormal progress of labor), 3) breech presentation, and 4) fetal distress.

Today the traditional "once a cesarean always a cesarean" thesis is being widely challenged, with the American College of Obstetricians and Gynecologists (ACOG), and others, recommending that women with a previous c-section be given a chance to deliver naturally if possible.

Dr. Emanuel A. Friedman, Professor of Obstetrics and Gynecology at Beth Israel Hospital in Boston, and a recognized authority, suggests that about 50 percent of cesareans for arrest disorders, the second leading reason for c-sections, are unnecessary.

The "obstetrician impatience factor" is also cited for the increased incidence of cesareans. The impatience factor, speeding up normal labor through aggressive use of drugs and other interventions, has been seen in studies demonstrating that c-sections are performed more frequently in the evening or when there are fewer obstetricians to share round-the-clock availability for labor and delivery.

The economic factor also may influence cesarean rates. An

analysis of hospitals grouped by ownership revealed that of the four categories, federal government hospitals have the lowest cesarean rate, at 17.0 percent; state and local government hospitals at 21.1 percent; not-for-profit hospitals at 22.4 percent; and for-profit hospitals at 25.3 percent. The for-profit's cesarean rate was almost 49 percent higher than that of federal government hospitals.

Further, the increased costs associated with unnecessary c-sections are passed on to a society already suffering from grossly inflated health expenditures. Former ACOG President Dr. Richard Schwarz has estimated that a drop of only one percent in the national cesarean rate would save $115 million annually.

Finally, it is commonly believed that concern about malpractice is a major cause of the high cesarean section rate. Avoidance of malpractice suits has served as one of several impediments that prevent physicians from heeding the results of research and the recommendations of their own professional leadership urging fewer cesareans.

However, the Public Citizen Health Research Group charges that "concern for legal issues cannot be allowed to cover up for, or even cause, bad medical practice."

SSU Censored Researcher:
Jennifer Burns

COMMENTS: Responding on behalf of the Public Citizen Research Health Group, Mary Gabay said the release of the group's report, "Unnecessary C-Section," initially received a substantial amount of mass media coverage. However, she attributed the media's interest to the attention being given health care reform at the time and the report's estimate that the cost of unnecessary c-sections was over $1.3 billion, a figure which seemed to play a central role in the stories reported by the mass media.

Gabay noted that "While the issue of the cost of all this unnecessary surgery is an important one, our own focus for this story centered on what the variation in cesarean rates says about the quality of medical care women receive during labor and delivery and on how women can avoid an unnecessary c-section. These issues appear to be of secondary importance, if they are discussed at all, in stories that appear in the mass media."

On the other hand, "In-depth coverage of this story by the mass media might have done more to: increase women's awareness of the risks associated with cesarean surgery and of the steps they can take to avoid an unnecessary c-section; and encourage women to take an active interest in the care they will receive during labor and delivery. Women need to know that discussing with their doctors their concerns about cesarean section and other forms of medical intervention that may occur during labor and delivery is not only appropriate, it can ensure that women choose an obstetrician (or midwife) whose philosophy of obstetric care compares favorably with their own, leading to better childbirth experiences for women."

Gabay feels that certain physicians and hospitals have most to gain from the limited coverage given the subject. "Certainly, those physicians who don't want to be questioned by their patients about treatment decisions or held accountable for their overutilization of this major surgery benefit most by limiting coverage of this story.

"Hospitals also benefit from the limited coverage. The medical literature includes several examples of how hospitals have addressed the problem of high cesarean rates by instituting one or more measures designed to reduce the use of cesarean surgery. However, rather than take responsibility for unnecessary surgery taking place within their walls, some hospitals may instead continue allowing the performance of unnecessary surgery, due to the strong pull of financial incentives. Media coverage can increase the pressure on those hospitals named as having high c-section rates to pursue changes that can result in lower cesarean rates."

Gabay notes that the Florida legislature has taken steps to reduce the number of unnecessary cesareans and hopes that other state legislatures will follow Florida's lead and take a more proactive role toward ending the costly and dangerous epidemic of unnecessary cesarean surgery.

Legalizing Carcinogens in Our Food

Source:
IN THESE TIMES
Date: 3/21/94
Title: "Risky Business: A Proposed
EPA reform may leave
Americans even more exposed to
the dangers of pesticides"
Author: William K. Burke

SYNOPSIS: The only U.S. law that entitles Americans to a carcinogen-free food supply is being threatened by the Environmental Protection Agency and Congress.

The law is known as the Delaney Clause after Rep. James Delaney (D-NY) who insisted in 1958 that the Food, Drug and Cosmetics Act include language that prohibits cancer-causing chemicals in

America's processed food. While the law has threatened the multi-billion-dollar pesticide industry during the past 36 years, it has rarely hampered it.

Under Delaney, if a pesticide is shown to be a carcinogen, the government must ban it from use in all processed foods. And while it is quite specific, the pesticide industry (with the government's help) had found ways around the law until 1992 when the Natural Resources Defense Council won a federal lawsuit that compelled the EPA to begin enforcing Delaney.

To avoid doing this, and to appease the chemical industry, the Clinton EPA proposed a legislative reform package that would replace Delaney with a system known as "risk assessment." Under this system, the government weighs the "risks" posed by a given pesticide against the chemical's "benefits." In this case, a risk is negligible if only one in a million consumers develop cancer from a pesticide-treated food.

Critics point out that Americans already consume the residues of more than 300 EPA-registered pesticides—about 70 of which are known to cause cancer. Yet the proposed risk-assessment process falsely assumes that ill effects from exposure to a single toxin from a single source can be precisely calculated and then regulated. But this risk assessment process ignores the fact that causes of cancer can't be pinpointed that exactly. A typical American already runs a one-in-four risk of cancer.

Jay Feldman, of the National Coalition Against Misuse of Pesticides, points out that "Delaney is the building block to a sound public policy to prevent cancer." In fact, Feldman argues that the need for stringent restriction of cancer-causing agents has never been greater.

Nonetheless, environmentalists warn that once the Delaney Clause becomes history, which some expect to happen in 1995, the right of U.S. agribusiness to spread cancer will be secured. Congress and the EPA will be left to squabble over how many cancer deaths are too many.

Environmental writer William K. Burke concludes that "Without strong, unequivocal laws to guide it, the EPA has tended to negotiate with polluters rather than regulate their pollution. By proposing to replace the Delaney Clause with the dubious science of risk assessment, the Clinton EPA risks repeating that sorry history."

When the 103rd Congress adjourned on October 8, 1994, there already were two bills in Congress that would eliminate the Delaney Clause.

SSU Censored Researcher:
Paul Giusto

COMMENTS: Environmental writer William Burke reports, "Efforts to repeal the Delaney Clause and promote the 'risk assessment' approach to regulating environmental hazards were not heavily covered last year. The *Washington Post* has run editorials favoring the replacement of strict consumer protection laws like Delaney with risk assessment."

One of the problems in persuading editors to cover the issue, Burke said, is "that the risk assessment story lacks a sexy hook until you understand some of the complexities behind the concept. Over the last seven years freelancing I have learned that there is no better way to make an assignment editor's eyes glaze over and ears slam shut than to explain to him or her the complexities of environmental policy.

"The fact is that the promotion of risk assessment is an attempt by corporations addicted to pollution to use false science to promote policies that are bad for the nation's long-term economic and physical health. But the idea of balancing 'risks versus benefits' sound pseudo-scientific enough to pass through a political system ruled by centrists and right wingers who think pragmatism means fulfilling the desires of the most powerful lobbyists.

"One in four Americans will die prematurely from cancer. Yet few Americans know that the industry and government scientists who assure them their food supply is safe have no idea how the 70 carcinogenic pesticides legally applied to America's food interact. The effects of these combined exposures are difficult if not impossible to study, therefore the risks of such combined exposures are simply ignored in the regulatory process. As a result most mass media reports on pesticides focus on the risk from one pesticide in one use. So we get stories about pesticides being regulated because they cause cancer in a few rats. This lack of depth of coverage provides grist for the mills of the writers leading the current anti-environmental charge. It also prevents any serious discussion of what it means to our country to have a food supply system addicted to pesticides."

Burke charges that the grocers, food production lobbyists and pesticide companies that are paying for the effort to kill the Delaney Clause in Congress will all directly benefit if the law is changed.

Burke concludes, "If the Delaney Clause is overturned it will not represent a step towards an updated and sensible pesticide policy, which seems to be how the mainstream press intends to help sell risk assessment. Rather the end of Delaney will be one more marker that America's food supply has become one of history's great chemistry experiments."

21 CENSORED

Illegal Toxic Burning at Super-Secret Air Force Facility

Sources:
LEGAL TIMES
Date: 9/5/94
Title: "Target of Suit Doesn't (Officially) Exist"
Author: Benjamin Wittes

PROJECT ON GOVERNMENT OVERSIGHT (POGO)
Dates: 8/2/94, 8/16/94, September 1994
Titles: "Government Hides Illegal Disposal of Toxic Waste Through Secrecy" and "High Levels of Dioxins Found in Former Worker at Secret Air Force Base"
Author: Scott H. Amey

SYNOPSIS: The United States government has used secrecy and over-classification to hide the illegal burning of toxic materials at an Air Force facility so secret that the federal government does not even admit it exists.

While the government doesn't even acknowledge the presence of the Air Force facility in southwestern Nevada, Groom Lake Air Force Base has served for years as a test site for "black"—or officially non-existent—military aircraft such as the U-2 and SR-71 Blackbird spy planes. Critics charge that a Mach 8 spy plane called Aurora is now being tested there. The Air Force denies such a plane exists.

Were it not for the death of a civilian worker at Groom Lake, it is doubtful much information about the super-secret base and its activities would be coming to light even now. Workers at the Groom Lake AFB, also known as "Area 51," are challenging the secrecy laws that have, until now, prevented them from speaking out against the illegal waste disposal.

The workers have revealed that materials used in the process of building the Stealth Fighter were regularly burned in open air pits, including highly toxic composites, electronic equipment, tires, hardeners, solvents, resins, coatings, scrap metal, and paints. Workers performed these and other duties without having been allotted protective gear or clothing. The open pits have been described as being 100 yards long, 12 to 20 yards across, and 12 to 20 feet deep.

Robert Frost, a former sheetmetal worker at Groom Lake, died in 1989. He suffered from several mysterious symptoms including a skin rash that turned his hands and neck red and caused his face to split open and bleed. Helen Frost believes her husband's death was accelerated due to the burning of unconfirmed toxic materials in open pits.

Tissue samples taken before and after Frost's death revealed levels of dioxin and furans (immune system suppressants) far in excess of the normal limits for residents in industrialized countries. Dr. Peter Kahn, of Rutgers University, examined the tissue samples and determined that dioxin and furans were a contributing factor in the death of Robert Frost.

Helen Frost contacted The Project on Government Oversight (POGO), a non-profit government watchdog, to look into the matter. After initial research, POGO formed an alliance with law professor Jonathan Turley, director of the Environmental Crimes Project at George Washington University. The two organizations have filed suits against the federal government to stop the government's willful disregard of federal environmental laws, to expose the military's cynical use of secrecy laws to silence workers under the guise of "national security" and to help the many people who may be suffering from exposure to toxic materials. The suits will test just how far the federal courts will go in allowing the military to use secrecy to circumvent environmental and other statutes.

Meanwhile the military has requisitioned almost all the land within sight of Groom AFB to pre-vent civilians from catching glimpses of what goes on there.

SSU Censored Researcher: Marilyn Leon

COMMENTS: Author Benjamin Wittes said, "While papers and television have talked about Groom Lake's existence, (Professor Jonathan) Turley's suit has gone almost unnoticed. Groom Lake has received a lot of very poor coverage—particularly focused on the UFO angle. Larry King did a live show from Groom Lake, talking to 'UFO historians' and 'experts,' but largely ignoring the public interest angle. *The New York Times Magazine* ran a cover story on the base but ignored the suit almost completely and got some basic facts wrong.

"Other than the Las Vegas dailies, the print media have been utterly uninterested in the suit. I have not seen a story on the suit in any major newspaper, nor have the newspapers covered well the broader issues of over-classification and improper classification.

"Groom Lake is an open secret, but only among people who know where to look for information about it. Ironically, the only thorough reporting of goings on at the base has come from *Jane's Defense Weekly* and other defense industry press.

"Groom Lake is the principle example of abuse of the classification/secrecy system, which, as a problem, needs public attention and pressure. The continued classification of the existence of the facility is both an affront to the public's intelligence and a surefire means of undermining its confidence in government. When 'blackness' is used—as it appears to have been at Groom Lake—to cover up massive abuse of domestic regulations, the public needs to stand as guardian to the integrity of those regulations. Needless to say, it can't do so without access to the little information aviation writers and other journalists have been able to glean about the base.

"The 'black' world is an area prone to government abuse—simply by virtue of the inherent absence of public oversight. Suits like Turley's are a brute force means of assuring that oversight does continue. The more the public understands about Groom Lake, the more it understands the limitations of American democracy in the secret world of the military.

"I do not believe there has been any effort/conspiracy to suppress coverage of either the base or the suit (except insofar as the government refuses to comment on the base). Having said this, it is certainly in the Air Force's interest for exposure of the issue to be limited.

"The principle problem, however, in getting this matter to the attention of the public, has been the laziness of the press —not its complicity in any governmental grand design."

As noted above, The Project On Government Oversight (POGO) joined with law professor Jonathan Turley to sue the government over environmental abuse and secrecy. Following are comments on this issue by Scott H. Amey on behalf of POGO.

"Groom Lake has been reported on extensively regarding two issues: the possibility that UFOs are kept at the super-secret Air Force facility, and the government's impending withdrawal of public land overlooking the base." Amey points out that despite that coverage, the public remains unacquainted with the overall scope and possible impact of the story on current and former Groom Lake workers, surrounding communities, and workers at other government facilities. "Most importantly," Amey adds, "this story affects U.S. citizens, who should be aware of the government's use of 'national security' to hide these illegal activities.

"The consequences of the secrecy surrounding 'black programs' can be observed in the government's ability to hide illegal activities at this base—a base that does not even officially exist. Exposure through the mass media would educate the general public about the dangers of excessive government secrecy. Workers at this facility cannot publicly dissent—not only against government waste and abuse, but even against flat-out illegal practices. Public education through the mass media would also help force the government to provide its workers with a physically and environmentally safe workplace.

"In the case of Groom Lake, the federal government is the sole beneficiary of the limited media coverage this story has received. Exposure would hinder the government's ability to keep this base a secret, as well as, of course, the illegal handling of toxic materials. Our goal is to expose the military's cynical use of secrecy laws to silence workers under the guise of 'national security;' to stop the government's willful disregard of federal environmental laws; and to assist the workers and local residents in obtaining the appropriate medical attention. However, it is not the objective of our work, or the law suits, to jeopardize national security.

"The federal government has made it illegal for citizens to take pictures of the facility from as far as twelve miles away or for workers to admit the facility exists. Yet, Russian satellite photos of the base can be purchased on the open market in the U.S., and the Open Skies Treaty reveals its location to the rest of the world. Lack of media attention only serves the government in its efforts to cover up their illegal practices from the American public."

In an update, POGO reports that on November 1, 1994, it filed a change of venue motion to move the law suit filed against the EPA from Nevada back to the District of Columbia where it was originally filed. Also, on November 10, 1994, the government accepted POGO's motion to strike its use of the military secrets privilege. As a result, the government is limited in its use of the "national security" defense to block POGO's jurisdiction or have the suits dismissed.

On December 26, 1994, the McClatchy News Service reported that two mountain peaks that provide a distant vista of the base may soon be off-limits to the public, as requested by the Air Force. There was no mention of the illegal burning of toxic materials at the base nor of Turley's suit.

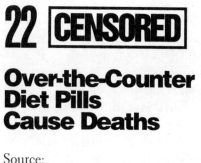

22 CENSORED

Over-the-Counter Diet Pills Cause Deaths

Source:
MUCKRAKER
Date: October 1994
Title: "Over-the-Counter Diet Pills and Cerebral Hemorrhages"
Author: Diana Hembree

SYNOPSIS: On the morning of October 12, 1990, 41-year-old Arlette Cannata took a popular diet pill called Acutrim, advertised as a safe and effective way to lose weight. Later that day she collapsed, was rushed to a local hospital, and died minutes later of a cerebral hemorrhage, or stroke.

An autopsy found the pill's active ingredient, phenylpro-panolamine, in her bloodstream, and a physician at Johns Hopkins University School of Medicine later concluded the stroke was caused by the drug.

Arlette Cannata's case is just one of a number in a decades-long controversy surrounding the use of over-the-counter diet pills and cold medications containing phenyl-propanolamine hydrochloride (PPA). The drug has a chemical structure similar to that of amphetamine, or speed, and like speed, can trigger a sharp rise in blood pressure, sometimes resulting in stroke. PPA is found in many brands of popular diet pills such as Acutrim and Dexatrim, as well as in cold remedies such as Contac and Dimetapp.

This rare but alarming side effect has sparked a controversy within federal health agencies over whether to tighten restrictions on the widely available drug. It also has raised larger questions about whether such decisions are made quickly and effectively enough to protect consumers.

A year after Cannata's death, Food and Drug Administration officials learned that drug-industry data show 92 people had suffered PPA-linked strokes during an 11-year period. More than a dozen medical case reports have linked PPA to life-threatening strokes in previously healthy individuals; some strokes have occurred even at the recommended dosages.

Dr. Thaddeus Prout, an associate professor at the Johns Hopkins University School of Medicine, defied "anyone to find another unregulated drug with such a record of disaster." PPA, he said, "should be returned to the logical and safe place for purchase: the pharmacy."

Dr. Sidney Wolfe, of the Public Citizen Health Research Group, said that "Over-the-counter diet pills should not be on the market—they're dangerous." He also criticized the slowness of the FDA's review process as "unacceptable .... This has been going on for two decades."

While most people who take the drug report no problems, for years medical experts have warned that a small number of PPA users have severe reactions to it, including seizures, psychosis, and strokes. Many others have reported less severe symptoms, ranging from headaches and nausea to anxiety and irregular heartbeats. Experts point out that some medical conditions increase the risk of PPA-induced strokes and that people being treated for high blood pressure, diabetes, and heart, thyroid, or kidney disease should not take diet pills.

Drug manufacturers contend problems with PPA products are overstated and insist the drug is both safe and effective.

In a study published by the *Western Journal of Medicine*, James McDowell, a neurologist, noted that these drugs seem to pose a danger even to healthy people, and added, "I can't understand why there hasn't been more outcry over this."

SSU Censored Researcher:
Jessica Nystrom

COMMENTS: Investigative journalist Diana Hembree said that to date her story about over-the-counter diet pills and cerebral hemorrhages has not been carried by a wire service, the television networks, or a newsweekly. "Besides appearing in the Center for Investigative Reporting's internal publication, *Muckraker*, the story has been sold to a handful of outlets: the *Philadelphia Inquirer*, Fox-TV's 'Front Page,' and the *San Francisco Chronicle* (where it appeared on 12/4/94). I feel the story is still underreported because there has been no wire pickup or network coverage to date.

"The millions of Americans who take PPA-containing diet pills—the majority of whom are women—would greatly benefit from wider exposure of this subject. They would know they may be risking their lives each time they take over-the-counter PPA diet pills, which have been known to cause strokes in previously healthy individuals even at the correct dosage. As one doctor told me, physicians always have to weigh a drug's potential risks against its benefit. In the case of PPA, however, the doctor concluded that the risk of stroke completely outweighed any possible benefits. 'Diet pills are not a crucial drug like penicillin,' he added, 'and they haven't even been proven effective.'"

Hembree said the large pharmaceutical companies that make PPA, and their directors, benefit from the lack of media coverage. "By settling nearly all diet pill/stroke lawsuits out of court, with gag orders and sealed records, non-prescription drug manufacturers have effectively prevented news of stroke dangers from reaching the public. Such secrecy has also delayed the push for better regulation of such drugs."

In an update, Hembree stated that the Food and Drug Administration (FDA) "is overseeing a study of PPA and stroke by the Nonprescription Drug Manufacturers' Association, which will complete its study in 1995. The

FDA will pull PPA products off the shelves if the trade association documents a stroke risk. However, the FDA already has criticized the trade association for what critics called apparent sabotage of the epidemiological study—not including a 'control' group, for example. Although this omission has since been remedied, such maneuvers have left some health advocates wary of the study."

23 CENSORED

Buying and Selling Permits to Pollute

Source:
SAN FRANCISCO CHRONICLE
Date: 3/21/94
Title: "Selling Dirty Air Is Big Business: One firm's smog is another's gold"
Author: Jonathan Marshall

SYNOPSIS: Where "plastics" was once the hot word for young business entrepreneurs, the word today might be "pollution."

Under a national initiative, passed into law in the 1990 Clean Air Act amendments, it is now possible to make a good living helping companies buy and sell permits to pollute.

Joshua Margolis, director of the Air Trade Services Group at Dames & Moore, a nationwide environmental consulting firm, is making such a living buying and selling dirty air credits. His clients include oil refineries, electric utilities, cogeneration firms, printers, wood products manufacturers, and many other industries covered by air pollution laws.

As Jonathan Marshall, economics editor of the *San Francisco Chronicle* points out, this is no small business. "Firms pay hundreds of thousands of dollars for the right to spew some pollutants into the air—sometimes more per pound than the price of filet mignon."

Under federal law, a polluting company that seeks to move into or expand in a polluted area must first obtain emissions reductions, or "offsets," from existing plants in the same locale. In some areas, it is possible for a company to reduce its polluting emissions and then "bank" those credits for later sale to a company that needs them.

And the process seems to be working. In 1994, a New Jersey utility, which was cleaning up its exhaust, sold credits to emit smog-forming nitrogen oxides to another utility expanding in Connecticut. And when Shell Oil (like other refineries) came under state and federal mandates to modify its Martinez, California, refinery to produce cleaner gasoline and diesel fuel, it bought 55 tons of sulfur dioxide credits from Gaylord Container. Gaylord had acquired the credits when it purchased and eventually closed a pulp paper plant several years earlier.

Marshall reports that prices for credits vary widely because there are relatively few big transactions in any given year. "In the Bay Area last year," Marshall reported, "credits for nitrogen oxide emissions sold for $6,500 to $20,000 a ton, according to William de Boisblanc, an official at the air district. Shell paid about $5,500 per ton for its sulfur dioxide credits."

David Ryan, spokesman for the Environmental Protection Agency supports the concept. "Acid rain emissions are now a commodity, like a stock or bond," he notes. "We think this market will bring down the cost of meeting national acid rain objectives."

Margolis is optimistic about the future for selling pollution. He said such programs to achieve pressing environmental goals at the least cost to industry and consumers are the wave of the future. However, not everyone agrees. Some critics charge that the process amounts to a license to kill, or at least to pollute.

Like they say, it's a dirty business but someone's got to make a profit out of it.

SSU Censored Researcher: Jennifer Burns

COMMENTS: Investigative journalist Jonathan Marshall said, "I think media attention has been discouragingly slight considering the revolution underway in environmental regulation that my article discusses.

"There are at least two key issues raised by the introduction of markets for pollution 'permits.' One is the tremendous potential such markets have for giving polluting firms an incentive to clean up their emissions at the lowest possible costs to themselves, their workers and their customers. The other is whether it is desirable to give firms, in effect, a license to pollute and whether their compliance can be monitored. Unless the public is informed about these tradeoffs it cannot contribute intelligently to a debate that has profound implications for their pocketbooks and their health."

Marshall notes that while no one has an obvious interest in suppressing coverage of this subject, its technical nature deters a lot of journalists. "That's one reason I chose to profile one of the key players in these markets rather than offer a more general and abstract account of how they work. However, one-sided discussions of this topic are all too common: industry neglects to talk about the potential for abuse in these markets and some environmentalists neglect to talk about the costs and failures of traditional 'command and control' regulation."

Marshall adds that he continues to follow and write about little publicized developments in this field including a proposal by the Environmental Defense Fund to clean up selenium contamination in the San Joaquin River by establishing a water pollution market and auctions of air pollution credits in southern California that could help clean the air without costing large numbers of jobs.

Meanwhile, a *New York Times* story on November 17, 1994, reported that the domestic concept of trading air pollution allowances may eventually lead to an international trade in pollution allowances.

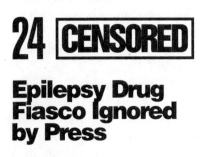

24 CENSORED

Epilepsy Drug Fiasco Ignored by Press

Source:
Personal letter and documents
Date: 10/11/94
Author: Stephen Bertman

SYNOPSIS: On August 2, 1993, the Food and Drug Administration (FDA) approved the first new epilepsy drug in more than ten years. The approval was announced with considerable fanfare at a press conference held at the National Press Club Ballroom in Washington, DC. On August 4, *The New York Times* reported that the drug, felbamate, will be used to prevent partial seizures in adults. The *Times* noted that some 2.5 million Americans have epilepsy, a chronic brain disorder that can cause seizures, and 125,000 new patients are diagnosed each year.

The FDA said that in clinical trials, felbamate reduced the frequency of seizures *and had minimal side effects.* (Emphasis added.) David A. Kessler, the Commissioner of Food and Drugs, said "Felbamate provides a new weapon against the debilitating effects of epilepsy." The *Times* reported that Wallace Labs of Cranbury, N.J., would market the new drug under the brand name Felbatol. It quoted the company as saying "An estimated 500,000 to 700,000 epilepsy patients suffer seizures that cannot be controlled by current medications."

Just a year later, on August 2, 1994, *The New York Times* published a seven-column-inch story headlined "Carter-Wallace Stock Falls." The lead paragraph read: "Carter-Wallace Inc.'s shares plummeted yesterday, losing nearly a third of their value, after the company warned doctors to quit treating patients with an epilepsy drug linked to two deaths." The story then reported that the manufacturer sent letters to some 240,000 doctors recommending that patients discontinue taking the drug, Felbatol, then went on to discuss the impact this action would have on Carter-Wallace shares and sales.

A *Wall Street Journal* (WSJ) article, also published August 2, 1994, was headlined "Carter-Wallace Stock Plummets as FDA Warns Against Firm's Epilepsy Drug." The WSJ article reported that "The (Felbatol) drug is the third Carter-Wallace pharmaceutical product hit by regulatory action this year. Production of Organidin, an expectorant, was halted in June after the FDA had raised concerns about its safety last year. In April, the company ended production of Deprol, an antidepressant, after the FDA withdrew its approval because it lacked evidence of efficacy." Organidin and Felbatol were the company's two biggest-selling drugs, representing about a third of its health-care sales of $296.6 million in the last fiscal year.

On October 5, 1994, in a follow-up story, *The New York Times* reported that Carter-Wallace was virtually abandoning all its drug research. It also noted that since the FDA approved the drug for the market, six people using Felbatol have died—four from blood disorders and two others of liver failure.

This story was submitted to Project Censored by Stephen Bertman, of West Bloomfield, Michigan. Aware of a patient who suffered multiple grand-mal seizures and other serious side effects, following withdrawal from Felbatol on her doctor's advice, Bertman attempted to research the issue and found "Except for articles in *The Wall Street Journal* and on the financial (!) pages of *The New York Times*, the story and, in particular, its tragic human impact have remained unreported."

Project Censored researchers confirmed the limited coverage.

SSU Censored Researcher:
Dave Lake
COMMENTS: Stephen Bertman, who originally brought this story to the attention of Project Censored, said, "The story received only minimal coverage in terms of the human cost of what had happened and who was responsible. There were no follow-ups on victims; no coverage whatsoever of withdrawal causing grand-mal seizures."

25 CENSORED

Deadly "Mad Cow Disease" Spreads to North America

Sources:
THE ANIMAL'S AGENDA
Date: March/April 1994
Title: "Eating beef in Britain is
  becoming risky business"
Author: Joyce D'Silva

IN THESE TIMES
Date: 1/24/94
Title: "How Now Mad Cow?"
Author: Joel Bleifuss

SYNOPSIS: A new and ghastly disease which turns the brain sponge-like and has been attacking dairy cows in England for years, has now appeared in North America. Nicknamed "Mad Cow Disease," bovine spongiform encephalopathy (BSE) has infected more than 120,000 cattle since it was discovered in 1985.

BSE attacks the animal's central nervous system and makes the animal fall, act confused, or act aggressive. It is thought that British cattle contracted the virus-like agent that causes this degenerative brain disease by eating protein feed supplements made from the rendered carcasses of sheep that were infected with scrapie, the sheep form of transmissible spongiform encephalopathy.

While it has not been proven that humans can contract the disease from BSE-infected cattle, humans are susceptible to three brain diseases similar to BSE. The most common of these, though still rare, is Creutzfeldt-Jakob disease (CJD), a horrendous condition that leads to rapid dementia and death within a year after its first symptoms appear. CJD has an incubation period of up to 30 years. So far two British dairy farmers, whose herds were infected with BSE, have died from CJD, and a teenage girl whose favorite food is beefburgers also is said to have developed the disease. Since 1989, the number of Britons who succumb to CJD each year has increased by 100 percent. Nonetheless, the official position of both the British and U.S. governments is that BSE poses no risk to humans.

The recent discovery of a case of BSE on a ranch in Alberta, Canada, has increased fears that a BSE epidemic threatens North America. The cow that contracted BSE had been imported to Canada from England in 1987. It was one of 175 cows Canada imported from England between 1982 and 1989, when both the United States and Canada banned the importation of British cattle. Before the ban went into effect, the United States imported 459 cattle from Britain during this time period. According to the U.S. Department of Agriculture, as of August 23, 1991, 205 of the British cattle imported into the U.S. were still alive, 66 were untraceable, and 188 had died or been slaughtered, and then rendered. In response to the BSE case in Canada, the USDA is now retracing the whereabouts of the 205 cattle still alive in 1991.

The occasional occurrence of BSE in U.S. cattle would not pose a public health risk were it not for two factors. First, almost all dead cow material that is not consumed as human food is rendered into bone and protein meal, some of which is then fed back to cattle in the form of high-protein feed supplements. Second, in the late '70s, the rendering industry here and in Britain began rendering animal carcasses with fewer solvents and at lower temperatures, a change that allows the virus-like agent that causes transmissible encephalopathies to survive intact. This is how the scrapie agent began to infect the British cattle population.

In 1989, British government experts predicted 17,000 to 20,000 cases of BSE by 1993. The actual number of cases was 120,476 by the end of February 1994.

**SSU Censored Researcher:
Kate Kauffman**

COMMENTS: The "Mad cow disease" story is regularly covered in the European press, according to investigative author Joel Bleifuss. "In Great Britain stories about the disease and the controversy over whether it poses a risk to humans appear weekly." But, Bleifuss adds, "I am the only U.S. journalist who has been reporting on the controversy within the FDA and the USDA on how to respond to the threat posed by the disease.

"Cattle infected with mad cow disease were certainly imported from Britain into the U.S. before the 1989 ban on such imports went into effect. And some of those cattle have undoubtedly died from the disease and then been rendered into animal protein feed supplements. These supplements, infected with the agent that causes mad cow disease, then have been fed to other cows, setting off a cycle like the one that has devastated the British beef industry. Because the USDA and FDA still permit the practice of feeding cows back to other cows, the U.S. cattle industry faces an increasingly greater threat of contamination. Further, those humans who have eaten meat from infected animals have been subjected to a potential, if at present unquantifiable, risk.

"The short-term interests of the beef, rendering and feed industries are all served by keeping this story quiet," Bleifuss noted. "Public officials at the FDA and USDA who have failed to act have also benefited from the lack of coverage."

COMPARING PROJECT CENSORED
WITH THE ASSOCIATED PRESS

Following is a comparison of Project Censored's top ten *Censored* stories of 1994, as selected by our judges, with the Associated Press's top ten news stories of the year, as selected by AP newspaper and broadcast news executives across the country.

PROJECT CENSORED	ASSOCIATED PRESS
1. OSHA'S Deadly Secrets	1. O.J. Simpson
2. Conservatives' Secret Plans	2. November Elections
3. DOD Pays for Mergers	3. Baseball Strike
4. Toxic Incinerators	4. Mother & Drowned Sons
5. Retreat on Ozone Crisis	5. Nancy Kerrigan/Tonya Harding
6. Secret AEC Radiaton Memo	6. Aristide's Return to Haiti
7. Tons of Fish Wasted Annually	7. Universal Health Insurance
8. The Return of Tuberculosis	8. Northridge, CA, Earthquake
9. Pentagons' Secret HAARP Plan	9. Rwanda
10. Spousal Violence Language	10. Palestinians in Gaza Strip

The most immediate distinction between the two lists is that, not surprisingly, no single story appears on both lists. But while Haiti appears on this year's AP list of major news stories, the background story of Haitian "drugs, thugs, and the CIA" was on our *Censored* list of stories in 1993.

However, the most glaring distinction between the two lists is found in the kinds of stories appearing on either list. The Associated Press list reflects stories that tend toward sensationalism while the *Censored* list reflects stories that impact on the health, wealth, well-being, and safety of the public.

The top AP "news" story of 1994 was O.J. Simpson, a football legend accused of a double murder; the top *Censored* story of the year was the failure of a federal agency to inform nearly 170,000 American workers that they were subject to health risks from on-the-job exposure to hazardous materials.

Instead, O.J. Simpson was the top "junk food news" story of 1994. In fact, three of the top five "news" stories cited by the Associated Press are found on the list of "junk food news" stories cited by news ombudsmen in Chapter 5—O.J. Simpson, #1; Nancy Kerrigan/Tonya Harding, #2; the baseball strike, #20.

The #2 stories on either list also provide for an interesting comparison. The Associated Press story—the November elections—described the "tumultuous November elections that left Democrats in disarray and Republicans in triumph," according to the Associated Press.

However, the #2 *Censored* story—the conservatives' plans—revealed the secret plans of a powerful group of ultra-conservatives that helped cause the dramatic shift in political power in November 1994.

Overall, comparing this year's two lists of stories should make it abundantly clear why it is long overdue for news editors and directors to redefine what they mean by news—instead of simply relying on the sensationalistic old "man bites dog" definition.

As noted in the Preface, real news is reliable information about events that affect the lives and well-being of the public—information such as that cited among Project Censored's top ten stories of the year. And when the news media start providing the public with information they can use, journalists will discover that the public will treat them with the respect and trust the profession will then deserve.

THE CENSORED SUBJECTS OF 1994

Domestic issues, led by environmental and health stories, dominated the list of *Censored* subjects of 1994. Environmental and health issues combined to account for 12 of the 25 top stories. Considering that environmental issues tend also to impact on the public well-being, i.e. pollution, toxic incineration, etc., it is clear that health issues constituted a top overlooked category of subjects for the year.

In fact, this was the largest number of health issues to make the top 25 list in any single year. Perhaps investigative authors and publications were drawn to the subject because of the attention devoted to health care by politicians.

One of our judges noted that while the lapdog nature of the press with regard to international issues has always been apparent, the extension of this to domestic issues, as evidenced by this year's selections, should be a matter of great concern. Another judge commented on how a number of this year's underreported stories relate to environmental dangers that can affect millions of lives.

Several judges expressed concern about the lack of international subjects among this year's selections. There were four international stories cited in 1993 and none in 1992. However, a number of updates on global issues, cited in previous years, are noted in Chapter 4, "Censored Déjà

Vu." It was almost as if the media were trying to catch up with what they'd missed in the past; for example, recent developments on a number of critical international issues, including the Persian Gulf, Guatemala, El Salvador, Haiti, and East Timor are reported in Chapter 4.

Following are the top 25 stories of 1994 separated by category.

ENVIRONMENT
 #4—Poisoning Ourselves with Toxic Incinerators
 #5—Clinton's Retreat on Ozone Crisis
 #7—Wasting 60 Billions Pounds of Fish Annually
 #12—Oil Spill Covered Up by Unocal
 #20—Legalizing Carcinogens in our Food
 #23—Buying and Selling Permits to Pollute
HEALTH
 #8—The Return of Tuberculosis
 #16—Fallibility of the AIDS Test
 #19—Cesarean Sections Epidemic
 #22—Over-the-Counter Diet Pills Cause Deaths
 #24—Epilepsy Drug Fiasco Ignored by Press
 #25—Deadly "Mad Cow Disease"
POLITICS
 #1—OSHA's Deadly Secrets
 #2—Ultra-conservatives' Secret Plans
 #13—The NRC's Dirty Secret
MILITARY
 #6—1947 AEC Memo Censored Radiation Issue
 #9—The Pentagon's Mysterious HAARP Project
 #21—Illegal Toxic Burning at Secret Air Base
CORPORATE
 #3—Secret Plan Subsidizes Defense Industry Mergers
 #14—Faulty Nuclear Fuel Rods Spell Potential Disasters
 #18—Collusion Between Drug Companies and Pharmacists
CRIME
 #10—Media's "Language of Love" Masks Spousal Violence
 #11—Treasury Department Ignores S&L Crimes
EDUCATION
 #15—DARE Program Cover-up Continues
 #17—Censoring Tomorrow's Journalists Today

COMMENTS BY JUDGES

Following are reflections on this year's Censored selections by some of the judges who helped select the top ten stories of 1994:

DONNA ALLEN, founding editor of *Media Report to Women* and a *Censored* judge since 1980, said the #10 story, "News Media Mask Spousal Violence in the 'Language of Love'," reminds us that the news media often go beyond the traditional concept of censorship. "Are they 'news' media reporters or apologists for and therefore promoters of, violence?

"In the midst of world violence, and when single murders can become front page and nightly news continuing stories—like soap operas—it is shocking that the public has not been told the dimensions of this domestic violence. Why does the public not know that four women die *daily* at the hands of their husbands and that every 12 seconds in this country, some man batters his current or former wife or girlfriend. If violence is 'news' why is it not news if it happens to women. Now that it is recognized by law as being unacceptable, why are the news media still describing how she was dressed, what she might have done to cause the attack, how jealous or overcome by love he was, in other words trying to make violence to women acceptable, excusable, even justified.

"It seems more like promotion and encouragement of violence than news reporting. This nomination raises a serious media fault in not only failure to report (censorship) but worse, teaching tolerance of illegal violence. We need much more information on this journalistic and ethical shortcoming of the news media. Selection of this nomination by Project Censored should encourage the media to focus on this major source of violence in the U.S. and in the world."

BEN BAGDIKIAN, professor emeritus, Graduate School of Journalism, University of California, Berkeley, and a *Censored* judge since 1976, said, "Once again, the main media have provided varying degrees of privileged sanctuary for bad news about industries and conservatives. There are always a few underplayed stories that could be attributed to ignorance. But almost all reflect an ingrained habit of regarding negative stories about corporate life and conservatives as not important news to highlight."

RICHARD BARNET, senior fellow, Institute for Policy Studies, was hoping for more digging into the hidden aspects of mainstream politics, but, on the whole, felt this was an interesting collection of nominations.

SUT JHALLY, professor of communication and executive director of The Media Education Foundation, University of Massachusetts, said three things stand out about the stories nominated for 1994: "(1) While the subservience of the press to corporate power continues unabated, this seems to have been joined by subservience to state power over domestic issues. Many of the stories concern cover-ups or lack of action by government agencies. Such non-activities have serious impacts upon citizen interests. While the lapdog nature of the press with regard to international issues has always been apparent, the extension of this to domestic issues should be a matter of great concern.

"(2) I am glad to see the definition of 'censorship' expanded to include not merely absence/presence but also framing. For example, regarding spousal violence, while this has been pushed onto the public agenda by the hard work of progressive groups, the definition of the issues by the press had deflected attention away from its serious consequences and possible responses.

"(3) the absence of international stories from the list this year is notable, especially considering the whole focus on Haiti. While Haiti has not been ignored, the framing of the crisis, Aristide and the military by the mainstream media did a disservice to citizens trying to understand the issues around 'intervention'."

RHODA A. KARPATKIN, president of the Consumers Union, nonprofit publisher of *Consumer Reports*, shared her thoughts on censorship and this year's nominations. "From the superficial to the sensational, Americans are bombarded with massive amounts of information every day, much of it packaged in the form of news. News gathering and distribution have become a multi-billion dollar industry in this country. Yet all too often, the 'news' fails to constitute useful or even intelligible information for citizens. The important things we need to know may be mentioned only in passing, reported out of context, or just not reported at all.

"Far from suffering from an 'information glut,' citizens are actually suffering from a serious 'information deficit.' There are two problems. One, Americans are simply not being informed about many critical problems and issues to begin with—period. Two, the media may provide some coverage of an important problem or issue, but the reporting is only cursory; it scratches the surface, and deals with irrelevant fringe matters. The facts and issues are not related in a way that empowers the citizen to make sense of what is really happening.

"The consequences of the growing American information deficit are serious:

■ In the 1980s, the American media slept soundly while the public got taken to the cleaners by the savings and loan industry.

■ In 1993 and 1994, the media failed to adequately inform consumers about the vital importance of health care reform, which by all rights should be one of our nation's highest domestic priorities. The health care system is in serious crisis; it unconscionably excludes a large segment of the population, and with costs out of control, no consumer can feel secure, even when covered. Yet for the most part, the media failed to challenge the notion that health care reform could be weakened or delayed without serious consequences for consumers, in terms of coverage, costs and choice of doctor. Journalists could have done a far better job at examining the real-life problems in the health care system, investigating the lobbying strategies of the powerful interests who oppose reform, and reporting of the full range of legislative alternatives.

■ In example after example, including many of this year's Project Censored nominations, the mass media continue to dodge their responsibility to report on public and private abuses of power. These include the promotion of unsafe products by pharmaceutical companies, and the cover-up of environmental hazards and pollution by government agencies. These types of wrongdoing are frequently fueled or exacerbated by unchecked conflicts of interest. Among other things, reporters need to investigate the sources and implications of private money in political campaigns, and the myriad other ways in which private interests seek to promote their interests at public expense.

"Project Censored shines a light on unreported and underreported stories to help bring them to wider public attention. As citizens, we not only need to think about the particular stories nominated for this year's selections, we need to think about the process that causes them to be ignored or suppressed to begin with. In a democratic society, the media have a critical role and responsibility to help citizens learn about what is really going on. Since the heady days of Watergate and the Pentagon Papers, it seems that many reporters, editors and publishers have lost their zeal to dig under the surface, and relate the facts that citizens need to know in a coherent and compelling way."

FRANCES MOORE LAPPÉ, co-director of the Center for Living Democracy, said, "With each passing year I become more outraged by the narrow purview of the primary media through which most Americans learn news affecting them. I find markedly less and less news in *The New York Times*, for example.

"A striking feature of many of this year's underreported stories is that they relate to environmental dangers that can touch millions—dangers from which a democratic government should be protecting people. The ever-louder calls for 'smaller government' will continue to ring true to people who aren't made aware of the hazards from which a truly accountable government can and should be protecting us.

"Many of this year's stories are about the failure of government and government regulation. The challenge for media is to demonstrate not just these failures, but the possibilities for truly accountable government. Only then will Americans stop arguing over 'big' or 'small' and start talking about effective and accountable. Unfortunately, equally unreported are stories of citizens making both governments and corporations accountable—the stories that can make Americans believe that it's possible."

WILLIAM LUTZ, professor of English at Rutgers University, said, "Once again Project Censored brings to light the important stories that the media have ignored. These are stories that affect our lives as individuals and the political life of the nation. Many of these stories aren't 'sexy'— they don't deal with personalities or scandal, but each and every one of them does deal with matters of life and death—our lives, our families' lives, our neighbors' lives, and the very life of this nation. These are stories that *deserve* better coverage, that *demand* better coverage."

JULIANNE MALVEAUX, Ph.D., economist and columnist, King Features and Pacifica Radio, and a first-time *Censored* judge, noted that a number of the top 25 nominated stories are concerned with health and science themes. "Tuberculosis, cesarean section operations, errors in HIV antibody tests, nuclear reactor problems, the impact of incineration, and similar stories all deal with areas that are central to human existence, yet at the periphery of public discourse. It seems, and I may be reaching, that part of the reason these stories have been 'censored' is because people are not as facile in discussions about science and health issues as they are about political and social issues.

"Information is power. Burying information either directly enriches some people at the expense of others, or indirectly maintains a profit relationship that would be altered given full information. Drug companies that subsidize prescription decisions, federal plans to make defense contractors even larger than they already are, a faulty epilepsy drug whose flaws are buried in the financial pages are all examples of the economic consequences of controlling the flow of information.

"Each of the *Censored* stories is the basis for an important public information campaign, as millions of people are affected by the facts uncovered in each. Each has the potential for front page news. But, as the Unocal story illustrates, powerful interests would be embarrassed or financially threatened by wider dissemination of the *Censored* stories. We know more about the murders of Nicole Brown Simpson and Ronald Goldman than we need to, and far more about the private lives of British royalty than we care to, but we know less than we need to know about the way our government works and about the way scientific information is disseminated. In some ways this is a statement about who chooses the headlines, what sells papers or rivets attention to a broadcast, and whether the role of the press is to inform, educate, or merely titillate.

"My review of the 25 nominated stories confirms my sense that we are all losers when substantive information is nudged (or pushed) aside for sensationalist headlines. The work that Project Censored does should motivate people to view the media as something that is 'of the people, by the people, and for the people,' and to agitate for better coverage and wider dissemination of the information that concerns us."

JACK NELSON, a professor in the Graduate School of Education at Rutgers University, and a *Censored* judge since 1976, commented specifically on the #2 story, "Powerful Group of Ultra-Conservatives has Secret Plans for Your Future." "Although the threat of ultra-conservatives has been on the horizon of American politics for a long time, their success in elections has created a setting for serious problems. This makes their secrecy, and their platform, much more significant in American life (and world-wide) and creates an urgent need for full exposition by the media. It took too long during the McCarthy period to sound the public alarm. They are smarter now—are the media?"

MICHAEL PARENTI, political analyst, author and lecturer, said the most important stories for him were "those that dealt with the life and death of the planet itself, the dangers to the ozone layer, the oceans, the atmosphere. These were heavily represented in the selections for 1994. Stories on unsafe products and the like were also important but of more limited scope in regard to impact and potential victimization.

"I included the story about the Council on National Policy (the #2 story), the right-wing cabal with its agenda for the USA —because I continually encounter people who do not believe that those with money and power consciously plan to protect and advance their power. And if one suggests that they do, then one is called a 'conspiracy theorist.' So the story is important.

"My one complaint is that there were no offerings regarding the continually suppressive and undemocratic features of U.S. foreign policy. In the last year, the CIA-backed wars in Angola and Mozambique have caused over ten times more deaths than have occurred in Bosnia in the last three years. There is also the suppressed story of the U.S. role in death squads in Latin America and elsewhere, and the U.S. role in Haiti over the last 80 years, etc. The U.S. public knows almost nothing about these."

HERBERT I. SCHILLER, visiting professor of media ecology, New York University, and professor emeritus, University of California, San Diego, is troubled by what the 1994 nominations portend for the future of our society. "This year's Project Censored nominations strongly suggest that an irresponsible, and largely unaccountable, alliance of private corporate interests and governmental power, are rapidly making the country (and the world) unlivable. The extent of the havoc already created is appalling. How these tendencies may be reversed is the overriding issue of this era. The prognosis is less than cheerful."

SHEILA RABB WEIDENFELD, president of D.C. Productions, Ltd., and a founding member of the *Censored* panel of judges in 1976, said, "Once again, Project Censored directs our attention to otherwise overlooked stories that affect our health, well-being, and economic security.

"Two of this year's stories underline the disturbing tendency of the mass media to gloss over issues. Project Censored exposes the media's propensity, for example, to treat spousal abuse lightly by masking such violence in the 'language of love.'

It is also disturbing that with all the information available, unnecessary cesarean sections still are being performed. Stories like these emphasize the contribution Project Censored makes to a better informed society."

"God forbid that any book
should be banned.
The practice is as
indefensible as infanticide."
—Rebecca West

CHAPTER 3

Top Censored Books of 1994

Books have often been hailed as the last pure vehicle for critical minds to expose controversial and possibly even uncomfortable ideas to the general public. As advertisers, accountants, and censors have come to wield increasing influence on the mass media, book lovers have held to the belief that the book publishing industry, once led by proud, independent individuals and families, would not succumb to the bottom line, as did newspapers, magazines, radio, and television.

This cherished belief was seriously questioned in 1983 with the first edition of *The Media Monopoly*, by Ben Bagdikian, which described the growing concentration of media ownership which included the publishing industry.

Bagdikian's fourth edition, published in 1992, confirmed that book publishing has now succumbed to corporate control. While there are some 2,500 companies that publish one or more books a year, the industry is dominated by just six corporations that gross more than half of all book revenues.

The six companies (and some of their subsidiaries) are: Paramount Communications (Macmillan, Simon & Schuster, Ginn & Company); Harcourt Brace Jovanovich (Academic Press); Time Warner (Little, Brown; Scott, Foresman); Bertelsmann, A.G. (Doubleday, Bantam Books);

Reader's Digest Association (Condensed Books); Newhouse (Random House).

The extraordinary influence of media monopolization was highlighted in September 1994 when St. Martin's Press tried to buy advertising space in *Vanity Fair* for a new book titled *Newhouse*, an unflattering biography of S.I. Newhouse. As it turns out, Newhouse owns Conde Nast which owns *Vanity Fair* which rejected the ad. And that's the way you play the media monopoly game.

At the same time, independent bookstores were being squeezed out by the chains which are primarily interested in blockbuster bestsellers they can bank on. Best-selling author Stephen King has also noted that independent bookstores are disappearing while the chains are guilty of censorship, making it nearly impossible for yet-to-be discovered authors to get published.

As the book publishers dwindled down to a "precious" few and the chain bookstores grew more powerful, Project Censored started receiving more and more nominations of books as censored stories. As a result, we decided to add a new chapter to the annual *Censored* Yearbook dealing solely with books.

As with our criteria for other censored issues, we are limiting our nominations to non-fiction books that have been published, but have not received the media exposure they deserve. Also, while we recognize the censorship of many classic books, we'll limit the nominations to recently published non-fiction books exploring critical issues.

The American Library Association Intellectual Freedom Committee publishes the *Newsletter on Intellectual Freedom*, a bimonthly on censorship which regularly features books, including the classics, that are "Targets of the Censor" at libraries, public schools, and universities. The *Newsletter*, cited in Appendix A, The CENSORED! Resource Guide, is available for subscription.

Think of what you would have lost if you had not been able to read books such as the following—which are just some of the books targeted by censors, as cited by the ALA *Newsletter* in 1994: *The Adventures of Huckleberry Finn, The Adventures of Tom Sawyer, The Autobiography of Malcolm X, Brave New World, The Catcher in the Rye, Clan of the Cave Bear, The Grapes of Wrath, The Hobbit, I Know Why the Caged Bird Sings, Dracula, Jurassic Park, Little House on the Prairie, The Lord of the Rings* trilogy, *Of Mice and Men*, and *The Red Pony*.

The ALA *Newsletter* also noted two books dealing specifically with book censorship: *Banned in the U.S.A.: A Reference Guide to Book Censorship in Schools and Libraries*, by Herbert N. Foerstel, published by Greenwood Press, 231 p., 1994; *Censored Books: Critical Viewpoints*, Edited by Nicholas J. Karolides, Lee Burress, and John M. Kean, published by Scarecrow Press, 498 p., 1993.

Nominations cited in this first year's compilation of *Censored* books are drawn from two basic sources: a Project Censored survey of 75 publishers cited in the *Alternative Publishers of Books in North America*, a catalog compiled by Byron Anderson, Project Coordinator for Alternatives in Print, at Northern Illinois University Libraries, DeKalb, Illinois; and from books nominated directly to Project Censored by authors, publishers, librarians, educators, and the general public.

Catalog compiler Byron Anderson said the publishers included in the catalog were considered significant presses in terms of "producing incisive and penetrating publications in distinct interest areas." The catalog was published in 1994 by Crises Press, Inc., 1716 SW Williston Road, Gainesville, FL 32608.

We plan to include an expanded selection of books censored in 1995 in next year's *Censored* Yearbook; if you know of any books that should be included, please write CENSORED BOOKS, Project Censored, Sonoma State University, Rohnert Park, CA 94928, for a listing application.

In most cases, in the listing of books that follows, the information concerning the book and author has been provided by the publisher; in some cases, the information has been excerpted from a review. In addition to basic information about the book—its price, availability, length, etc.— where available, we have included a brief description of the book's subject, some information about the author, and why the publisher feels it is important for the public to know about the book.

BHOPAL: The Inside Story
Carbide workers speak out
on the world's worst industrial
disaster
by T.R. Chouhan & Others

SUBJECT: For the first time, T.R. Chouhan, a former worker in Union Carbide's pesticide plant in Bhopal, India, tells the inside story of what it was like to work in a dangerous chemical plant destined to go down in history as the site of the world's worst industrial disaster. The book also provides personal experiences, including eye-witness accounts of the disaster, from 15 other workers. Among these workers is the person

Union Carbide apparently has accused of causing the disaster by sabotage. He denies the accusation and Chouhan gives a critique to show why Carbide's sabotage theory is not only incorrect, but slanders the workers in the Bhopal plant.

AUTHOR: T. R. Chouhan is a former plant operator in Union Carbide's pesticide plant in Bhopal, India.

IMPORTANCE: The publisher said it is important for the public to know about this book because the perpetrator of the world's worst industrial disaster, Union Carbide Corporation, continues to deny responsibility for this historic and terrible tragedy, trying instead to blame a "disgruntled" worker with false charges of "sabotage."

AVAILABLE: Through the publisher's order department: 800/316-APEX. Pbk: ISBN 0-945257-22-8; price: $11.50; 112 pages.

PUBLISHER:
THE APEX PRESS
Suite 3C
777 United Nations Plaza
New York, NY 10017
Tel: 212/972-9877
Fax: 212/972-9878

BY INVITATION ONLY: How the Media Limit Political Debate
by David Croteau and
William Hoynes

SUBJECT: What are the corporate constraints on the media's "objectivity"? While the Right portrays the media as liberal loose cannons, Hoynes and Croteau have done the studies that show the media to be servants of the powerful. Who gets on the talk shows? By examining "Nightline," "MacNeil/Lehrer" and several other shows, the authors reveal that the marketplace of ideas is tightly regulated by government spokespeople and right wing-think tanks whose mostly white male members appear time and time again, while the broad range of opinions in our diverse democracy are ignored. Even the Public Broadcasting System, touted as the alternative provider of in-depth analysis, draws heavily from industry and government representatives to parrot the official line.

AUTHORS: David Croteau is a sociologist and author of *Politics and the Class Divide: Working People and the Middle Class Left*; William Hoynes teaches sociology at Vassar College and is the author of *Public Television for Sale: Media, the Market, and the Public Sphere.*

IMPORTANCE: The publishers suggest *By Invitation Only* is "Critical reading for students of journalism;" we would add that it also is critical reading for journalists and for everyone who believes what those white male pundits are saying on the tube.

AVAILABLE: At bookstores or from the publisher: 800/497-3207. Pbk: ISBN 1-56751-044-2; price:

$9.95; 250 pages Hbk: ISBN 1-56751-045-0; price: $29.95
PUBLISHER:
COMMON COURAGE PRESS
P.O. Box 702
Monroe, ME 04951
Tel: 207/525-0900;
Fax: 207/525-3068

BREACH OF TRUST: Physician Participation in Executions in the United States
by The American College of Physicians; Human Rights Watch; National Coalition to Abolish the Death Penalty; Physicians for Human Rights

SUBJECT: Despite an American Medical Association policy prohibiting participation by physicians in capital punishment, doctors continue to be involved in executions all across the United States. Indeed, of the thirty-six states with death penalty laws, all but a few require that a physician be present at executions. This report documents the extent of physician participation in executions. It reviews state laws and regulations, as well as professional ethics regarding this issue. The report shows how laws and regulations often mandate physician participation in executions. The authors provide policy recommendations to ensure that current laws do not require physicians to violate professional ethics.

AUTHOR: American College of Physicians is a professional association of physicians trained in internal medicine; Human Rights Watch is an organization that conducts regular, systemic investigations of human rights abuses in 70 countries; National Coalition to Abolish the Death Penalty leads and coordinates the movement to end state killings in the United States; Physicians for Human Rights is an organization of physicians and other health professionals that works to investigate and prevent human rights violations throughout the world.

IMPORTANCE: The public should know about the conflict between state laws and codes of medical ethics. Furthermore, the public should be aware that most medical professional groups oppose participation in executions as a threat to the public trust in physicians. Participation contradicts the fundamental role of physicians as comforters and healers. This is important for the public to know as citizens, voters, and patients.

AVAILABLE: Directly from Human Rights Watch, the publisher. Pbk: ISBN 1-56432-125-8; price: $10.00; 72 pages
PUBLISHER:
HUMAN RIGHTS WATCH
485 Fifth Avenue
New York, NY 10017-6104
Tel: 212/972-8400
Fax: 212/972-0905

CLEARCUT: The Tragedy of Industrial Forestry
Edited by Bill Devall

SUBJECT: *Clearcut* is a 300-page exhibit-format book documenting some of the most horrific clearcuts in North America. It was originally conceived by Doug Tompkins, whose Foundation for Deep Ecology, a grant-giving organization, was created to address continuing ecological crises. *Clearcut* is the most comprehensive collection of photos portraying the destructive impact of industrial forestry. The photographs in the book were carefully selected from thousands; although all forest types in North America are represented, priority is given to photos of clearcuts few people have seen. The massive clearcuts in the book are primarily from the back country, away from the scrutiny of those who drive along major highways—and represent only a small sample of the vast destruction that has taken place in the forests of North America.

AUTHORS: *Clearcut* is co-published by Sierra Club Books and Earth Island Press; Edgar Boyles is Photo Editor; Douglas Tompkins, Project Director; and Bill Devall, Editor. The book includes contributions by David Brower, Chris Maser, Colleen McCrory, Jan Wilder-Thomas, and Galen Rowell. Dozens of writers and photographers were commissioned for the project.

IMPORTANCE: *Clearcut* stands as a sad testimony for the need to show what has really happened to North America's wilderness. The book documents the destruction of North American forests and also presents realistic approaches towards creating a new public policy that returns human society into balance with the forest ecosystem. The book threatened industrial forestry interests to the point where the Alta California Alliance, one of the largest northern California Forestry associations, reportedly encouraged its members to steal copies of the book from public libraries.

AVAILABLE: *Clearcut* is available through local book stores; ask for it by title and as published by Sierra Club Books. Copies also are available through the Patagonia mail order catalog: 1/800/638-6464. Hbk: ISBN 0-9637749-0-5; price: $30.00; 300 pages

PUBLISHERS:
SIERRA CLUB BOOKS
100 Bush Street
San Francisco, CA 94104
Tel: 415/291-1600
Fax: 415/291-1602
EARTH ISLAND PRESS
300 Broadway
San Francisco, CA 94133
Tel: 415/788-3666
Fax: 415/788-7324

DARK VICTORY: The United States, Structural Adjustment, and Global Poverty

by Walden Bello, Shea Cunningham, and Bill Ray

SUBJECT: *Dark Victory* reveals three wrenching global developments that unfolded in the 1980s and early 1990s. First, the book examines the universalization of structural adjustment programs via the World Bank and International Monetary Fund (IMF) and shows their destructive effects on people and the environment. Next, the authors show how the United States has used "trade warfare" against the "Newly Industrializing Countries" (NICs) of Asia to economically resubordinate them in a U.S.-dominated global economy. And finally, they show how a "frontal attack on organized labor, draconian downsizing, and domestic deregulation" were central elements of this global strategy to reassert U.S.-corporate dominance.

AUTHORS: Walden Bello, Principal Research Analyst, is author of many books by Food First including *Dragons in Distress: Asia's Miracle Economies in Crisis, People and Power in the Pacific: The Struggle for the Post-Cold War Order,* and *Development Debacle: The World Bank in the Philippines.* Shea Cunningham is a Research Associate of Food First and Bill Ray is an expert on Africa.

IMPORTANCE: *Dark Victory* reveals a shocking inhumane global trend that is threatening both human existence and the fate of our environment. The book is an exceptional resource tool that the public can use to raise its voice and cut-off the flow of tax dollars into the IMF and the World Bank. It will awaken the public to some of the primary causes of perpetual poverty, labor exploitation, and environmental degradation. *Dark Victory* is a vital resource for students, educators, policy makers, and the concerned public in the United States and elsewhere.

AVAILABLE: At all bookstores or directly from the publisher: 800/274-7826. Pbk: ISBN 0-935028-61-7; price: $12.95; 148 pages

PUBLISHER:
FOOD FIRST BOOKS
398-60th Street
Oakland, CA 94618
Tel: 510/654-4400
Fax: 510/654-4551

DEATH BY DENIAL: Preventing suicide in gay and lesbian teenagers

Edited by Gary Remafedi

SUBJECT: A federal study in 1989 found that teenagers struggling with issues of sexual orientation were three times more likely than their peers to attempt suicide. The report was swept aside by the Bush administration, yet the problem didn't go away. *Death by Denial* presents the full findings of that report and of several other studies. It also documents the difficulties faced by teenagers who are coming out and proposes ways to ease that process.

AUTHOR: Gary Remafedi, M.D., M.P.H., is executive director of the Youth and AIDS Project at the University of Minnesota and an internationally recognized authority on adolescent homosexuality and its public health implications.

IMPORTANCE: The Bush administration chose to look the other way when a federal report found that teenagers struggling with issues of sexual orientation are three times more likely than their peers to attempt suicide. The findings of the studies in this book will open eyes and could save lives.

AVAILABLE: At booksellers nationwide or directly from the publisher: 800/8-ALYSON. Pbk: ISBN 1-55583-260-1; price: $9.95; 205 pages

PUBLISHER:
ALYSON PUBLICATIONS INC.
40 Plympton Street
Boston, MA 02118
Tel: 617/542-5679
Fax: 617/542-9189

AN EYE FOR AN EYE:

The Untold Story of Jewish Revenge Against Germans in 1945
by John Sack

SUBJECT: This controversial and disturbing book presents a dramatic account of the appalling events that accompanied the end of World War II. In 1945, the Soviet Union, which occupied Poland and parts of Germany, established the Office of State Security and deliberately recruited survivors of the Holocaust to carry out a policy of de-Nazification. The author describes how the Office rounded up German men, women, and children and took them to cellars, prisons, and 1,255 concentration camps, where inmates subsisted on starvation rations, where typhus ran rampant, and where torture was commonplace.

AUTHOR: John Sack has been a journalist for 48 years. He was a newspaper reporter in North and South America, Europe, Africa, and Asia, a magazine writer, a contributing editor of *Esquire*, a writer, producer, and special correspondent for CBS News, its bureau chief in Spain, a war correspondent in Korea, Vietnam, and Iraq, and author of seven non-fiction books, including *M* and *Lieutenant Calley*.

IMPORTANCE: "The topic of Jewish participation in these acts of oppression is controversial, but, in my view, only two questions need to be raised. The first concerns the motivation of the author and here I am convinced that Mr. Sack has tried, as he himself writes, to tell 'something more than the story of Jewish revenge: the story of Jewish redemption.' The second is whether the story is true and what it is based on. Here, too, I am satisfied that the author is a serious researcher."—Antony Polonsky, professor of East European Jewish History, Brandeis University (excerpted from book jacket).

AVAILABLE: At booksellers nationwide. Hbk: ISBN 0-465-04214-7; price: $23.00; 252 pages

PUBLISHER:
BASIC BOOKS
10 East 53rd Street
New York, NY 10022
Tel: 212/207-7000

FARM LABOR ORGANIZING:
Trends and Prospects
by Maralyn Edid

SUBJECT: In vivid language, Maralyn Edid tells the story of farmworkers' struggle to organize unions. She traces their intermittent efforts to bargain effectively with employers over wages and working conditions and explores the reasons why migrant and seasonal farmworkers have felt compelled to unionize. She also documents the obstacles that impede their chances for success,

including the erosion of dramatic worker gains made in the 1970s during the Reagan-Bush era. After tracing the history of farm labor unions, Edid analyzes the legal issues that have complicated their emergence. She also addresses the possibilities for labor law reform and discusses the impact such changes might have on the people who grow and harvest our food.

AUTHOR: Maralyn Edid has worked as a reporter for Crain's *Chicago Business* and *Business Week* magazines. She is now on the extension faculty at the School of Industrial and Labor Relations at Cornell University.

IMPORTANCE: The plight of farmworkers is invisible to most people in the United States who eat the food laborers grow and pick. As a matter of conscience, the public should learn about the efforts of farmworkers to organize. For all those concerned about the plight of farmworkers, Edid's book fills a void left by the media whose sporadic attention died with Cesar Chavez. She builds the case that protecting farmworkers is a necessary step in enfranchising oppressed racial and ethnic groups and recent immigrants.

AVAILABLE: At some bookstores; distributed by Ingram and by Inland Book Co.; or directly from the publisher: 607/255-2264; and available in Canada through Scholarly Book Services in Toronto.

Pbk: ISBN 0-87546-321-5; price: $12.95; 144 pages
PUBLISHER:
ILR PRESS
Cornell University
Ithaca, NY 14853-3901
Tel: 607/255-3061
Fax: 607/255-2755

HEAR MY TESTIMONY

by María Teresa Tula
Translated and edited by
Lynn Stephen

SUBJECT: *Hear My Testimony* is the riveting testimony of a woman awakened to politics in a land torn apart by years of war. Following in the footsteps of Rigoberta Menchú and others who have sought to tell their story through personal narrative, María Teresa Tula describes her childhood, marriage, and growing family as well as her awakening political consciousness, activism, imprisonment, and torture. The human side of the civil war in El Salvador and decades of repression come to the fore in this woman's tale of extraordinary courage and ordinary labor.

AUTHOR: María Teresa Tula has lived in Washington, D.C., since 1987 where she is a human rights organizer for CO-MADRES and is still waiting to resolve her case for political asylum. Lynn Stephen lives in Boston, where she is an associate professor of anthropology

at Northeastern University. She works with a women's solidarity organization, Mujeres Sin Fronteras, and is the author of *Zapotec Women.*

IMPORTANCE: María Teresa Tula's testimony is followed by several contextual chapters, which offer recent Salvadoran political, economic, and social history, and a discussion of women's grassroots organizing in El Salvador during the past 25 years. A final chapter discusses the process of testimonial production, focusing on the politics of publishing and collaborative projects.

AVAILABLE: At booksellers or from Inbook!: 800/243-0138. Pbk: ISBN 0-89608-484-1; price: $14.00; 224 pages Hbk: ISBN 0-89608-485-X; price: $30.00
PUBLISHER:
SOUTH END PRESS
116 Saint Botolph Street
Boston, MA 02115
Tel: 617/266-0629
Fax: 617/266-1595

KEEPING THE RABBLE IN LINE
NOAM CHOMSKY INTERVIEWS

With David Barsamian

SUBJECT: In a gripping series of interviews from 1992 to 1994, Noam Chomsky outlines his views on a wide range of topics including: Global Warming, Free Trade & International Capital, Health Care,

Gun Control & the Death Penalty, The Democracy deficit, Clinton's Foreign Policy, and many other issues.

AUTHOR: Noam Chomsky, internationally renown professor of linguistics at the Massachusetts Institute of Technology, is the author of many important, and often undercovered books on U.S. political life and foreign policy.

IMPORTANCE: Once again, Noam Chomsky is right on target in these interviews on some of the most important issues of our time. Chomsky provides an extraordinary insight into and perspective on issues such as global warming, health care, and gun control that you won't find discussed by the mainstream pundits nor covered by the mainstream media.

AVAILABLE: At good independent bookstores or directly from the publisher: 800/497-3207. Pbk: ISBN 1-56751-032-9; price: $12.95; 256 pages Hbk: ISBN 1-56751-033-7; price: $29.95

PUBLISHER:
COMMON COURAGE PRESS
P.O. Box 702
Monroe, ME 04951
Tel: 207/525-0900
Fax: 207/525-3068

LAND OF WAR:
Memories From Israel
by Abraham Gal

SUBJECT: *Land of War* is a first person memoir on how "clandestine arms deals have compromised the security and the future of the state of Israel." It describes events and secret transactions which have placed Israel in jeopardy. Before the Gulf War, Israeli technology increasing the efficiency of the Scud missile was shipped to Iraq, Iran and Syria. And an Israeli manufacturer sold the airborne warfare system, TS Mark II, to Iraq via Pakistan to conceal its destination and deceive company employees. Bribes intended for Iraqi army officers and supplied by certain Israeli Defense Ministry officials were disbursed. During the Gulf War, Iraqi intelligence threatened to leak information about the payoff, effectively blocking retaliatory action by Israel.

AUTHOR: Abraham Gal was a defense industry engineering contractor in Israel for the past twelve years. He is now a journalist living in Southern California where he is working on his next book.

IMPORTANCE: Abraham Gal's intent is to alert the Israeli people to a situation which has placed Israel's security and very existence in danger and make them aware that certain powerful officials have put personal gain above the welfare of their country.

AVAILABLE: Directly from the publisher: TEL & Fax: 818/ 705-7335. Hbk: ISBN 0-9636437-0-3; price: $19.80; 320 pages

PUBLISHER:
GILAR PRESS
P.O. Box 18061
Encino, CA 91416
Tel: 818/705-7335
Fax: 818/705-7335

MACROCOSM USA: Possibilities for a New Progressive Era

Edited by Sandi Brockway
Foreword by Marilyn Ferguson

SUBJECT: *Macrocosm USA* is an environmental, political, and social solutions handbook with directories. It has been likened to "a huge issue of the *Utne Reader*" and called "the best resource guide since the Whole Earth Catalog," only without advertisements. A directory and interdisciplinary reader that contains fourteen chapters, it will assist readers in understanding the issues and getting involved. Readers will discover how to take part in rearranging economic priorities; improving our environmental, political, and social landscape; and making democracy more than an empty promise for future generations.

AUTHORS: Edited by Sandi Brockway, other authors include: Denis Hayes, Jim Hightower, John Bowker, Carl Pope, Rosalie Bertell, Theodore Roszak, Francis Moore Lappé, Marilyn Ferguson, Mary Catherine Bateson, Donella Meadows, Winona LaDuke, Lois Gibbs, Hazel Henderson, Helen Caldicott, Ram Dass, Fritjof Capra, William Greider, Richard Neville, Chief Oren Lyons, Terry Tempest Williams, John Stockwell, Thomas Berry, John Gatto, and many more.

IMPORTANCE: Theodore Roszak, author of *The Voice of the Earth*, said "...the best example I've seen of a citizen-friendly information service, *Macrocosm USA* genuinely serves the values of democracy." The *Utne Reader* said "There is no guide to the social change movements comparable to this; it seems destined to become indispensable."

AVAILABLE: Updated supplement published March 1995; directly from the publisher: 805/927-8030. Pbk: ISBN 0-9632315-5-3; price: $24.95; 432 pages

PUBLISHER:
MACROCOSM USA, INC.
P.O. Box 185
Cambria, CA 93428-0185
Tel: 805/927-8030
Fax: 805/927-1713

THE ME IN THE MIRROR
by Connie Panzarino

SUBJECT: This is the dynamic and moving memoir of a severely disabled activist and artist who has been living with a rare muscular disease, Spinal Muscular Atrophy III, since birth. Beginning in early childhood, the author tells of the complexities and challenges of growing up disabled and offers a fascinating exploration of her family relationships—in particular with a mother on whom she was dependent for survival and a sister who also had SMA. She then recounts her teenage and early adult years—a time in which her sexuality and political activism emerge and a period of great personal growth. Reflecting on recent years, Panzarino explores her long-term relationship with Ron Kovic, her eventual turn to lesbianism, and her continuing work as a disability rights activist.

AUTHOR: Connie Panzarino is an art therapist, a writer, and a disability and lesbian rights activist. She has published numerous articles on disability and has been featured in the anthologies *Lesbian Land, Time Without Work,* and *Riding Desire.*

IMPORTANCE: The publisher says that every able bodied person should read this book. "We can never truly appreciate what the handicapped go through in this society until we read their words. It is not the most talked about or glamorous issue but one that everyone must understand to make this a more humane and inclusive world."

AVAILABLE: Bookstores nationally and from the publisher. Pbk: ISBN 1-878067-45-1; price: $12.95; 220 pages

PUBLISHER:
SEAL PRESS
3131 Western Ave., #410
Seattle, WA 98121
Tel: 206/283-7844
Fax: 206/285-9410

A MORE PERFECT UNION:
Why Straight America Must Stand Up for Gay Rights
by Richard D. Mohr

SUBJECT: *A More Perfect Union* establishes that without equal citizenship for gay and lesbian Americans, the rights of straight Americans are hollow and tenuous. Gay and lesbian Americans must be allowed the same rights granted to other Americans: to a workplace without harassment, to marriage by choice, to service in the armed forces, and to the custody of their own or adopted children. Denying these and other fundamental rights to gay and lesbian Americans deprives the society of their free expression, and supports an atmosphere of ignorance, mistrust, and hatred. The book also outlines suggestions for public and governmental responses to the AIDS epidemic; it concludes by offering a ten-step plan of what straight Americans can do to support gays and lesbians in their search for freedom.

AUTHOR: Richard D. Mohr is professor of philosophy at the University of Illinois at Urbana. He is the author of *Gays/Justice* and *Gay Ideas: Outing and Other Controversies* which won the *Lambda Book Report* Editor's Choice Award for 1992; he also has written for the *Advocate*, the *Nation*, and the *Boston Globe*.

IMPORTANCE: Gay and lesbian visibility has increased dramatically in the past few years, yet Americans who might sympathize with their cause are often unaware of how they can help. Other Americans are misinformed about lesbian and gay issues, and feel that, in their case, equal rights are special privileges. For too many years, misunderstanding has formed the basis of legislation and popular opinion about American gays and lesbians. A *More Perfect Union* shows that, by opposing the freedom of gays and lesbians, straight Americans jeopardize their own rights.

AVAILABLE: At bookstores everywhere or from the publisher: 617/742-2110. Hbk: ISBN 0-8070-7932-4; price: $15.00; 140 pages

PUBLISHER:
BEACON PRESS
25 Beacon Street
Boston, MA 02108-2892
Tel: 617/742-2110
Fax: 617/742-3097

NETWORKS OF POWER: Corporate TV's Threat to Democracy
by Dennis W. Mazzocco
Foreword by Herbert I. Schiller

SUBJECT: This book is a startling exposé of the increasing threat to free speech and democratic government. A broadcast insider with twenty years of working experience with the major networks, Dennis Mazzocco describes the ways that an ever-expanding U.S.-based multinational media cartel veils the machinations of the corporate state by dominating worldwide markets for TV, radio, newspapers, and other media. Challenging the disingenuous claims of network executives about democracy and public interest, Mazzocco argues that media practice is more often guided by the nefarious pursuit of power, privilege, and profits.

AUTHOR: Dennis W. Mazzocco was a producer/director at ABC and NBC for fifteen years. He is the recipient of four Emmy awards, three Cine Gold awards for documentary excellence, and a George Foster Peabody award. He is currently pursuing a Ph.D. in Communication at the University of California, San Diego.

IMPORTANCE: Besides sounding a warning, the author offers specific suggestions for making the mass media a more democratic and less elitist service to the general public. This book will be of interest to concerned citizens, media workers, students, cultural critics, and political activists. "Coming from the television industry, Dennis Mazzocco gives readers a history of the relentless convergence of concentrating power and pressured profits on television and radio. Rest assured, many of his criticisms are voiced privately by many an anchor, producer and reporter throughout television and radio land. It is time for the public audience to save them from themselves."—Ralph Nader

AVAILABLE: Directly from the publisher: 800/533-8478. Pbk: ISBN 0-89608-472-8; price: $14.00; 200 pages Hbk: ISBN 0-89608-473-6; price: $30.00

PUBLISHER:
SOUTH END PRESS
116 Saint Botolph Street
Boston, MA 02115
Tel: 617/266-0629
Fax: 617/266-1595

THE SILICONE BREAST IMPLANT CONTROVERSY:
What Women Need To Know
by Frank B. Vasey, M.D.,
and Josh Feldstein

SUBJECT: This book provides important information on how silicone implants cause illness, the specific symptoms of silicone-induced disorders, the risks and benefits of having implants removed, and how government politics and corporate interests affect female medical care. It contains interviews with 20 women affected by silicone implants.

AUTHOR: Dr. Frank B. Vasey is a leading spokesperson on the dangers of implants, has appeared as an expert witness for government committees, and has served as an advisor to the Food and Drug Administration. He is a widely published rheumatologist and Professor of Medicine at the University of South Florida College of Medicine. Josh Feldstein is a medical writer.

IMPORTANCE: Women who have implants should know the likely consequences of what will happen with silicone in their bodies, and women considering implants should be aware of the dangers. Doctors and health care professionals should also be more aware of the symptoms of silicone-related diseases. "Silicone survivors," as they call themselves, say the widely publicized Mayo Clinic study claiming implants are safe was flawed in many ways: two of them being that the study was partially funded by plastic surgeons (who profit from implants) and that the study did not cover implant ruptures.

AVAILABLE: In some bookstores and directly from the publisher: 408/722-0711. Hbk: ISBN 0-89594-610-6; price: $20.95; 153 pages

PUBLISHER:
THE CROSSING PRESS
P.O. Box 1048
Freedom, CA 95019
Tel: 408/722-0711
Fax: 408/722-2749

STUBBORN HOPE:
Religion, Politics, and Revolution in Central America
by Phillip Berryman

SUBJECT: Chronicling more than a decade of war, revolution, and social change, Phillip Berryman offers a current and comprehensive analysis of the interplay between religion and politics in Central America. Focusing on Nicaragua, El Salvador, and Guatemala, Berryman shows how during the 1980s each country became the setting for a profound drama of faith and oppression, revolution, and retrenchment. Of particular significance is the growing influence of evangelicals and Pentecostals, challenging the traditional status of the Catholic Church.

AUTHOR: Phillip Berryman is author of *Liberation Theology* and *The Religious Roots of Rebellion,* as well as numerous articles on religion and politics in Latin America. He worked in Central America for many years in the 1960s and is generally regarded as an expert on Central American religion and politics.

IMPORTANCE: In this original and journalistic approach, assessing the meaning of Central American history for North Americans, Berryman gives readers an insight into history and an opportunity to learn from its lessons.

AVAILABLE: Directly through the publisher and through Meakin & Associates, Canada; Fowler Wright Books, U.K.; Word of Life, Australia; Peeters Louvain, Belgium/Europe; David Phillip Publishers, South Africa. Hbk: ISBN 0-88344-962-5; price: $22.95; 276 pages

PUBLISHER:
ORBIS BOOKS
Walsh Bldg.
Box 308
Maryknoll, NY 01545-0308
Tel: 914/941-7636
Fax: 914/945-0670

URBAN INDIANS:
Drums from the Cities
by Dr. Gregory W. Frazier

SUBJECT: This is the first book to ever tell the full story of more than one-half of the Indian and Alaska Native population of America who live off the reservations in urban areas. Forced into the cities by poorly designed government programs, the nearly one million urban Indians and Alaska Natives have had to fight to maintain their cultural identity and their lives. Meanwhile, for more than 40 years, the government has worked diligently in its hopes that the Indians would be consumed or "assimilated" into city life. The book features studies of urban Indian life, corruption in federal government programs, and failures by federal bureaucrats to maintain the public trust when dealing with the First Americans. The book also provides an analysis of federal Indian policy from 1950 through the Reagan-Bush era; current census data on American Indians and Alaska Natives; confidential correspondence and legal case findings; an exposé of governmental abuse and mismanagement at the Departments of Labor and Health and Human Services.

AUTHOR: Dr. Gregory W. Frazier is an American Indian (Crow) activist. For nearly 20 years, he has lobbied for and represented the urban Indians and Alaska Natives. He was a Presidential Appointee by President Jimmy Carter and has served as a consultant to numerous federal agencies. For ten years, he was the elected leader of the urban Indians and Alaska Natives in America. In the 1980's he was the target of several federal efforts by the Reagan/Bush administration to remove him from his leadership posts. Described as a "Twentieth Century warrior," he is the foremost expert on urban American Indian/Alaska Native policy in America today. He lives on the Crow Indian reservation in Montana and writes about matters concerning American Indians and Alaska Natives.

IMPORTANCE: The publisher hails the book as "absolutely essential to any student or historian concerned with American Indian/Alaska Native policy or anyone interested in the Indians/Alaska Natives of today. Acclaimed as one of the most informative and inclusive publications of its kind, *Urban Indians* was almost not published as the government raced to prevent it from becoming public when it learned that the author was preparing to expose many of the problems with the federal Indian and Alaska Native programs."

AVAILABLE: Directly from the publisher: 303/231-6599. Pbk: ISBN 0-935151-17-6; price: $19.95 plus $3 S/H; 500 pages

PUBLISHER:
ARROWSTAR PUBLISHING
100134 University Park Station
Denver, CO 80250-0134
Tel: 303/231-6599

THE USES OF HAITI
by Paul Farmer
Introduction by Noam Chomsky

SUBJECT: Will current U.S. efforts to restore democracy in Haiti succeed? In this up-to-the-minute exposé, Paul Farmer exposes the myriad forces that have long kept the majority of Haitians poor, sick, and silenced. Farmer demonstrates that U.S. policy towards Haiti, moving in well-worn tracks, has always undermined democratic movements even as it buttressed a corrupt military and business elite. *The Uses of Haiti* offers a sharp contrast to journalistic accounts, which are shown by Farmer to be sharply constrained by both conventional wisdom and the dictates of the powerful.

AUTHOR: Paul Farmer, author of *Aids and Accusation*, is assistant professor at the Harvard Medical School and a fellow at Boston's Brigham and Women's Hospital. He conducts his research and medical practice in rural Haiti, where he specializes in community-based efforts to improve the health of the poor.

IMPORTANCE: As Noam Chomsky remarks in his 30-page introduction, *The Uses of Haiti* "tells the truth about uncomfortable matters—uncomfortable, that is, for the structures of power and the doctrinal framework that protects them from critical scrutiny. It tells the truth about what has been happening in Haiti, and the U.S. role in its bitter fate."

AVAILABLE: At good independent bookstores or directly from the publisher: 800/497-3207. Pbk: ISBN 1-56751-034-5; price: $14.95 CLOTH: ISBN 1-56751-035-3; price: $29.95; 432 pages
PUBLISHER:
COMMON COURAGE PRESS
P.O. Box 702
Monroe, ME 04951
Tel: 207/525-0900
Fax: 207/525-3068

ZR RIFLE:
The Plot to Kill Kennedy and Castro
by Claudia Furiati

SUBJECT: This book discusses a conspiracy between key figures in the CIA, the Mafia, and anti-Castro Cuban exiles to assassinate President Kennedy. The material is based on Cuban intelligence sources and includes the first ever interview with General Fabian Escalante, Cuban counterintelligence chief. Author Claudia Furiati names CIA officers and Cuban exiles. The book proves that

Oswald did visit the Cuba Embassy in Mexico and offers evidence that Oswald was a CIA operative. The book's major thesis is that the CIA program code named ZR Rifle or Executive Action was aimed at assassinating foreign heads of government. From this program, came a plan to kill Castro and later to kill Kennedy.

AUTHOR: Claudia Furiati, Brazilian film-maker and journalist, is a graduate in history and social communication from the Catholic University in Rio de Janeiro. She has made numerous documentaries for cinema and television, and has been widely published in Brazilian and other Latin American journals and magazines.

IMPORTANCE: Filmmaker Oliver Stone notes: "This book is an important contribution to the literature on the Kennedy assassination. By getting the Cuban Government to open up its files, Claudia Furiati has added to our understanding of these historic events. Her book adds new pieces to the puzzle and gives us a clear picture of what really happened." The publisher adds: "At the very minimum, this book gives us the Cuban version of these events. As such, it should have been given the same publicity that KGB versions of Russian-related events have been given."

AVAILABLE: Directly from the U.S. distributor, the Talman Company: 800/537-8894. Pbk: ISBN 1-875284-85-0; price: $14.95; 180 pages

PUBLISHER:
OCEAN PRESS
GPO Box 3279
Melbourne, Victoria 3001
Australia

U.S. DISTRIBUTOR:
Talman Co.
131 Spring Street
New York, NY 10012
Fax: 212/431-7215

"Plus ça change,
plus c'est la même chose."
—Alphonse Karr

CHAPTER 4

Censored Déjà Vu of 1994

Project Censored annually sounds an alarm on disturbing social, environmental, economic, political, and other issues that may emerge in the alternative media but do not attract the attention of the mass media. The thesis is that by bringing early national attention to these problems, we will be better able to resolve them before they get out of control. Unfortunately, too often the warnings issued by America's alternative press go unheeded.

On the plus side, however, each year we do find issues that were cited in the past that have finally attracted the attention of the national news media and been put on the national news agenda.

There were several major issues brought to the attention of mainstream audiences in 1994 that provide some insight into the time it takes for a story to become widely known. One was a story that took decades to come out; another was a story that took less than a year to emerge; and a third represents an issue that has been trickling out over the years but became a deluge in 1994. In all three cases, it is interesting to note that there are still parts of each story that remain untold.

THE RADIATION ISSUE: While intentional radiation releases and human radiation experiments, involving thousands of people including unsuspecting subjects and professional scientists, occurred frequently as part of the nation's Cold War nuclear programs between the 1940s and 1975, it was not until late 1993 that the national news media told the

American people about it. As FAIR's newsletter *EXTRA!* noted, "Government-sponsored radiation experiments on humans hit the front pages of major newspapers last year as if they were breaking news" (May/June 1994). "Federal Radiation Tests on Americans" was the #8 *Censored* story of 1986. Finally, in 1994, human radiation tests became a major news story. The public exposure brought public reaction and government investigation. Toward the end of the year, the President's Advisory Committee on Human Radiation Experiments said it had documented at least 400 cases of human experiments and had indications of some 1,000 more. It also confirmed that hundreds of intentional releases of radiation had occurred (*Associated Press*, 10/22/94). Despite the large number of people involved, this is a story that took decades to emerge and even then the whole story was not told, as our 1994 *Censored* story about the "1947 AEC Memo" revealed. As additional Cold War records were declassified through the year, it became obvious that there was still much more to be known. On December 23, the Associated Press reported that the U.S. government developed radiation weapons not only for defense but also for offensive use on a vast scale. Contemplated offensive uses included combining radioactive materials with germ and chemical warfare weapons. Tests of radiation weapons reportedly started in October 1949 with bigger-scale field tests scheduled through 1953.

THE DARE ISSUE: The failure of the DARE (Drug Abuse Resistance Education) program was the #23 *Censored* story of 1993 and in less than a year it was a front page story. However, like the radiation issue, this also

THIS MODERN WORLD by TOM TOMORROW

I HAD THE STRANGEST DREAM LAST NIGHT, SPARKY... CRACK COCAINE WAS *LEGAL*...AND PEOPLE WERE SMOKING IT *EVERYWHERE*...

ANOTHER *HIT*, DARLING?

...THERE WERE ALL SORTS OF *BILLBOARDS* AND *ADVERTISEMENTS* PROMOTING THE DRUG'S *USE*...

HEY KIDS! SMOKE C

It's fun!

Cocaine

Crack

Come to where the flavor is. Cocaine.

became a *Censored* story of 1994 when it was revealed how the *Washington Post* and the Department of Justice had helped to cover-up the failure of the program.

THE TOBACCO ISSUE: While the hazards of cigarette smoking were known as early as 1938, it is only in recent decades that information concerning them have increasingly become known to the American people, with 1994 possibly representing a culmination of publicly known hazards.

Following are just some of the tobacco revelations that attracted media attention in 1994: the year started with a January 1994 cover story in the *Washington Post* "Health" section warning that "30 Years after the Surgeon General's Report, Cigarettes Still Kill More than 1,000 Americans a Day;" on February 24, U.S. Surgeon General Joycelyn Elders attacked "Joe Camel" and cigarette advertising and warned of the dangers of smoking for young people (*Washington Post*, 2/25/94); U.S. Rep. Henry Waxman charged that Philip Morris Co. stopped publication of a 1983 study revealing nicotine was addictive (*Knight-Ridder* Newspapers, 4/1/94); tobacco companies release a secret list of 599 chemicals (some of which reportedly cause liver damage and convulsions in animals) they add to cigarettes (*Associated Press*, 4/13/94); the April 18 cover of *U.S. News & World Report* asked "Should Cigarettes Be Outlawed?;" a former tobacco company scientist revealed that ten years earlier, Philip Morris shut down a research lab that was close to producing a safe cigarette substitute (*USA Today*, 4/29/94).

Two former tobacco company researchers confirmed that their work on secretive nicotine addiction experiments had been suppressed (*Time*,

5/9/94); a cover story in USA Today, 5/19/94, revealed how tobacco industry executives had covered-up the dangers of smoking tobacco for decades; an investigation by the Los Angeles Times reported that Brown & Williamson Tobacco Corporation gave nearly $1 million to filmmakers and stars, including at least $300,000 to Sylvester Stallone, from 1979 to 1983, to get them to hype its brands in their films (Associated Press, 5/20/94); new documents obtained by USA Today revealed that tobacco executives had valid research linking second-hand smoke to health problems 13 years earlier (6/6/94); the head of the Food and Drug Administration charged that a major tobacco company genetically altered tobacco plants in order to double the amount of nicotine found in them (Boston Globe, 6/22/94); an article in Weekly Reader, a publication circulated to some 8 million fifth-graders nationally, was attacked for promoting a cigarette industry viewpoint. Weekly Reader is part of K-III Communications, a unit of Kohlberg Kravis Roberts & Co., the largest shareholder of cigarette maker RJR Nabisco (USA Today, 8/11/94); interest groups, led by Philip Morris Tobacco and the National Smokers Alliance, spent more than $2.3 million to get a smoking regulation initiative, Proposition 188, which would weaken California smoking regulations, on the California ballot (Associated Press, 8/31/94).

A new book, Mortality from Smoking in Developed Countries 1950-2000, published by Britain's Imperial Cancer Research Fund, the World Health Organization, and the American Cancer Society, reported that worldwide smoking now kills three million people each year, about six people every minute (Associated Press, 9/20/94); health ministers from Europe and Asia urged a ban on cigarette ads, but experts at the ninth World Conference on Tobacco and Health in Paris accused powerful tobacco interests of preventing them from stopping advertising to which children are susceptible (Associated Press, 10/13/94); two former technicians for a Tobacco Institute consulting firm said field measurements of indoor smoke levels were faked to show tobacco smoke wasn't a problem (USA Today, 11/2/94); on election day, November 8, 1994, California voters defeated Proposition 188, on which the tobacco industry had spent another $18 million, by more than two-to-one (San Francisco Examiner, 11/9/94); unfortunately, however, as Newsday reported on November 11, all this may have been a last hurrah for the anti-tobacco forces due to the shift to Republican control in the next Congress. Rep. Thomas Bliley, R-VA, now in line to head the House health and environment subcommittee, said he would stop the hearings on tobacco conducted by outgoing Chair Rep. Waxman. Bliley, whose district includes Philip Morris, said, "I don't think we need any more legislation regulating tobacco."

OTHER DÉJÀ VU STORIES OF 1994

SOLVING THE RADIOACTIVE SMOKE ALARM PROBLEM—One of the *Censored* stories of both 1977 and 1978 pointed out that a leading smoke detector operated with Americium-241, an element more radioactive than plutonium-239 with a half life of 460 years. It warned consumers to return used detectors to the manufacturer for transmittal to an official nuclear waste disposal site. Today's radioactive detectors, while noting they contain 1 microcurie of Americium-241, a radioactive material, have no warning about disposal but assure consumers that "The purchaser is exempt from any regulatory requirements."

GLOBAL DUMPING IS ALIVE & WELL IN CHINA—A group of women journalists from China visited the San Francisco-based Center for Investigative Reporting (CIR) in August, 1993, where they were shown CIR's 1990 documentary, "Global Dumping Ground," which was the subject of the #21 *Censored* story of 1990. Returning to China, they tracked down the original toxic waste king, Joe Chen, to discover he had moved his scrap business to another site in China and boasted of running 10 factories with more to come, according to CIR's *Muckraker*, Winter 1994.

SAVINGS & LOAN DEBACLE BURIED IN UNMARKED GRAVE—The #2 *Censored* story of 1990 reported that the Resolution Trust Corporation (RTC) engineered a solution to the savings and loan failures that could be more costly than the original crime. On January 13, 1994, the *Associated Press* reported that RTC was failing woefully in its efforts to recoup an estimated $200 billion lost in Texas alone. In fact, the RTC failed to issue a single subpoena in 99 of 122 investigations of thrift officials; not a single RTC case ever reached a jury; and one of the RTC's most effective attorneys in Texas quit in disgust telling Congress his bosses "just wanted to bury the S&L mess in an unmarked grave."

IRAN-CONTRA CRIMES SWEPT UNDER THE RUG—What should have been the political crime of the decade—a network of retired spies, secret arms deals with a terrorist state, official knowledge of cocaine smuggling into the U.S. by mercenary pilots, millions of dollars laundered through Switzerland, buying guns for rebels in Nicaragua, misuse of power by the administration, lies to Congress and the American people—was quietly swept under the rug on January 19, 1994, the day after independent counsel Lawrence Walsh released his 2,507-page final report on the Iran-contra scandal. The lead sweeper was *The New York Times* which headlined its front page analysis of the report "The Scandal That Fell Flat." Follow-up media analyses by the *Columbia Journalism Review, EXTRA!*, and others revealed that other mainstream media, including the *Washington Post*, PBS, NBC, and the *Wall Street Journal*, were eager to adopt the same "sweep it away" attitude. In the final analysis, the real crime may not have been Iran-contra but the failure of the media to hold the guilty accountable. *For a copy of the $60 three-volume "Final Report of the Independent Counsel for Iran-contra Matters," call (202) 783-3238 or write the Superintendent of Documents, P.O. Box 371954, Pittsburgh, PA 15250-7954.*

PBS WINS COVETED LEMON AWARD—The Public Broadcasting Service received a special lemon award on January 27, 1994, "for commercial excess" from the Center for Science in the Public Interest which annually presents the Harlan Page Hubbard Memorial Awards for deceptive advertising. PBS, which is prohibited by law from promoting products or services, was cited for running commercial-type advertisements instead of brief sponsor credits. PBS was the subject of one of the *Censored* stories of 1980 titled "Public Loses Broadcasting System—PBS Goes Commercial." A year earlier the #8 *Censored* story cited PBS as the Petroleum Broadcasting System.

CRYING OVER SPILLED MILK—On February 4, 1994, the Monsanto Company started selling bovine somatrotropin, or BST, to dairy farms. BST, a bioengineered version of a natural cow hormone, will boost milk production in dairy cows by up to 30 percent. The #22 *Censored* story of 1985 revealed that more than a million of America's dairy cows were slaughtered in an ill-conceived, secretive plan to *reduce* milk production to maintain prices. Monsanto reportedly has a stake of $500 million in BST.

DEATH OF CONSPIRACY INVESTIGATOR CASOLARO RE-OPENED—*San Francisco Chronicle* staff writers Michael Taylor and Jonathan Littman reported that the Clinton administration has quietly launched a nationwide investigation into the alleged suicide of writer Danny Casolaro (2/11/94). Casolaro was exploring a web of connections among Reagan-Bush era scandals including the S&L collapse, the October

Surprise, Iran-contra, the Wackenhut Corp., BCCI, and the Inslaw software theft. "The Strange Death of Daniel Casolaro" was the #11 *Censored* story of 1991. The November/December issue of *Mother Jones* reported that Rep. Charlie Rose, (D-NC), introduced legislation to authorize the U.S. Court of Federal Claims to hear the Inslaw theft case, "to address what is clearly one of the greatest wrongs ever inflicted upon American citizens by the federal government."

WORLD'S OZONE LAYER IS DECLINING—The #4 *Censored* story of 1990 warned about threats to the world's protective ozone layer including damage from NASA's space shuttle flights. The United Nations World Meteorological Organization, meeting in Geneva, confirmed that the stratospheric ozone layer has declined by about 10 percent in the last 25 years, as reported by Jane Kay in the *San Francisco Examiner*, February 22, 1994. One of the scientists lamented, "We've been warning of this for a long time, but nobody believed it. ... Now, we see it." On March 1, the *Los Angeles Times* reported a study at Oregon State University that provided the first evidence that the thinning ozone layer directly harms wild animals. And on December 19, 1994, scientists at NASA's Goddard Space Flight Center reported the first conclusive evidence that the Earth's protective ozone layer is being eroded by man-made chemical products and not by natural events like volcanic eruptions.

AMERICA'S SUPER-SECRET SPY COURT HITS PERFECT RECORD OF 7,500!—The #2 *Censored* story of 1982 exposed a little-known U.S. Foreign Intelligence Court which had heard 962 requests for electronic surveillance on Americans in the U.S. since the court was launched in 1979 and had approved all 962 requests. A "Déjà Vu" brief in the 1993 Yearbook revealed that the court had approved all 6,546 requests it had received by the end of 1991. This extraordinary record finally made TV prime time on March 4, 1994, when Dan Rather in an "Eye On America" segment on *CBS News* told viewers, "Chances are you've never heard of this court because it's a secret court." The latest score was 7,500 requests and 7,500 approvals. Dan didn't ask the key question: do we really need to support a secret federal court that merely rubber stamps all requests?

STINGER MISSILES STILL ELUDE THE CIA—The #22 *Censored* story of 1993 revealed how the CIA was desperately trying to buy back hundreds of surface-to-air Stinger missiles it secretly gave Afghan guerrillas only a few years ago. On March 4, 1994, the *Washington Post* reported that the supposedly covert CIA buy-back program was "plagued by failures, miscalculations and wasted money." While Congress has now authorized more than $65 million in secret funds for the buy-back program ($10 million more than a year earlier), the *Post* reported that the CIA has recovered only a fraction of the missiles and doesn't know who has most of the rest of them. On October 26, 1994, a report by the General Accounting Office confirmed that the Army can't account for 40 Stinger missiles.

U.S. COMPANIES STILL USING BANNED PESTICIDES IN THIRD WORLD—The #3 *Censored* story of 1976 warned how hundreds of thousands of people in the Third World were poisoned annually by pesticides banned in the U.S. In February 1994, some 16,000 plaintiffs from 12 countries, most from Costa Rica, filed a class-action suit against the U.S. companies that manufactured the hazardous DBCP pesticide which banana companies headquartered in the U.S. continued to use even after it was banned in America. (Reported by David Scanlan, *San Francisco Chronicle* Foreign Service, 3/15/94.) Experts now believe as many as 100,000 banana workers worldwide have been made sterile by the banned pesticide.

AMERICA'S DEADLY DOCTORS DISCIPLINED—On April 13, 1994, the *Associated Press* reported that the Federation of State Medical Boards had disciplined 3,078 doctors in 1993, an increase of 107 doctors over the previous year. A Federation spokesperson said "There is far more scrutiny of doctors today than ever before. But we do need better monitoring." This is something of an understatement considering that the #8 *Censored* story of 1993 reported that some five to 10 percent of all U.S. doctors (some 30,000 to 60,000) could be hazardous to your health according to a study by the Public Citizen's Health Research Group. In early December, 1994, the California Medical Board reluctantly released data revealing that at least one of every 49 California doctors has been found guilty of questionable or dangerous medical practices.

17 U.S. WORKERS DIE ON THE JOB DAILY—The *Associated Press* reported on April 15, 1994, that in the 10-year period from 1980 to 1989, 63,589 workers, an average of 17 a day, died from occupational injuries. A spokesperson from the Centers for Disease Control and Prevention and the National Institute for Occupational Safety and Health said "The take-home message is that occupational deaths is a serious public health problem, but one that can be prevented." If these deaths could be prevented, it's too bad no one was listening 18 years ago. The #7 *Censored* story of 1976 warned that the untold number of injuries, disease, and deaths caused by work hazards in America's industries is an on-going story that gets little, if any, mass media coverage.

DANGERS OF HALCION CONCEALED—In the April 1992 issue *of America's CENSORED Newsletter*, we wondered why the press was so disinterested in the fact that George Bush, the president of the United States, was taking a reportedly dangerous prescription sleeping pill called Halcion. On April 30, 1994, the *Houston Chronicle* revealed that the Upjohn Co., producers of Halcion, had "engaged in an ongoing pattern of misconduct" involving the sleeping pill according to a U.S. Food and Drug Administration report which wasn't released until two years after the investigators were pulled off the case. The investigators said they found evidence of possible criminal wrongdoing by Upjohn which they thought should be turned over to a grand jury, but that they were reassigned and their findings never reached a grand jury.

GULF WAR SYNDROME NOW BIG NEWS—The May issue of *Esquire* featured a six-page article titled "Walking Wounded" that explored the mysterious illness now called the Gulf War Syndrome—a major news story of 1994. In October, when we were once again sending troops to the Persian Gulf, *The New York Times*, *USA Today*, and others were reporting that scientists still couldn't explain what made thousands of gulf war veterans sick. The May 1992 issue of *America's CENSORED Newsletter* reported how the Military Families Support Network had been trying to get the media to pay attention to a mysterious illness that was found among many Gulf veterans. The *Los Angeles Times* (11/14/94) reported that ten babies of Gulf War veterans already have died from heart defects and liver cancer at the Army's Fort Bragg base in North Carolina. Some reports estimate that as many as 65 percent of the children born to Gulf War soldiers are afflicted in some form or another. A report by the U.S. Senate Veterans Affairs Committee, released on December 8, 1994, revealed that the Pentagon knew the risks of using experimental and potentially dangerous drugs and vaccines on the troops before the Gulf War but used them anyway.

SWEEPING GRENADA UNDER THE RUG—The #12 *Censored* story of 1983 cited President Ronald Reagan's invasion of Grenada as a case study of governmental censorship. The #14 *Censored* story of 1987 revealed a score of abuses documented by the Committee for Human Rights in Grenada that occurred there since our invasion in 1983. In early May 1994, as reported by *The New York Times* (5/2/94), the Clinton administration decided Grenada was of little strategic importance to the U.S. and said it planned to close the U.S. embassy there. Only after protests by Grenadian officials and some members of Congress, the administration changed its mind and left the embassy open.

ACID RAIN WARNING IGNORED IN MEXICO—The #8 *Censored* story of 1977 warned of the ecological damage resulting from acid rain caused in part by coal burning. Nonetheless, and despite environmental assurances of the North American Free Trade Agreement, two massive coal-fired power plants near Piedras Negras, in Mexico, are on-line to go fully operational in 1995. The plants have no emission control devices or scrubbers and are expected to annually produce some 200,000 tons of acid-rain-producing sulfur dioxide which will be carried northwest across the border and over the Big Bend National Park, according to a report in *The Texas Observer* (May 6, 1994).

THE SPECTER OF STERILITY CONFIRMED ... AGAIN—The #7 *Censored* story of 1978 revealed how workers exposed to a pesticide in a California chemical plant were found to be sterile. A follow-up study by the National Institute for Occupational Safety and Health confirmed a reduction in sperm count due to exposure to pesticides, herbicides, fungicides, etc. The #13 *Censored* story of 1992 reported another study, published in the *British Medical Journal* that documented a significant decline in sperm due to environmental pollution. Now the results of new Danish research, published in the *London Independent* (5/8/94), reveal that male subjects in 20 countries are producing only half as much sperm now as in the late 1930's. Again, pesticides appear to be the problem. Ironically, none of this appears to have impressed President Clinton, who postponed legislation which would have protected the nation's agricultural workers from exposure to pesticides until 1995.

MORE BAD NEWS FROM THE DRUG WAR FRONT—The #4 *Censored* story of 1989 charged that the "government's war on drugs is more hype than reality." On May 12, 1994, *USA Today* reported that the latest report on the drug war revealed that despite the $52 billion in federal anti-drug spending in the prior five years, there is higher use and less fear of drugs now. White House drug czar Lee Brown conceded that things are "not getting any better."

THE GREATEST GOLD HEIST IN HISTORY—Even seasoned *Censored* supporters were slightly skeptical of the #4 *Censored* story of 1993 which warned that, under the Mining Act of 1872, corporations could mine federal lands containing billions of dollars of gold without paying royalties or fees to U.S. taxpayers—and buy the land for as little as five dollars an acre. The author of that story, Jonathan Dushoff, lamented the lack of media coverage and said more coverage could save taxpayers tens of billions of dollars. It didn't happen. On Monday, May 16, 1994, Interior Secretary Bruce Babbitt gave American Barrick Resource Corp., a Canadian mining company, ownership of the country's largest gold deposit, Nevada's Goldstrike mine, for a payment of only $9,000 to the U.S. Treasury. The mine is estimated to hold up to $10 billion in gold.

INTEGRATING TRADITIONAL AND ALTERNATIVE CANCER CURES—Published by MIT Press in June 1994, *Choices in Healing: Integrating the Best of Conventional and Complementary Approaches to Cancer*, by Michael Lerner, explores the longtime controversy over alternative cancer therapies. Lerner, a MacArthur Prize Fellow for his work in public health, says it shouldn't be an either/or proposition. After 10 years of worldwide research, Lerner concludes that the most effective cure may be a combination of conventional and alternative therapies and that the latter deserve more research funding. The #20 *Censored* story of 1990 explored whether groups like the American Medical Association and the American Cancer Society, which have vested economic interests in the medical status quo, have successfully fought research into alternative cancer cures.

ADL SPY CASE QUIETLY ENDS—The #20 *Censored* story of 1993, which documented how the Anti-Defamation League of B'nai B'rith was charged with civil rights violations including domestic spying on a massive scale, came to a quiet conclusion on May 27, 1994, as reported by the *San Francisco Bay Guardian* (6/1/94). The prosecution accepted a no contest plea to a misdemeanor charge after the FBI refused to cooperate in the case.

FIRST REPORT ON VIETNAM'S OWN TOLL—For the first time, the Vietnamese government reported that three million Vietnamese soldiers and civilians, from both North and South Vietnam, died during the Vietnam War (*San Francisco Examiner*, 6/26/94). A *Censored* story of 1976 reported that while some 46,000 U.S. military were killed during the war (now estimated at 47,382), a Veterans Administration report, dated June 1976, revealed that some 101,000 U.S. Vietnam veterans had died since returning to civilian life with suicide being one of the leading causes of deaths.

WASTE DISCOVERED IN DOD PROCUREMENT SYSTEM!—On June 29, 1994, acknowledging an inefficient and wasteful defense procurement system, Secretary of Defense William Perry announced a major overhaul to save billions of dollars annually (*Los Angeles Times*, 6/30/94). The #10 *Censored* story of 1983 reported that despite occasional press exposés of a 15-cent bolt that costs taxpayers hundreds of dollars, DOD's fraud-susceptible contracting system continues from year to year.

LYNDON LAROUCHE: FROM PRISON STRIPES TO PIN STRIPES—The #15 *Censored* story of 1982 asked "Who is Lyndon LaRouche and why should we know about him?" and warned about his increasing power among ultra-right, anti-Jewish, single-issue cults and groups. LaRouche was released from a federal penitentiary on January 26, 1994, after serving five years of a 15-year sentence for fraud and conspiracy. The July/August 1994, issue of *Worth* featured an eight-page article warning its readers that the elderly are a "Soft Touch for Smooth LaRouchies." Taxpayers also are a soft touch since LaRouche will be getting matching funds for his 1996 presidential campaign according to May 1994 issue of *Esquire*.

LAW OF THE SEA TREATY NOW MORE BUSINESS FRIENDLY—The #9 *Censored* story of 1976 reported that while a 1969 United Nations' resolution stated that the ocean floor is a "common heritage of mankind," private multinational corporations were fighting the Law of the Sea treaty in an effort to gain greater control over the estimated 1.5 trillion tons of mineral wealth on the ocean floor. On July 1, 1994, *The New York Times* reported that Secretary of State Warren Christopher said the administration had negotiated changes that made the treaty friendlier to business and would sign the treaty after more than two decades of negotiations.

NORPLANT: DREAM CONTRACEPTIVE TURNS INTO NIGHT-MARE—In 1991, Norplant was hailed as a "dream contraceptive" when it went on the market; in 1992, Norplant was the #17 Censored story which warned that the press had ignored serious questions about its safety, testing methods, and potential for social control of poor women; on July 8, 1994, The New York Times announced that some 400 women were seeking to join a class-action lawsuit against Wyeth-Ayerst Laboratories, the company that sells Norplant. The women claim they suffered severe pain, scarring, and permanent injury when their doctors removed the six matchstick-size capsules. While the capsules are designed to remain in the arm for five years, about 20 percent of the Norplant users try to remove them in the first year, either because of side effects like irregular menstrual bleeding or because they want to get pregnant.

TAX-FUNDED DRUGS COST TAXPAYERS MORE—The #4 Censored story of 1993 charged that America's corporations were the real welfare cheats and pointed out how drug manufacturers developed new drugs with taxpayer funds but paid no royalties to the U.S. Treasury. As if that were not unethical enough, on July 12, 1994, the Associated Press reported that Americans pay much more for drugs developed with tax dollars than those developed by the drug companies themselves. The Taxpayer Assets Projects, a consumer group, revealed that the median wholesale price for company-financed drugs was $1,626 while tax-funded drugs cost $4,854.

AMERICAN INDIANS END FIVE-MONTH WALK FOR JUSTICE—The Associated Press reported (7/16/94) that American Indian activist Dennis Banks and some 400 others celebrated the end of a five-month "Walk for Justice" across the country at the Lincoln Memorial. The leaders of 21 tribal nations demanded that President Clinton free Leonard Peltier, the subject of Censored stories of 1985 and 1987, who was accused of killing two FBI agents at Wounded Knee, S.D., and has been imprisoned for 18 years.

SELENIUM POLLUTION STUDY URGED—Environmentalists asked California state water quality regulators to monitor Southern California refineries for selenium discharges that may be poisoning coastal waters. The extraordinary scope of selenium poisoning was the #7 Censored story of 1993. Early in 1994, San Francisco Chronicle correspondent Lloyd

Carter reported that poisonous selenium levels are rising at the Kesterson National Wildlife Refuge (2/21/94). On December 20, 1994, scientists reported finding dead and deformed duck embryos, similar to those found earlier at Kesterson, in a showcase marsh operated by Chevron USA in Northern California.

RIGGED STAR WARS TEST CONFIRMED—*The New York Times* revealed on July 23, 1994, that a Star Wars test in 1984 was rigged to make it appear that the ballistic missile-defense system worked when it didn't. Sen. David Pryor, D-Ark., said it was "an outrage that Congress did not find out about it until 10 years had passed and $35 billion was spent." The #7 *Censored* story of 1985 was "Phony 'Star Wars' Test Results," which described how administration officials covered-up scientific failures with the Star Wars program. Despite this, following the November elections, Robert Wright, a senior editor of *The New Republic*, reported that Star Wars was back, as the National Security Restoration Act, one of the 10 bills in the Republicans' Contract with America.

TRAGIC TRUTH ABOUT GUATEMALA—On July 24, 1994, news services reported that human rights workers had uncovered mass grave sites in northern Guatemala believed to hold the bodies of as many as 1,000 peasants killed in the early 1980s during the army's repressive campaign against rebels. The #5 *Censored* story of 1982 warned that while the Guatemalan human rights situation may be the worst in Central America, we're getting no information as to what was happening there. The tragedy in Guatemala was raised again by Project Censored in 1988 with "What's Happening in Guatemala?" and in 1989 with the #5 *Censored* story titled "Guatemalan Blood on U.S. Hands" which revealed official U.S. military support of the human rights violations by repressive Guatemalan military forces.

ALZHEIMER'S AND ELECTROMAGNETIC FIELDS—The *Los Angeles Times* reported (7/31/94) three new studies, two from Finland and one in the United States, that reveal people with a high occupational exposure to electromagnetic fields (EMFs) are three times more likely to develop Alzheimer's diseases than those without significant exposure. EMFs previously have been implicated in triggering leukemia, brain tumors, and breast cancer. One of the top 25 *Censored* stories of 1978 was titled "High Voltage: Hazards Over Our Heads."

CHERNOBYL'S TRAGEDY CONTINUES—The "hidden tragedy of Chernobyl," the #5 *Censored* story of 1993, was explored in a well-written nine-page article appearing in the August, 1994, issue of *Harper's Magazine*. Author Alan Weisman reports that "Government officials knew all along that people were plowing radioactive dust, eating radioactive vegetables, and feeding radioactive hay to their cows," but were more concerned with the political consequences of acknowledging the extent of the tragedy than with public safety.

U.S.—STILL THE WORLD'S LEADING MERCHANT OF DEATH—The Congressional Research Service reported that U.S. munitions manufacturers now account for 72.6 percent of all new arms sales to Third World countries (*Associated Press*, 8/3/94). Among our best customers are Saudi Arabia, Kuwait, China, South Korea, and Iran. The #4 *Censored* story of 1992 noted that the U.S. had become the world's leading merchant of death.

PACIFIC ATOLL TARGETED AS WORLD'S NUKE DUMP—The president of the Marshall Islands in the South Pacific has offered one of them as an international dump for nuclear waste and warheads (*Associated Press*, 8/17/94). While environmentalists and neighboring countries are aghast at the idea, the #19 *Censored* story of 1992, titled "Poison in the Pacific," spelled out what was already in the works.

ENVIRONMENTAL RACISM STILL A REALITY—Despite *Censored* warnings about environmental racism as early as 1982 (#10—Toxic Waste Firms Target Indian Reservations), a study reported by the *Associated Press* (8/25/94) revealed that American Indians, blacks, Hispanics, and Asians were still more likely to live by commercial hazardous waste facilities in 1993 than a decade earlier.

NUCLEAR TERRORISM MAKES TIME COVER—The August 29, 1994, cover of *Time* magazine confronted its readers with the threat of nuclear terrorism warning " ... no one knows who might buy smuggled plutonium— and hold the world hostage." The #6 *Censored* story of 1976 was titled "Missing Plutonium and Inadequate Nuclear Reactor Safeguards."

MILITARY FINALLY STARTS TOXIC CLEANUP—The September/ October 1994 issue of *World Watch* reports that the U.S. military, in an effort to avoid any more Rocky Flats coverups, is starting to clean up the toxic messes on its bases and claims to have undergone a "culture change." The #2 *Censored* story of 1985 warned how the military, not subject to EPA regulations, was generating more than a half million tons of hazardous waste annually.

DEATH SQUADS STILL ROAM EL SALVADOR—Documents obtained by the *Pacific News Service* (PNS) revealed that the newly elected Salvadoran government and ARENA, the right-wing governing party, have been involved in financing and directing death squad assassinations, as reported by Allan Nairn, of PNS, in *Random Lengths*, 9/1/94. The subject of the #4 *Censored* story of 1984 was CIA-trained death squads in El Salvador.

GHOSTS OF DAN QUAYLE PAST—On September 20, 1994, the Associated Press reported that the Council on Competitiveness released a report which showed that the United States has regained its competitiveness. AP referred to the Council, chaired by Paul Allaire, chairman and chief executive officer of Xerox Corp., as "a nonprofit organization of top leaders in business, education and labor." The Council was the #12 *Censored* story of 1991 which exposed Dan Quayle, then vice president, as a lobbyist for big business in Washington. Ironically, Carol Browner, administrator of the EPA, had declared the Council on Competitiveness out of business on July 9, 1994.

CONGRESS GETS WAKE-UP CALL RE POISONED WATER—Fourteen years after the #10 *Censored* story of 1980 tried to warn people about "Poisoned Water," Congress passed legislation strengthening the 1974 Safe Drinking Water Act which established standards to limit pollution in drinking water supplies (*Washington Post*, 9/28/94). The congressional action also followed the March 1993 outbreak of waterborne disease caused by the parasite cryptosporidium, in Milwaukee, which resulted in 104 deaths and more than 400,000 illnesses.

CHLAMYDIA NOW INFECTS MORE THAN 4 MILLION AMERICANS ANNUALLY—Chlamydia, the most common sexually transmitted disease, is even more widespread than previously believed according to the Centers for Disease Control and Prevention (*Associated Press*, 10/11/94). Chlamydia, which can cause infertility and pelvic inflammatory disease in women, was the #20 *Censored* story of 1984 which warned that it was causing sterility in up to 100,000 women annually.

BREAKING INTERNATIONAL OIL EMBARGO IS NOTHING NEW—
On October 15, 1994, *CounterPunch*, an alternative publication based in Washington, DC, revealed how both the Bush and Clinton administrations knew that Texaco's Caribbean subsidiary illegally distributed oil in Haiti, breaking the embargo and propping up military dictators. The #5 *Censored* story of 1976 revealed how Mobil oil supplied oil to Rhodesia (now Zimbabwe) thereby breaking an international embargo and supporting a regime "condemned by virtually every nation on earth."

DRUGS, THUGS, THE CIA, & HAITI CONFIRMED—The #10 *Censored* story of 1993, titled "Haiti: Drugs, Thugs, the CIA, and the Deterrence of Democracy," revealed Haitian involvement in drug trafficking and CIA involvement with the Haitian military. *Time* magazine, on 10/17/94, revealed that Emmanuel "Toto" Constant, head of the FRAPH, a brutal gang of thugs known for murder, torture, and beatings, was on the payroll of both the CIA and the U.S. Defense Intelligence Agency. Earlier, the *Associated Press* reported (5/21/94) that Justice Department prosecutors had evidence that top Haitian military officers were involved in cocaine smuggling and that U.S. intelligence agencies may have cooperated with the smugglers.

TIME REPORTS FOWL SMELLING SCANDAL—The #10 *Censored* story of 1989 warned that the number of cases of salmonella had risen to 2.5 million a year due in part to the lax poultry inspection practices of the U.S. Department of Agriculture (USDA). The October 17, 1994, issue of *Time* reported a scandal involving lax USDA inspection practices and President Clinton's Agriculture Secretary Mike Espy who was under investigation for accepting alleged favors from Tyson Foods Inc., the world's largest chicken processor. Espy submitted his resignation. On 10/26/94, the *Associated Press* reported that the USDA dropped proposed new rules for improving inspection practices.

PENTAGON'S SECRET BLACK BUDGET EXPOSED—ACCIDENTALLY!—The "Pentagon's Secret Billion-Dollar Black Budget" was the #7 *Censored* story of 1990. The top-secret, highly-classified data about U.S. spy activities, estimated at some $28 billion in the current fiscal year, were revealed in Steven Aftergood's *Secrecy & Government Bulletin*, November 4, 1994. Believe it or not, the Pentagon had forgotten to delete the secret numbers from subcommittee hearing transcripts before they were made public.

A SUNNY FORECAST FOR A MONOPOLY ON THE SUN—The #9 *Censored* story of 1980 warned how a powerful elite of multi-national corporations were quietly buying into the solar industry in an apparent effort to control development of alternative energy sources. In a two-page spread on November 7, 1994, *Time* heralded a "sunny forecast" for solar energy, noting that renewable power sources were always cleaner than fossil fuels and may soon be just as cheap. Shell International Petroleum in London predicts that renewable power, particularly solar, will dominate world energy production by 2050. Surprise!

NURSING HOMES FINALLY GET STRONGER REGULATIONS—On November 11, 1994, the *Washington Post* reported that the Department of Health and Human Services issued final regulations on how to clean up abuses and substandard care in the nation's nursing homes. The tighter rules came too late for some patients including two who died at a nursing home in Visalia, California. The home was owned by Charles Wick, President Reagan's biggest single private fund-raiser in 1980 (later named director of the U.S. Information Agency). Following an unannounced visit, the home was cited by a state inspector for having "the worst nursing home conditions" he had ever seen. In early 1984, an investigative reporter sold the story to *ABC-TV News* which spent several months investigating and filming it. Then, just before the story was ready for final edit, there were reports of heavy pressure on *ABC*, including a call directly from the Reagan White House, not to run the story. The story did not run but, it did become part of our #9 *Censored* story of 1984.

THIS MODERN WORLD by TOM TOMORROW

POLITICIANS ARE PROFESSING *OUTRAGE* AT THE DISCOVERY OF A RUSSIAN SPY IN THE CIA... EVEN THOUGH INTELLIGENCE SOURCES CONCEDE THAT THE CIA CONTINUES TO SPY ON *RUSSIA*...

WELL THAT'S *DIF-FERENT*-- BECAUSE-- UM-- BECAUSE--

--BECAUSE WE'RE *AMERICANS!*

RICK AMES IS ACCUSED OF BETRAYING HIS COUNTRY FOR FINANCIAL GAIN-- BY REVEALING THE NAMES OF SOVIET CITIZENS WHO WERE WORKING FOR THE CIA...

--SOVIETS WHO WERE, IN OTHER WORDS, BETRAYING *THEIR* COUNTRY-- PRESUMABLY FOR FINANCIAL GAIN...

FRANKLY I'M NOT SURE *ANYONE* SHOULD BE LAYING CLAIM TO THE MORAL *HIGH GROUND* HERE...

TRAGEDY OF EAST TIMOR FINALLY MAKES WORLD HEADLINES
—In mid-November, 1994, as President Clinton and other foreign leaders arrived for an Asia-Pacific trade summit, protesters from East Timor focused the world's attention on Indonesia's human rights record. The slaughter of East Timorese natives by Indonesia after it invaded the tiny island in 1975 was the #7 Censored story in 1979 and the #3 Censored story of 1985.

CORPORATE WELFARE CHEATS CHALLENGED—On November 23, 1994, *USA Today* reported that Robert Reich, secretary of labor, called for a cut in "corporate welfare." Reich cited dozens of subsidies and tax breaks for energy, mining, agriculture, transportation, aerospace, high-tech, and finance industries that could be cut, saving hundreds of billions of dollars. "The Real Welfare Cheats: America's Corporations" was the #4 *Censored* story of 1993. By December 1, 1994, Reich's plan to cut subsidies had gathered bipartisan Congressional support.

NUKE CLEANUP A $23 BILLION BOMB—Despite $23 billion in government spending since 1989, the nation's nuclear waste problem is worse than ever according to a *Los Angeles Times* report on November 27, 1994. Radioactive waste is now stored in some 9,000 production buildings, tank farms, ponds, burial pits and other sites across the country. "Burying America in Radioactive Waste" was the #3 *Censored* story of 1981.

"As for modern journalism,
it is not my business to defend it.
It justifies its own existence
by the great Darwinian principle
of the survival of the vulgarest."
—Oscar Wilde

CHAPTER 5

The Junk Food News Stories of 1994

In discussing the Junk Food News stories last year, I noted that while the media have assumed unparalleled power in our society, they have squandered it on matters of little import.

This would never appear more true than in 1994. It will come as no surprise to anyone that the unprecedented and unchallenged "junk food news" story of the year was the O.J. Simpson trial.

Indeed, even with the reams of self-serving analytic explanations by the press itself as to why the O.J. Simpson trial was an important story and deserved the coverage it received, the News Ombudsmen of America overwhelmingly chose the Simpson trial for this distinction.

THE SIMPSON PHENOMENON

Around midnight, Sunday, June 12, the bodies of O.J. Simpson's ex-wife Nicole Brown and an acquaintance, Ronald Lyle Goldman, were discovered dead at her condominium. *KCBS TV/2*, in Los Angeles, reportedly broke the story at ll:30 a.m., Monday, and the scent of blood immediately attracted an unrelenting pack of media attack dogs. Within a week, the media were being criticized for their coverage and the chase had hardly begun. Now it is generally agreed that the Simpson case has become the most sensationalized media event in history.

The Simpson case provided the media with a challenge which they managed to fail at every turn. Following is a brief summary of just some of the media phenomena arising from the O.J. Simpson case of 1994:

On Friday, June 17, an estimated 95 million Americans watched the bizarre slo-mo-escort of Simpson's white Bronco on Southern California freeways. For comparison, about 118 million Americans tuned in for the first day of the Gulf War on January 16, 1991.

Within a week, the media were unashamedly on their way to no-holds-barred sleaze coverage with "exclusive" interviews with "best friends" of O.J. or Nicole, with an "eyewitness" to O.J.'s reported flight from the scene, and even with an instant phone poll to determine whether authorities should pursue the death penalty if O.J. is convicted. The trial had not yet started.

The potential appeal of the case was established on June 21 when a "Turning Point" interview with the police who arrested O.J. was rated No. 1 for the week, with 25.4 million viewers—the first top ranking ever for the television newsmagazine.

On June 27, *Time* magazine featured a cover photo of O.J. Simpson that had been computer-altered to make Simpson look darker-skinned and more heavily bearded, raising questions of racism.

THIS MODERN WORLD by TOM TOMORROW

All three television networks, ABC, CBS, and NBC acknowledged they would interrupt regular daytime programming starting Thursday, June 30, to cover the pretrial court hearing live.

For those who wish to relive the pretrial hearing, Turner Home Entertainment produced a 60-minute video of the highlights of the preliminary hearing selling for $24.93.

On June 30, USA *Today* editorially criticized both the defense attorneys and the prosecutors for generating the publicity they complained about; however, the Simpson case was the cover story in that same issue of USA *Today* and was featured on four other news pages.

Less than three weeks after the bodies were discovered, a CD-ROM, featuring the complete "O.J. Simpson Story", was advertised for $29.95 by the Bureau of Electronic Publishing.

The case also created a lucrative bull market for "witnesses" who were willing to sell their stories. David Perel, an editor at the *National Enquirer*, told *The New Yorker*, "If someone has a great story to sell, and it can be exclusive for us, the price may be in the hundreds of thousands of dollars, and we're going to pay it."

By mid-July, in the rush to get an exclusive, *KCBS-TV2* broadcast an erroneous report that prosecutor Marcia Clark was at O.J. Simpson's house before a search warrant was issued; a few days later the station publicly apologized.

Unwilling to wait for the end of the trial and the final verdict, in late July the *Philadelphia Daily News* published four endings, with four dif-

ferent murderers, written by four mystery novelists. One media critic said it was a response to the "instantaneous sensationalization that you see on television."

Not all media were quick to capitalize on the tragedy. In July, Hugh Hefner announced that *Playboy* would not release its videotape, "Minimum Maintenance Fitness for Men," which featured Simpson, even though it cost about $250,000 to produce.

In early August, Tony Miller, Acting Secretary of State in California, asked Superior Court Judge Lance Ito for a "time out" in the trial on November 7 and 8 so it wouldn't distract voters from the November 8 elections. No time out was called and the California voters did not appear to be distracted from the polls.

On August 18, Fox Broadcasting announced it would air "The O.J. Simpson Story" movie on September 13, and added it was not apologetic about producing the movie. On August 20, Fox announced it would *not* run its O.J. movie as previously advertised. Fox CEO Rupert Murdoch mentioned something about making it difficult for Simpson to obtain a fair trial.

Time magazine reported on September 5 that Simpson hired a Los Angeles law firm to prevent his good name from being exploited by bootleg T-shirt makers, trading card producers, and other non-authorized entrepreneurs seeking to make a quick buck.

By October 3, the *Los Angeles Daily News* was able to report that O.J. Simpson had been on the cover of the tabloids for 15 weeks straight, an unprecedented achievement.

While Judge Lance Ito made no secret of his disdain for the media, even to the extent of barring the *Los Angeles Daily News* from his courtroom at one point, he inexplicably allowed *KCBS-TV* to broadcast a five-part interview series with him, even as the trial was underway.

During the week of October 17, two new books were published. One was the widely heralded *Crossing the Threshold of Hope* by John Paul II; the other was the sleazy tell-all *Nicole Brown Simpson: The Private Diary of a Life Interrupted*, by Faye D. Resnick. The Resnick book outsold the Pope book in the first week, according to the *USA Today* best-selling books list reported October 26. A week later, the Pope book topped the list while the Resnick book dropped to third. The November 10 *USA Today* listing had the Pope book still in first place while the Resnick book dropped to 16. The Pope book remained the best seller on November 17 and the Resnick book slid to #39. The November 23 best-seller list showed the Pope had slipped to second place while Faye D. Resnick disappeared from the top 50 list.

On October 22, M. L. Stein, writer for *Editor & Publisher*, the authoritative trade journal of the newspaper industry, reported that "The massive 'media army' camped outside the Los Angeles Criminal Courts Building might give the impression that the O.J. Simpson murder trial is one big stage show in a city whose reputation is built largely on entertainment." Looking at the uniquely American scene from an international perspective, Oddivar Stenstrom, a reporter for TV-2, a national TV network in Norway, told Stein his main interest was in covering the "media madness," rather than the trial itself.

In an art imitates life twist, cartoonist Garry Trudeau lampooned the "media circus" in L.A. in a "Doonesbury" series chronicling the experiences of an aspiring author going to "O.J. City" to get material for his book.

On November 7, when Judge Ito announced a camera would be allowed in the courtroom for the O.J. trial, CNN announced it would scrap its normal daytime schedule to cover the trial live once it gets underway. Paul Thayer, director of the journalism program at Mercy College in New York, charged that CNN is "losing sight of its own responsibility as a news network" by replacing news coverage with trial coverage.

It was not until the week of November 7 that the O.J. Simpson case failed to rank as one of the top ten stories of the week on the weekday nightly newscasts of *ABC World News Tonight*, *CBS Evening News*, and *NBC Nightly News*. From the week of June 13 through November 4, the Simpson case dominated the network newscasts, according to the authoritative *Tyndall Report* which monitors television news.

In reviewing the coverage during the summer months, Andrew Tyndall, publisher of the *Report* said, "Before the trial even starts, from the murders, the indictment, the Ford Bronco's notorious freeway ride, the preliminary hearings to the pre-trial jockeying, the O.J. Simpson case has gained more minutes on the nightly news in just three months than any other story in the whole of 1994." It was often the top ranked story of the week, beating out other issues such as the November elections, Iraq/Kuwait, Israeli/Arab peace negotiations, universal health care legislation defeat, Haiti, the budget deficit, and Yugoslavia.

For comparative purposes, the *Report* noted that the 520 minutes the network devoted to Simpson during those three months exceeded "the entire 498 minutes accorded to the Los Angeles riots—including the first

Rodney King beating trial, the arson fires, the deaths of 55, and the subsequent rebuilding efforts—in the whole of 1992."

Time magazine heralded "Yet Another O.J. Shocker!" on November 28 when it reported that in the previous week the *National Enquirer* published an issue whose cover made no mention of O.J. Simpson.

While the press will maintain to its last drop of ink that its primary motivation in all this is to give the public what it needs to know, we must note that the Simpson story had some peripheral fringe benefits for the media.

For example, Nielsen Media Research figures during the summer revealed how prime-time "news" magazines, such as "Dateline," "20/20," "60 Minutes," "PrimeTime Live," and "Turning Point," were all getting an extra ratings boost from the Simpson coverage; producers at "Inside Edition" estimated a 60% rise in ratings over expected summer numbers; O.J. coverage gave ABC, NBC, CBS, and CNN huge daytime ratings; newsstand sales of magazines and newspapers also skyrocketed: *Time* estimated sales up 50% in one week, both *Newsweek* and *People Magazine* expected two of their O.J. covers to be top sellers in 1994, *USA Today* circulation sales on big O.J. days were up about 100,000 over the previous week, and the nation's three top tabloids, the *National Enquirer*, the *Star*, and the *Globe* each boasted circulation gains from 10 percent to 20 percent during the July-September period.

The cover story of the August *ASNE Bulletin*, trade journal of the American Society of Newspaper Editors (ASNE) asked, how did the press do in covering the murder charges against O.J. Simpson? The journal concluded that while most editors offered no apologies for their coverage of the trial, some feel the press must revive traditional standards for dealing with sensational crimes.

The range of responses to the question of the media's performance ranged from an editor who defended the public's "need to know" even *more* about the O.J. Simpson case, to an editor who reminded his colleagues of Joseph Pulitzer's warning about too much sensationalism.

Jane Healy, managing editor of the *Orlando* (FL) *Sentinel*, admitted that the media have gone absolutely nuts on O.J. but said the coverage was absolutely justified. Healy pointed out how the press coverage had given the public lessons about the preliminary hearing judicial process, the Fourth Amendment, and domestic violence. However, she pointed out, the biggest problem was that the press hadn't been able to carve out enough of a niche of O.J. coverage for itself. Recognizing that cameras in the courtroom give television a big advantage, Healy suggested that smart newspapers could help their readers find O.J. specials on TV and use TV as a "huge promotional device for our next day's paper and then complement its coverage in a big way." She concluded, "Bring on the trial."

On the other hand, William F. Woo, editor of the *St. Louis Post-Dispatch*, was concerned that too much sensationalistic coverage can create a cynical populace. Woo reminded us of the warning issued by the *Post-Dispatch* founder, Joseph Pulitzer, in 1907: "A cynical, mercenary, demagogic press will produce in time a people as base as itself." Noting the journalism trend toward tabloidization, Woo rejected the argument that the press has a responsibility to present what the public says it wants rather than what it knows the public needs. Pulitzer, Woo said, understood the problem when he spoke of the need for a press "with trained intelligence to know the right and courage to do it," and about the connection between a cynical, mercenary press and a people as base as itself. Woo concluded, "And that is what we journalists today are fast forgetting."

Joann Byrd, ombudsman for the *Washington Post*, warned that the O.J. reporting contained "every possible failing in journalism," in an *American Journalism Review* article analyzing the media coverage (September 1994). She pointed out how reporters went with stories based on rumors, many of which proved false; how they speculated that Simpson must be guilty because he didn't act innocent; how they were willing to be manipulated by either side in the case if they got the story first; and how tabloid media paid potential witnesses for their stories, thereby compromising their testimony.

Tony Snow, a Washington correspondent for *The Detroit News* and a former speechwriter for President George Bush, defended the O.J. coverage saying "If journalism is supposed to cover the stuff of everyday life, this story has it all. That's why the saga of the football player, his former wife and her ill-fated visitor will remain front-page news—and should."

Less charitable about the media coverage was Hal Boedeker, TV critic for the *Miami Herald*, who said the television coverage of the Simpson story "reveals the medium's penchant for vampirism, feeding on reality, sucking it dry and reinventing it as more promotion and programming."

Sanford J. Ungar, dean of the School of Communication at The American University, in Washington, DC, warned that the media are jeopardizing their traditional standards by sensationalizing the sensational. He pointed out that "a decade or so ago, the newspapers and the networks still measured their success—at least some of the time—by revealing tragedy rather than living off it."

But perhaps the best advice for a public gasping for fresh air in the cesspool of O.J. coverage came from Michelle Malkin, a columnist for the *Los Angeles Daily News*. Acknowledging that you can't expect Nielsen-driven media executives to practice restraint, Malkin said, "It will be up to the individual to rescue himself from the dregs of the Simpson spectacle."

But even for those able to drag themselves away from the Simpson spectacle, there was an abundance of other junk food news stories of the year waiting to distract them.

THE TOP 10 JUNK FOOD NEWS STORIES OF 1994

Incredibly, even without O.J., 1994 proved to be yet another vintage year for Junk Food News—the sensationalized, personalized, and homogenized inconsequential trivia served up in abundance by the nation's media.

Indeed, by the end of the year, two of the nation's leading journalists, Pulitzer Prize-wining *Los Angeles Times* Washington Bureau chief Jack Nelson and NBC Nightly News television anchor Tom Brokaw, acknowledged that journalism has run amok in scandal and sensationalism while important news is often ignored.

To provide a record of Junk Food News stories, at the end of each year, I survey members of the national Organization of News Ombudsmen to solicit their selections for the most over-reported, least deserving news stories of the year.

Following are the top ten Junk Food News stories of 1994 as cited by the news ombudsmen. As you read them, compare how much you heard about them last year with how much you heard about the top ten *Censored* stories cited in Chapter 2.

1. THE O.J. SIMPSON CASE
2. TONYA HARDING
3. ROSEANNE
4. MICHAEL JACKSON & LISA MARIE PRESLEY
5. THE BRITISH ROYALS
6. JOHN WAYNE & LORENA BOBBITT
7. MICHAEL FAY'S SINGAPORE CANING
8. INFORMATION SUPER-HIGHWAY
9. WHITEWATERGATE
10. WOODSTOCK II

Rounding out the top 25 JFN nominations of 1994 were Generation X, Rush Limbaugh, Oprah, The Wonder Bra, Heidi Fleiss, Joey Buttafuoco, Barbie's 35th Birthday, Kurt Cobain, Burt & Loni, Baseball Strike, Howard Stern, World Cup Fever, Rolling Stones Tour, Nixon's Legacy, and the Flesh-Eating Virus.

Top-ranked Junk Food News stories of the past:

1984 Clara Peller's "Where's the beef?"
1985 Coca-Cola's new old classic Cherry Coke
1986 Clint Eastwood's campaign for mayor of Carmel
1987 The tribulations of Jim and Tammy Faye
1988 The trapped whales of Alaska
1989 Zsa Zsa Gabor's cop-slapping trial
1990 The marital woes of Donald and Ivana Trump
1991 The William Kennedy Smith rape trial
1992 Dan Quayle's misspelling of potato
1993 Amy Fisher & Joey Buttafuoco

Following are explanations suggested by some of the news ombudsmen who participated in the selection of the top 1994 Junk Food News subjects as to why the media tend to sensationalize such stories as those cited above:

"Gatekeepers in print and broadcast news are 1) too young to know better, and 2) are not being trained to use mature judgment about story selection. The reliable, well-edited newspaper or news program, the one that does not go overboard with the pack but saves personnel, time and space for a more important story, will profit most in the long run."—Richard P. Cunningham, Department of Journalism, New York University.

"None of the other stories this year hold a candle to O.J. —and the trial is just beginning. The O.J. story is the mirror image of the Bobbitt saga, but without the personality slapstick. And with murder, rather than just mayhem. Justification: if the public loved/hated Lorena and John Wayne, they'll really love/hate Nicole and O.J."—Lynn Feigenbaum, *The Virginian-Pilot* & *The Ledger-Star*, Norfolk, Virginia.

"With television setting the information agenda for most of the other media, and with the proliferation of TV 'magazine' shows that devour personality stories, no wonder emphasis falls on such coverage. TV is primarily an entertainment medium that delivers audience to advertisers. Shows are audience-and-advertising driven. The print media are responsive to public interest in entertainment news as well, but are better able to make certain the stage is shared with news the public needs."—Jerry Finch, *The Richmond Times-Dispatch*, Richmond, Virginia.

"First, because the media follow the TV model; second, because they follow the news agency bulletins that insist on a particular subject and the papers feel obligated to accept it; and finally, due to the fact that people tend to talk about these issues."—Roger Jimenez, *La Vanguardia*, Barcelona, Spain.

"Most of these stories have significance to only a few people—particularly those involved. So it's a chicken and egg question: have the media made peeping Toms (and Tammys) of the public, or have the public's interests in celebrities' private lives made peeping Toms of the media? Whichever came first, each has created an insatiable appetite in the other and both are stuffed with irrelevancies, gossip, innuendo, and sleaze. We are choking on our garbage."—Jean Otto, *Rocky Mountain News*, Denver, Colorado.

"Because the public devours these kinds of stories and we get caught up in the frenzy."—Phil Record, *Fort Worth Star-Telegram*, Fort Worth, Texas.

"All these stories appeal to basic human emotions—curiosity (i.e., whodunit); greed, sex, nostalgia, crime and punishment and so on. In their competitive zeal to satisfy these interests, media go overboard and lose perspective, failing to recognize when the public interest has waned and people tire of endless repetition."—Gordon Sanderson, *London Free Press*, London, Ontario, Canada.

"The media tend to sensationalize these stories because of a competitive panic, compounded by inertia, that causes stories to keep on rolling along. Editors should stop and think."—Emerson Stone, The RTNDA Magazine, *The Communicator*, Greenwich, Connecticut.

"Editors and producers are governed by mass media group-think, ratings, and circulation."—Jim Stott, *The Calgary Herald*, Calgary, Alberta, Canada.

"The news organizations give these stories too much coverage because the readers love them. The mainstream organizations rarely sensationalize them, i.e., rarely distort them until they simply are not true."—Robert Walker, *The Gazette*, Montreal, Quebec, Canada.

"These stories sell the paper! Besides, readers find them interesting."—Gayle Williams, Gannett Suburban Newspapers, White Plains, New York.

In an article in the November/December issue of *The Quill*, ombudsman Emerson Stone offered an additional piece of advice to the nation's news editors, "The Simpson case poses a textbook challenge for journalists in editorial selection and restraint. Militating against moderation are the high ratings drawn by the original barrage of print and broadcast coverage, both traditional and tabloid. If news coverage is to be based mainly on polls of what people want, in the form of ratings and newspaper sales, editors have little reason to come to the office."

WHAT IS AN OMBUDSMAN?

The ombudsmen, who annually name the top Junk Food News stories of the year for Project Censored, are members of one of the most select clubs in America—the Organization of News Ombudsmen (ONO). Their responsibility is awesome—to make the newspaper more accountable to its readers. And while there are some 1,650 daily newspapers in America, there were just 38 official U.S. ombudsmen cited as ONO members in 1994.

Following is an explanation of what an ombudsman is by Art Nauman, longtime ombudsman at *The Sacramento Bee* in California and former president of ONO. It is excerpted, with his permission, from his column in *The Bee* on October 10, 1994.

"WHAT DOES THE WORD OMBUDSMAN MEAN?

"Scandinavian in origin, ombudsman ("om-BUDZ-man") means one who investigates complaints, reports findings, and helps to achieve fair settlements. A news ombudsman (there are 57 of us around the world) typically is independent of the news staff. He or she checks out complaints about fairness, accuracy, balance and good taste in news, feature and sports stories, photos and graphic displays. Generally, anything in the paper's news and feature columns, including photos and graphics, is fair game for ombudsman queries and critique.

"WHY HAVE AN OMBUDSMAN?

"To help make the paper more accountable to its readers. After all, newspapers enjoy protections and privileges given by the people—in the Constitution—to no other business enterprise. To say it another way, a newspaper is a major social and economic force in its community that potentially affects how people think and act. It should be willing to expose and critique its news-gathering process in the same way it continually demands that other community institutions account for themselves.

'HOW DOES THE BEE'S OMBUDSMAN FUNCTION?

"Nearly every complaint or comment, whether telephoned, mailed or passed along orally, is checked out. In the 19 years of its life, this office has fielded thousands of comments and criticisms. Nearly every one gets an answer of some kind, even when I find I can't agree.

"Typically, if the complaint involves a story written by a *Bee* reporter, a memo from this office that states the case will go to the journalists involved. If a response seems appropriate, I'll invite one. If the complaints involve wire stories, calls or letters go to those editors. After I've heard from everybody who had a hand in the story, I'll report back to the reader, and usually include my own opinion. If the complaint is journalistically significant or unusual, was generated by a goodly number of readers, or was just plain interesting to me, I'll write about it in my column.

"IF YOU FIND THAT A REPORTER HAS ERRED OR AN EDITOR HAS DISPLAYED LOUSY JUDGMENT, DO YOU DISCIPLINE THE SINNER?

"Absolutely not. That's not my function. That's a job for supervising editors. The ombudsman speaks only for himself, not for the newspaper's ownership or news management team. I simply offer these people what I think to be an accurate reflection of what readers are saying to me—frequently coupled with my own opinions formed in the safe haven of hindsight, and based on 39 years of experience as a reporter, editor and columnist.

"BUT HOLD ON, YOU'RE ON THE NEWSPAPER'S PAYROLL HOW INDEPENDENT CAN YOU REALLY BE?

"The paper provides me with an office separate from the newsroom, a secretary, computer, telephone and fax. Then I'm left totally alone. In my 14 years of ombudsmanship, I've not once been ordered by anybody what to write. That fulfills a pledge made by the late editor C.K. McClatchy when he created the position in 1975. He promised publicly in a front page story that the ombudsman would be independent, that he would have license to speak his mind about the paper, and that there would be no interference from management.

"Before its publication, my column goes through *The Bee's* copy desk for the normal checking for spelling, style and grammar. Otherwise, what the reader sees is all Art Nauman and nobody else. There have been arguments with staffers of the column's conclusions, sometimes even unpleasant moments. But this comes with the territory. The point is, the independence is real. Without it, the job would be worthless hypocrisy and I would have given it up years ago.

"DOES THE OMBUDSMAN FUNCTION DO ANY GOOD?"

"I'm not always sure, but I want to believe that in the long run it does. You can't measure the effectiveness of the ombudsman's job in concrete terms as you can other functions here. Its value lies in the sheer act of candid ventilation, this weekly hanging out of family laundry.

"Surely, this has to have a salutary impact on the journalists, bringing them in closer touch with their readers, whom they dare not disdain, underestimate or ignore.

"And I hope it will help readers to understand that a daily newspaper is an amalgam produced at an often frenetic pace by a group of generally sincere mortals who, inescapably, are fallible."

If you are not fortunate enough to be a subscriber to a daily newspaper like *The Sacramento Bee* that feels a responsibility to its readers and supports a strongly independent ombudsman like Art Nauman, you might want to ask your newspaper to consider adding an ombudsman to its staff. John Sweeney, public editor of *The News Journal*, of Wilmington, Delaware, and president of the Organization of News Ombudsmen, feels that too many newspapers not only lack an ombudsman but any form of media criticism. In an interview in the November/December issue of *The Quill*, Sweeney said, "People want to know about the institutions that govern their lives, but we pretend they have no business knowing what's going on with us; no wonder they don't trust us."

Possibly the only encouraging aspect of the O.J. Simpson case is that it is forcing the news industry to rethink its role and responsibility to the public. That would be a major first step toward correcting the problem.

THIS MODERN WORLD by TOM TOMORROW

But, as we should know by now, we cannot rely solely on the media to heal themselves. Further, since we all will benefit from a more responsible media, we all really should help bring it about.

To do this, the corporate media owners should start to earn their unique First Amendment privileges. Editors should rethink their news judgment. Journalists should persevere in going after the hard stories. Journalism professors should emphasize ethics and critical analysis and turn out more muckrakers and fewer buckrakers. The judicial system should defend the freedom-of-the-press provision of the First Amendment with far more vigor. And the public should show the media it is more concerned with the high crimes and misdemeanors of its political and corporate leaders than it is with the crimes and gossip of celebrities.

The effort will be well worth it. America today is not the nation it once was—nor is it the nation it could be. We need a free and aggressive press more now than ever before, a press that will stand up to those who would control it and assume again the independence it once celebrated.

Indeed, the effort is not merely worth it; it is critical. Few have said it better than Joseph Pulitzer, who warned, "We are a democracy, and there is only one way to get a democracy on its feet...and that is by keeping the public informed about what is going on."

Pulitzer did not have O.J. Simpson in mind when he said that.

"Those who cannot remember the past
are condemned to repeat it."
—George Santayana

CHAPTER 6

An Eclectic Chronology of Censorship from 605 B.C. to 1995

The following eclectic chronology culls information and events from a variety of sources, both traditional and nontraditional.

A thorough reading of this chronology should make it clear that censorship is not merely an occasional social aberration, but rather a threat that has been with us from the earliest recorded times. As A. Holmes said, "If history without chronology is dark and confused, chronology without history is dry and insipid." I hope you find this neither dry nor insipid.

A thorough reading also should persuade you that censorship historically has been a tool of a powerful elite which attempts to control society through the manipulation of thought, speech, and all other forms of expression. There are, to my knowledge, very few examples, if any, where the poor or powerless are able to use censorship as a tool to influence decisions affecting themselves, let alone a wealthy and powerful elite.

In addition, this chronology should provide you with insights into how we as a society have supported rules, regulations, leaders and institutions that have fostered censorship.

Finally, I hope the following persuades you that freedom of expression is never permanently secured; it must be fought for and won each day. Project Censored is but one of many combatants who have fought against censorship. While the battle is never-ending, it is truly worthy.

A CENSORED CHRONOLOGY

605 B.C. Perhaps the earliest recorded case of censorship occurred when Jehoiakim, the king of Judah, burned Jeremiah's book of prophecies. This prescient event, found in the Bible (Jeremiah 36, 1-32), may also be the earliest example of self-censorship since Jeremiah had written the book at Jehoiakim's bidding.

500 B.C. While we revere the Greeks for their respect for freedom of speech, censorship was not unknown. In the fifth century B.C., poets, philosophers, musicians, authors, and others were subject to bans, persecution, and exile.

443 B.C. Most dictionaries trace censorship back to ancient Rome when two magistrates, called "censors," were appointed to conduct an annual census to register citizens and to assess their property for taxation and contract purposes. The censors also were authorized to censure and penalize moral offenders thought to be guilty of vice and immorality by removing their voting rights and tribe membership. This form of censorship was discontinued in 22 B.C. when emperors took over the censorial powers.

399 B.C. The ultimate form of censorship is death, and Socrates—one of the first philosophers to express a rational defense of freedom of speech—became an early victim of it. After he was tried and convicted of impiety and of corrupting youth, Socrates was put to death. Ironically, his best-known pupil, Plato, outlined the first comprehensive system of censorship, particularly of the arts. In *The Republic*, Book II, Plato warned against allowing children to hear any casual tales by casual persons and called for the establishment of a censorship system for writers of fiction.

221 B.C. About two centuries after the appointment of censors in Rome, the Chinese launched their own office of censorship under the Ch'in dynasty (221-206 B.C.) Originally designed to critique the emperor's performance, the office of censor soon was used by the emperor to investigate and punish official corruption. The institution eventually became a huge bureaucracy that effectively ended with the overthrow of the Ch'ing dynasty in 1911.

213 B.C. One of China's most famous monarchs, Tsin Chi Hwangti, built the Great Wall of China (214-204 B.C.) He also exercised a most impressive act of censorship in 213 B.C. by ordering all books in China destroyed, except those concerning science, medicine, and agriculture. In addition, he executed 500 scholars and banished thousands of others.

48 B.C. The famous Alexandrian Library was burned on orders from Julius Caesar and some 700,000 rolls of manuscripts were lost forever. An effort was made to rebuild it, and this later library, known as the "Daughter Library," was destroyed in A.D. 389 by an edict of the Emperor Theodosius.

A.D. 58 In Acts 19:19 of the Bible, the apostle Paul praised converts who burned books (worth 50,000 pieces of silver) in the purifying fires of orthodoxy, providing modern-day Christian censors with scriptural authorization for their book burning.

A.D. 95 Following-up on Paul's advice, the "Apostolic Constitutions," written by St. Clement of Rome, warned Christians that the Scriptures provided everything a true believer needed to read.

A.D. 499 Under Pope Gelasius, the concept of the Papal Index, a list of books unsuitable for Roman Catholics, first appeared. It was formalized in 1564 and still exists to this day.

1215 On June 15, King John of England, under pressure from English barons, sealed the Magna Carta at Runnymede, guaranteeing certain civil and political liberties to the English people.

1231 The Inquisition, an open season for censors, was launched by the Roman Catholic Church as a formal way of discovering heresy and punishing heretics. Thousands of scriptures were inspected, reviewed, and often destroyed by the Inquisitors—self-described defenders of the Truth of the Sacred Text—from 1231 to 1596. For almost four centuries, book burners also were empowered to burn authors at the stake.

1450 Johann Gutenberg invented the printing press, with its movable type, thereby providing the technological breakthrough for the intellectual revolution of the Renaissance and its challenge to the institution of censorship. It also threatened the tight control secular and religious leaders exercised over the production and distribution of information.

1501 In an effort to protect the Church of Rome against heresy, Pope Alexander VI issued an edict banning the printing of books. Not unlike their colleagues in the Roman Catholic Church, leaders of the Protestant Reformation (including John Knox, Martin Luther, and John Calvin) persecuted heretics and papists. In England, Henry VIII burned copies of William Tyndale's *New Testament* and had Thomas More beheaded for refusing to acknowledge the king's power over religion. In 1529, Henry VIII issued an official list of banned books, some 30 years before the widely known Roman Catholic Index was institutionalized. By 1586, prior restraint had run rampant in England where all books had to be read and approved by the Archbishop of Canterbury or the Bishop of London prior to publication.

1512 Nicolaus Copernicus published "Commentarious," his hypothesis on the revolutions of the heavenly bodies. It stated that the earth was not the center of the universe but revolved around the sun. The theory, which contradicted the geocentric theory favored by the Catholic church, was condemned and placed on the Papal Index in 1616.

1517 Protesting papal censorship, the sale of indulgences, and other papal expedients, Martin Luther, an ordained priest, posted his 95 theses on the door of the Palast Church in Wittenberg, laying the foundations for the German Reformation and the Lutheran Church. Luther later was one of the prohibited authors cited in an abortive early version (1559) of the *Index of Prohibited Books*, formally authorized and published by the Roman Catholic Church in 1564.

1541 Concerned about nude figures in Michelangelo's fresco, "The Last Judgment," in the Sistine Chapel, Pope Paul IV ordered artists to paint over the more provocative parts to protect the innocent. During a major four-year restoration that was completed in 1993, Vatican authorities decided not to remove the draperies or "breeches" painted on to the Sistine nudes 452 years earlier. Gianluigi Colalucci, head of the Vatican Museum's restoration project, explained, "The decision we took is of a historic nature, not an aesthetic one; we have chosen to respect the acts of the Council of Trent." It now appears the world will never again see the fresco exactly as Michelangelo painted it.

1564 After abortive attempts dating back more than a thousand years, the papacy successfully issued the formal *Index Librorum Prohibitorum* (Index of Prohibited Books) as authorized by the Council of Trent. Approximately 500 pages in length, it listed books and authors condemned by the Roman Catholic Church. While it survived until 1774 in France and 1834 in Spain, the Index (as it is known colloquially) remains in force for Roman Catholics up to present day. It is the longest running, and possibly most effective, example of censorship in world history.

1633 Galileo Galilei was forced by the Inquisition to renounce and reject *Dialago*, published in 1632, which supported the theories of Copernicus concerning the revolutions of the planet. *Dialago* was added to the infamous Index where it remained until 1822.

1643 The British Parliament reintroduced the Licensing Act, ending a brief respite from censorship which occurred in 1640 with the abolishment of the Court of Star Chamber. It was this renewal of book licensing which instigated John Milton's eloquent plea for free speech a year later.

1644 *Areopagitica; a Speech of Mr. John Milton For the Liberty of Unlicenc'd Printing, To the Parlament of England,* published in 1644, is considered to be the English-speaking world's first and most powerful statement urging freedom of expression. Some of its better known excerpts include:

> *Who kills a man kills a reasonable creature, God's image; but he who destroys a good book, kills reason itself. Give me the liberty to know, to utter, and to argue freely according to conscience, above all liberties. Though all the winds of doctrine were let loose to play upon the earth, so Truth be in the field, we do injuriously, by licensing and prohibiting to misdoubt her strength. Let her and Falsehood grapple; whoever knew Truth put to the worse in a free and open encounter?*

While Milton's eloquent statement is rightfully credited with being the genesis of press freedom in America, his treatise actually dealt with the right to license, or prior restraint, not with post-publication censorship. The latter finally was addressed by the First Amendment to the Constitution of the United States in 1791.

1690 A small, three-page newspaper, measuring just six by nine-and-one-half inches, titled "Numb. 1, PUBLICK OCCURRENCES Both FOREIGN and DOMESTICK, Boston, Thursday Sept. 25th, 1690," is generally agreed to be the first newspaper published in America. There was no "Numb. 2" because the governor and council issued a statement four days after its publication declaring their "high resentment and Disallowance of said Pamphlet, and order that the same be Suppressed and called in; strictly forbidding any person or persons for the future to Set forth any thing in Print without License first obtained." They found that the editor, Benjamin Harris, had printed "Reflections of a very high nature: As also sundry doubtful and uncertain Reports." While this was an inauspicious beginning for a free press in the New World, there remain many reflections of a very high nature (Iran-contra, Iraqgate, BCCI, etc.) that continue to be subject to censorship today.

1695 Because of increasing resistance, partially generated by Milton's *Areopagitica*, the Licensing Act in England was not renewed in 1695, a date which has come to signify the establishment of freedom of the press in England. However, this did not mark the end of censorship in that country. Prior censorship, through licensing, was replaced with punitive (or post-publication) censorship, a form that, though preferable to prior censorship, is still found in most societies to this day. This is not to say that prior censorship is no longer attempted: consider the case of *The Progressive* magazine, the target of the first case of press prior restraint in America (*U.S. v. Progressive*, 1979).

Again, in 1988, the Supreme Court's *Hazelwood* decision gave school administrators prior restraint control over student newspapers.

1735 The John Peter Zenger case provided a classic example of an attempt at punitive, or post-publication, censorship in America; but it established that truth was a defense against charges of libel. Zenger was arrested and charged with seditious libel for criticizing New York Governor William Cosby in his *New York Weekly Journal*. At the age of 80, Andrew Hamilton, one of the leading attorneys in the colonies, took on the case pro bono, considering the issue to be critical to the future of liberty. Putting Milton's *Areopagitica* at the core of the defense, Hamilton won the case with the presumption that truth could not be libel. The case is often referred to as the birth of freedom of the press in America.

1764 The *Hartford* (Connecticut) *Courant*, the oldest continuously published newspaper in the United States, was founded on October 29. The oldest U.S. daily newspaper, the *New York Post*, was founded in 1801.

1765 The British Stamp Act of 1765 taxed all printed materials circulated in the colonies; the Taunted Acts of 1766 placed duties on American imports of glass, lead, paint, tea, and paper. Together these documents outraged colonial journalists and encouraged press protests until all duties, except those on tea, were removed in 1770. The famed Boston Tea Party (planned at the home of an editor of the *Boston Gazette*) followed in 1773. Then, in rapid succession, the British reacted with the Intolerable Acts of 1774, the First Continental Congress met that same year, and the first shot of the War of Independence was fired in 1775.

1776 In Philadelphia, on July 4, the Declaration of Independence was signed by representatives from the thirteen states of America. It opened with these words: "When in the Course of human events it becomes necessary for one people to dissolve the political bonds which have connected them with another...;" and it continued, "We hold these truths to be self-evident, that all men are created equal, that they are endowed by their Creator with certain unalienable Rights, that among these are Life, Liberty and the pursuit of Happiness..." These eloquent words, with their emphasis on liberty and equality, paved the way for a free society granting free speech and a free press.

1787 The Constitution of the United States was drafted in 1787, ratified in 1788, and went into effect on the first Wednesday of March 1789, thereby formally establishing the United States of America.

1789 The French Revolution of 1789 specifically enshrined the freedoms of "speech, thought, and expression" in Clause 11 of its Declaration of the Rights of Man.

1791 On December 15, the first ten amendments, known collectively as the Bill of Rights, were added to the Constitution. These provisions established a formal contractual agreement between the government and its citizens, encompassing specific concerns not addressed in the Constitution. Foremost among these is Article I, dealing with the freedoms of religion, speech, the press, and the right of petition: "Congress shall make no law respecting an establishment of religion, or prohibiting the free exercise thereof; or abridging the freedom of speech, or of the press; or the right of the people peaceably to assemble, and to petition the Government for a redress of grievances." What might be most remarkable about this most extraordinary document is not what it says but what it does not say. There are no restrictions, contingencies, exclusions, or other provisos dealing with heresy, blasphemy, pornography, obscenity, defamation, national security, sedition, public morals, racism, sexism, libel, slander, political correctness, or a host of other social concerns that have threatened to dilute the strength of the First Amendment for more than 200 years.

1798 The ink was barely dry on the Bill of Rights when Congress enacted the Alien and Sedition Acts of 1798. The legislation would punish anyone who spoke, wrote, or published "Any false scandalous and malicious (speech) against the government of the United States" or used speech that would bring the President or Congress "into contempt or disrepute." Although the acts expired in 1801, it wasn't until 1964 that the Supreme Court declared them "inconsistent with the First Amendment."

1802 The English Society for the Suppression of Vice was launched in England, paving the way for similar groups in the United States later in the 19th century.

1818 Dr. Thomas Bowdler, an early British version of Jerry Falwell, was an unsuccessful physician consumed with cleansing the language of any indelicate words or phrases. Specifically, he wanted to eliminate from Shakespeare "whatever is unfit to be read aloud by a gentleman in the company of ladies." In 1818, in London, he published his "Family Shakespeare" which was also widely distributed in the United States. The expurgated version of Shakespeare led to the term "bowdlerized," referring to this form of censorship.

1841 Ralph Waldo Emerson published his famed essay, "Self-Reliance." In this tribute to free expression, he wrote, "The virtue in most request is conformity. Self-reliance is its aversion. ... Whoso would be a man must be a non-conformist. ... A foolish consistency is the hobgoblin of little minds, adored by little statesmen and philosophers and divines."

1842 At the age of 24, Karl Marx began his career as a working journalist with an essay titled "Remarks on the Latest Prussian Censorship Instruction." Censored by German authorities, it was published a year later by a German-exile press in Switzerland. Marx went on to decry censorship for protecting the interests of the elite and perpetuating the domination of the powerless by the powerful. Ironically, communist societies subsequently used censorship to protect the interests of the elite and to dominate the powerless. Marx himself went on to become one of the most censored authors of modern times, particularly, of course, in capitalist societies.

1842 While Marx was being censored in Germany, the U.S. Congress passed the Tariff Law of 1842, prohibiting "all indecent and obscene prints, paintings, lithographs, engravings, and transparencies" from being imported. In 1857, the law was expanded to include images, figures, and photographs, in order to prevent the importation of Greek statues of "questionable" taste into the U.S.

1856 French novelist Gustave Flaubert was charged with immorality and lasciviousness for publishing *Madame Bovary*. When Flaubert was acquitted, the book, which otherwise might have reached a small audience, became an instant bestseller. The first American edition was published in 1896.

1857 In England, the Obscene Publications Act of 1857 led to an early definition of obscenity. It was also known as the Campbell Act, named for its proponent, the Lord Chief Justice. To assure passage of his bill, Campbell defined an obscene work as one written for the single purpose of corrupting the morals of youth and designed to shock the sense of decency in any well-regulated mind.

1859 In his famous essay "On Liberty," John Stuart Mill, who believed every man is competent to choose what he will read or hear, recorded his thesis on the expression of thought: "Who can compute what the world loses in the multitude of promising intellects combined with timid characters, who dare not follow out any bold, vigorous, independent train of thought, lest it should land them in something which would admit of being considered irreligious or immoral? ... No one can be a great thinker who does not recognize that as a thinker it is his first duty to follow his intellect to whatever conclusions it may lead. ... There is always hope when people are forced to listen to both sides. It is when they attend only one that errors harden into prejudices and truth itself ceases to have the effect of truth, by being exaggerated into falsehood."

1861 During the Civil War, the U.S. War Department warned journalists against providing any military information that would aid the enemy. The order was generally disregarded, though, leading to casualties. However, more responsible correspondents and editors proved able to report on the war while still concealing information of value to the enemy. In the North, the greatest censorship came from angry mobs who attempted to destroy newspapers with which they disagreed.

1861 William Makepeace Thackeray, founder and editor of *The Cornhill Magazine*, rejected Elizabeth Barrett Browning's poem, "Lord Walter's wife," as one of many poems and stories he thought to be indecent or indelicate.

1873 The New England Watch and Ward Society and the New York Society for the Suppression of Vice were founded for the purpose of pressuring publishers, editors, and news agents into rejecting controversial writers.

1873 Anthony Comstock was America's answer to England's Thomas Bowdler. Comstock, a religious fanatic whose motto was "Morals, Not Art or Literature," joined with the YMCA to found the New York Society for the Suppression of Vice. As head of this organization, he was given a monopoly by New York to eliminate vice in the state. He also succeeded in getting Congress to pass what was known as The Comstock Act of 1873 which consolidated various statutes and regulations dealing with "obscene, lewd, and lascivious" publications and specifically barred birth-control material from the mail.

Comstock was extraordinarily successful in "fighting vice." In 1874, he reported that in a two-year period, his society had seized 130,000 pounds of bound books along with 60,300 "articles made of rubber for immoral purposes." When he retired in 1915, he estimated that he had destroyed over 160 tons of "obscene" literature.

One of his great successes was the suppression of Paul Chabas' "September Morn," a romantic painting of a young nude girl bathing on the shore of a lake. The censored painting led to a controversy over the distinction between "nude" and "naked" that persisted for nearly 120 years. Finally, in 1992, Anne-Imelda Radice, acting head of the National Endowment for the Arts in the United States, announced her personal ability to differentiate between "nude" and "naked."

1885 The board of trustees of the Concord Public Library in New Hampshire censored a book which "deals with a series of adventures of a very low grade of morality; it is couched in the language of a rough dialect, and all through its pages there is a systematic use of bad grammar. ... The book is flippant and irreverent. ... It is trash of the veriest sort." Mark Twain, the author of this dangerous book, *The Adventures of Huckleberry Finn*, responded by saying, "That will sell 25,000 copies for us, sure."

1896 A simple kiss in a play, "The Widow Jones," when seen magnified to a larger than life scale on a screen in the May Irwin-John C. Rice film "Kiss," resulted in the first known attempt at film censorship.

1900 The turn of the century marked the Golden Age of Muckraking—a brief glowing uncensored moment in history when journalists exposed the ills of society, publishers provided the soapbox, people reacted with indignation, and politicians responded with corrective legislation. The first two decades of the 20th century were distinguished by the clamorous, sometimes sensationalized, efforts of investigative writers like Rheta Child Doss, Finley Peter Dunne, Frank Norris, Upton Sinclair, Lincoln Steffens, and Ida Tarbell. Their investigative style of journalism intrigued readers, exposed the widespread corporate and political corruption of the times, and paved the way for many of the social reforms that followed. While President Theodore Roosevelt applied the term "muckrakers" to journalists in a pejorative manner, today it is considered a mark of distinction among some reporters and authors such as Jessica Mitford. Unfortunately, except for the contributions of a few notable journalists, like Drew Pearson, George Seldes, and I.F. Stone, contemporary America has not enjoyed a comparable period of socially aware, concerned, and effective journalism.

1909 Appearing before the Select Committee of both Houses of Parliament which was considering censoring stage plays in 1909, George Bernard Shaw opened his testimony by citing his qualifications as a witness: "I am by profession a playwright...I am not an ordinary playwright in general practice. I am a specialist in immoral and heretical plays. My reputation has been gained by my persistent struggle to force the public to reconsider its morals. ... I object to censorship not merely because the existing form of it grievously injures and hinders me individually, but on public grounds." The statement, titled "The Necessity of Immoral Plays." was rejected by the Committee. Shaw subsequently published it as part of the preface to *The Shewing-Up of Blanco Posnet.* Shaw also pointed out, in *The Rejected Statement, Part I,* that "Assassination is the extreme form of censorship."

1911 From 1911 to 1926, the Hearst media empire used its various propaganda techniques to persuade the U.S. to declare war against Mexico. The public would have had a better understanding of Hearst's clamorous propaganda if it had known that his real motivation was to protect his family's land-holding of some 2500 square miles in Mexico against possible expropriation.

Apparently impressed by Hearst's endeavors, Colonel Robert Rutherford McCormick, owner of the *Chicago Tribune,* sent reporter George Seldes to Mexico in 1927 to cover the "coming war" with the United States. Seldes never did find a "war," but he did write a series of ten columns on the situation in Mexico. The first five echoed the official State Department line, supporting American business interests; the second five reported the other side of the issue which Seldes had observed or verified himself. Despite promises to publish all ten columns, the *Tribune* ran only the first five; disgusted with this obvious act of censorship, Seldes quit the *Tribune*.

1912 The first radio-licensing law was passed by Congress and signed by William Howard Taft. It authorized the Secretary of Commerce and Labor to assign wavelengths, time limits, and broadcast licenses. The only control at the time was a loose form of self-censorship by the stations whose taboos included lewd jokes and any discussion of birth control.

H.V. Kaltenborn, who lectured on current events over WEAF in New York became one of the first broadcasters to become embroiled in a controversy over the content of a radio talk. Kaltenborn had criticized Secretary of State Charles Evans Hughes regarding the way he had dealt with the Russians.

This led to a request from Washington, through the American Telephone and Telegraph Company, which leased the telephone lines to WEAF, that Kaltenborn be taken off the air. Recognizing the threat to its own best interests, WEAF acquiesced, and Kaltenborn left the station. AT&T saw nothing wrong with its actions; in fact, it acknowledged that it had "constant and complete" cooperation with governmental agencies and had indulged in censorship to maintain this cooperative relationship. The government's first attempt at electronic censorship was a resounding success.

Undaunted by the threat of censorship, radio expanded rapidly; by 1927 there were 733 stations and considerable interference on the broadcast bands. The near-chaotic situation ended with the passage of the Federal Radio Act of 1927, establishing the Federal Radio Commission (FRC). The Federal Communications Commission (FCC) was later established with passage of the Federal Communications Act of 1934.

1914 *The Woman Rebel*, a feminist newspaper edited by Margaret Sanger, advocated the practice of birth control. After five issues, it was stopped by the U.S. Post Office, which had the authority to censor the press at the time.

1917 The National Civil Liberties Bureau was founded and renamed the American Civil Liberties Union (ACLU) in 1920. The organization was created to deal with civil liberties problems arising out of World War I, including the Espionage and Sedition Acts, conscientious objectors, and political prisoners. It gained national recognition in the mid-1920s by defending the accused individuals in the Scopes trial, the Sweet case, and the Sacco-Vanzetti case. In 1988, it attracted national attention when presidential candidate George Bush resorted to red-baiting by referring derisively to "card-carrying members" of the ACLU.

1917 World War I kept Congress busy churning out legislation designed to prevent any conceivable sign or sound of disloyalty from occurring. First, the Espionage Act of June 15 provided heavy fines and imprisonment for anyone encouraging disloyalty or obstructing recruitment; in practice, it made it easier to jail Wobblies, communist sympathizers, and radicals. Next, on October 6, came the Trading-with-the-Enemy Act, which called for the censorship of all messages sent abroad and required domestic media containing articles in a foreign language to file sworn translations with local postmasters.

1918 Following on the heels of the two paranoia-induced decrees cited above came the Sedition Act of May 16. This made it unlawful to "utter, print, write, or publish any disloyal, profane, scurrilous, or abusive language about the form of the government of the United States, of the Constitution of the United States, or the uniform of the Army or Navy of the United States." As if this were not sufficient, President Woodrow Wilson authorized the formation of the Committee on Public Information (CPI), a propaganda machine headed up by George Creel, a journalist.

Now, for the first time, the brute forces of official censorship were buttressed by the slick techniques of propaganda, self-censorship, and disinformation, in what Creel called "a fight for the mind of mankind." And it worked. While the press eventually rejected CPI's manipulative efforts, most newspapers reportedly published all 6,000 press releases sent out by the CPI News Division.

In late November, *The Nation* magazine warned of the apparent control of the press not merely by the government and its legislation but also by the patriotic desire of the press itself to support the government in its efforts. This cheerleading function of the press was most recently observed during the Persian Gulf War in 1991.

1918 Lenin reintroduced censorship in the Soviet Union as a temporary emergency measure to protect the incipient Bolshevik regime against hostile propaganda, demonstrating how censorship is often rationalized as necessary for self-protection.

1918 The biggest censored story of World War I started on November 11, Armistice Day, when journalist George Seldes and three colleagues broke the Armistice regulations and drove into Germany to see what was happening.

Through luck and bravado, they managed to get an interview with Field Marshal Hindenburg. When Seldes asked him what ended the war, Hindenburg replied it was the American infantry attack in the Argonne that won the war. Without it, Germany would have held out much longer. As a form of punishment for breaking regulations, Seldes' story of

Hindenburg's confession was suppressed by military censors, with the support of other U.S. journalists angry because they had been scooped.

The historic interview was never published, except by Seldes, who believed it could have altered the course of history. Hitler built Nazism on what Seldes called a total lie, i.e. that Germany did not lose the war on the battlefield but rather because of the Dolchstoss, or stab-in-the-back "by civilians," "by the Socialists," "by the Communists," and "by the Jews." Had the world known of Hindenburg's confession, Hitler might not have so easily manipulated German citizens into supporting his cause. We'll never know what might have been because of a military censor.

1918 While there were many victims of the repressive censorship laws of World War I, Eugene V. Debs was one of the most famous. Founder of the Social Democratic Party in the United States and five-time presidential candidate (between 1900 and 1920), Debs was tried for espionage for opposing the war effort. His citizenship was revoked and he was sentenced to ten years in prison. While in jail in 1920, he ran for president as the Socialist candidate and received nearly a million votes. President Harding commuted his sentence on Christmas Day 1921.

1919 In a Supreme Court ruling in the espionage case *Schenck v. United States*, Justice Oliver Wendell Holmes, delivering the unanimous opinion of the Court, supported the ruling with the now-famed example of censorship warranted by a clear and present danger—"The most stringent protection of free speech would not protect a man in falsely shouting fire in a theatre and causing a panic."

1920 Walter Lippmann, an outstanding journalist, author, and ethicist of the time, issued an early warning about latter day journalists and media moguls in his essay, "Journalism and the Higher Law"—"Just as the most poisonous form of disorder is the mob incited from high places, the most immoral act the immorality of a government, so the most destructive form of untruth is sophistry and propaganda by those whose profession it is to report the news. The news columns are common carriers. When those who control them arrogate to themselves the right to determine by their own consciences what shall be reported and for what purpose, democracy is unworkable. Public opinion is blockaded."

1922 The Motion Picture Producers and Distributors of America (MPPDA) was formed as a self-censoring response to outside critics. The MPPDA, chaired by Will Hays, former Postmaster General and Chairman of the Republican National Committee, paved the way for the creation of a formal motion picture code in 1930.

1924 In *Literature and Revolution*, Leon Trotsky established the role of art in a revolutionary society as a service to the revolutionary state, with artists allowed to create in relative freedom but, of course, always under "watchful revolutionary censorship."

1925 John T. Scopes, a young high school teacher, was convicted of violating Tennessee's law that prohibited the teaching of biological evolution (Darwin's theory). In one of the most famous courtroom confrontations in American history, famed liberal attorney Clarence Darrow defended Scopes while William Jennings Bryan assisted the state with the prosecution. Scopes later was released on a technicality by the Tennessee State Supreme Court.

1927 The seeds for repressive censorship measures in Germany were sown when the Reichstag passed a morality law to protect young people from indecent prints and pictures. In the guise of maintaining morality among the youth, the law was used by the police to enter private homes, to supervise dancing in homes, and to protect children from parents. By the time the National Socialists came to power in 1933 with the appointment of Adolph Hitler as Chancellor, modern art was banned and leaders of the Expressionist movement were exiled.

1929 Boston earned its "Banned in Boston" epithet in late 1929 when a wave of censorship swept through the city resulting in what was called a "memorable wholesale book holocaust." Among the 68 books by prominent authors banned during that period were *What I Believe* by Bertrand Russell, *Oil* by Upton Sinclair, *An American Tragedy* by Theodore Dreiser, *Elmer Gantry* by Sinclair Lewis, *The Sun Also Rises* by Ernest Hemingway, and *Antic Hay* by Aldous Huxley.

1930 The Motion Picture Producers and Distributors of America (MPPDA) adopted its first Motion Picture Production Code (also known as the Hays Code after the head of the MPPDA). At first, adhering to it was strictly voluntary. Then, in 1933, in response to the National Legion of Decency—founded by the Catholic Church, which had started to review movies—the MPPDA established a stronger code and began to review all scripts. Acceptable films were given a Hays Office seal of approval.

In 1968, again in reaction to outside efforts at censorship, the Motion Picture Association of America (MPPDA became MPAA in 1948) developed a formal, but still voluntary, rating system of four categories: G for general audiences; PG for parental guidance suggested; R for restricted (children under 17 must be accompanied by a parent or guardian); and X (no one under 17 admitted). In 1984, the MPAA added a fifth category: PG-13 (parental guidance suggested for children under 13). In 1990, the X rating was revised to NC-17 (no children under 17 admitted). The X rating had become so popular among promoters of hard-core pornography, it was no longer suited for general use by the theaters.

Finally, in mid-1992, the MPAA revamped its ratings once again, this time to include explanations as to why films are given ratings other than G. For example, the MPAA gave the film "Christopher Columbus—The Discovery" a PG-13 rating, noting that it included "some action violence" and "nudity."

Since its inception in 1930, the MPAA has claimed that the ratings code is not designed to censor a film but rather to warn parents about the content of a film.

1933 James Joyce's celebrated novel *Ulysses* broke the historic barrier of customs censorship when the New York Federal District Court and the Circuit Court of Appeals ruled that it was not obscene within the meaning of federal statutes. Judge John Woolsey, of the District Court, said, "although it contains...many words usually considered dirty, I have not found anything that I consider to be dirt for dirt's sake."

1934 The Federal Communications Act established the Federal Communications Commission (FCC) to succeed the earlier Federal Radio Commission, granting it the right to renew a license as long as the broadcaster operated in the "public interest, convenience, and necessity." It was explicitly stated that the FCC would not have the authority of censor; however, it did have the authority to withhold a license from a broadcaster not operating in the "public interest." Thus, while the FCC could not prohibit liquor advertising, it could emphasize that a station that did advertise liquor, which children could hear, would have to prove that it was acting in the public interest to do so when its license came up for renewal. Not surprisingly, stations have not accepted liquor advertising since.

Although the FCC was not allowed to practice censorship, it wasn't long before advertisers discovered that they were not subject to the same restrictions. Cream of Wheat, which sponsored best-selling author Alexander Woollcott on CBS, received some complaints from listeners that Woollcott had made derogatory remarks about Adolph Hitler. When the author refused the advertiser's request to refrain from such remarks, his series was canceled.

1937 Automobile safety, essentially, has been a censored subject since the 1930s. Auto manufacturers haven't liked to acknowledge that driving can be hazardous to your health. Yet, in January 1937, Dr. Clair Straith, a plastic surgeon who specialized in treating facial injuries from auto accidents, published an article in the *American Medical Association Journal* warning of the dangers and suggesting ways the industry could make cars safer. Nonetheless, Detroit ignored the warnings and continued to stress power and speed.

Nearly three decades later, Ralph Nader, in *Unsafe At Any Speed*, wrote, "It is more than coincidental that radio, television, newspapers and magazines have so long ignored the role of vehicle design in producing...collisions." Not one out of 700 newspapers accepted the offer to run a serialization of his book. In September 1993, Health and Human Services Secretary Donna E. Shalala attributed a decrease in deaths from motor vehicle accidents to an increased use of safety belts and other safety devices and added, "We're now seeing how effective injury control programs and highway design can be."

1938 Information concerning the hazards of cigarette smoking was available as early as 1938 but was ignored, or censored, or played down by the media to such an extent that, even two decades later, only 44 percent of the public thought smoking was a cause of lung cancer. In 1994, 56 years after the hazards of smoking were first known, the national news media unleashed a torrent of information and exposés about the hazards of smoking, as noted in the introduction to "censored déjà vu stories" in Chapter 4. Ironically, even in the face of well-documented data, the tobacco manufacturers continue to deny such health hazards. Nonetheless, in 1994, cigarette consumption fell to its lowest level since World War II.

1938 The infamous House Un-American Activities Committee (HUAC) was founded under the chairmanship of Congressman Martin Dies, Jr. (D-TX) to "expose communist infiltration" in the Congress of Industrial Organizations (CIO) and in FDR's New Deal administration. This powerful congressional body was particularly successful in using the principle of guilt by association.

1938 *Fortune* magazine sent a copy of an editorial about hunger in America to six New York City daily newspapers; it warned of the dangers to a democracy when a third of its citizens were starving. The *New York Post* featured the editorial on its front page and noted that four of the six dailies, including *The New York Times*, completely ignored the story.

The issue continued to attract media attention even three years later when Senator Robert M. La Follette addressed the Senate saying that 45 million people were below the safety line in nutrition; in addition, "Twenty million families must live on not more than eight or nine cents per person per meal. About 14 percent of all American families must live on an average of five cents per person per meal." Again, *The New York Times*, which proudly claims that it prints "all the news that's fit to print," failed to report a word of this the next day.

1938 On Halloween night, October 31, CBS's "Mercury Theater on the Air" broadcast a realistic dramatization of H.G. Wells' science fiction masterpiece, *War of the Worlds*. The response by terrified listeners across the country confirmed the potential power of radio. While many listeners in 1938 believed alien creatures from Mars were invading the planet, an inferior 1994 clone, "Without Warning," a CBS-TV movie depicting the destruction of the earth by asteroids, failed to generate a similar panic.

1939 Communist dictator Joseph Stalin redefined the role of the artist in Russia to require active participation in the political guidance of the country. To accomplish this, Russian artists were expected to practice self-censorship in the interest of the state; those who didn't cooperate often vanished suddenly.

1940 On May 20, 1940, George Seldes—America's Emeritus Journalist and the most censored journalist in history—published Volume I, Number 1, of *In Fact*, a biweekly newsletter for "the millions who want a free press." The premiere issue exposed a secret meeting of 18 prominent American leaders who decided to "do their utmost to abrogate existing neutrality legislation," reprimanded the press for its failure to reveal how a major soap manufacturer had been caught "fooling the American people through fake advertising," and warned readers about Father Coughlin and his anti-Semitic hate campaign. George Seldes, hailed as the grandfather of the alternative press and the creator of modern investigative journalism, celebrated his 104th birthday in September 1994. He also is a former Project Censored judge.

1940 Morris Ernst, one of the nation's leading crusaders against censorship, compiled and categorized a comprehensive list of works censored in the United States. The list included some of the world's greatest classics, including works by Homer, Shakespeare, Whitman, and Darwin.

1940 The American Library Association (ALA) established the Committee on Intellectual Freedom, now called the Office for Intellectual Freedom, one of the nation's leading advocates of the First Amendment and free speech. Part of the committee's responsibility is to guard, protect, defend, and extend intellectual freedom.

1940 "The Outlaw," a sexy western starring a sultry Jane Russell in a push-up bra designed by Howard Hughes, was denied the film industry's "seal of approval" because, as one judge put it, Jane Russell's breasts "hung over the picture like a thunderstorm spread out over a landscape." While the film is now available in the 95 and 103 minute versions, no one appears to have a copy of the original uncensored 117-minute version. And it wasn't until 1994 that the push-up bra, re-introduced as the Wonderbra, attained the "junk food news" stature it deserved.

1941 The Manhattan Project, the research effort that led to the atomic bomb, was launched in total secrecy. Within a few years, more than a half-million people across the U.S. were involved in one of the most secretive scientific projects in history. The successful information-control practices employed by the Manhattan Project paved the way for the news management, manipulation, and obfuscation which has since characterized the nation's nuclear research, in peacetime as well as wartime. The longtime cover-up of the human radiation experiments, as noted in the introduction to Chapter 4, Censored Déjà Vu, is but one example of the "success" of those information-control techniques.

1941 An extraordinary two-year U.S. Senate investigation of the concentration of economic power in the U.S. concluded that the National Association of Manufacturers (representing large corporations) and the United States Chamber of Commerce were receiving favored treatment from the press. Although similar charges often have been made since then, America's corporate elite and the press continue to deny that such favored treatment exists.

1941 World War II censorship was initiated when President Franklin Delano Roosevelt created the U.S. Office of Censorship with Byron Price, former executive news editor of *The Associated Press*, as director. Price had the authority to censor all international communications, including mail, cable, and radio. At its peak, the postal section of his office had more than 10,000 employees. Nonetheless, there was little public outrage over censorship during WWII, the result of Price's successful efforts to encourage editors and publishers to practice "voluntary cooperation" with the censorship program.

That effort, along with the Office of War Information (OWI), a propaganda organization headed up by Elmer Davis, formerly with *CBS News* and *The New York Times*, co-opted the traditional negative reaction to information control. The fact that American citizens were more united behind the nation during WWII than WWI also aided the censorship effort. The Office of Censorship closed on August 15, 1945, a few hours after the surrender of Japan. Shortly after the end of the war, the OWI was succeeded by the United States Information Service, under the auspices of the State Department.

1947 "A Free and Responsible Press," a comprehensive and critical report on the status of the media, was issued by the Commission on Freedom of the Press, headed by Dr. Robert M. Hutchins, Chancellor of the University of

Chicago. The study, funded by a $200,000 grant from Henry Luce, owner of *Time* and *Life*, found free speech to be in grave danger—not so much from the government as from those who controlled access to the media. The report warned, "One of the most effective ways of improving the press is blocked by the press itself. By a kind of unwritten law the press ignores the errors and misrepresentation, the lies and scandals, of which its members are guilty." Not surprisingly, the landmark report was given a lukewarm reception by the press. Commenting on the press coverage of the Commission's report, Hutchins said, "Some treated it unfairly, some used untruthful headlines, and some just plain lied about it."

1947 The Dead Sea Scrolls, dating from approximately 22 B.C. to A.D. 100, were discovered in Wadi Qumran. They were almost immediately subjected to censorship by controlled access, which continued until 1991 when biblical scholars forced official researchers to share the information. Since then, access to the scrolls has increased, and by 1994 the Israel Antiquities Association was releasing microfiche and CD-ROM editions.

1947 Charlie Chaplin's "Monsieur Verdoux," a satirical film criticizing munitions makers and military leaders and espousing a more humanistic morality, drew protests and pickets by veterans and religious groups. The outcry resulted in the film's withdrawal from distribution. Chaplin, one of the world's greatest filmmakers and actors, whose impersonation of "the little tramp" created laughter everywhere it was shown, left the U.S. for a self-imposed exile in Switzerland.

1947 Prompted by allegations that the government was infiltrated by communist spies, President Harry S Truman issued an executive order establishing a loyalty-security program for government employees. The program paved the way for one of the nation's most repressive political periods, from 1949 to 1953, which came to be known as the McCarthy era, named after Senator Joseph McCarthy (R-Wisconsin). McCarthy, who incessantly charged that "card-carrying communists" had infiltrated our government from top to bottom, was one of the most feared and controversial men in U.S. Senate history. Following an historic television interview with consummate journalist Edward R. Murrow (see 1954), McCarthy was censured by the U.S. Senate on a vote of 67-22 and died a discredited disgrace in 1957.

1948 The Library Bill of Rights was adopted by the American Library Association to resist "all abridgment of the free access to ideas and full freedom of expression." With the First and Fourteenth Amendments to the Constitution as its foundation, the Bill took an unequivocal stand on the freedom to read and supported democracy in full measure, stating, "There should be the fullest practicable provision of material presenting all points of view concerning the problems and issues of our times, international, national, and local." America's librarians are the nation's first line of defense in the ongoing battle against censorship.

1948 Alfred Kinsey published *Sexual Behavior in the Human Male*, the first of the "Kinsey Reports," which influenced public attitudes toward sex, helped promote sexual freedom and expression, and, at the same time provided a major target for censors. The second report, *Sexual Behavior in the Human Female*, was published in 1953.

1948 The Universal Declaration of Human Rights was adopted by the General Assembly of the United Nations as "Article XIX." It holds that freedom of expression is not the property of any political system or ideology but is, rather, a universal human right, now defined and guaranteed in international law. Article 19 also became the name of an international human rights organization founded in England in 1986.

1949 Apparently seeing a threat of communism in certain murals on the walls of public buildings, Richard Nixon, then a Republican Congressman from California, wrote, "I believe a committee should make a thorough investigation of this type of art in government buildings with the view of obtaining removal of all that is found to be inconsistent with American ideals and principles." Nixon went on to even greater efforts at censorship as his career progressed.

1952 The Television Code, adopted by the National Association of Broadcasters, spoke eloquently about commercial television's responsibility to augment the "educational and cultural influence of schools, institutions of higher learning, the home, the church, museums, foundations, and other institutions devoted to education and culture." It also addressed the medium's specific responsibilities toward children and the community. The Code has since been subject to a number of interpretations and revisions. Potential dangers of censorship by the networks, affiliates, advertisers, and the government have yet to be addressed.

1953 On January 17, 1953, I.F. Stone published the first issue of *I.F. Stone's Weekly* in Washington, DC. Following in the footsteps of George Seldes, whom he cited as a mentor, Stone used his extraordinary investigative skills to criticize the U.S. government and its policies. The *Weekly* was an early and clamorous opponent to U.S. involvement in the Vietnam War. Stone's wit, wisdom, and outspoken criticism attracted more than 70,000 subscribers by the time the final issue was published in December 1971. They also attracted the attention of J. Edgar Hoover, the late FBI director, who ineffectually monitored Stone's activities for four decades.

1953 President Dwight D. Eisenhower, often maligned for his military background, warned of censorship during a talk at Dartmouth College: "Don't join the book burners. Don't think you are going to conceal faults by concealing evidence that they ever existed. Don't be afraid to go into your library and read every book as long as it does not offend your own ideas of decency. That should be the only censorship." In June 1953, in a letter to the American Library Association Convention, President Eisenhower wrote: "As it is an ancient truth that freedom cannot be legislated into existence, so it is no less obvious that freedom cannot be censored into existence."

1954 The evening of March 9, 1954, has been called television's finest hour. It was the night that Edward R. Murrow, on his weekly program "See It Now," permitted Senator Joseph R. McCarthy to destroy himself in front of millions of viewers. Murrow concluded his program saying, "The actions of the junior senator from Wisconsin have caused alarm and dismay amongst our allies abroad and given considerable comfort to our enemies. And whose fault is that? Not really his; for he didn't create this situation of fear, he merely exploited it and rather successfully. Cassius was right. 'The fault, dear Brutus, is not in our stars but in ourselves.'"

Referring to the years the press had permitted McCarthy to decimate Americans' civil rights, Murrow later said, "The timidity of television in dealing with this man when he was spreading fear throughout the land is not something to which this art of communication can ever point with pride. Nor should it be allowed to forget it." McCarthy was surely not the first demagogue to intimidate the press; nor will he be the last.

1957 The Supreme Court made its first significant effort to define obscenity. Until now it had worked with what was known as the Hicklin rule, a carry-over description of obscenity from British law, which ruled that obscenity had a tendency to deprave and corrupt those whose minds were open to such immoral influences (such as children) and into whose hands it might fall. In 1957, the Supreme Court replaced this extraordinarily strict interpretation of obscenity with what came to be known as the Roth-Memoirs Test. This ruling established three tests, or standards, for ruling a work obscene: 1) The dominant theme of the material, taken as a whole, appeals to an average person's prurient interest in sex; 2) the material is patently offensive because it affronts contemporary community standards, assuming a single national standard, relating to sexual matters; and 3) the material is utterly without redeeming social value. This test for obscenity, while less restrictive than Hicklin, permitted a wide range of legal maneuvering and remained in effect until 1973.

1958 In defending the absolutist theory of the First Amendment, which holds that "no law" means no law, William O. Douglas, Supreme Court Justice, wrote: "The First Amendment does not say that there is freedom of expression provided the talk is not 'dangerous.' It does not say that there is freedom of expression provided the utterance has no tendency to subvert. It does not put free speech and freedom of the press in the category of housing, sanitation, hours of work, factory conditions, and the like, and make it subject to regulation for the public good. Nor does it permit legislative restraint of freedom of expression so long as the regulation does not offend due process. All notions of regulation or restraint by government are absent from the First Amendment. For it says in words that are unambiguous, 'Congress shall make no law...abridging the freedom of speech, or of the press.'"

1959 D.H. Lawrence's novel, *Lady Chatterly's Lover*, first published in Italy in 1928, was banned by the Federal Post Office Department when published in New York in 1959. The New York Postmaster withheld some 200,000 copies of a circular announcing the new Grove Press edition of the book. The Federal Courts subsequently ruled that the book was not hard-core pornography and dismissed the banning restriction. *Lady Chatterly's Lover* and James Joyce's *Ulysses* are among the most important contemporary censorship cases. Both books, by noted literary artists, were subjected to obscenity charges; both were tried, appealed, and approved in federal courts; and both remain controversial to this day.

1959 Clarifying the distinction between freedom and pornography in a capitalist system versus a communist system, Soviet premier Nikita Khrushchev said, "This is a dance (the Can-Can) in which girls pull up their skirts. ... This is what you call freedom—freedom for the girls to show their backsides. To us it's pornography. The culture of people who want pornography. It's capitalism that makes the girls that way. ... There should be a law prohibiting the girls from showing their backsides, a moral law."

1960 A classic example of the misguided foolishness of news media self-censorship was provided by the events surrounding the Bay of Pigs disaster. In November 1960, editors of *The Nation* magazine tried to interest major news media in an article charging that the U.S. was preparing to invade Cuba, but no one took the story. While reports of the impending invasion were widely known throughout Central America, the American press followed the lead of *The New York Times* which dismissed the reports as "shrill...anti-American propaganda." Following the tragic, ill-fated invasion, President John F. Kennedy, who had persuaded the *Times* to withhold the story, acknowledged that had the press fulfilled its traditional watchdog role and reported the pending invasion, it would have saved the nation from a disastrous decision and the subsequent national disgrace; he told *The New York Times*: "If you had printed more about the operation, you could have saved us from a colossal mistake."

1960   *The New York Times vs Sullivan*—a landmark case in libel law, introduced the concept of malice in journalism. On March 29, 1960, *The New York Times* published a full-page ad signed by some 64 people who charged that thousands of black Southern students engaging in nonviolent protests had been deprived of their constitutional rights. The ad specifically cited an event that occurred in Montgomery, Alabama. L.B. Sullivan, the commissioner of public affairs in Montgomery at the time, filed a libel suit against The New York Times Company and others. In finding for *The Times*, Supreme Court Justice William J. Brennan Jr., said: "We are required in this case to determine for the first time the extent to which the constitutional protections for speech and press limit a State's power to award damages in a libel action brought by a public official against critics of his official conduct." In doing so in this case, the court ruled that it would be more difficult, under law, for a public official to win a libel suit than it is for a private citizen. The ruling now requires that the public official must prove that the statement was made with "actual malice"—that is, with knowledge that it was false, or with reckless disregard as to whether it was false. The 1981 movie, "Absence of Malice," starring Sally Field and Paul Newman, popularized this court decision regarding libel.

1963   Whatever the truth may be behind the assassination of President John F. Kennedy, the news media cannot justify their early and uncritical endorsement of the Warren Commission Report. Their initial attempts to silence the critics of the official version smacked of raw censorship. When a leading scholar offered to write an analysis of the commission's operations, *The New York Times* rejected the offer, saying, "The case is closed." Mark Lane's book on the same subject, *Rush To Judgment*, was not rushed to print. Lane could not find a publisher for 15 months and it was only published after the media decided the issue was acceptable for coverage as a "newsworthy controversy."

Lane's second book, *A Citizen's Dissent*, published in early 1968, records how his pleas for a national examination of the evidence were rejected by *Look, Life*, the *Saturday Evening Post* and others. When *UPI* was offered advance proof sheets, they replied they "would not touch it." This book provides what may be the most exhaustive and documented study ever undertaken of the mass media's use of hidden bias on one issue. Not surprisingly, three years after publication, Lane reported that he hadn't been able to discover "one newspaper story in the mass media noting that the book had been published." Lane said that several media representatives told him: "We will bury that book with silence." And they did.

Incredibly, the media's conspiracy-like efforts to attack anything critical of the original Warren Commission Report's interpretation of the assassination was still in evidence in 1991. The press, in what appeared to be a well-orchestrated campaign, left no stone unturned in its criticism of film producer and director Oliver Stone and his movie, "JFK," which did not support the commission's findings. The effort was so exceptional, Stone had to hire one of the nation's leading public relations firms, Hill & Knowlton, to counteract the attacks and defend himself.

Indicative of the extent of censorship surrounding the Kennedy assassination was the way Abraham Zapruder's eight-millimeter film of the assassination was handled. This extraordinary bit of footage, which recorded the actual assassination, raised serious questions about the Warren Commission's version of the event. The film, originally purchased by Time Inc. and later sold back to Zapruder, was not shown on national television until 1975, when it was aired on Tom Snyder's late-night "Tomorrow" show. In November 1994, the Zapruder film was placed in the Library of Congress' registry of American film. It was the first amateur film to be so honored.

1963 "The CBS Evening News" with Walter Cronkite was expanded to 30 minutes, becoming network TV's first half-hour nightly newscast. The evening TV news originally started in the mid-fifties as a 15 minute dose of headlines. In 1980, Ted Turner created the first 24-hour-a-day news programming with Cable News Network (CNN).

1966 In passing the Freedom of Information Act (FOIA), Congress established the American public's "right to know." It was signed into law by President Lyndon Johnson and went into effect on July 4, 1967. Unfortunately, years of information control and manipulation, as well as disdain for the FOIA by the Reagan/Bush administrations, encouraged federal agencies to find ways to circumvent it. Today, it can be extremely time-consuming and expensive for the public—as well as the press—to use it.

1966 At 10 a.m., on February 10, the U.S. Senate Foreign Relations Committee began hearings on the Vietnam war with the testimony of Ambassador George F. Kennan. Over the objections of Fred W. Friendly, president of *CBS News*, the network aired a fifth *CBS* rerun of "I Love Lucy" instead of the hearings. Because of that decision, Friendly quit *CBS* and subsequently wrote *Due to Circumstances Beyond Our Control...* to tell what happened. The book begins with a quotation: "What the American people don't know can kill them." And it did. More than 58,000 Americans died in Vietnam, and many tens of thousands of returned Vietnam veterans have died from war-related problems since.

1968 Dr. Paul Ehrlich's book *The Population Bomb* created a stir with its prediction that mass famines would plague the world within 20 years. Ehrlich warned that to avoid the tragedy of overpopulation, birth rates must be curbed. In 1971, media critic Robert Cirino, referring to Ehrlich's book, was equally prescient with his warning that "Experts have been making urgent pleas for controlling population and pollution for the last twenty-five years. But did the news media alert us in time?" Ehrlich's prediction has been tragically fulfilled with the African famines of the 1980s and 1990s, yet his warning continues to go unheeded. The earth's population is now growing at a rate of more than 100 million a year, and few people, including the press, seem to be aware that this is indeed a problem.

1968 The Columbia University Center for Mass Communications in New York offered all three networks a documentary using U.S. Army footage which depicted the horrifying effects of the atomic bomb on individual Japanese victims. The Army had suppressed the film since 1945 and only released it at the insistence of the Japanese government. The film was described by Columbia University Professor Sumner J. Glimcher as "perhaps the best argument for people to live in peace." All three networks rejected the offer to run the documentary, telling the University they just weren't interested; nor did they use the Army's film, which also was available to them, to produce a documentary of their own.

1968 On March 16, some 570 South Vietnamese civilians were slaughtered in Mylai by the U.S. military. Although the massacre was reported over the radio in South Vietnam and in French publications, neither the U.S. press nor that of any other country challenged the official Pentagon version that 128 "Reds" had been killed. Ronald Ridenhour, a former soldier, spent six months investigating the tragedy and talking to witnesses before trying to interest federal officials and the media in the story. He contacted the President, Secretary of State, Secretary of Defense, numerous congressmen, *Life, Look, Newsweek, Harper's*, major newspapers, two wire services, and at least one of the networks. Neither the politicians nor the media were interested.

By September 1969, nearly 18 months after the tragedy, David Leonard, a reporter for the *Columbus Enquirer*, followed up on a lead about Lt. William Calley Jr., and published a front-page story about him. Again the media ignored it, and the story died. In October, Seymour Hersh, then a freelance writer in Washington, DC, investigated the report and tried to sell his version to several publications, including *Life* and *Look*. Again they were not interested. He finally sold the story to the *Dispatch News Service*, which released it on November 13; at last, the media put the tragic massacre on the national agenda.

1968 On September 24, "60 Minutes" was launched on the CBS television network. The weekly hour-long program became known for its hard-hitting investigative reports and went on to become the most popular show in the history of television. The "father" of television news magazines celebrated its 26th anniversary in 1994.

1968 The critical need for mass media coverage of social problems, and the potential impact such coverage can have, was made clear when *CBS-TV News* broadcast a documentary, titled "Hunger in America." The documentary stirred a public debate, made hunger a national issue overnight, and had a lasting impact. The U.S. Department of Agriculture expanded its food program to more counties, increased its monthly surplus of food going to the poor, and called for an expansion of the food stamp program.

1968 "The Final Report: President's Task Force on Communications Policy," published December 7, was highly critical of the nation's commercial television system. It strongly recommended creating a television communications system that would ensure a diversity of ideas and tastes, so that all minorities and majorities could be represented on television. President Johnson refused to make the report public before he left office, and the new president, Richard Nixon, delayed its release for another four months, until May 1969. Neither Johnson nor Nixon should have been worried; when the media finally did get the report, they essentially suppressed the potentially explosive information. The *Los Angeles Times* "covered" the report in a two-inch article on Page 2 under the daily news roundup; *The New York Times* reported it under a small headline in the middle of Page 95.

1969 "The Smothers Brothers Comedy Hour," a weekly entertainment program, was canceled by CBS for failing to cooperate with the network's program-previewing policies. According to the brothers, the program was often censored by CBS, with up to 75 percent of a program being edited out before being aired. In one classic case of broadcasting censorship, as cited by Robert Cirino in his book *Power to Persuade*, CBS asked Pete Seeger, the famed folk singer who was blacklisted by broadcasters for 17 years, to drop the following verse from one of his songs on the Smothers Brothers program. It referred to the position in which the U.S. found itself in Vietnam in 1967:

> *But every time I read the papers*
> *That old feeling comes on;*
> *We're waist deep in the Big Muddy*
> *And the big fool says to push on.*

When Seeger refused to drop the verse, CBS censored the entire song, prompting Seeger to say, "It is wrong for anyone to censor what I consider my most important statement to date. ... I think the public should know that the airwaves are censored for ideas as well as for sex."

1969 In a letter to *The New York Times*, Charles Tower, chairman of the National Association of Broadcasters Television Board, proposed an interesting new definition of censorship. Tower criticized *The Times* for attacking CBS-TV for "censoring" social commentary on the Smothers Brothers show (see above). He suggested, "There is a world of difference between the deletion of program material by Government command and the deletion by a private party (such as a broadcaster). ... Deletion by Government command is censorship. ... Deletion of material by private parties ... is not censorship." While Tower's definition was spurious as well as self-serving, there are probably some who would support his thesis, even now.

1969 The U.S. Supreme Court granted specific protection for student expression rights. The Court's decision in *Tinker v. Des Moines Independent Community School District*, often called the "black armbands case," allowed students to wear black armbands as a symbolic expression of protest against the Vietnam war. The Court declared that neither students nor teachers "shed their constitutional rights to freedom of speech or expression at the schoolhouse gate."

1969 In August, the outrageous but historic three-day Woodstock Music and Art Fair in New York State paved the way for future rock festivals by showing it was possible to overcome censorship rules and regulations set-up by local authorities to prevent such festivals. In August 1994, a commercialized, plastic, 25th anniversary version of Woodstock failed to generate any reported efforts at censorship but it did become a nomination for "junk food news story" of 1994.

1969 On November 13, during a speech in Des Moines, Iowa, Vice President Spiro Agnew launched a series of scurrilous and unsubstantiated attacks on the nation's media, accusing them of favoring liberals. His stand was applauded by the vast majority of media owners who shared Agnew's opinion. These accusations are still used today to support the pervasive myth of "the liberal American media."

1970 Agnew continued his verbal assault, attacking the underground press, rock music, books, and movies for luring American youth into a drug culture. He told his audience, "You need a Congress that will see to it that the wave of permissiveness, the wave of pornography, and the wave of moral pollution never become the wave of the future in our country." In a speech in Las Vegas, he specifically criticized radio stations for playing songs that contain "drug culture propaganda." On March 5, 1971, the FCC issued a notice to broadcasters, holding them responsible for airing songs that would "promote or glorify the use of illegal drugs" and made it abundantly clear that any station ignoring this notice could lose its license.

1970 On May 4, four students protesting the Cambodian incursion during the Vietnam War were killed by the National Guard on the Kent State University campus in Ohio, a tragic example of the ultimate form of censorship—assassination.

1970 *How To Talk Back To Your Television Set*, a strident criticism of television by Nicholas Johnson, a former member of the FCC, cites a series of CBS-TV documentaries that were "shelved, turned down, or killed," including "a 'hard-hitting' documentary on homosexuals gutted before showing by the management. ... an 'in-depth investigation' of Saigon corruption, also tabled. ... film footage of North Vietnam rejected for broadcast. ... an hour production on [the] black middle class, dumped ... a project on 'Police Brutality,' turned into 'an industrial promo film for sponsor IBM' ... a probe of the military industrial complex, ultimately devoted to 'the nomenclature of military rockets.'" Johnson also noted that CBS had pending for several years a project on "Congressional ethics"; he wondered whether we'd ever see it. The relevancy of the subjects of those censored documentaries to today's social problems is self-evident.

1970 The President's Commission on Obscenity and Pornography failed to find evidence linking obscene materials to criminal behavior, a conclusion that led both President Richard M. Nixon and the U.S. Senate to reject the report. The lesson was not lost on President Ronald Reagan, who later appointed Attorney General Edwin Meese to direct his own Commission on Pornography in 1985.

1971 Robert Cirino, a secondary school teacher in San Fernando, California, published an extraordinary book, *Don't Blame the People: How the news media use bias, distortion and censorship to manipulate public opinion*. After being rejected by mainstream publishers, Cirino published the book himself. Following its success as a college textbook, it was picked up and published by Random House in 1972. Cirino's closing paragraph sums up the role of the press in America and suggests a solution:

"The effort to improve the quality of life in America has to be first the fight to save America from the distorted view of reality presented by the communication industry. It is a fight to restore the average man's participation in government by really letting him decide important questions. It is the average man, the man who doesn't have large corporate interests to protect, that is the strength of a democracy. His reasoning ability and sense of justice enacted into decisions and policies constitute the type of government envisioned by those who wrote America's Declaration of Independence. There has never been a better idea of governing a nation. Our major mistakes have not been the result of democracy, *but of the erosion of democracy made possible by mass media's manipulation of public opinion.* This erosion could only be stopped in the unlikely event that the Courts, the Congress and the American people were to demand that all political viewpoints have equal control over access to a mass communication system that is not for sale to anyone."

1971 On June 13, *The New York Times* started to print the Pentagon Papers, part of a top-secret 47-volume government study of decision-making on Vietnam. Two days later, *The Times* was barred from continuing the series. In pleading its right to publish the papers before the Supreme Court, *The Times*, in effect, appeared to abandon the First Amendment in proposing the establishment of guidelines for prior restraint. Supreme Court Justice William O. Douglas warned *The Times*: "The First Amendment provides that Congress shall make no laws abridging the freedom of the press. Do you read that to mean that Congress can make some laws abridging freedom of the press?" It was, added Justice Douglas, "a very strange argument for *The Times* to be making." On June 30, the Supreme Court, by a 6-3 vote, told *The Times* it could go ahead and print the rest of the material.

1971 In December, I.F. Stone, marking the end of a special era in journalism, published the last issue of *I.F. Stone's Weekly.* In his essay, "Notes On Closing, But Not In Farewell," Stone wrote: "To give a little comfort to the oppressed, to write the truth exactly as I saw it, to make no compromises other than those of quality imposed by my own inadequacies, to be free to follow no master other than my own compulsions, to live up to my idealized image of what a true newspaper man should be and still be able to make a living for my family—what more could a man ask?"

1971 "The Selling of the Pentagon," a hard-hitting CBS documentary, told the American people how much money the Pentagon was spending to buy a favorable public image for itself. Congress, particularly Rep. F. Edward Hebert, chair of the House Armed Services Committee, and members of the Nixon administration were outraged. When CBS-TV rebroadcast the show about a month later, it had to add 15 minutes of rebuttal from Hebert (who called it "un-American"), Vice President Spiro Agnew (who called it a "vicious broadside against the nation's defense establishment"), and Secretary of Defense Melvin Laird (often caricatured with a missile head). The House Committee on Interstate and Foreign Commerce unsuccessfully attempted to subpoena the film, and a committee vote to request a contempt citation against CBS had to be voted down.

1972 The break-in of the Democratic National Committee offices in the Watergate complex by the Republican CREEP (Committee to Re-elect the President) in June sparked one of the biggest political cover-ups in modern history. And the press, to its lasting shame, was an unwitting, if not willing, partner in the cover-up. The break-in, by CREEP employees known as the "plumbers," was described as a "two-bit burglary" not worthy of press attention. It didn't manage to get on the national news agenda until after November, when Richard Nixon was re-elected with a landslide vote. Carl Bernstein and Bob Woodward, both with the *Washington Post*, eventually made it a national story. Bernstein noted that out of some 2,000 full-time reporters for major news organizations, just 14 were assigned to the story on a full-time basis, even six months after the break-in. When Walter Cronkite tried to do an extraordinary two-part series on Watergate on the "CBS-TV Evening News," *before* the election, a phone call from the Nixon White House to Bill Paley, chair of CBS, resulted in Cronkite's scheduled program being reduced. The power of a President to directly intervene and censor the nation's leading broadcast news organization was revealed. Ironically, 21 years after the Watergate break-in, when the government released three additional hours of the tapes to the public, Nixon was heard plotting to deflect the blame for the break-in and calculating that Watergate was "a Washington son-of-a-bitching story" most Americans would shrug off.

1972 The Supreme Court ruled that dancing, even topless dancing, was a type of expression entitled to protection under the First Amendment. This judicial ruling encouraged the growth of topless, and eventually bottomless, dancing in bars throughout America.

1972 The Supreme Court ruled that the Central Intelligence Agency could preview its employees' speeches and publications to protect against any disclosure of classified information. In 1980, this ruling was expanded to include pre-publication review of all materials, including unclassified information. This decision was based on a case involving a former CIA agent who published a book criticizing U.S. actions during the Vietnam War. The book contained no classified information.

1972 The first issue of the *Index On Censorship* was published, acknowledging that "the need for such a magazine would become clear in the next few years"—and it has. *The Index*, an international advocate of free expression, focuses on the censorship, banning, and exile of writers and journalists throughout the world. In 1994, it was relaunched with a new format but without a change in its focus on international censorship.

1973 Beginning with the case of *Miller v. California*, the Supreme Court refined the Roth-Memoirs 1957 definition of obscenity, replacing national standards with local community standards. What is known as the Miller Test for obscenity is used today by American courts to determine whether a work is, by law, obscene. Written material is legally obscene under the following three conditions: 1) An average person, applying contemporary local community standards, finds that the work, taken as a whole, appeals to prurient interest; 2) The work depicts, in a patently offensive way, sexual conduct specifically defined by applicable state law; and 3) The material lacks serious literary, artistic, political, or scientific value.

1973 "Sticks and Bones"—a dramatic, filmed version of an award-winning stage drama about the homecoming of a blind Vietnam veteran and his callous reception—was scheduled to be shown on CBS on March 9. Just four days before air date, CBS executives postponed the program, saying it would be "unnecessarily abrasive to the feelings of millions of Americans whose lives or attention were dominated at the time by the returning POWs and other veterans." Joseph Papp, producer of the film, called the postponement "a cowardly cop-out, a rotten affront to freedom of speech." When the drama was finally shown five months later, only 91 affiliate stations carried it (less than half of the 184 that normally would carry the network's programs). Many advertisers canceled their commercials.

1975 Ruling on the constitutionality of a Tennessee ban on the rock musical "Hair," the U.S. Supreme Court decided that live theater had legal protection against prior restraint, as was the case with books, movies, and other forms of expression.

1976 Project Censored, the national media research project focusing on news media censorship, was founded by Carl Jensen, Ph.D., at Sonoma State University, Rohnert Park, California. The top ten *Censored* stories of 1976 were:
1. Jimmy Carter and the Trilateral Commission
2. Corporate Control of DNA
3. Selling Banned Pesticides and Drugs to Third World Countries
4. The Oil Price Conspiracy
5. The Mobil Oil/Rhodesian Connection
6. Missing Plutonium and Inadequate Nuclear Reactor Safeguards
7. Workers Die for American Industry
8. Kissinger, the CIA, and SALT
9. Worthless or Harmful Non-prescription Drugs
10. The Natural Gas "Shortage"

1976 On June 2, Don Bolles, investigative reporter for the *Arizona Republic* was permanently "censored" when his car exploded in the parking lot of the Hotel Chardon in Phoenix. Bolles was investigating a lead dealing with massive land frauds, political payoffs, the underworld, and corporate crime. Following the assassination, nearly 100 journalists, organized as the Investigative Reporters and Editors Inc. (IRE), produced a 23-installment series on crime and corruption in Arizona. John Harvey Adamson, who admitted to planting the dynamite under Bolles' car, testified that Bolles was killed as a favor to Kemper Marley, one of Arizona's richest and most powerful figures and a target of Bolles' exposés. Ironically, in 1993, the University of Arizona named one of its buildings after Kemper Marley following a $6 million contribution to the university. Marley died in 1990 at 83.

1977 The FCC outlawed a monologue, "Seven Words You Can't Say On Radio" by comedian George Carlin, from being broadcast on radio or television. While the words still have shock value in print, they're surely not strangers on television, particularly on cable. The seven words that assured Carlin of lasting First Amendment fame were "shit," "piss," "fuck," "cunt," "cocksucker," "motherfucker," and "tits."

1977 When the ACLU defended the rights of the Nazi party to demonstrate in Skokie, near Chicago, 15 to 20 percent of ACLU members dropped their membership in protest. While the Illinois Appellate Court gave the Nazis permission to demonstrate but not to wear the swastika, the Illinois Supreme Court subsequently ruled that the Nazis had a right to display the swastika.

1977 The problem of decommissioning nuclear power plants—one of Project Censored's top ten censored stories of 1977—wasn't discovered until some of the original plants and reactors had to be shut down. In two cases, the costs for dismantling the plant ran almost as high as the original construction costs. Decommissioning nuclear power plants remains an unresolved and under-covered issue in 1995.

1978 The specter of sterility was raised when researchers discovered that the average sperm count among American men had dropped substantially since a landmark study done less than 30 years earlier. The research revealed that the probable causes were industrial and agricultural chemicals similar to the DBCP pesticide (which, earlier, had led to male sterility at a chemical plant), and that the trend may represent a potential sterility threat to the entire male population. The threat, one of the top ten *Censored* stories of the year, wasn't dramatic enough to attract the attention of the mass media at the time. However, in mid-September, 1992, a new study made front-page news when a growing number of scientists concluded that changes in sexuality, including reduced fertility, may have occurred in humans exposed to chemical pollution. Nonetheless, a "20/20" segment on ABC-TV on August 26, 1994, concluded that still more studies were needed.

1979 The longest period of government censorship by prior restraint of a publication in U.S. history began March 9. A Federal District Court in Wisconsin imposed a temporary restraining order on *The Progressive*, a Wisconsin-based monthly magazine, censoring publication of the article, "The H-Bomb Secret: How We Got It, Why We're Telling It." The government claimed that the description of how a hydrogen bomb was designed would help foreign countries produce H-bombs more swiftly. But the government finally acknowledged the true intent of the First Amendment on September 17, when it ruled the magazine could publish the article.

1979 To find cheap labor and to escape U.S. health and safety regulations, increasing numbers of major American corporations set up branches or contracted jobs under "sweatshop" conditions in Third World countries. This story—one of the top ten *Censored* stories of 1979—attracted national attention during the 1992 presidential election year, as unemployment plagued workers in the U.S., and health problems and environmental pollution threatened workers in Third World countries.

1980 The top *Censored* story of 1980, "Distorted Reports of the El Salvador Crisis," launched more than a decade of top ten *Censored* stories dealing with underreported or biased reports of U.S. intervention in Central America.

1981 The American people were told that the over-regulation of business and the "declining moral fiber of the American worker" had caused the worst economic crisis since the depression. But Maurice Zeitlin, a UCLA economic sociologist, testifying before the California Senate Committee on Industrial Relations, charged that we no longer had a competitive economy, and that monopoly, militarism, and multinationalization were at the root of our economic crisis. His testimony, cited as the top *Censored* story of 1981, also suggested that we could expect more of the same until the root causes are examined and changed.

1982 President Reagan established an oppressive system of security classification with his Executive Order 12356. It reversed a trend toward openness on the part of previous administrations by eliminating what was known as the balancing test. Now it was no longer necessary to weigh the public's need to know against the need for classification. In addition, the Executive

Order reduced the threshold standard for classification. That same year, Project Censored cited Reagan as "America's Chief Censor" for his efforts to reduce the amount of information available to the public about the operation of the government, the economy, the environment, and public health, and for his attempts to weaken the Freedom of Information Act.

1982 *The Media Monopoly*, by Ben Bagdikian, was published, revealing that just 50 corporations control half or more of the media in America.

1983 National Security Decision Directive 84 (NSDD 84), issued by the Reagan Administration in March, required all government personnel with access to classified materials to sign a lifetime secrecy pledge.

1984 Fulfilling the Orwellian expectations of the year, President Reagan implemented NSDD 84—the largest censoring apparatus ever known in the United States. For the first time in history, millions of federal employees were required to submit their speeches, articles, and books for prepublication review by their superiors for the rest of their lives. Under pressure from Congress, the administration suspended the pre-publication review provision in September 1984, but a 1986 General Accounting Office report on its impact concluded that the suspension had little effect, and that pre-publication review was alive and well in America.

1984 On September 14, CBS reporter Mike Wallace appeared on the "Phil Donahue Show" and predicted that one of the segments he was working on for "60 Minutes" could possibly change the course of the presidential election. The story focused on one of Ronald Reagan's closest friends, Nevada Senator Paul Laxalt, who was high on Reagan's list of potential Supreme Court nominees. Journalists investigating Laxalt found he had accepted political contributions from supporters linked to organized crime, received highly questionable loans, tried to limit FBI investigations into Nevada gaming operations and owned a Carson City casino that engaged in illegal skimming operations. After being contacted by Laxalt and his attorney, CBS decided not to run the story. And although the story didn't have a chance to change the course of the 1984 election, as predicted by Wallace, Ronald Reagan never nominated Laxalt to the Supreme Court.

1985 President Ronald Reagan appointed Attorney General Edwin Meese to head his Commission on Pornography. The members, reportedly handpicked for their support of censorship, spent considerable time investigating erotic films, books, and magazines protected by the First Amendment. Based on the testimony of the Rev. Donald Wildmon, executive director of the National Federation of Decency, the commission sent a letter to 26 major corporations, including K-mart, Southland (7-Eleven stores), and Stop N Go Stores, that accused them of selling and distributing pornography by selling publications such as *Playboy* and *Penthouse*. A U.S. District Court subsequently ruled that the commission had threatened the First Amendment rights of magazine publishers and distributors and ordered the letter withdrawn. In 1994, a U.S. District Court in Los Angeles struck a blow for readers' rights when it overturned a ban on sexually explicit magazines at Los Angeles fire stations, saying the First Amendment gives firefighters the right to read publications such as *Playboy*.

1985 The drive for profits, coupled with the apparent collapse of the FCC, led to a frenzy of media mergers and paved the way for an international information monopoly. Consumer advocate Ralph Nader warned of the increased threat of censorship resulting from conglomerate self-interest: "Self-censorship is alive and well in the U.S. media."

1986 The American Library Association (ALA) charged the Reagan administration with efforts to eliminate, restrict, and privatize government documents; with launching an official new "disinformation" program that permitted the government to release deliberately false, incomplete and misleading information; and with developing a new category of "sensitive information," restricting public access to a wide range of previously unclassified data. While the ALA charges were accurate and well-documented, they were ignored by the major news media.

1986 FAIR, Fairness & Accuracy In Reporting, an anti-censorship organization based in New York, was formed to shake up the establishment-dominated media. It draws attention to important news stories that have been neglected or distorted by the media, and defends working journalists when they are muzzled.

1986 Article 19, an international human rights organization named after Article XIX of the Universal Declaration of Human Rights (see 1948), was founded in London to document and fight censorship on an international basis. The UN declaration holds that "Everyone has a right to freedom of opinion and expression; this right includes freedom to hold opinions without interference and to seek, receive and impart information and ideas through any media regardless of frontiers."

1986 The final report of Attorney General Edwin Meese's Commission on Pornography was released. As expected, it simply ignored the First Amendment. But what can you expect from Edwin Meese, the subject of a 1984 *Censored* story that charged him with directing a secret operation involving a variety of illegal and unconstitutional activities while a California state official in the late '60s and early '70s. The effort was aimed at subverting the anti-war movement in California.

1987 The continuing centralization of media ownership raised critical questions about the public's access to a diversity of opinion as Ben Bagdikian updated his 1982 book, *The Media Monopoly*. He found that just 26 corporations now controlled the majority of America's media enterprises. Bagdikian also predicted that by the 1990s, a half dozen giant firms would control most of the world's media.

1988 In what many consider to be an unconstitutional ruling, the U.S. Supreme Court's *Hazelwood* decision provided renewed support for censorship through the use of prior restraint. In essence, the court gave high school administrators the power to censor student publications in advance. The ruling reversed a long-time trend of First Amendment support for freedom of expression issues on high school campuses. Oddly enough, this violation of the First Amendment has been ignored by the major news media. Despite widespread on-going student protest, it is still unchallenged in 1995.

1988 Top *Censored* story of this election year revealed how the major mass media ignored, overlooked, or undercovered at least ten critical stories reported in America's alternative press that raised serious questions about the Republican candidate, George Bush. The stories dated from his reported role as a CIA "asset" in 1963 to his Presidential campaign's connection with a network of anti-Semites with Nazi and fascist affiliations in 1988.

1988 Author Salman Rushdie's novel, *The Satanic Verses*, was attacked by Muslims for sacrilege and blasphemy. On February 14, 1989, the Ayatollah Khomeini issued a "fatwa," or death sentence, on Rushdie who went into hiding. Khomeini died four months later of cancer. On February 14, 1994, the fifth anniversary of Khomeni's death sentence, Iranian leaders publicly renewed their pledge to find and kill Rushdie, saying the late Khomeini's death decree would never be rescinded. In a similar case, feminist author Taslima Nasrin went into hiding in her native Bangladesh in June 1994 after Muslim extremists offered a $5,000 reward for her death. Extremist groups were infuriated by a report that Nasrin had called for a revision of the Koran, the Islamic holy book. Nasrin said she was misquoted but had called for changes in strict rules that limit Bangladeshi women to housework and child-rearing. On August 10, Nasrin fled to Sweden where she vowed to continue her fight against Muslim extremism.

1989 Fulfilling his 1987 predictions about world media conglomerates, Ben Bagdikian revealed in a well-documented article in *The Nation* that five global media lords already dominated the fight for hundreds of millions of minds throughout the world. Further, these media monopolies conceded that they may control most of the world's important newspapers, magazines, books, broadcast stations, movies, recordings, and video cassettes by the turn of the century. The Big Five of 1989:

Time Warner Inc., the world's largest media corporation
German-based Bertelsmann AG, owned by Reinhard Mohn
Rupert Murdoch's News Corporation Ltd., of Australia
Hatchette SA, of France, world's largest producer of magazines
U.S.-based Capital Cities/ABC Inc.

1990 In April, for the first time in history, an American museum and its director faced criminal charges for pandering obscenity. Their crime was a display of erotic photographs by Robert Mapplethorpe. The director, Dennis Barrie, and the Contemporary Arts Center in Cincinnati were both acquitted of pandering in October. Cincinnati earned its name "Censornati."

1990 The flawed coverage of events leading up to the Persian Gulf crisis was the top *Censored* story of the year. Traditional press skepticism of government/military activities was the first casualty in the days immediately following Iraq's invasion of Kuwait as the U.S. media became cheerleaders for the Bush Administration.

1991 For the second year in a row, the top *Censored* story of the year focused on the Gulf War. It revealed how the networks rejected uncensored videotape footage of the heavy Iraqi civilian damage, the result of American-led bombing campaigns. Instead, the networks continued to publicize the Pentagon-approved, high-tech, smart-bomb, antiseptic, non-threatening version of the war. The second overlooked story of the year revealed a number of specific Gulf War issues that didn't receive the coverage they deserved, while the #6 story provided photographic evidence that challenged President Bush's original explanation for our rapid deployment in the Gulf.

1991 On May 24, the Supreme Court, in a ruling as unconstitutional as its earlier *Hazelwood* decision, upheld a Reagan administration interpretation of Title X, the Public Health Services Act, that prohibited abortion counseling at federally funded family planning clinics. The 1987 interpretation suggested that Title X "required physicians and counselors to withhold information about abortion even from patients who were at medical risk from continuation of the pregnancy." The Court ruled that the word "abortion" cannot be uttered in any of America's 4,500 federally supported clinics that provide aid and counseling to millions of poor women. In essence, the United States Supreme Court ruled that First Amendment free speech rights are a function of federal funding. The abortion "gag rule" was repealed by President Clinton in January 1993.

1991 The introduction to the *Article 19 Yearbook of 1991* (see 1986) provides some sobering statistics about censorship on an international scale. In 62 of the 77 countries surveyed for the report, people were detained for peacefully expressing their opinions. In 27 of the countries, people, including journalists, were reportedly tortured, killed, or otherwise maltreated on account of their opinions.

1991 In the introduction to Volume IV of *The Right To Know*, published in 1992 by the DataCenter, in Oakland, California, Zoia Horn, a long-time champion of intellectual freedom and the public's right to know, made the following comments about how we "celebrated" the 200th anniversary of the Bill of Rights in 1991: "The 200th anniversary of the Bill of Rights should have been the occasion for a reaffirmation of democratic principles. Unfortunately, it fizzled into just another public relations campaign profiting Philip Morris, Inc., the sponsor of a widely viewed exhibit. Many people polled during the Persian Gulf war saw no contradiction between the censorship and manipulation of the media by the Pentagon, and the Bill of Rights. Indeed, previous polls have revealed that people on the street, asked to read the Bill of Rights, thought it was a communist document, and thus rejected parts of it. Ignorance of our basic democratic tenets requires a serious, massive, educational campaign at all age levels, through all mediums of communication."

1992 The Department of Defense and a group of self-selected media executives agreed on nine out of ten ground rules for press coverage of America's next military engagement. The contested and unresolved issue concerned prior restraint on the part of the military. The policy, which apparently "supplements" the First Amendment, evolved from the pool concept of censorship developed by the Reagan administration for the Grenada War, subsequently refined by the Bush administration for the Panama invasion, and finally given a full-scale test during the Gulf War—where it failed.

1992 The Center for the Study of Commercialism (CSC) invited 200 media outlets to a press conference to be held on March 11 in Washington, DC. The purpose was to reveal how advertisers, one of the nation's most powerful media voices, influence, corrupt, and censor a free press. Not a single radio or television station or network sent a reporter and only two newspapers, the *Washington Post* and the *Washington Times*, bothered to attend. The *Post* didn't run a story on the press conference while the *Times* (also known as the Capital's Moonie Paper since it is owned by Sun Yung Moon) ran one but didn't name the advertisers cited in the CSC study. The well-documented study, which has been seen by few Americans, was titled "Dictating Content: How Advertising Pressure Can Corrupt A Free Press."

1992 In the June introduction to "Less Access To Less Information By and About the U.S. Government: XVIII," the American Library Association, Washington Office, reflected on how the Reagan/Bush administrations have significantly limited access to public documents and statistics and warned that it might get worse, given the increasing commercialization of what was once public information. By contrast, in the June 1993 introduction, the ALA reported that in its first year in office, "the Clinton Administration has improved public access to government information." However, it also added, there are still barriers to access.

1993 In his latest update on the increasing monopolization of the media, the Fourth Edition of *The Media Monopoly*, Ben Bagdikian reported that fewer than 20 corporations now own and control the majority of the media in America.

1993 Franklyn S. Haiman, John Evans Professor Emeritus of Communication Studies at Northwestern University and leading First Amendment scholar, systematically challenges the criminalization of purely expressive behavior, sometimes referred to as speech act theory, because it is felt to be offensive, provocative, or even dangerous. In his book *"Speech Acts" and the First Amendment*, Haiman persuasively argues that controlling speech is neither constitutional nor effective as a means of preventing antisocial conduct.

1993 Reminiscent of an attempt to censor a film titled "Kiss," nearly a century ago (see 1896), the director of a children's theater in Dallas ordered a kiss eliminated from a wedding scene after a businessman complained because the actor was black and the actress was white. The actor went ahead and kissed his "bride" in the production of "Ramona Quimby" anyway, and, after a flood of complaints, the director officially reinstated the kiss in the performance. The specious grounds for kiss-censorship moved from race to gender in 1994 when a kissing scene between two men on the May 18 episode of television's "Melrose Place" was cut from the final production.

1993 An ABC-TV movie about a Marine held hostage during the Vietnam war was itself held hostage for more than two years. "The Last P.O.W.: The Bobby Garwood Story" was finally broadcast on June 28, about two and a half years after its originally scheduled air date. ABC reportedly felt "it was inappropriate to air it" in early 1991 during the Gulf War since it raised questions about patriotism. The rationale sounds much the same as that given for the CBS censorship of "Sticks and Bones" in 1973.

1993 Robert Maynard, 56, a high school dropout who rose to become the first African-American owner-publisher of a major metropolitan daily newspaper, died of cancer. Before buying the *Oakland Tribune*, Maynard was a pioneering black journalist and founder of the Institute for Journalism Education in Oakland, which has trained more than 600 minority journalists to be reporters, editors and managers. Maynard also had served as a judge for Project Censored.

1993 The Uniform Defamation Act, a complex and widely criticized approach to reforming libel law across the country, was replaced with a version more acceptable to the media. The Uniform Correction or Clarification of Defamation Act of 1993 allows for the publication of a correction or clarification to mitigate damages, or even to settle a claim completely, and it sets up a framework and timetable for the process.

1993 In September, the Pontifical Council for Social Communications, of the Roman Catholic Church, based in Vatican City, announced that it was going to take a long, very official look at truth and ethics in advertising. While advertising industry officials claim they are not concerned, others recall the impact of the National Legion of Decency, founded by the Catholic Church in 1933, on the film industry.

1993 IRE (Investigative Reporters & Editors) announced one of its most ambitious projects ever with the development of a computerized bulletin board service that would provide a comprehensive news and information library available to journalists throughout the world.

1993 The top *Censored* story of the year focused on the failure of the mass media to widely report that the United States had become one of the most dangerous places in the world for young people. A study by the United Nations Children's Fund revealed that nine out of ten young people murdered in industrialized countries are slain in the U.S.

1994 In late March, 70 leading editors, publishers, politicians, lawyers, and scholars at the First Hemispheric Conference on Free Expression, meeting in Mexico City, declared that "A society of free individuals cannot remain free without free speech and freedom of the press." Asserting there must be no law abridging freedom of speech or press, and supporting it with ten basic principles, the historic document reinforces the Universal Declaration of Human Rights adopted on December 10, 1948, by the General Assembly of the United Nations as "Article XIX" (see 1948). The Inter American Press Association, meeting in Guatemala City a week after the Hemispheric conference, declared its support for the declaration and endorsed a plan to ask the leaders of all governments in the Western Hemisphere to sign the document.

1994 On May 3, the right of reviewers and other journalists to express their opinions was upheld in a remarkable ruling by the U.S. Court of Appeals for the District of Columbia. Admitting to a "mistake of judgment," the court reversed its ruling of February 18 which found *The New York Times* guilty of libeling author Dan E. Moldea in a review of his book on the National Football League and organized crime. In doing so, the Court reinforced the First Amendment rights of journalists, as well as reviewers, to publish their opinions.

1994 In an historic, unanimous First Amendment decision, issued on June 13, the Supreme Court advanced the free speech rights of all Americans. The court unanimously ruled that cities may not bar residents from posting signs on their own property. The case began when the community of Ladue, Missouri, refused to permit a resident to display an 8 x 11 *inch* sign in an upstairs window of her house. The simple little sign read: "For Peace in the Gulf."

1994 The U.S. Supreme Court ruled that television cable operators have the same rights and protections under the Constitution as other media. In ruling on the *Turner Broadcasting System Inc. v. Federal Communications Commission* case, the Court concluded that cable programmers and cable operators engage in and transmit speech and thus are entitled to the protection of the First Amendment.

1994 On July 29, the Interactive Digital Software Association announced a video game rating system for games on cartridges, compact discs, and diskettes, based on samples of content. The categories include Early Childhood, ages 3+; Kids to Adults, ages 6+; Teens, ages 13+; Mature, ages 17+; and Adults only.

1994 On August 15, the "Voice of America," the official U.S. Information Agency (USIA) propaganda arm of the U.S. Department of State, started to offer digital audio newscasts in 15 foreign languages over the Internet, the reputedly uncontrollable international network of computer networks. Since the USIA is officially prohibited from distributing program materials in the U.S., the Internet carries a disclaimer warning that the material is "provided exclusively for recipients outside the United States."

1994 *Amerika*, the monthly magazine published by the U.S Information Agency, was another casualty of the end of the Cold War when it folded in September 1994 after 38-years of publication. William Harwood, deputy public affairs office at USIA, said the publication, originally designed to counter Soviet propaganda, "was about the only thing you could read that wasn't filled with propaganda."

1994 One of the most important libel trials in modern media history continued through 1994. Psychoanalyst Jeffrey Masson had sued journalist Janet

Malcolm for libel by misquoting him in a 1983 *New Yorker* magazine article. The first round ended in June 1993, when a jury found that five quotes attributed to Masson had been fabricated or distorted and that Malcolm was aware that two of them were libelous. The second round ended in September 1993, when a U.S. District Judge dismissed Masson's suit against the *New Yorker* but granted a new libel trial to Malcolm. The third round ended November 2, 1994, when a federal jury cleared Malcolm of libeling Masson. However, this might not be the end of the decade-long libel suit since Masson announced a week later that he would seek a third trial. And on November 29, 1994 the *San Francisco Chronicle* reported that Masson was hired to co-teach an ethics class at the University of California journalism school in Berkeley. Stay tuned.

1994 President Bill Clinton signed an executive order on November 10 approving the declassification of 44 million documents stored at the National Archives. There are still some 281 million pages of classified material from before 1964 and hundreds of millions more held by the Pentagon, Central Intelligence Agency, and other executive branch agencies.

1994 The Supreme Court limited the range of free speech on November 14 when it reversed a Circuit Court of Appeals ruling that said City College of New York violated Professor Leonard Jeffries' free-speech rights when it removed him as chairman of CCNY's black-studies department. Jeffries was accused of making an anti-Semitic speech.

1994 In late December, Random House announced it would publish A *Long Fatal Love Chase*, a novel by Louisa May Alcott that had been censored more than a century earlier for being too sensational.

1994 On December 20, the British Broadcasting Corporation, a state-owned television company, announced it would launch a 24-hour international information and news service, called the BBC World Channel, on U.S. cable television, starting on Cable USA, a Midwestern cable network.

1994 The top *Censored* story of the year revealed that the National Institute for Occupational Safety and Health (NIOSH) had still not notified some 169,000 American workers that they had been exposed to hazardous materials at their worksites as discovered during NIOSH studies in the early 1980s.

THE WRITER AND THE ASTERISK

A writer owned an Asterisk,
And kept it in his den,
Where he wrote tales (which had large sales)
Of frail and erring men;
And always, when he reached the point
Where carping censors lurk,
He called upon the Asterisk
To do his dirty work.

Stoddard King (1889-1933)

BIBLIOGRAPHY TO CHRONOLOGY

American Library Association, Washington Office. "Less Access To Less Information By and About the U.S. Government: XVIII and XXI." Washington, DC.: American Library Association, June 1992 and June 1993.

Attorney General. "Commission on Pornography Final Report, July 1980, Vol. I & II." Washington, DC: U.S. Department of Justice, 1980.

Bagdikian, Ben H. *The Information Machines: Their Impact on Men and the Media.* New York: Harper & Row, 1971.

Bagdikian, Ben H. *The Effete Conspiracy and Other Crimes By the Press.* New York: Harper & Row, 1972.

Bagdikian, Ben H. *The Media Monopoly.* Boston: Beacon Press, 1983, 1992.

Bartow, Edith Merwin. *News and These United States.* New York: Funk & Wagnalls Company, 1955.

Black, Jay, and Jennings Bryant. *Introduction to Mass Communication,* Third Edition. Dubuque, Iowa: Wm. C. Brown Publishers, 1992.

Boyle, Kevin, ed. *Article 19: Information, Freedom and Censorship.* New York: Times Books, 1988.

Busha, Charles H., ed. *An Intellectual Freedom Primer.* Littleton, Colorado: Libraries Unlimited, Inc., 1977.

Cirino, Robert. *Don't Blame the People.* Los Angeles: Diversity Press, 1971. (Later published by Random House, 1972.)

Cirino, Robert. *Power To Persuade: Mass Media and the News.* New York: Bantam Books, 1974.

Curry, Richard O., ed. *Freedom at Risk: Secrecy, Censorship, and Repression in the 1980s.* Philadelphia: Temple University Press, 1988.

D'Souza, Frances, Editorial Team Director. *Article 19: Information Freedom and Censorship.* Chicago: American Library Association, 1991.

DeGrazia, Edward. *Censorship Landmarks.* New York: R.R. Bowker Co., 1969.

Downs, Robert B., ed. "The First Freedom." Chicago: American Library Association, 1960.

Emery, Edwin. *The Press and America: An Interpretative History of the Mass Media,* Third Edition. Englewood Cliffs, New Jersey: Prentice-Hall, Inc., 1972.

Ernst, Morris L. and Alexander Lindey. *The Censor Marches On.* New York: Da Capo Press, 1971.

Friendly, Fred. *Due To Circumstance Beyond Our Control...* New York: Vintage Books, 1967.

Goetz, Philip W. *The New Encyclopædia Britannica.* Chicago: Encyclopædia Britannica, Inc., 1991.

Haiman, Franklyn S. *"Speech Acts" and the First Amendment.* Carbondale: Southern Illinois University Press, 1993.

Hentoff, Nat. *The First Freedom: The Tumultuous History of Free Speech in America.* New York: Delacorte Press, 1980.

Hoffman, Frank. *Intellectual Freedom and Censorship: An Annotated Bibliography.* Metuchen, New Jersey: Scarecrow Press, 1989.

Horn, Zoia, Nancy Gruber, and Bill Berkowitz, eds. *The Right To Know, Volume 4.* Oakland, California: Data Center, 1992.

Hoyt, Olga G. and Edwin P. *Freedom of the News Media.* New York: The Seabury Press, 1973.

Jansen, Sue Curry. *Censorship: The Knot That Binds Power and Knowledge.* New York: Oxford University Press, 1988.

Jenkinson, Clay. "From Milton to Media: Information Flow in a Free Society." Media&Values. Spring 1992.

Johnson, Nicholas. *How To Talk Back To Your Television Set.* New York: Bantam Books, 1970.

Kendrick, Alexander. *Prime Time: The Life of Edward R. Murrow.* Boston: Little, Brown and Company, 1969.

Kent, Allen and Harold Lancour, eds. *Encyclopedia of Library and Information Science, Volume 4.* New York: Marcel Dekker, 1970.

Knight, Arthur. *The Liveliest Art: A Panoramic History of the Movies.* New York: New American Library, 1957.

Lee, Martin A. and Norman Solomon. *Unreliable Sources: A Guide to Detecting Bias in News Media.* New York: Lyle Stuart, 1990.

Lippmann, Walter. *Liberty and the News.* New York: Harcourt, Brace and Howe, 1920.

Liston, Robert A. *The Right To Know: Censorship in America.* New York: Franklin Watts, Inc., 1973.

McCormick, John and Mairi MacInnes, eds. *Versions of Censorship.* Garden City, New York: Anchor Books, 1962.

McKeon, Richard, Robert K. Merton, and Walter Gellhorn. *The Freedom to Read: Perspective and Program.* New York: R. R. Bowker Company, 1957.

Minor, Dale. *The Information War.* New York: Hawthorn Books, Inc., 1970.

Mott, Frank Luther. *American Journalism: A History of Newspapers in the United States through 260 Years: 1690 to 1950.* New York: The Macmillan Company, 1950.

The New York Public Library. *Censorship: 500 Years of Conflict.* New York: Oxford University Press, 1984.

Parenti, Michael. *Inventing Reality: The Politics of the Mass Media.* New York: St. Martin's Press, 1986.

Pember, Don R. *Mass Media Law, Fifth Edition.* Dubuque, Iowa: Wm. C. Brown Publishers, 1990.

Powledge, Fred. *The Engineering of Restraint: The Nixon Administration and the Press.* Washington, DC: Public Affairs Press, 1971.

Project Censored. "The 10 Best Censored Stories: 1976-1994." Rohnert Park, CA: Censored Publications, 1976-1994.

Rivers, William L., and Wilbur Schramm. *Responsibility in Mass Communication: Revised Edition.* New York: Harper & Row, 1969.

Seldes, George. *Lords of the Press.* New York: Julian Messner, Inc., 1938.

Seldes, George. *Witness to a Century: Encounters With the Noted, the Notorious, and the Three SOBs.* New York: Ballantine Books, 1987.

Sills, David L. ed. *International Encyclopedia of the Social Sciences, Volume 2.* New York: The Macmillan Company & The Free Press, 1968.

Stephens, Mitchell. *A History of News From the Drum to the Satellite.* New York: Viking, 1988.

Stone, I.F. "Notes On Closing, But Not In Farewell." I.F. Stone's Bi-Weekly, December 1971.

Tebbel, John. *The Media in America.* New York: Thomas Y. Crowell Company, 1974.

Theiner, George. *They Shoot Writers, Don't They?* London: Faber and Faber, 1984.

Wallraff, Günter. *Wallraff: The Undesirable Journalist.* London: Pluto Press Limited, 1978.

Widmer, Kingsley, and Eleanor. *Literary Censorship: Principles, Cases, Problems.* Belmont, California: Wadsworth Publishing Company, 1961.

APPENDIX A

CENSORED Resource Guide

One of Project Censored's long-standing goals is to improve the lines of communication between the public and the media that serve the public. Just knowing where to direct concerns, compliments, ideas or even offers to help is a question many people have when trying to reach either the alternative or establishment media.

With this in mind, Project Censored assembled a simple, easy-to-use and dependable resource guide for anyone who wants to contact the media to follow-up on these stories or to get actively involved in doing something about an issue or the media.

Following is a collection of names, addresses, phone and fax numbers, when available, for a variety of organizations, individuals, and electronic and print media outlets that might prove useful.

Although this information was current as of late 1994, you may want to double-check to ensure the names, addresses, etc., are still accurate. If you are aware of any changes and/or corrections to the list, please send them to Censored Resource Guide, Sonoma State University, Rohnert Park, CA 94928.

We plan to update the list in the 1996 edition of CENSORED! If you have any additions that should be included, please send them to the same address.

TABLE OF CONTENTS—CENSORED RESOURCE GUIDE

ALTERNATIVE BROADCAST/FILM/VIDEO PRODUCERS & ORGANIZATIONS

8MM NEWS COLLECTIVE
c/o Squeaky Wheel
372 Connecticut Street
Buffalo, NY 14213
Tel: 716/884-7172

THE 90'S CHANNEL
2010 14th Street, #209
Boulder, CO 80302
Tel: 303/442-8445
Fax: 303/442-6472

ALTERNATIVE RADIO
2129 Mapleton
Boulder, CO 80304
Tel: 303/444-8788
Fax: 303/546-0592

ALTERNATIVE VIEWS
Box 7297
Austin, TX 78713
Tel: 512/477-5148
Fax: 512/471-4806

AMERICA'S DEFENSE
MONITOR
1500 Massachusetts Ave., NW
Washington, DC 20005
Tel: 202/862-0700
Fax: 202/862-0708
E-Mail: cdi @ igc.apc.org

BLACK PLANET PRODUCTIONS/
NOT CHANNEL ZERO
P.O. Box 435, Cooper Station
New York, NY 10003-0435
Tel: 212/886-3701
Fax: 212/420-8223

CALIFORNIA NEWSREEL
149 9th Street, Suite 420
San Francisco, CA 94103
Tel: 415/621-6196

COMMON GROUND
Stanley Foundation
216 Sycamore Street, Suite 500
Muscatine, IA 52761
Tel: 319/264-1500

CUBA VA FILM PROJECT
12 Liberty Street
San Francisco, CA 94110
Tel: 415/282-1812
Fax: 415/282-1798

DIVA-TV
c/o ACT-UP
135 W. 29th Street, #10
New York, NY 10001
Tel: 212/564-2437

EARTH COMMUNICATIONS
(Radio For Peace International)
SJO 577, P.O. Box 025216
Miami, FL 33102-5216
Tel: 506/249-1821 (Costa Rica)
Fax: 506/249-1095 (Costa Rica)

EDUCATIONAL VIDEO CENTER
60 E. 13th Street, 4th Fl.
New York, NY 10003
Tel: 212/254-2848

EL SALVADOR MEDIA PROJECT
335 W. 38th Street, 5th Fl.
New York, NY 10018
Tel: 212/714-9118
Fax: 212/594-6417

EMPOWERMENT PROJECT
3403 Highway 54 West
Chapel Hill, NC 27516
Tel: 919/967-1963
Fax: 919/967-1863

ENVIROVIDEOS
P.O. Box 629000
El Dorado Hills, CA 95762
Tel: 1/800/227-8955

FILMFORUM
6522 Hollywood Blvd.
Los Angeles, CA 90028
Tel: 213/466-4143
Fax: 213/466-4144

FREE RADIO BERKELEY/
FREE COMMUNICATIONS
COALITION
1442 A Walnut Street, #406
Berkeley, CA 94709
Tel: 510/644-3779
or 510/464-3041
E-Mail: frbspd @ crl.com

GLOBALVISION
1600 Broadway
New York, NY 10019
Tel: 212/246-0202

INDEPENDENT TELEVISION
SERVICE
190 Fifth Street East, Suite 200
St. Paul, MN 55101
Tel: 612/225-9035
Fax: 612/225-9102

LABOR BEAT
37 S. Ashland Avenue
Chicago, IL 60607
Tel: 312/226-3330

MEDIA DEMOCRACY PROJECT
c/o Made in USA Productions
330 W. 42nd Street, Suite 1905
New York, NY 10036
Tel: 212/695-3090
Fax: 212/695-3086

MEDIA NETWORK/
ALTERNATIVE MEDIA
INFORMATION CENTER
39 W. 14th Street, #403
New York, NY 10011
Tel: 212/929-2663
Fax: 212/929-2732

NATIONAL ASIAN AMERICAN
TELECOMMUNICATIONS
ASSOCIATION
346 9th Street, 2nd Fl.
San Francisco, CA 94103
Tel: 415/863-0814
Fax: 415/863-7428

NATIONAL FEDERATION OF
COMMUNITY BROADCASTERS
666 11th Street, NW, Suite 805
Washington, DC 20001
Tel: 202/393-2355

PACIFICA NETWORK NEWS
702 H Street, NW, Suite 3
Washington, DC 20001
Tel: 202/783-1620
Fax: 202/393-1841

PACIFICA RADIO ARCHIVE
3729 Cahuenga Blvd., West
North Hollywood, CA 91604
Tel: 818/506-1077
Fax: 818/985-8802

PAPER TIGER TV/DEEP DISH
339 Lafayette Street
New York, NY 10012
Tel: 212/420-9045
Fax: 212/420-8223

P.O.V. (Point Of View)
330 W. 19th Street, 11th Fl.
New York, NY 10011-4035
Tel: 212/989-8121
Fax: 212/989-8230

RISE AND SHINE
PRODUCTIONS
300 West 43rd Street, 4th Fl.
New York, NY 10036
Tel: 212/265-2509

TELEMUNDO NETWORK
2470 West 8th Avenue
Hialea, FL 33010
Fax: 305/888-7610

THIRD WORLD NEWSREEL
Camera News, Inc.
335 West 38th Street, 5th Fl.
New York, NY 10018
Tel: 212/947-9277
Fax: 212/594-6417

UNPLUG
360 Grand Avenue
P.O. Box 385
Oakland, CA 94610
Tel: 510/268-1100

VIDEO DATABANK
112 S. Michigan Avenue, 3rd Fl.
Chicago, IL 60603
Tel: 312/345-3550
Fax: 312/541-8072

THE VIDEO PROJECT:
FILMS AND VIDEOS FOR
A SAFE AND SUSTAINABLE WORLD
5332 College Avenue, Suite 101
Oakland, CA 94618
Tel: 510/655-9050
or: 1/800-4-PLANET
Fax: 510/655-9115

"VIEWPOINTS" SERIES
c/o PBS
1320 Braddock Place
Alexandria, VA 22314-1698
Tel: 703/739-5000
PBS Comment Line: 1-800/356-2626

ZEITGEIST FILMS, LTD.
247 Centre Street, 2nd Fl.
New York, NY 10013
Tel: 212/274-1989
Fax: 212/274-1644

ALTERNATIVE & ELECTRONIC NEWS SERVICES

ACTIVIST NEWS NETWORK
P.O. Box 51170
Palo Alto, CA 94303
Tel: 415/493-4502
Fax: 415/493-4564

ALTERNET-Alternative News Network
77 Federal Street
San Francisco, CA 94107
Tel: 415/284-1420
Fax: 415/284-1414
CompuServe ID: 71362,27

CALIFORNIA ALTERNATIVE
NEWS BUREAU
2210 21st Street
Sacramento, CA 95616
Tel: 916/737-1234
Fax: 916/737-1437

INSIGHT FEATURES
Networking for Democracy
3411 Diversey, Suite 1
Chicago, IL 60647
Tel: 312/384-8827
Fax: 312/384-3904

INTERNET
(See Library and Reference Sources)

INTERPRESS SERVICE
Global Information Network
777 United Nations Plaza
New York, NY 10017
Tel: 212/286-0123
Fax: 212/818-9249

LATIN AMERICA DATA BASE
Latin American Institute
University of New Mexico
801 Yale Blvd., NE
Albuquerque, NM 87131-1016
Tel: 800/472-0888
or 505/277-6839
Fax: 505/277-5989

NEWS INTERNATIONAL
PRESS SERVICE
6161 El Cajon Blvd., #4
San Diego, CA 92115
Tel: 619/696-9531
Fax: 619/231-4186

PACIFIC NEWS SERVICE
450 Mission Street, Room 506
San Francisco, CA 94105
Tel: 415/243-4364

PEACENET; ECONET;
CONFLICNET; LABORNET
INSTITUTE FOR GLOBAL
COMMUNICATIONS
18 DeBoom Street
San Francisco, CA 94107
Tel: 415/442-0220
Fax: 415/546-1794

PEOPLE'S NEWS AGENCY
7627 16th Street, NW
P.O. Box 56466
Washington, DC 20040
Tel: 202/829-2278
Fax: 202/829-0462
E-mail Internet: prout wdc @ igc.apc.org

ALTERNATIVE PERIODICALS & PUBLICATIONS

14850 MAGAZINE
Public Communications, Inc.
104 N. Aurora Street, Suite 3
Ithaca, NY 14850
Tel: 607/277-1021
Fax: 607/277-0801

ACROSS THE LINE
Seeds of Peace
P.O. Box 12154
Oakland, CA 94604
Tel: 510/420-1799

THE ADVOCATE
6922 Hollywood Blvd., 10th Fl.
Los Angeles, CA 90028
Tel: 213/871-1225
Fax: 213/467-6805

AFRICA NEWS
P.O. Box 3851
Durham, NC 27702
Tel: 919/286-0747
Fax: 919/286-2614

AGAINST THE CURRENT
Center for Changes
7012 Michigan Avenue
Detroit, MI 48210
Tel: 313/841-0161
Fax: 313/841-8884

AKWESASNE NOTES
Mohawk Nation
P.O. Box 196
Rooseveltown, NY 13683-0196
Tel: 518/358-9531
Fax: 613/575-2935

ALERT: Focus on Central America
CISPES
P.O. Box 12156
Washington, DC 20005
Tel: 202/265-0890
Fax: 202/265-7843

ALTERNATIVE PRESS REVIEW
C.A.L. Press
P.O. Box 1446
Columbia, MO 65205-1446
Tel: 314/442-4352

ALTERNATIVES
Lynne Rienner Publishers
1800 30th Street, Suite 314
Boulder, CO 80301-1032
Tel: 303/444-6684
Fax: 303/444-0824

AMICUS JOURNAL
40 W. 20th Street
New York, NY 10011
Tel: 212/727-2700
Fax: 212/727-1773

BLACK SCHOLAR
P.O. Box 2869
Oakland, CA 94609
Tel: 510/547-6633
Fax: 510/547-6679

CANADIAN DIMENSION
707-228 Notre Dame Avenue
Winnipeg, MB R3B 1N7
Canada
Tel: 204/957-1519
Fax: 204/943-4617

CITIZENS CLEARINGHOUSE FOR
HAZARDOUS WASTES
P.O. Box 6806
Falls Church, VA 22040

CITY PAPER
Baltimore's Free Weekly
812 Park Avenue
Baltimore, MD 21201
Tel: 410/523-2300
Fax: 410/523-2222

COMMON CAUSE MAGAZINE
2030 M Street, NW
Washington, DC 20036
Tel: 202/833-1200
Fax: 202/659-3716

CONNECT
The Center for Media Literacy
1962 South Shenandoah Street
Los Angeles, CA 90034
Tel: 310/559-2944
Fax: 310/559-9396

COUNTERPUNCH
Institute for Policy Studies (IPS)
Newsletter Project
1601 Connecticut Ave., NW
Washington, DC 20009

COVERTACTION QUARTERLY
1500 Massachusetts Ave., NW, #732
Washington, DC 20005
Tel: 202/331-9763
Fax: 202/331-9751

CRESTED BUTTE
CHRONICLE & PILOT
P.O. Box 369
Crested Butte, CO 81224
Tel: 303/349-6114

CUBA ADVOCATE
1750 30th Street, #152
Boulder, CO 80301
Tel: 303/447-2286

CULTURAL DEMOCRACY
P.O. Box 7591
Minneapolis, MN 55407
Fax: 612/721-2160

CULTURAL SURVIVAL
QUARTERLY
Cultural Survival, Inc.
46 Brattle Street
Cambridge, MA 02138
Tel: 617/441-5400
Fax: 617/441-5417

THE DAILY CITIZEN
P.O. Box 57365
Washington, DC 20037
Tel: 202/429-6929
Fax: 202/659-1145

THE DAYTON VOICE
915 Salem Avenue
Dayton, OH 45406-5879
Tel: 513/275-8855
Fax: 513/278-2778

DEADLINE
Center for War, Peace
and the News Media
New York University
10 Washington Place, 4th Fl.
New York, NY 10003
Tel: 212/998-7960
Fax: 212/995-4143

DE TODO UN POCO
2830 5th Street
Boulder, CO 80304
Tel: 303/444-8565
Fax: 303/545-2074

DEFENSE MONITOR
1500 Massachusetts Ave., NW
Washington, DC 20005
Tel: 202/862-0700
Fax: 202/862-0708
E-Mail: cdi @ igc.apc.org

DENVER WESTWORD
P.O. Box 5970
Denver, CO 80217
Tel: 303/296-7744

DISSENT
521 Fifth Avenue
New York, NY 10017
Tel: 212/595-3084

DOLLARS AND SENSE
1 Summer Street
Somerville, MA 02143
Tel: 617/628-8411
Fax: 617/628-2025

E: THE ENVIRONMENTAL
MAGAZINE
P.O. Box 5098
Westport, CT 06881
Tel: 203/854-5559
Fax: 203/866-0602

EARTH ISLAND JOURNAL
300 Broadway, Suite 28
San Francisco, CA 94133-3312
Tel: 415/788-3666
Fax: 415/788-7324

ENVIRONMENTAL ACTION
6930 Carroll Avenue, Suite 600
Takoma Park, MD 20912
Tel: 301/891-1106
Fax: 301/891-2218

ENVIRONMENTAL IMPACT
REPORTER
P.O. Box 1834
Sebastopol, CA 95473
Tel: 707/823-8744

ESSENCE MAGAZINE
1500 Broadway
New York, NY 10036
Tel: 212/642-0600

EXTRA!
Fairness and Accuracy in Reporting
130 W. 25th Street
New York, NY 10001
Tel: 212/633-6700
Fax: 212/727-7668

FACTSHEET 5
c/o Seth Friedman
P.O. Box 170099
San Francisco, CA 94117-0099

FOOD FIRST NEWS
Institute for Food & Development Policy
398 60th Street
Oakland, CA 94618
Tel: 510/654-4400

FREE THINKER FORUM
Project Freedom
P.O. Box 14447
St. Louis, MO 63178
Tel: 618/637-2202

FRONT LINES RESEARCH
Public Policy Institute
Planned Parenthood Federation of
America
810 Seventh Avenue
New York, NY 10019
Tel: 212/261-4721
Fax: 212/261-4352

GENDER & MASS MEDIA
Stockholm University-JMK
P.O. Box 27861
S-115 93
Stockholm, Sweden

GLOBAL EXCHANGES
2017 Mission Street, Room 303
San Francisco, CA 94110
Tel: 415/255-7296

GLOBAL PESTICIDE CAMPAIGNER
Pesticide Action Network
116 New Montgomery, #810
San Francisco, CA 94105
Tel: 415/541-9140
Fax: 415/541-9253

GRASSROOTS ECONOMIC
ORGANIZING NEWSLETTER
P.O. Box 5065
New Haven, CT 06526
Tel: 203/389-6194

GREEN MAGAZINE
P.O. Box 381
Mill Harbour
London E14 9TW
England

HEALTH LETTER
2000 P Street, NW
Washington, DC 20036

HIGH COUNTRY NEWS
P.O. Box 1090
Paonia, CO 81428
Tel: 303/527-4898

THE HUMAN QUEST
Churchman Co., Inc.
1074 23rd Avenue N.
St. Petersburg, FL 33704-3228
Tel: 813/894-0097

HURACAN
P.O. Box 7591
Minneapolis, MN 55407

IN CONTEXT
P.O. Box 11470
Bainbridge Island, WA 98110
Tel: 206/842-0216
Fax: 206/842-5208

THE INDEPENDENT
540 Mendocino Avenue
Santa Rosa, CA 95401
Tel: 707/527-1200
Fax: 707/527-1288

INDEX ON CENSORSHIP
Writers & Scholars Educational Trust
33 Islington High Street
London N1 9LH
United Kingdom
Tel: 071-278 2313
Fax: 071-278 1878

IN THESE TIMES
2040 N. Milwaukee Avenue, 2nd Fl.
Chicago, IL 60647-4002
Tel: 312/772-0100
Fax: 312/772-4180

IRE JOURNAL
INVESTIGATIVE REPORTERS
& EDITORS
P.O. Box 838
University of Missouri
School of Journalism
Columbia, MO 65205
Tel: 314/882-2042
Fax: 314/882-5431

ISSUES IN SCIENCE &
TECHNOLOGY
1636 Hobart Street, NW
Washington, DC 20009
Tel: 202/986-7217
Fax: 202/986-7221

KLANWATCH
P.O.Box 548
Montgomery, AL 36104
Tel: 205/264-0286
Fax: 205/264-0629

LATIN AMERICAN
PERSPECTIVES
2455 Teller Road
Newbury Park, CA 91320
Tel: 805/499-0721
Fax: 805/499-0871

LEFT BUSINESS OBSERVER
250 W. 85th Street
New York, NY 10024-3217
Tel: 212/874-4020

LEGAL TIMES
1730 M Street, NW, Suite 802
Washington, DC 20036
Tel: 202/457-0686

LIES OF OUR TIMES
Institute for Media Analysis
145 W. 4th Street
New York, NY 10012
Tel: 212/254-1061
Fax: 212/254-9598

LONDON INDEPENDENT
40 City Road
London EC1Y 2DB
England

MEDIA AND VALUES
Media Action Research Center
475 Riverside Drive, Suite 1901
New York, NY 10115
Tel: 212/865-6690
Fax: 212/663-2746

MEDIACULTURE REVIEW
77 Federal Street
San Francisco, CA 94107
Tel: 415/284-1420
Fax: 415/284-1414

THE METRO TIMES
743 Beaubien, Suite 301
Detroit, MI 48226
Tel: 313/961-4060
Fax: 313/961-6598

MOTHER JONES
731 Market Street, Suite 600
San Francisco, CA 94103
Tel: 415/665-6637
Fax: 415/665-6696

MS. MAGAZINE
230 Park Avenue
New York, NY 10169
Tel: 212/551-9595

MUCKRAKER
Center for Investigative Reporting
568 Howard Street, 5th Fl.
San Francisco, CA 94105-3008
Tel: 415/543-1200
Fax: 415/543-8311

MULTINATIONAL MONITOR
P.O. Box 19405
Washington, DC 20036
Tel: 202/387-8034
Fax: 202/234-5176

THE NATION
72 Fifth Avenue
New York, NY 10011
Tel: 212/242-8400
Fax: 212/463-9712

NATIONAL CATHOLIC REPORTER
P.O. Box 419281
Kansas City, MO 64141
Tel: 816/968-2200
Fax: 816/968-2280

NATIONAL REVIEW
150 E. 35th Street
New York, NY 10016
Tel: 212/679-7330
Fax: 212/696-0309

THE NEW REPUBLIC
1220 19th Street, NW
Washington, DC 20036
Tel: 202/331-7494
Fax: 202/331-0275

NEW TIMES, INC.
P.O. Box 5970
Denver, CO 80217

NEW YORK NATIVE
That New Magazine, Inc.
P.O. Box 1475
Church Street Station
New York, NY 10008

NEWSLETTER ON
INTELLECTUAL FREEDOM
American Library Association
50 E. Huron Street
Chicago, IL 60611
Tel: 312/280-4223
Fax: 312/440-9374

NORTHERN SUN NEWS
P.O. Box 581487
Minneapolis, MN 55458-1487
Tel: 612/729-8543

OUT
The Soho Building
110 Greene Street, Suite 800
New York, NY 10017
Tel: 212/334-9119
Fax: 212/334-9227

PACIFIC SUN
P.O. Box 5553
Mill Valley, CA 94942
Tel: 415/383-4500
Fax: 415/383-4159

PBI/USA REPORT
Peace Brigades Int'l/USA
2642 College Avenue
Berkeley, CA 94704
Tel: 510/540-0749
Fax: same; call first

PEACE REVIEW:
The International
Quarterly of World Peace
1800 30th Street, Suite 314
Boulder, CO 80301-1032
Tel: 303/444-6684
Fax: 303/444-0824

THE PEOPLE'S WARRIOR
P.O. Box 488
Rockwall, TX 75087
Tel: 1-800/771-1992
or 214/771-1991

PERCEPTIONS MAGAZINE
11409 Jefferson Blvd.
Culver City, CA 90230
Tel: 310/313-5185
or 800/276-4448
Fax: 310/313-5198

THE PROGRESSIVE
409 E. Main Street
Madison, WI 53703
Tel: 608/257-4626
Fax: 608/257-3373

PROPAGANDA REVIEW
Media Alliance
814 Mission Street, Suite 205
San Francisco, CA 94103
Tel: 415/546-6334

PUBLIC CITIZEN
2000 P Street, NW, Suite 610
Washington, DC 20036
Tel: 202/833-3000

RACHEL'S HAZARDOUS
WASTE NEWS
c/o Environmental Research
  Foundation
Box 5036
Annapolis, MD 21403-7036
Tel: 410/263-1584
Fax: 410/263-8944

RECONSTRUCTION
1563 Massachusetts Avenue
Cambridge, MA 02138
Tel: 617/495-0907
Fax: 617/496-5515

THE RECORDER
625 Polk Street
San Francisco, CA 94102

RETHINKING SCHOOLS
1001 E. Keefe Avenue
Milwaukee, WI 53212
Tel: 414/964-9646
Fax: 414/964-7220

REVOLUTIONARY WORKER
P.O. Box 3486
Chicago, IL 60654

ROC-ROCK OUT CENSORSHIP
P.O. Box 147
Jewett, OH 43986

ROLLING STONE
1290 Ave. of the Americas, 2nd Fl.
New York, NY 10104
Tel: 212/484-1616
Fax: 212/767-8203

SAFE FOOD NEWS
Food and Water,Inc.
RR1, Box 114
Marshfield, VT 05658
Tel: 802/426-3700
Fax: 802/426-3711

THE SAN FRANCISCO BAY
GUARDIAN
520 Hampshire
San Francisco, CA 94110
Tel: 415/255-3100
Fax: 415/255-8762

SANTA BARBARA NEWS PRESS
715 Anacapa Street
Santa Barbara, CA 93101
Tel: 805/564-5200

SANTA ROSA SUN
1275 Fourth Street, #608
Santa Rosa, CA 95404
Tel: 707/544-3448
Fax: 707/544-4756

SECRECY & GOVERNMENT
BULLETIN
Federation of American Scientists
307 Massachusetts Avenue, NE
Washington, DC 20002
Tel: 202/675-1012

SF WEEKLY
425 Brannan Street
San Francisco, CA 94107
Tel: 415/541-0700
Fax: 415/777-1839

S.O.A. WATCH
P.O. Box 3330
Columbus, GA 31903

SOJOURNERS
2401 15th Street, NW
Washington, DC 20009
Tel: 202/328-8842
Fax: 202/328-8757

SOUTHERN EXPOSURE
P.O. Box 531
Durham, NC 27702
Tel: 919/419-8311
Fax: 919/419-8315

SPIN
6 West 18th Street
New York, NY 10011
Tel: 212/633-8200
Fax: 212/633-9041

SPIRIT OF CRAZY HORSE
Leonard Peltier Defense Committee
International Office
P.O. Box 583
Lawrence, KS 66044
Tel: 913/842-5774
Fax: 913/842-5796

THE SPOTLIGHT
300 Independence Avenue, SE
Washington, DC 20003
Tel: 202/544-1794

STRATEGIES
Strategies for Media Literacy
1095 Market Street, Suite 617
San Francisco, CA 94103
Tel: 415/621-2911

TEXAS OBSERVER
307 West 7th Street
Austin, TX 78701-2917
Tel: 512/477-0746

THIRD FORCE
Center for Third World Organizing
1218 East 21st Street
Oakland, CA 94606-9950
Tel: 510/533-7583

TIKKUN
251 W. 100th Street, 5th Fl.
New York, NY 10025
Tel: 212/864-4110
Fax: 212/864-4137

TURNING THE TIDE
People Against Racist Terror
P.O. Box 1990
Burbank, CA 91507

U. THE NATIONAL COLLEGE
MAGAZINE
1800 Century Park East #820
Los Angeles, CA 90067-1503
Tel: 310/551-1381
Fax: 310/551-1859

UNCLASSIFIED
Association of National Security Alumni
2001 S Street, NW, Suite 740
Washington, DC 20009
Tel: 202/483-9325

URGENT ACTION BULLETIN
Survival International
11-15 Emerald Street
London WC1N 3QL
United Kingdom
Tel: 0171-242 1441
Fax: 0171-242 1771

UTNE READER
1624 Harmon Place, Suite 330
Minneapolis, MN 55403
Tel: 612/338-5040

VILLAGE VOICE
36 Cooper Square
New York, NY 10003
Tel: 212/475-3300
Fax: 212/475-8944

WAR AND PEACE DIGEST
War and Peace Foundation
32 Union Square East
New York, NY 10003-3295
Tel: 212/777-6626
Fax: 212/995-9652

WASHINGTON FREE PRESS
1463 E. Republican Street, #178
Seattle, WA 98112
Tel: 206/233-1780
E-Mail: freepres @ scn.org

THE WASHINGTON
SPECTATOR
London Terrace Station
P.O. Box 20065
New York, NY 10011

WELFARE MOTHER'S VOICE
Welfare Warriors
4504 North 47 Street
Milwaukee, WI 53218

WHO CARES: A JOURNAL
OF SERVICE AND ACTION
511 K Street, NW, Suite 1042
Washington, DC 20005

WHOLE EARTH REVIEW
27 Gate Five Road
Sausalito, CA 94965
Tel: 415/332-1716
Fax: 415/332-3110

WILD FOREST REVIEW
P.O. Box 86373
Portland, OR 97286
Tel: 503/788-1998

WILLAMETTE WEEK
Portland's Newsweekly
822 SW 10th Avenue
Portland, OR 97205
Tel: 503/243-2122
Fax: 503/243-1115

WIRED MAGAZINE
520 Third Street, 4th Fl.
San Francisco, CA 94107
Tel: 415/222-6205
Fax: 415/222-6209

WORLD PRESS REVIEW
200 Madison Avenue, Suite 2104
New York NY 10016
Tel: 212/889-5155
Fax: 212/889-5634

WORLD WATCH
Worldwatch Institute
1776 Massachusetts Avenue, NW
Washington, DC 20036
Tel: 202/452-1999
Fax: 202/296-7365

YO!-YOUTH OUTLOOK
Pacific News Service
450 Mission Street, Room 506
San Francisco, CA 94105
Tel: 415/243-4364

Z MAGAZINE
116 Botolph Street
Boston, MA 02115
Tel: 617/787-4531
Fax: 508/457-0626

FREE PRESS/RIGHT-TO-KNOW PUBLICATIONS & ORGANIZATIONS

THE ADVOCACY INSTITUTE
1730 Rhode Island Ave., NW
Suite 600
Washington, DC 20036-3118
Tel: 202/659-8475

ALLIANCE FOR CULTURAL
DEMOCRACY
P.O. Box 7591
Minneapolis, MN 55407
Fax: 612/721-2160

ALTERNATIVE PRESS CENTER
P.O. Box 33109
Baltimore, MD 21218
Tel: 410/243-2471
Fax: 410/235-5325

AMERICAN LIBRARY
ASSOCIATION OFFICE FOR INTEL-
LECTUAL FREEDOM
50 E. Huron Street
Chicago, IL 60611
Tel: 312/280-4223
or 800/545-2433
Fax: 312/440-9374

ARTICLE 19: INTERNATIONAL
CENTRE AGAINST
CENSORSHIP
33 Islington High Street
London N1 9LH
England
Tel: 071-278 9292
Fax: 071-713 1356

ASSOCIATION OF
ALTERNATIVE
NEWSWEEKLIES
c/o The New Times
1201 East Jefferson, Suite A-260
Phoenix, AZ 85034
Tel: 602/229-8487
Fax: 602/253-5871

BILL OF RIGHTS JOURNAL
175 Fifth Avenue, Room 814
New York, NY 10010
Tel: 212/673-2040
Fax: 212/460-8359

CALIFORNIA FIRST
AMENDMENT COALITION
926 J Street, Suite 1406
Sacramento, CA 95814-2708
Tel: 916/447-2322
Fax: 916/447-2328

CALIFORNIANS AGAINST
CENSORSHIP TOGETHER (ACT)
1800 Market Street, Suite 1000
San Francisco, CA 94103
Tel: 510/548-3695

CENTER FOR MEDIA
EDUCATION
1511 K Street, NW, Suite 518
Washington, DC 20005
Tel: 202/628-2620
Fax: 202/628-2554

CENTER FOR THIRD WORLD
ORGANIZING
1218 East 21st Street
Oakland, CA 94606-9950
Tel: 510/533-7583

CIVIC MEDIA CENTER
1636 West University Avenue
Gainesville, FL 32603
Tel: 904/373-0010

CIVIL LIBERTIES
American Civil Liberties Union
132 W. 43rd Street
New York, NY 10036
Tel: 212/944-9800
Fax: 212/869-9065

COALITION vs PBS
CENSORSHIP
P.O. Box 485
Santa Monica, CA 90406-0485
Tel: 310/288-6693
Fax: 310/315-4773

COMMITTEE TO PROTECT
JOURNALISTS
330 Seventh Ave., 12th Fl.
New York, NY 10001
Tel: 212/465-1004
Fax: 212/465-9568

CULTURE WATCH
Data Center
464 19th Street
Oakland, CA 94612
Tel: 510/835-4692
Fax: 510/835-3017

DATA CENTER
Right-to-Know Project
464 19th Street
Oakland, CA 94612
Tel: 510/835-4692
Fax: 510/835-3017

ENVIRONMENTAL RESEARCH
FOUNDATION
Box 5036
Annapolis, MD
Tel: 410/263-1584
Fax: 410/263-8944

FEMINISTS FOR FREE
EXPRESSION
2525 Times Square Station
New York, NY 10108
Tel: 212/713-5446

FIRST AMENDMENT CENTER
Society of Professional Journalists
1050 Connecticut Avenue, NW
Suite 1206
Washington, DC 20036
Tel: 202/628-1411

FIRST AMENDMENT
CONGRESS
1445 Market Street, Suite 320
Denver, CO 80202
Tel: 303/820-5688
Fax: 303/534-8774

FREEDOM FORUM
1101 Wilson Blvd.
Arlington, VA 22209
Tel: 703/528-0800
Fax: 703/284-3570

FREEDOM FORUM
First Amendment Center
1207 18th Avenue South
Nashville, TN 37212
Tel: 615/321-9588

FREEDOM FORUM
Media Studies Center
Columbia University
2950 Broadway
New York, NY 10027-7004
Tel: 212/678-6600
Fax: 212/678-6663

FREEDOM OF EXPRESSION
FOUNDATION
5220 S. Marina Pacifica
Long Beach, CA 90803
Tel: 310/985-4301
Fax: 310/985-2369

FREEDOM OF INFORMATION
CENTER
20 Walter Williams Hall
University of Missouri at Columbia
Columbia, MO 65211
Tel: 314/882-4856
Fax: 314/882-9002

FREEDOM OF INFORMATION
CLEARINGHOUSE
P.O. Box 19367
Washington, DC 20036
Tel: 202/833-3000

FREEDOM WRITER
Institute for First Amendment Studies
P.O. Box 589
Great Barrington, MA 01230
Tel: 413/274-3786

FREE PRESS ASSOCIATION
P.O. Box 15548
Columbus, OH 43215
Tel: 614/291-1441

FREE RADIO BERKELEY/
FREE COMMUNICATIONS
COALITION
1442-A Walnut Street, #406
Berkeley, CA 94709
Tel: 510/464-3041
E-Mail: frbspd @ crl.com.

FUND FOR FREE EXPRESSION
485 Fifth Avenue
New York, NY 10017
Tel: 212/972-8400
Fax: 212/972-0905

THE GAP MEDIA PROJECT
142 W.S. College Street
Yellow Springs, OH 45387
Tel: 513/767-2224
Fax: 513/767-1888

THE GIRAFFE PROJECT
P.O. Box 759
Langley, WA 98260
Tel: 206/221-7989

GOVERNMENT
ACCOUNTABILITY PROJECT
810 First Street, NE, Suite 630
Washington, DC 20002-3633
Tel: 202/408-0034
Fax: 202/408-9855

HEAL
Hanford Education Action League
1720 North Ash Street
Spokane, WA 99205
Tel: 509/326-3370

HISPANIC EDUCATION
AND MEDIA GROUP
P.O. Box 221
Sausalito, CA 94966
Tel: 415/331-8560

INFACT
256 Hanover Street
Boston, MA 02113
Tel: 617/742-4583

INTER AMERICAN
PRESS ASSOCIATION
2911 NW 39th Street
Miami, FL 33142
Tel: 305/634-2465
Fax: 305/635-2272

THE INVESTIGATIVE
REPORTING FUND
P.O. Box 7554
Asheville, NC 28802
Tel: 704/259-9179
Fax: 704/251-1311

LABOR NEWS FOR
WORKING FAMILIES
I.I.R., 2521 Channing Way
Berkeley, CA 94720
Tel: 510/643-6814
Fax: 510/642-6432

LEONARD PELTIER DEFENSE
COMMITTEE
P.O. Box 583
Lawrence, KS 66044
Tel: 913/842-5774

LEONARD PELTIER FREEDOM
CAMPAIGN
c/o International Action Center
39 West 14th Street, Room 206
New York, NY 10011
Tel: 212/633-6646
Fax: 212/633-2889

MEDIA ACTION
RESEARCH CENTER
P.O. Box 320
Nashville, TN 37202
Tel: 615/742-5451
Fax: 615/742-5419

MEDIA COALITION/
AMERICANS FOR
CONSTITUTIONAL FREEDOM
1221 Avenue of the Americas,
24th Fl.
New York, NY 10020
Tel: 212/768-6770
Fax: 212/391-1247

MEDIA/ED
The Media Education Foundation
26 Center Street
Northhampton, MA 01060
Tel: 413/586-4170
Fax: 413/586-8398

MEDIA REPORT TO WOMEN
10606 Mantz Road
Silver Spring, MD 20903
Tel: 301/445-3230

MEIKLEJOHN CIVIL LIBERTIES
INSTITUTE
P.O. Box 673
Berkeley, CA 94701
Tel: 510/848-0599
Fax: 510/848-6008

NATIONAL COALITION
AGAINST CENSORSHIP
275 7th Avenue, 20th Fl.
New York, NY 10001
Tel: 212/807-6222
Fax: 212/807-6245

NATIONAL COMMITTEE AGAINST
REPRESSIVE LEGISLATION
3321 12th Street, NE
Washington, DC 20017
Tel: 202/529-4225

OMB WATCH
1742 Connecticut Avenue, NW
Washington, DC 20009-1171
Tel: 202/234-8494
Fax: 202/234-8584

PEOPLE FOR THE
AMERICAN WAY
2000 M Street, NW, Suite 400
Washington, DC 20036
Tel: 202/467-4999
Fax: 202/293-2672

POLITICAL RESEARCH
ASSOCIATES
678 Massachusetts Ave., Suite 702
Cambridge, MA 02139-3355
Tel: 617/661-9313

PROGRESSIVE MEDIA
PROJECT
409 East Main Street
Madison, WI 53703
Tel: 608/257-4626
Fax: 608/257-3373

PROJECT ON GOVERNMENT
OVERSIGHT
2025 Eye Street, NW, Suite 1117
Washington, DC 20006-1903
Tel: 202/466-5539
Fax: 202/466-5596

REPORTERS' COMMITTEE
FOR FREEDOM OF THE PRESS
1735 Eye Street, NW, Suite 504
Washington, DC 20006
Tel: 202/466-6312

STUDENT PRESS
LAW CENTER
P.O. Box 27904
Washington, DC 20038-7904
Tel: 202/466-5242

THE THOMAS JEFFERSON CENTER
FOR THE PROTECTION OF
FREE EXPRESSION
400 Peter Jefferson Place
Charlottesville, VA 22901-8691
Tel: 804/295-4784
Fax: 804/296-3621

UNDERGROUND PRESS
CONFERENCE
Mary Kuntz Press
P.O. Box 476617
Chicago, IL 60647
Tel: 312/486-0685
Fax: 312/226-1168

WORLD PRESS FREEDOM
COMMITTEE
c/o The Newspaper Center
11600 Sunrise Valley Drive
Reston, VA 22091
Tel: 703/648-1000
Fax: 703/620-4557

WOMEN'S INSTITUTE
FOR FREEDOM OF THE PRESS
3306 Ross Place, NW
Washington, DC 20008-3332
Tel: 202/966-7783

JOURNALISM/MEDIA ANALYSIS PUBLICATIONS & ORGANIZATIONS

ACCURACY IN MEDIA
AIM
4455 Connecticut Avenue, NW
Suite 330
Washington, DC 20005
Tel: 202/364-4401
Fax: 202/364-4098

ADBUSTERS:
A Magazine of Media
and Environmental Strategies
The Media Foundation
1243 W. Seventh Avenue
Vancouver, British Columbia
Canada V6H 1B7
Tel: 604/736-9401
Fax: 604/737-6021

AMERICAN JOURNALISM REVIEW
8701 Adelphi Road
Adelphi, MD 20783
Tel: 301/431-4771
Fax: 301/431-0097

AMERICAN SOCIETY OF
JOURNALISTS AND AUTHORS
1501 Broadway, Suite 302
New York, NY 10036
Tel: 212/997-0947
Fax: 212/768-7414

AMERICAN SOCIETY OF
NEWSPAPER EDITORS
P.O. Box 4090
Reston, VA 22090-1700
Tel: 703/648-1144
Fax: 703/476-6125

ASIAN AMERICAN
JOURNALISTS ASSOCIATION
1765 Sutter Street, Room 1000
San Francisco, CA 94115
Tel: 415/346-2051
Fax: 415/931-4671

THE ASPEN INSTITUTE
Communications and Society Program
1333 New Hampshire Avenue, NW
Suite 1070
Washington, DC 20036
Tel: 202/736-5818
Fax: 202/467-0790

ASSOCIATION OF AMERICAN
PUBLISHERS
220 E. 23rd Street
New York, NY 10010
Tel: 212/689-8920
Fax: 212/696-0131

ASSOCIATION OF HOUSE
DEMOCRATIC PRESS
ASSISTANTS
House of Representatives
2459 Rayburn Bldg.
Washington, DC 20515
Tel: 202/225-1554
Fax: 202/225-4951

BAY AREA CENSORED
Media Alliance
814 Mission Street, Suite 205
San Francisco, CA 94103
Tel: 415/546-6334

BLACK PRESS INSTITUTE
2711 E. 75th Place
Chicago, IL 60649
Tel: 312/375-8200
Fax: 312/375-8262

BLACK WOMEN
IN PUBLISHING
P.O Box 6275
FDR Station
New York, NY 10150
Tel: 212/772-5951

CENTER FOR
INVESTIGATIVE REPORTING
568 Howard Street, 5th Fl.
San Francisco, CA 94105-3008
Tel: 415/543-1200
Fax: 415/543-8311

CENTER FOR MEDIA
AND PUBLIC AFFAIRS
2100 L Street, NW, Suite 300
Washington, DC 20037-1526
Tel: 202/223-2942
Fax: 202/872-4014

CENTER FOR MEDIA
EDUCATION
1511 K Street, NW, Suite 518
Washington, DC 20005
Tel: 202/628-2620
Fax: 202/628-2554

CENTER FOR MEDIA LITERACY
1962 South Shenandoah Street
Los Angeles, CA 90034
Tel: 310/559-2944
Fax: 310/559-9396

CENTER FOR THE STUDY
OF COMMERCIALISM
1875 Connecticut Avenue, NW
Suite 300
Washington, DC 20009-5728
Tel: 202/332-9110
Fax: 202/265-4954

CENTER FOR WAR,
PEACE AND THE NEWS MEDIA
New York University
10 Washington Place, 4th Fl.
New York, NY 10003
Tel: 212/998-7960
Fax: 212/995-4143

CHRISTIC INSTITUTE
5276 Hollister Avenue
Santa Barbara, CA 93111
Tel: 805/967-8232
Fax: 805/967-5060

CITIZENS FOR MEDIA LITERACY
34 Wall Street, Suite 407
Asheville, NC 28801
Tel: 704/255-0182
Fax: 704/254-2286

COLUMBIA JOURNALISM REVIEW
700 Journalism Building
Columbia University
New York, NY 10027
Tel: 212/854-1881
Fax: 212/854-8580

COMMUNICATIONS
 CONSORTIUM AND
 MEDIA CENTER
1333 H Street, NW, Suite 700
Washington, DC 20005
Tel: 202/682-1270
Fax: 202/682-2154

CULTURAL ENVIRONMENT
MOVEMENT
P.O. Box 31847
Philadelphia, PA 19104
Tel: 215/573-7099
Fax: 215/898-2024

DOWNS MEDIA EDUCATION
CENTER
P.O. Box 1170
Stockbridge, MA 01262
Tel: 413/298-0262
Fax: 413/298-4434

EDITOR AND PUBLISHER
11 W. 19th Street
New York, NY 10011
Tel: 212/675-4380
Fax: 212/929-1259

ESSENTIAL INFORMATION
P.O. Box 19405
Washington, DC 20036
Tel: 202/387-8030
Fax: 202/234-5176

FAIRNESS AND ACCURACY
IN REPORTING
130 W. 25th Street
New York, NY 10001
Tel: 212/633-6700
Fax: 212/727-7668

FORBES MEDIA CRITIC
P.O. Box 762
Bedminster, NJ 07921
Tel: 908/781-2078
or 1/800/825-0061

FUND FOR INVESTIGATIVE
JOURNALISM
1755 Massachusetts Avenue, NW
Washington, DC 20036
Tel: 202/462-1844

GAY AND LESBIAN PRESS
ASSOCIATION
P.O. Box 8185
Universal City, CA 91608
Tel: 818/902-1476

GLAAD
Gay and Lesbian Alliance
Against Defamation
150 W. 26th Street, Suite 503
New York, NY 10001
Tel: 212/807-1700
Fax: 212/807-1806

GLAAD MEDIA WATCH/SFBA
1360 Mission Street, Suite 200
San Francisco, CA 94103
Tel: 415/861-2244
Fax: 415/861-4893
E-Mail: glaad sfba @ aol.com

THE INDEPENDENT
Association of Independent
Video and Film (AIVF)
625 Broadway, 9th Fl.
New York, NY 10012
Tel: 212/473-3400
Fax: 212/677-8732

INSTITUTE FOR
ALTERNATIVE JOURNALISM
77 Federal Street
San Francisco, CA 94107
Tel: 415/284-1420
Fax: 415/284-1414
CompuServe: 71362, 27

INSTITUTE FOR MEDIA ANALYSIS
145 W. 4th Street
New York, NY 10012
Tel: 212/254-1061
Fax: 212/254-9598

INVESTIGATIVE
JOURNALISM PROJECT
Fund for Constitutional Government
122 Maryland Avenue, NE, Suite 300
Washington, DC 20002
Tel: 202/546-3732
Fax: 202/543-3156

INVESTIGATIVE
REPORTERS & EDITORS
P.O. Box 838
University of Missouri
School of Journalism
Columbia, MO 65205
Tel: 314/882-2042
Fax: 314/882-5431

JOURNALISM QUARTERLY
George Washington University
Journalism Program
Washington, DC 20052
Tel: 202/994-6226

MEDIA ACCESS PROJECT
2000 M Street, NW, Suite 400
Washington, DC 20036
Tel: 202/232-4300
Fax: 202/223-5302

MEDIA ALLIANCE
814 Mission Street, Suite 205
San Francisco, CA 94103
Tel: 415/546-MEDIA
Fax: 415/546-6218

MEDIAFILE
814 Mission Street, Suite 205
San Francisco, CA 94103
Tel: 415/546-6523
Fax: 415/546-6218

THE MEDIA INSTITUTE
1000 Potomac Street, NW,
Suite 204
Washington, DC 20007
Tel: 202/298-7512
Fax: 202/337-7092

MEDIA WATCH
P.O. Box 618
Santa Cruz, CA 95061-0618
Tel: 408/423-6355
Fax: 408/423-6355

NATIONAL ALLIANCE
FOR MEDIA EDUCATION
655 13th Street, Suite 210
Oakland, CA 94612
Tel: 510/451-2717

NATIONAL ASSOCIATION OF
BLACK JOURNALISTS
11600 Sunrise Valley Drive
Reston, VA 22091
Tel: 703/648-1270
Fax: 703/476-6245

NATIONAL ASSOCIATION OF
HISPANIC JOURNALISTS
National Press Bldg., Suite 1193
Washington, DC 20045
Tel: 202/662-7145
Fax: 202/662-7144

NATIONAL CONFERENCE
OF EDITORIAL WRITERS
6223 Executive Boulevard
Rockville, MD 20852
Tel: 301/984-3015

NATIONAL NEWSPAPER
ASSOCIATION
1627 K Street, NW, Suite 400
Washington, DC 20006
Tel: 202/466-7200
Fax: 202/331-1403

NATIONAL TELEMEDIA COUNCIL
120 East Wilson Street
Madison, WI 53703
Tel: 608/257-7712

NATIONAL WRITERS UNION
873 Broadway, Room 203
New York, NY 10003
Tel: 212/254-0279

NEWSPAPER ASSOCIATION
OF AMERICA
11600 Sunrise Valley Drive
Reston, VA 22091
Tel: 703/648-1000
Fax: 703/620-4557

THE NEWSPAPER GUILD
8611 Second Avenue
Silver Spring, MD 20910
Tel: 301/585-2990

NEWSPAPER RESEARCH JOURNAL
Scripps Hall School of Journalism
Ohio University
Athens, OH 45701
Tel: 614/593-2590
Fax: 614/593-2592

NEWSWORTHY
Minnesota News Council
822 Marquette Ave., Suite 200
Minneapolis, MN 55402
Tel: 612/341-9357

ORGANIZATION OF
NEWS OMBUDSMEN
c/o Art Nauman
Sacramento Bee
P.O. Box 15779
Sacramento, CA 95852
Tel: 916/442-8050

PR WATCH
Center for Media and Democracy, Inc.
3318 Gregory Street
Madison, WI 53711
Tel: 608/233-3346
Fax: 608/238-2236

PROJECT CENSORED
Communications Studies
Sonoma State University
1801 E. Cotati Avenue
Rohnert Park, CA 94928-3609
Tel: 707/664-2500
Fax: 707/664-2108

PROJECT CENSORED CANADA
Department of Communication
Simon Fraser University
Burnaby, BC V5A 1S6
Canada
Tel: 604/291-3687
Fax: 604/291-4024

PUBLIC MEDIA CENTER
446 Green Street
San Francisco, CA 94133
Tel: 415/434-1403
Fax: 415/986-6779

PUBLIC MEDIA MONITOR
Council for Public Media
P.O. Box 4703
Austin, TX 78765

QUILL
Society of Professional Journalists
16 S. Jackson Street
P.O. Box 77
Greencastle, IN 46135-0077
Tel: 317/653-3333
Fax: 317/653-4631

ROCKY MOUNTAIN MEDIA WATCH
Box 18858
Denver, CO 80218
Tel: 303/832-7558

ST. LOUIS JOURNALISM REVIEW
8380 Olive Boulevard
St. Louis, MO 63132
Tel: 314/991-1699
Fax: 314/997-1898

SOUTHWEST ALTERNATE MEDIA
PROJECT
1519 West Main
Houston, TX 77006
Tel: 713/522-8592
Fax: 713/522-0953

STRATEGIES FOR MEDIA LITERACY
1095 Market Street, Suite 617
San Francisco, CA 94103
Tel: 415/621-2911
Fax: 415/255-9392

TIMES MIRROR CENTER
FOR THE PEOPLE & THE PRESS
1875 Eye Street, NW, Suite 1110
Washington, DC 20006
Tel: 202/293-3126

TYNDALL REPORT
135 Rivington Street
New York, NY 10002
Tel: 212/674-8913
Fax: 212/979-7304

WOMEN IN COMMUNICATIONS
3717 Columbia Pike, Suite 310
Arlington, VA 22204
Tel: 703/920-5555
Fax: 703/920-5556

LIBRARY & REFERENCE SOURCES

THE ACTIVIST'S ALMANAC:
The Concerned Citizen's Guide
to the Leading Advocacy Organizations
in America
By David Walls, 1993
Simon & Schuster Fireside Books
New York

ALTERNATIVE PRESS INDEX
Alternative Press Center, Inc.
P.O. Box 33109
Baltimore, MD 21218
Tel: 410/243-2471
Fax: 410/235-5325

CENTER FOR DEFENSE
INFORMATION
Library for Press and Public
1500 Massachusetts Avenue, NW
Washington, DC 20005
Tel: 202/862-0700
Fax: 202/862-0708
E-Mail: cdi @ igc.apc.org

CONNECTING TO THE INTERNET
O'Reilly & Associates, 1993
103 Morris Street, Suite A
Sebastopol, CA 95472
Tel: 707/829-0515

DIRECTORY OF ELECTRONIC
JOURNALS, NEWSLETTERS AND
ACADEMIC DISCUSSION LISTS
by Kovacs and Strangelove
Association of Scientific
and Academic Publishing
1527 New Hampshire Avenue, NW
Washington, DC 20036

ECOLINKING: EVERYONE'S GUIDE
TO ONLINE INFORMATION
by Don Rittner, 1992
Peachpit Press
2414 6th Street
Berkeley, CA 94710

ENCYCLOPEDIA OF ASSOCIATIONS
1993 ed., 4 vols.
Gale Research Inc., Detroit and London

ERIC
Clearinghouse on Information &
Technology
Syracuse University
Schools of Information
Studies/Education
4-194 CST
Syracuse, NY 13244-4100
Tel: 315/443-3640

FROM RADICAL TO
EXTREME RIGHT
A bibliography of current periodicals
of protests, controversy, advocacy and
dissent
by Gail Skidmore and Theodore Jurgen
Spahn, 1987, 3rd ed.
Scarecrow Press, Inc.
Metuchen, NJ, and London

GALE DIRECTORY OF PUBLICA-
TIONS AND BROADCAST MEDIA
1992 ed., 3 vols, plus supplement
Gale Research Inc., Detroit and London

THE INTERNATIONAL DIRECTORY
OF LITTLE MAGAZINES
AND SMALL PRESSES
Len Fulton, ed., 30th ed., 1994/95
Dustbooks
P.O. Box 100
Paradise, CA 95967

THE LEFT INDEX:
A QUARTERLY INDEX
TO PERIODICALS
OF THE LEFT
Reference and Research Services
Santa Cruz, CA

MACROCOSM USA: POSSIBILITIES
FOR A NEW PROGRESSIVE ERA
Sandi Brockway, ed., 1992
Macrocosm USA, Inc.
P.O. Box 185
Cambria, CA 93428-8030
Tel: 805/927-8030
Fax: 805/927-1713
BBS (MacroNet): 805/927-1987

FORBES MEDIA GUIDE
1400 Route 206 N.
P.O. Box 89
Bedminster, NJ 07921
Tel: 908/781-2078
Fax: 908/781-6635

NATIONAL FORUM ON
INFORMATION LITERACY
c/o American Library Association
50 East Huron Street
Chicago, IL 60611

THE PEOPLE'S RIGHT TO KNOW:
MEDIA, DEMOCRACY AND THE
INFORMATION HIGHWAY
by Frederick Williams
and John V. Paulik, eds.
Lawrence Erlbaum Associates, 1994.

PROGRESSIVE PERIODICALS
DIRECTORY
by Craig T. Canan
2nd ed., 1989
Progressive Education
P.O. Box 120574
Nashville, TN 37212

RIGHT-TO-KNOW NETWORK
(RTK NET)
OMB Watch
1742 Connecticut Ave., NW
Washington, DC 20009-1171
Tel: 202/234-8494
Fax: 202/234-8584

ULRICH'S INTERNATIONAL
PERIODICALS DIRECTORY
1992/93, 3 vols.
R.R. Bowker, New Providence, NJ

THE WHOLE INTERNET:
USER'S GUIDE AND CATALOG
by Ed Krol
O'Reilly & Associates, 1992
103 Morris Street, Suite A
Sebastopol, CA 95472
Tel: 707/829-0515

THE WORKING PRESS
OF THE NATION, 1995 ed.
Reed Reference Publishing
P.O. Box 31
New Providence, NJ 07974
Tel: 1/800/521-8110

NATIONAL BROADCAST AND CABLE MEDIA

48 HOURS
CBS News
524 W. 57th Street
New York, NY 10019
Tel: 212/975-4848

60 MINUTES
CBS News
524 W. 57th Street
New York, NY 10019
Tel: 212/975-2006

20/20
ABC News
147 Columbus Avenue
New York, NY 10023
Tel: 212/456-2020
Fax: 212/456-2969

ABC WORLD NEWS TONIGHT
47 W. 66th Street
New York, NY 10023
Tel: 212/456-4040

AMERICAN JOURNAL
CBS
402 E. 76th Street
New York, NY 10021
Tel: 1-800/EDI-TION

ASSOCIATED PRESS RADIO
NETWORK
1825 K Street, NW, Suite 710
Washington, DC 20006
Tel: 202/736-9500
Fax: 202/736-1199

CBS EVENING NEWS
524 W. 57th Street
New York, NY 10019
Tel: 212/975-3693

CBS THIS MORNING
524 W. 57th Street
New York, NY 10019
Tel: 212/975-2824

CHRISTIAN
BROADCASTING NETWORK
700 CBN Center
Virginia Beach, VA 23463-0001
Tel: 804/523-7111

CONUS COMMUNICATIONS
3415 University Avenue
Minneapolis, MN 55414
Tel: 612/642-4646

CNN
One CNN Center
Box 105366
Atlanta, GA 30348
Tel: 404/827-1500

CNN
Washington Bureau
820 First Street, NE
Washington, DC 20002
Tel: 202/898-7900

C-SPAN
400 N. Capitol Street, NW, Suite 650
Washington, DC 20001
Tel: 202/737-3220
Fax: 202/737-3323

CROSSFIRE
CNN
820 First Street, NE
Washington, DC 20002
Tel: 202/8989-7951

THE CRUSADERS
1011-F West Alameda Avenue
Burbank, CA 91506
Tel: 818/556-2155
Fax: 818/556-2111

DATELINE
NBC News
30 Rockefeller Plaza, Room 510
New York, NY 10112
Tel: 212/664-6170

DAY ONE
ABC News
147 Columbus Avenue, 8th Fl.
New York NY 10023
Tel: 212/456-6100

PHIL DONAHUE SHOW
30 Rockefeller Plaza
New York, NY 10019
Tel: 212/975-2006

ESPN
ESPN Plaza
Bristol, CT 06010
Tel: 203/585-2000

EYE TO EYE
CBS News
555 W. 57th Street
New York, NY 10019
Tel: 212/975-2000

FACE THE NATION
CBS News
2020 M Street, NW
Washington, DC 20036
Tel: 202/457-4481

FRONTLINE
125 Western Avenue
Boston, MA 02134
Tel: 617/783-3500
Fax: 617/254-0243

FRONT PAGE
FOX
10301 West Pico Blvd., 2nd Floor
Los Angeles, CA 90064
Tel: 310/284-3600

THE GERALDO RIVERA SHOW
555 West 57th Street
New York, NY 10019
Tel: 212/265-8520

GOOD MORNING AMERICA
ABC News
147 Columbus Avenue
New York, NY 10023
Tel: 212/456-5900
Fax: 212/456-7290

HIGHTOWER RADIO
P.O. Box 13516
Austin, TX 78711
Tel: 512/477-5588
Fax: 512/478-8536

HOME BOX OFFICE
1100 Avenue of the Americas
New York, NY 10036
Tel: 212/512-1329

INVESTIGATIVE REPORTS
Arts & Entertainment Network
235 E. 45th Street
New York, NY 10017
Tel: 212/661-4500

LARRY KING LIVE
CNN
820 First Street, NE
Washington, DC 20002
Tel: 212/898-7900

MACNEIL/LEHRER
NEWSHOUR
New York Office:
WNET-TV
356 W. 58th Street
New York, NY 10019
Tel: 212/560-3113

MACNEIL/LEHRER
NEWSHOUR
Washington Office:
Arlington, VA 22206
Tel: 703/998-2870

MEET THE PRESS
NBC News
4001 Nebraska Avenue, NW
Washington, DC 20016
Tel: 202/885-4200
Fax: 202/362-2009

MORNING EDITION:
ALL THINGS CONSIDERED
National Public Radio
2025 M Street, NW
Washington, DC 20036
Tel: 202/822-2000
Fax: 202/822-2329

BILL MOYERS
Public Affairs Television
356 W. 58th Street
New York, NY 10019
Tel: 212/560-6960

MTV NEWS
1515 Broadway, 24th Fl.
New York, NY 10036
Tel: 212/258-8000

NATIONAL PUBLIC RADIO
2025 M Street, NW
Washington, DC 20036
Tel: 202/822-2000
Fax: 202/822-2329

NBC NIGHTLY NEWS
30 Rockefeller Plaza
New York, NY 10112
Tel: 212/664-4971

NIGHTLINE (New York)
ABC News
47 W. 66th Street
New York, NY 10023
Tel: 212/456-7777

NIGHTLINE (Washington DC)
ABC News
1717 DeSales Street, NW
Washington, DC 20036
Tel: 202/887-7360

NOW
NBC News
30 Rockefeller Plaza
New York, NY 10112
Tel: 212/664-7501

PBS
1320 Braddock Place
Alexandria, VA 22314-1698
Tel: 703/739-5000
Fax: 703/739-0775
PBS Comment Line: 1/800/356-2626

PRI-PUBLIC RADIO
INTERNATIONAL
100 North Sixth Street, Suite 900 A
Minneapolis, MN 55403
Tel: 612/338-5000
Fax: 612/330-9222

PRIMETIME LIVE
ABC News
147 Columbus Avenue
New York, NY 10023
Tel: 212/456-1600

RADIO FREE EUROPE/
RADIO LIBERTY
1201 Connecticut Avenue, NW
Suite 1100
Washington, DC 20036
Tel: 202/457-6900
Fax: 202/457-6997

RELIABLE SOURCES
CNN
820 First Street, NE
Washington, DC 20002
Tel: 202/898-7900

RUSH LIMBAUGH
WABC Radio
2 Penn Plaza, 17th Fl.
New York, NY 10121
Tel: 212/613-3800
Fax: 212/563-9166

STREET STORIES
CBS News
555 W. 57th Street
New York, NY 10019
Tel: 212/975-8282

THIS WEEK WITH DAVID BRINKLEY
ABC News
1717 DeSales Street, NW
Washington, DC 20036
Tel: 202/887-7777

TODAY SHOW
NBC News
30 Rockefeller Plaza
New York, NY 10112
Tel: 212/664-4249

TURNER BROADCASTING SYSTEM
1 CNN Center
Atlanta, GA 30348-5366
Tel: 404/827-1792

TV NATION
Remote Broadcasting
1114 Ave. of the Americas
6th Floor, Grace Bldg.
New York, NY 10036
Tel: 212/221-6398
Fax: 212/221-6398

OPRAH WINFREY
Harpo Productions
P.O. Box 9909715
Chicago, IL 60690
Tel: 312/633-1000

NATIONAL COLUMNISTS

RUSSELL BAKER
The New York Times
229 W. 43rd Street
New York, NY 10036

DAVID BRODER
The Washington Post
1150 15th Street, NW
Washington, DC 20071

ALEXANDER COCKBURN
The Nation
72 Fifth Avenue
New York, NY 10011
Tel: 212/242-8400
Fax: 212/463-9712

ROBERT NOVAK
Chicago Sun Times
401 N. Wabash Avenue
Chicago, IL 60611
Tel: 312/321-3000
Fax: 312/321-3084

ELLEN GOODMAN
The Boston Globe
P.O. Box 2378
Boston, MA 02107
Tel: 617/929-2000

NAT HENTOFF
The Village Voice
36 Cooper Square
New York, NY 10003
Tel: 212/475-3300
Fax: 212/475-8944

JIM HIGHTOWER
P.O. Box 13516
Austin, TX 78711
Tel: 512/477-5588
Fax: 512/478-8536

MOLLY IVINS
Fort Worth Star-Telegram
P.O. Box 1870
Fort Worth, TX 76101
Tel: 817/390-7400
Fax: 817/390-7520

JAMES KILPATRICK
Universal Press Syndicate
4900 Main Street, 9th Fl.
Kansas, MO 64112
Tel: 800/255-6734 or 816/932-6600

MORTON KONDRACKE
ROLL CALL
900 Second Street, NE
Washington, DC 20002
Tel: 202/289-4900
Fax: 202/289-5337

MAX LERNER
New York Post
210 South Street
New York, NY 10002
Tel: 212/815-8000
Fax: 212/732-4241

JULIANNE MALVEAUX
c/o King Features Syndicate
216 E. 45th Street
New York, NY 10017

MARY MCGRORY
The Washington Post
1150 15th Street, NW
Washington, DC 20071
Tel: 202/334-6000

CLARENCE PAGE
Chicago Tribune
435 N. Michigan Avenue
Chicago, IL 60611
Tel: 312/222-3232

TOM PETERS
555 Hamilton Avenue
Palo Alto, CA 94031

ANNA QUINDLEN
New York Times
229 W. 43rd Street
New York, NY 10036
Tel: 212/556-1234

A.M. ROSENTHAL
New York Times
229 W. 43rd Street
New York, NY 10036
Tel: 212/556-1234

MIKE ROYKO
Chicago Tribune
435 N. Michigan Avenue
Chicago, IL 60611
Tel: 312/222-3232

WILLIAM SAFIRE
New York Times
1627 Eye Street, NW
Washington, DC 20006
Tel: 202/862-0330
Fax: 202/862-0340

GEORGE WILL
Newsweek
444 Madison Avenue
New York, NY 10022
Tel: 212/350-4000

NATIONAL PUBLICATIONS & NEWS SERVICES

ASSOCIATED PRESS
National Desk
50 Rockefeller Plaza
New York, NY 10020
Tel: 212/621-1600

BRITISH MEDICAL JOURNAL
B.M.A. House
Tavistock Square
London WC1H 9JR
England
Tel: 071/387-4499

CHICAGO TRIBUNE
435 N. Michigan Avenue
Chicago, IL 60611
Tel: 312/222-3232

CHRISTIAN SCIENCE
MONITOR
One Norway Street
Boston, MA 02115
Tel: 617/450-2000

FORTUNE
Time Warner, Inc.
Time & Life Building
Rockefeller Center
New York, NY 10020
Tel: 212/586-1212

HARPER'S MAGAZINE
666 Broadway
New York, NY 10012-2317
Tel: 212/614-6500
Fax: 212/228-5889

KNIGHT-RIDDER NEWS SERVICE
790 National Press Building
Washington, DC 20045
Tel: 202/383-6080

LOS ANGELES TIMES
Times-Mirror Square
Los Angeles, CA 90053
Tel: 800/528-4637

MCCLATCHY NEWS SERVICE
P.O. Box 15779
Sacramento, CA 95852
Tel: 916/321-1895

NATIONAL NEWSPAPER
ASSOCIATION
1525 Wilson Boulevard, Suite 550
Arlington, VA 22209-2434
Tel: 703/907-7900
Fax: 703/907-7901

NEWSWEEK
444 Madison Avenue
New York, NY 10022
Tel: 212/350-4000

NEW YORK NEWSDAY
235 Pinelawn Road
Melville, NY 11747
Tel: 516/843-2020

NEW YORK TIMES
229 W. 43rd Street
New York, NY 10036
Tel: 212/556-1234

NEW YORK TIMES
Washington Bureau
1627 Eye Street, NW, 7th Fl.
Washington, DC 20006
Tel: 202/862-0300
Fax: 202/862-0340

REUTERS INFORMATION SERVICES
1700 Broadway
New York, NY 10019
Tel: 212/603-3300
Fax: 212/603-3446

SAN FRANCISCO CHRONICLE
901 Mission Street
San Francisco, CA 94103
Tel: 415/777-1111
Fax: 415/512-8196

SAN FRANCISCO EXAMINER
110 Fifth Street
San Francisco, CA 94103
Tel: 415/777-2424
Fax: 415/512-1264

SCRIPPS/HOWARD NEWS SERVICE
1090 Vermont Avenue, NW, Suite 1000
Washington, DC 20005
Tel: 202/408-1484

TIME MAGAZINE
Time Warner, Inc.
Time & Life Building
Rockefeller Center
New York, NY 10020-1393
Tel: 212/522-1212

TRIBUNE MEDIA SERVICES
64 E. Concord Street
Orlando, FL 32801
Tel: 800/332-3068
or 407/420-6200

UNITED PRESS INTERNATIONAL
1400 Eye Street, NW
Washington, DC 20005
Tel: 202/898-8000

U.S. NEWS & WORLD REPORT
2400 N Street, NW
Washington, DC 20037
Tel: 202/955-2000
Fax: 202/955-2049

USA TODAY
1000 Wilson Boulevard
Arlington, VA 22229
Tel: 703/276-3400

WALL STREET JOURNAL
200 Liberty Street
New York, NY 10281
Tel: 212/416-2000

WASHINGTON POST
1150 15th Street, NW
Washington, DC 20071
Tel: 202/334-6000

Alternative Writer's Market

If you are a journalist merely rehashing yet another angle on the O.J. Simpson case, you probably have no problem getting your story published in one of the nation's many periodicals.

If, however, you are a journalist writing an exposé of the cozy relationship between *The New York Times* and the nuclear power industry, you probably will be hard-pressed to find a ready market for your work.

The traditional and authoritative resource for writers is the *Writer's Market: Where & How To Sell What You Write*, published annually by Writer's Digest Books. However, while the *Writer's Market* is a required resource for all freelance writers, it falls somewhat short when it comes to fulfilling the needs of investigative journalists.

For example, a natural market for a well-researched piece on how *The New York Times* has played a remarkably supportive role for nuclear power would be *Lies Of Our Times*, or LOOT, as it's known among its aficionados. The "Times" in *Lies Of Our Times*, is, of course, *The New York Times*, and LOOT has published innumerable articles about the cozy relationship between *The New York Times* and the nuclear power industry.

However, LOOT is not found in the *Writer's Market*, at least not in the 1995 edition of the *Writer's Market*. But LOOT is found in the "1995 Alternative Writer's Market."

Throughout its 19-year history, Project Censored has received numerous queries from journalists and authors seeking publishers for exposés that challenge the conventional wisdom of the establishment press.

It is this ongoing succession of queries that led to the development of the following guide.

All names and addresses have been updated where necessary in the second edition of the "Alternative Writer's Market" (AWM). This edition also includes a number of new publications and features some of the most promising markets open to investigative journalists.

If you know of any additional listings that should be included in the 1996 AWM, please write the "Alternative Writer's Market," Project Censored, Sonoma State University, Rohnert Park, CA 94928, for a listing application.

Also, if you are aware of any changes and/or corrections for the current list, please send them to the same address.

14850 MAGAZINE
104 N. Aurora Street
Ithaca, NY 14850
Tel: 607/277-1021 Fax: 607/277-0801
Editor-in-Chief: Corey Shane

14850 Magazine, named after its zip code but definitely not to be confused with a West Coast zip, is published monthly. About 95 percent of its articles are provided by freelance writers. It is interested in interviews, reviews, opinion, and think pieces, ranging from 800 to 1,600 words.

Rates: $30 in credit

Queries not required; send SASE for Writer's Guidelines; response time is two weeks.

Tips: "We like local stuff, but we're wide open; we've done pieces on JFK, Leonard Peltier, health care, censorship, and other political issues. We really publish a pretty broad array of material."—Editor-in-Chief Corey Shane

ALTERNATIVE PRESS REVIEW
P.O. Box 1446
Columbia, MO 65205-1446
Tel: 314/442-4352
Editor: Jason McQuinn

Alternative Press Review is a quarterly publication that monitors and reports on the activities and performance of America's alternative media. About 10 percent of its articles are provided by freelance writers. It is interested in articles, profiles, and book reviews covering alternative media and their relationship to society, radical movements, and mainstream media.

Rates: 2 cents per word for reprints or reviews; 5 cents per word for original articles.

Queries with published clips required; send SASE for Writer's Guidelines; response time is one to two months.

Tips: "We're looking for critical, perceptive assessments about alternative media organizations, conferences, publications, genre, movements; no puff pieces."—Editor Jason McQuinn

AMERICAN JOURNALISM REVIEW

8701 Adelphi Road
Adelphi, MD 20783
Tel: 301/431-4771 Fax: 301/431-0097
Editor: Rem Rieder

The **American Journalism Review**, formerly the Washington Journalism Review, is published ten times a year. About 80 percent of its articles are provided by freelance writers. It is interested in articles, analysis, book reviews, interviews, exposés, upwards of 2,000 words; short pieces of 500-700 words.

Rates: Features—20 cents a word; short features—$100.

Queries with published clips required; response time three to four weeks.

Tips: "Read the magazine before submitting **Queries**; know what we've done, what we do, what we're looking for. We're always looking for good ideas, especially investigations of media coverage."—Associate Editor Chip Rowe

CALIFORNIA ALTERNATIVE NEWS BUREAU

2210 21st Street
Sacramento, CA 95616
Tel: 916/737-1234 Fax: 916/737-1437
Editor: Tom Johnson

The **California Alternative News Bureau** is a monthly news service which includes 15 California alternative papers among its subscribers. About 50 percent of its articles are provided by freelance writers. It is interested in hard news, features, and profiles of statewide California interest. Articles range from 500 to 2,000 words.

Rates: $100 to $400 depending on quality and work involved.

Queries with published clips required; response time normally within a week.

Tips: "Take a story the mainstream papers have missed or downplayed, and, with lively writing tell Californians about it. No polemics, editorials. If you want your audience outraged, reflect it in your writing, not your lead."—Editor Tom Johnson

CANADIAN DIMENSION (CD)

228 Notre Dame Ave., Room 707
Winnipeg, Manitoba, R3B1N7
Canada
Tel: 204/957-1519 Fax: 204/943-4617
Office Manager: Yvonne Block

Canadian Dimension (CD), our first Canadian publication, relies on freelance writers for about 25% of its material. It is primarily interested in articles (2,000 words maximum) and book reviews (750 words maximum).

Rates: 10 cents per published word; maximum of $300 per article.

Queries not required; send SASE for Writer's Guidelines; response time is two months.

Tips: "We're looking for articles on issues affecting women, gays/lesbians, aboriginals, the environment, and labour."—Office Manager Yvonne Block.

CITY PAPER

Baltimore's Free Weekly
812 Park Avenue
Baltimore, MD 21201
Tel: 410/523-2300 Fax: 410/523-2222
Managing Editor: Jim Duffy

The City Paper is a weekly newspaper distributed free in the Baltimore area. About 50 percent of its articles are provided by freelance writers. It is interested in articles, profiles, book reviews, interviews, essays, exposés, all of which should have a strong Baltimore connection.
Rates: $25 to $400 depending on length.
Queries with published clips required; response time normally two weeks; send SASE for Writer's Guidelines.
Tips: "We are particularly interested in the issues, people, and character of Baltimore City."—Managing Editor Jim Duffy

COMMON CAUSE MAGAZINE

2030 M Street, NW
Washington, DC 20036
Tel: 202/833-1200 Fax: 202/659-3716
Editor: Vicki Kemper

Common Cause Magazine, longtime scourge of Washington's political highrollers, is published quarterly. About 15 percent of its articles are provided by freelance writers. It is primarily interested in investigative political pieces.
Rates: vary
Queries not required
Tips: "We're interested in articles about money in politics, political corruption, real-life impacts of government policy, and social issues."
—Editor Vicki Kemper

COVERTACTION QUARTERLY

1500 Massachusetts Ave., NW
Room 732
Washington, DC 20005
Tel: 202/331-9763 Fax: 202/331-9751
Editors: Terry Allen and Phil Smith

CovertAction Quarterly, a publication that lives up to its name, is naturally published quarterly. From 50 to 80 percent of its articles are provided by freelance writers. It is interested in substantive articles, well-researched (with footnotes), exposés, interviews, etc. Average article length is 4,000-5,000 words, sometimes longer.
Rates: negotiable
Queries with published clips required; send SASE for Writer's Guidelines; response time is 10 days.
Tips: "We're interested in stories about U.S. and allied intelligence operations (foreign and domestic), non-intelligence related topics demonstrating U.S. intervention or involvement, right-wing and/or racist activities, environmental issues, private (non-governmental) activities of a secret and/or detrimental nature."—Director of Research Louis Wolf

CULTURAL DEMOCRACY

P.O. Box 7591
Minneapolis, MN 55407
Fax: 612/721-2160

Cultural Democracy is a quarterly publication of the Alliance for Cultural Democracy, a 17-year-old national network of community and neighborhood based cultural workers.

Rates: None.

Queries not required; response time is two weeks to two months; send SASE for Writer's Guidelines.

Tips: "We are looking for writings that express the interconnection between cultural rights, community, arts, and ecology and ongoing, or historical, examples of projects or programs reflecting these concerns."

THE DAYTON VOICE
915 Salem Avenue
Dayton, OH 45406
Tel: 513/275-8855 Fax: 513/278-2778
Editor: Marrianne McMullen

The Dayton Voice is an alternative weekly that focuses primarily on local, state, or regional news and entertainment features surrounding the Dayton, Ohio, area. About 80 percent of its articles are provided by freelance writers. It is interested in investigative reporting, profiles, and popular culture features. Article length ranges from 500 to 2,500 words.

Rates: $30 to $50

Queries not required but preferred; send SASE for Writer's Guidelines; response time is two weeks.

DETROIT METRO TIMES
743 Beaubien, Suite 301
Detroit, MI 48226
Tel: 313/961-4060

The Detroit Metro Times is a weekly newspaper; about 70 percent of its material is provided by freelance writers. It is interested in articles, profiles, reviews, opinion pieces of 600 to 3,500 words on cutting edge culture and progressive political and social change. It is not interested in consumer news or mainstream religion, medicine, or sports.

Rates: None cited.

Queries with published clips required; response time two weeks.

Tips: "We are interested in feminism, progressive politics, analysis of U.S. government and corporate abuse, environmentalism, race relations, danger of the right-wing, media monopoly and manipulation, etc."
—Jim Dulzo

DOLLARS AND SENSE
1 Summer Street
Somerville, MA 02143
Tel: 617/628-8411 Fax: 617/628-2025
Editors: Betsy Reed and Marc Breslow

Dollars and Sense is a bimonthly magazine that focuses on economic issues and perspectives not normally found in *Forbes Magazine* or *The Wall Street Journal*. About 20 percent of its articles are provided by freelance writers. It will consider full-length features, interviews, and book reviews (200-600 words each) for publication.

Rates: Regrets that it cannot compensate authors at this time.

Queries required; response time is a month; send SASE for Writer's Guidelines.

Tips: "Articles on progressive economics and political economy will be of interest."—Editor Betsy Reed

EARTH ISLAND JOURNAL
300 Broadway, #28
San Francisco, CA 94133-3312
Tel: 415/788-3666 Fax: 415/788-7324
Editor: Gar Smith

Earth Island Journal is an environmentally-oriented quarterly magazine. Only about 5 percent of its articles are provided by freelance writers. However, half-page (500 words) and full page (1,000 words) stories are most likely to win consideration; feature-length reports (1,500-3,000 words) occasionally result from outside writers.
Rates: Year's free subscription in exchange.
Queries required; response time normally ten days to three months; send SASE for Writer's Guidelines.
Tips: "Our beat: 'Local News From Around the World.' First-person reports on under-reported environmental stories from abroad-particularly with a U.S. hook. Is some U.S. corporation causing harm overseas? Are there solutions from abroad that we can apply in the U.S.?"—Editor Gar Smith

ENVIRONMENTAL ACTION MAGAZINE
6930 Carroll Avenue, Suite 600
Takoma Park, MD 20912
Tel: 301/891-1100 Fax: 301/891-2218
Editor: Barbara Ruben

Environmental Action Magazine (EA) is a quarterly magazine that primarily explores the human environment. About 10 percent of its articles are provided by freelance writers. While it is mainly interested in book reviews and essays by established experts/leaders in particular fields, it does publish a few investigative pieces.
Rates: up to $300 but most authors are unpaid.
Queries with published clips and resume required; response time four to eight weeks.
Tips: "We stopped taking most freelance work in 1992 due to budget cuts and reduced frequency of the magazine. EA focuses primarily on the human environment (as opposed to wilderness issues) and on issues relating to the environmental movement itself. ... Issues in 1995 will focus on the history and progress of the environmental movement since Earth Day 1970, job creation and the environment, and ways to target corporate power."—Editor Barbara Ruben

EXTRA!
130 W. 25th Street
New York, NY 10001
Tel: 212/633-6700 Fax: 212/727-7668
Editor: Jim Naureckas

EXTRA! is a bimonthly news media review journal published by Fairness and Accuracy In Reporting, a national media watchdog organization. It is interested in well-documented articles related to issues of media bias.
Rates: Ten cents a word.
Queries not required; send SASE for Writer's Guidelines.
Tips: "Stories should focus more on the media than on the information not reported by the media. We look at media coverage of specific issues relating to government control of the media, corporate interference, racial and gender bias, etc."—Editor Jim Naureckas

FRONT LINES RESEARCH
Public Policy Institute
Planned Parenthood Federation of
America
810 7th Avenue
New York, NY 10019
Tel: 212/261-4721 Fax: 212/261-4352
Editor: Frederick Clarkson

Front Lines Research features "journalism with footnotes" in defense of reproductive health, education, and democracy. It is published bimonthly. About 20 percent of its articles are provided by freelance writers. It is interested in investigative, analytical, rigorous, footnoted, documentary features on the radical right. Maximum length is 2,000 words plus footnotes.

Rates: 10 cents per word plus expenses

Queries with published clips required; send SASE for Writer's Guidelines; response time is two weeks.

Tips: "Considerable expertise on the far-right is a pre-requisite. We are generally publishing definitive work in this field. The style is a mix of investigative journalism and academic journalism. I call it journalism with footnotes. Stories in this journal should be compelling reading and have a long shelf life."—Editor Frederick Clarkson

THE HUMAN QUEST
1074 23rd Avenue N.
St. Petersburg, FL 33704-3228
Tel: 813/894-0097
Editor: Edna Ruth Johnson

The Human Quest is a bimonthly national magazine that is "in the mail on the 25th of the month." 100 percent of its material is provided by freelance writers. Emphasis of The Human Quest is world peace; its religious conviction is spiritual humanism. It welcomes thoughtful articles ranging from 150 to 500 to 1,000 words in length.

Rates: None.

Queries not required; response time normally within a week; in lieu of formal guidelines, editor will "happily furnish a copy of the publication" on request.

Tips: "The Human Quest is an independent journal of religious humanism, under the sponsorship of The Churchman Associates, Inc. It is edited in the conviction that religious journalism must provide a platform for the free exchange of ideas and opinions; that religion is consonant with the most advanced revelations in every department of knowledge; that we are in a fraternal world community; and that the moral and spiritual evolution of man is only at the beginning."
—Editor Edna Ruth Johnson

THE INDEPENDENT FILM & VIDEO MONTHLY
625 Broadway, 9th Floor
New York, NY 10012
Tel: 212/473-3400 Fax: 212/677-8732
Editor: Patricia Thomson

The Independent Film & Video Monthly is a national magazine with about 90 percent of its articles provided by freelance writers. It is interested news articles, 500-800 words; profiles of film/video makers, distributors, festival directors, 700-1,000 words; business, legal, technical articles, 700-1,200 words; features 1,500-3,000 words.

Rates: news articles, $50; profiles, $100; features, 10 cents a word.

Queries with published clips required; response time from two weeks to two months.

Tips: "Interested in film/video-related articles that are not too theoretical or too mainstream. Recent features include 'The Money Game: Foundation Insiders Explain the Rules,' and 'Made in Japan: Current Trends in Japanese Independent Filmmaking.'"—Michele Shapiro.

INDEX ON CENSORSHIP
33 Islington High Street
London, England N1 9LH
Tel: 171-278-2313 Fax: 171-278-1878
Editor: Ursula Owen

Index on Censorship is an international bimonthly review and analysis of censorship issues. It is interested in articles, profiles, book reviews, interviews, opinion pieces, essays, exposés, etc. Also interested in factual news and analytic articles on censorship and freedom of expression issues. Articles range from 800 to 4,000 words.

Rates: £60 per 1,000 words for original pieces

Queries not required.

Tips: Special interests include "all areas concerned with freedom of expression and censorship, world-wide (including Britain)."—Editor Ursula Owen.

IN THESE TIMES
2040 N. Milwaukee
Chicago, IL 60647
Tel: 312/772-0100 Fax: 312/772-4180

Editor: James Weinstein; Managing Editor: Miles Harvey

In These Times (ITT) is a biweekly news and views magazine. About 50 percent of its articles are provided by freelance writers. It is interested in articles, profiles, book reviews, interviews, opinion pieces, essays, and exposés.

Rates: none cited.

Queries with published clips required; response time normally two to three weeks; send SASE for Writer's Guidelines.

Tips: "Writers should be familiar with the magazine before sending submissions. A huge percentage of our rejections are pieces that are submitted by writers who obviously haven't read ITT."—Managing Editor Miles Harvey

LIES OF OUR TIMES (LOOT)
145 West 4th Street
New York, NY 10012
Tel: 212/254-1061 Fax: 212/254-9598
Senior Editor: Edward S. Herman

Lies Of Our Times publishes ten issues a year and about 85 percent of its articles are provided by freelance writers. It is interested in articles, interviews, and exposés. Articles range from 1,000 to 2,000 words.

Rates: $75.

Queries required; response time about a month; send SASE for Writer's Guidelines.

Tips: "LOOT is interested in articles that critique the mainstream media's coverage of current issues—both national and international. Attention to how issues are framed, what sources are used, what information is omitted, what hidden premises shape reporting—are all of interest."—Nancy Watt Rosenfeld

MEDIAFILE
814 Mission Street, Suite 205
San Francisco, CA 94103
Tel: 415/546-6334 Fax: 415/546-6218
Editor: Larry Smith

Media/File is a bimonthly newspaper published by the Media Alliance, an organization of more than 3,000 San Francisco Bay Area media professionals. About 80 percent of its articles are provided by freelance writers. It is interested in articles and analyses relating to the media, with a specific interest in the San Francisco/Bay Area; book reviews on books about media; profiles of interesting media workers; and investigative media exposés encouraged.
   Rates: depends on experience; frequently trade.
   Queries not required but helpful along with published clips; response time normally in two weeks; send SASE for Writer's Guidelines.
   Tips: "Media, First Amendment, censorship issues are our bag."—Editor Larry Smith

MOTHER JONES
731 Market Street, Suite 600
San Francisco, CA 94103
Tel: 415/665-6637 Fax: 415/665-6696
Editor: Jeffrey Klein; Managing Editor: Katharine Fong

Mother Jones is a bimonthly magazine known for its investigative journalism and exposés, and its coverage of social issues, public affairs, and popular culture. Most of its articles are written by freelancers. It is interested in hard-hitting investigative reports exposing government, corporate, scientific, institutional cover-ups, etc.; thoughtful articles that challenge conventional wisdom on national issues; and people-oriented stories on issues such as the environment, labor, the media, health care, consumer protection, and cultural trends. 'Outfront' stories run 250-500 words; short features run 1,200-3,000 words, and longer features run 3,000-5,000 words.
   Rates: 80 cents per word for commissioned stories.
   Queries with published clips required; send SASE for Writer's Guidelines; please do not query by phone or fax.
   Tips: "Keep in mind that our lead time is three months and submissions should not be so time-bound that they will appear dated. We are not a news magazine."

MS.
230 Park Avenue
New York, NY 10169
Tel: 212/551-9595

Ms. is a bimonthly magazine that focuses primarily on women's issues and news. About 80 percent of its articles are provided by freelance writers. It is interested in articles, profiles, book reviews, opinion pieces, essays, and exposés. Article lengths: most departments, 1,200 words; features, 3,000-4,000 words; U.S. news, 1,000-2,000 words.
   Rates: between 70 cents and $1 per word, approximately.

Queries with published clips required; address **Queries** to Manuscripts Editor; response time about 12 weeks; send SASE for Writer's Guidelines.

MULTINATIONAL MONITOR
P.O. Box 19405
Washington, DC 20036
Tel: 202/387-8030 Fax: 202/234-5176
Editor: Robert Weissman

The Multinational Monitor is a monthly news magazine that focuses on the activities and escapades of multinational corporations. About 50 percent of its articles are provided by freelance writers. It is interested in articles, profiles, book reviews, interviews, essays, exposés, features and news items relating to multinational corporate issues. No fiction.

Rates: Ten cents a word.

Queries required; send SASE for Writer's Guidelines.

Tips: "Issues include all topics related to the activities of multinational corporations and their impact on labor, health, consumer issues and environment, especially in the Third World." —A. Freeman

THE NATION
72 Fifth Avenue
New York, NY 10011
Tel: 212/242-8400 Fax: 212/463-9712
Editor-in-Chief: Victor Navasky

The Nation is a weekly magazine (biweekly through the summer) dedicated to reporting on issues dealing with labor, national politics, business, consumer affairs, environmental politics, civil liberties, and foreign affairs. About 75 percent of its articles are provided by freelance writers. It is interested in articles, book reviews, opinion pieces, essays, and exposés.

Rates: $75 per Nation page

Queries with published clips required; normal response time is four weeks; send SASE for Writer's Guidelines.

Tips: "Leftist politics."—Dennis Selby

NATIONAL CATHOLIC REPORTER
P.O. Box 419281
Kansas City, MO 64141
Tel: 816/531-0538Fax: 816/531-7466
Editor: Tom Fox

The National Catholic Reporter is published weekly from September through May with the exception of Thanksgiving week and the first week in January. It publishes articles, profiles, book reviews, interviews, opinion pieces, essays, exposés, features and news items. About 50 percent of its articles are provided by freelance writers. Average length is from 750 to 1,500 words.

Rates: Fifteen cents a word.

Queries required.

NEWSLETTER ON INTELLECTUAL FREEDOM
50 E. Huron Street
Chicago, IL 60611
Tel: 312/280-4223 Fax: 312/440-9374
Editor: Judith F. Krug

The Newsletter On Intellectual Freedom is a bimonthly magazine published by the American Library Association (ALA). Book reviews are published in every issue of the NEWSLETTER. Interested reviewers should contact the ALA Office for Intellectual Freedom for guidelines. Articles focusing on intellectual freedom, freedom of the press, censorship, and the First Amendment will be considered for publication.

Rates: pro bono.

Queries required; send SASE for Writer's Guidelines.

Tips: "Authors should contact the Office for Intellectual freedom for information and guidelines."—Editor Judith Krug

THE PEOPLE'S WARRIOR
P.O. Box 488
Rockwall, TX 75087
Tel: 214/771-1991
Publisher: David Parker

The People's Warrior is a monthly publication which seeks to explore and profile legal or political corruption. About 90 percent of its articles are provided by freelance writers. All articles, profiles, book reviews, interviews, opinion pieces, essays, and exposés that deal with legal or political corruption will be given serious consideration. Manuscript length varies from two through ten typewritten, single-spaced pages.

Rates: $45 credit for 12-month subscription

Queries not required; response time is two weeks.

Tips: "We're particularly interested in well-documented articles which profile legal or political corruption."
—Publisher David Parker

THE PROGRESSIVE
409 E. Main Street
Madison, WI 53703
Tel: 608/257-4626 Fax: 608/257-3373
Editor: Matt Rothschild

The Progressive is a politically-oriented monthly magazine. About 80 percent of its articles are provided by freelance writers. It is interested in features, 2,500 words; activist profiles, 750 words; Q&A, 2,500 words; book reviews, 300-1,500 words; and exposés, 2,500-3,500 words.

Rates: Features, $300; book reviews, $150; interviews, $300; exposés, $300; and activist profiles, $100.

Queries preferred with published clips; normal response time is ten days; send SASE for Writer's Guidelines.

PUBLIC CITIZEN MAGAZINE
2000 P Street, NW
Washington, DC 20036
Tel: 202/833-3000 Fax: 202/659-9279
Editor: Peter Nye

Public Citizen Magazine is published six times a year and focuses on national policy issues and their impact on the public. About 15 percent of its articles are provided by freelance writers. It is interested in book reviews, 400 words (two reviews per magazine page); features up to 4,500 words; profiles of extraordinary individuals who work for improving their local community up to three pages.

Rates: negotiable, $400 tops; buys one-time rights only.

Queries required; normal response time is two weeks.

Tips: "Our articles deal with national

policy involving accountability of corporations and the government. It's best to read our magazine and be familiar with how our stories are published, their slant. We also rely heavily on facts, quotes, specific information."—Editor Peter Nye

SOJOURNERS
2401 15th Street, NW
Washington, DC 20009
Tel: 202/328-8842 Fax: 202/328-8757
Editor: Jim Wallis
Sojourners is published monthly (10 times a year) and about 25 percent of its articles are provided by freelance writers. It is interested in features on issues of faith, politics, and culture (1,800-3,200 words); book, film, and music reviews (600-1,000 words).
Rates: features, $100-$200; reviews, $40.
Queries not required; submit published clips; normal response time is six to eight weeks; send SASE for Writer's Guidelines.

SOUTHERN EXPOSURE
P.O. Box 531
Durham, NC 27702
Tel: 919/419-8311
Editor: Pat Arnow

Southern Exposure is a quarterly magazine that focuses on Southern politics and culture. About 50 percent of its articles are provided by freelance writers. It is interested in investigative journalism, essays, profiles, book reviews, oral histories, and features on Southern politics and culture.
Rates: $50-$250
Queries not required; submit published clips; normal response time is four to six weeks; send SASE for Writer's Guidelines. Send $5.00 for a sample copy.

ST. LOUIS JOURNALISM REVIEW
8380 Olive Boulevard
St. Louis, MO 63132
Tel: 314/991-1699 Fax: 314/997-1898
Editor: Charles L. Klotzer

The St. Louis Journalism Review is a regionally based but nationally oriented journalism review magazine published monthly except for combined issues in July/August and December/January. About 80 percent of its articles are provided by freelance writers. It is interested in articles, profiles, interviews, opinion pieces, essays, and exposés dealing with the news media.
Rates: $20 to $100.
Queries not required; normal response time is three to four weeks.
Tips: "While the St. Louis region is of primary interest, national and international pieces dealing with media criticism are considered."—Editor Charles L. Klotzer

TEXAS OBSERVER
307 W. 7th Street
Austin, TX 78701
Tel: 512/477-0746 Fax: Call first
Editor: Lou Dubose

Texas Observer, a publication that focuses on Texas but creates national waves, is published every two weeks. About 50 percent of its articles are provided by freelance writers. It is interested in articles, profiles, book reviews, interviews, essays, and exposés.

Rates: meager

Tips: "Texas-oriented politics and culture."—Associate Editor James Cullen

TIKKUN Magazine
251 W. 100th Street, 5th Floor
New York, NY 10025
Tel: 212/864-4110 Fax: 212/864-4137
Editor & Publisher: Michael Lerner

Tikkun is a bimonthly magazine that focuses on political and cultural issues. It is interested in articles, profiles, book reviews, interviews, opinion pieces, essays, exposés, features and news items; all types of material of varying lengths.

Rates: varies.

Queries not required; normal response time is four months.

Tips: "Political/cultural critiques—magazine has a liberal/progressive slant but does publish all sorts of viewpoints. A non-profit magazine."

U. THE NATIONAL COLLEGE MAGAZINE
1800 Century Park East, #820
Los Angeles, CA 90067
Tel: 310/551-1381 Fax: 310/551-1859
Managing Editor: Frances Huffman

U. The National College Magazine focuses on collegiate subjects and publishes 10 issues a year. About 90 percent of its articles are provided by freelance writers. It is looking for college news briefs: 300-400 words; feature articles: 1,000-2,000 words; profiles and interviews of celebrities, authors, athletes, politicians, etc.: 1,000 words; opinion pieces: 500-800 words; mini-features: 400-600 words; movie previews and music reviews: 100 words.

Rates: range from $25 to $100

Queries with published clips required (by phone, fax, or mail); send SASE for Writer's Guidelines; response time is one to two months.

Tips: "Our articles are written by college students and must have a college focus."—Managing Editor Frances Huffman

UTNE READER
1624 Harmon Place
Minneapolis, MN 55403
Tel: 612/338-5040
Managing Editor: Lynette Lamb

The Utne Reader is an eclectic bimonthly magazine that has earned the reputation of being the Reader's Digest of the alternative media. About 20 percent of its articles are provided by freelance writers. It is interested in short essays, articles, and opinion pieces.

Rates: $100-$500.

Queries not required; submit published clips; normal response time is two to three months; send SASE for Writer's Guidelines.

Tips: "We use unsolicited material most often in our 'Gleanings' section. Most of our other freelance articles are assigned. The majority of Utne Reader articles are reprinted from other publications."—Managing Editor Lynette Lamb

WASHINGTON SPECTATOR
541 E. 12th Street
New York, NY 10009
Tel: 212/995-8527 Fax: 212/979-2055

Editor: Ben Franklin;
Publisher: Phillip Frazer

The **Washington Spectator** is a small, but influential, political watchdog newsletter published 22 times a year. About 10 percent of its articles are provided by freelance writers. It is primarily interested in articles and exposés.
Rates: varies: 50 cents a word and up.
Queries with published clips required; normal response time is one week.
Tips: "Write a very brief (one page maximum) note as a first proposal."— Publisher Phillip Frazer

WILLAMETTE WEEK
822 SW 10th Avenue
Portland, OR 97205
Tel: 503/243-2122 Fax: 503/243-1115
Editor: Mark Zusman

Willamette Week is an alternative weekly newspaper published and distributed in the Portland, Oregon, area. About 50 percent of its articles are provided by freelance writers. It is interested in articles (if regional in perspective), interviews, book reviews, music reviews, profiles—again with a regional focus.
Rates: ten cents a word.
Queries with published clips required; normal response time is about three weeks; send SASE for Writer's Guidelines.

WRITER'S GUIDELINES
P.O. Box 608
Pittsburg, MO 65724
Fax: 417/993-5544
Publisher & Editor: Susan Salaki

Writer's Guidelines is a bimonthly magazine designed to help writers get published. About 99 percent of its articles are provided by freelance writers. It is interested in articles, book reviews, interviews, opinion pieces, and essays that will help writers.
Rates: depends on quality of material.
Queries not required; normal response time is two weeks; send SASE for Writer's Guidelines.
Tips: "Use a friendly relaxed style in your material but not chummy. Our objective is to help writers get published. If your article or essay contains information that will make that happen, we want to see it. We look for material the other writer publications usually overlook."—Editor Susan Salaki

APPENDIX C

Top 10 Censored! Reprints

1

Occupational Safety Agency Keeps Deadly Secrets

"UNFINISHED BUSINESS: OCCUPATIONAL SAFETY AGENCY KEEPS 170,000 EXPOSED WORKERS IN THE DARK ABOUT RISKS INCURRED ON JOB," by Public Citizen Health Research Group; Health Letter, March 1994

On February 2, 1994, Public Citizen's Health Research Group wrote to President Clinton urging him to immediately reverse Reagan-Bush policies and order acceleration of a program to individually notify nearly 170,000 workers of serious health risks they incurred through exposure to cancer-causing chemicals and other workplace hazards. Ten years have elapsed since Public Citizen wrote to President Reagan requesting that the federal government individually notify 240,450 workers exposed to hazardous materials at 258 worksites surveyed in 69 epidemiological studies funded and conducted by the National Institute for Occupational Safety and Health (NIOSH), a part of the Health and Human Services Department's Centers for Disease Control and Prevention (CDC). Today—a decade later—fewer than 30 percent of these workers covered by only a handful of studies have been notified.

Public Citizen has learned that, due to underfunding of its Screening and Notifications Section, NIOSH has individually notified a maximum of only 71,180 (29.6 percent) of the original 240,450 workers, leaving 169,270 still in the dark about health risks from on-the-job exposure. Those who were notified had been exposed at 55 (21.3 percent) of the 258 worksites. This failure to notify individuals in 60 of the 69 NIOSH studies has occurred despite notification recommendations from both NIOSH and CDC. A subcommittee of CDC's Ethics Advisory Committee concluded in 1983 that NIOSH has a duty to inform workers of exposure "particularly when NIOSH is the exclusive holder of information and when there is clear evidence of a cause and effect relationship between exposure and health risk." Many of the unnotified workers are unaware that they were exposed to substances (such as asbestos, silica and uranium) that were determined in these studies to increase the risk of cancer and other serious diseases, and thus have been denied an opportunity to take action to protect their health. Because of the long latent period between exposure to many industrial hazards and the development of overt disease, this information can still be useful to many workers. For example, upon learning that they were at increased risk workers could undergo screening that could lead to earlier detection of cancer.

The failure of the government to notify these workers has clear parallels to the current furor over subjects exposed to radiation in Department of Energy (DOE) studies. In both instances, the studies were funded by the U.S. government, the subjects were often unaware of their exposure, and the government has lists of the subjects by name. In fact, the NIOSH subjects are more clearly at increased health risk because the studies in which they were involved demonstrated an association between their occupational exposure and cancer and other diseases.

Although the NIOSH studies, unlike the DOE studies, were not experiments in which scientists administered hazardous material—they were studies of prior workplace exposure—for the federal government to fail to spend the amount of money it would take to notify each worker is unconscionable. It has been estimated that notification would cost $150 to $300 per person, or $25-50 million to cover all 169,270 still-unnotified workers.

NIOSH divided the original 69 studies into three categories (the agency's definition of each category is in parentheses):

Category A: ("Studies in which participants could gain direct medical/health benefits from notification"): 31 studies, 87 worksites, 104,821 workers.

Category B: ("Studies in which participants are potentially at high risk and should be notified but there are no known effective intervention methods"): 32 studies, 141 worksites, 128,246 workers.

Category C: ("Studies in which individual participant notification would stimulate improvements in working conditions"): 6 studies, 30 worksites, 7,383 workers.

Here, for comparison's sake, is the box score of NIOSH's accomplishments to date:

Category A: 9,250 workers notified (8.8 percent of total) at 20 sites (23.0 percent) in five studies (16.1 percent).

Category B: 61,930 workers notified (48.3 percent) at 35 sites (24.8 percent) in four studies (12.5 percent).

Category C: no workers notified (0.0 percent across the board).

Examples of Category A studies where no notification has occurred are: asbestos exposure in Globe, AZ (increased risk of lung cancer); dye exposure in Newton, NC (risk of cancer); and exposure to radiation in four states (22,000 workers at risk of lung cancer and respiratory disease).

It is perhaps revealing of NIOSH priorities that the vast bulk of notification efforts to date have been spent on Category B ("for which there are no known effective intervention methods") and only a relative trifle on Category A ("in which participants could gain direct medical/health benefits from notification"). Triage, the battlefield policy of treating those first who have the best chance of benefit, would suggest an opposite priority.

Despite the 1983 recommendations of its own scientific and ethical experts to notify exposed workers, the Reagan administration refused to fund a $4 million pilot notification program and opposed legislation that would have required such notification. Subsequently, NIOSH's Screening and Notifications Section began notifying subjects at a rate of three to five studies per year on a $300,000 annual budget. However, in addition to the 60 studies included in our original list for which NIOSH has done no notification, NIOSH has developed a backlog of 10-20 studies completed since 1984 for which notification has also not occurred. Most of the Section's efforts are going into notifying workers in the more recent studies. At this rate, notification will not be completed until most of the subjects have died, many from occupationally-acquired, potentially treatable health conditions. Public Citizen supports NIOSH's attempts to notify workers who were not included in the studies but nonetheless were exposed to the same industrial hazards in the workplaces studied.

Even at this snail's pace, evidence that notification is both feasible and potentially lifesaving has continued to accumulate. The most important notification program was conducted in Augusta, GA, among 1,385 workers exposed to beta-naphthylamine (BNA), which causes bladder cancer. Three of 13 workers with this disorder were discovered through the notification program. At least two additional cases have since occurred. A follow-up study of this cohort to determine whether more cases have occurred has only just begun, having been bottled up in the Bush administration's Office of Management and Budget for two years.

Three other aspects of the Augusta study are worthy of note. First, only 58 percent of screened workers had ever heard of BNA, and in this group only 41 percent were aware that BNA is harmful. Second, a psychological evaluation revealed no significant adverse effects from notification in those notified. Third, although 169 workers filed about $300 million in lawsuits, these were ultimately settled for $500,000, an average of less than $3,000 for each litigant. This should allay concerns raised by Reagan administration officials that notification would result in a flurry of lawsuits. But even if it did, Public Citizen believes the government has no business insulating industry from workers' legitimate claims for compensation from workplace illnesses.

The issue of radiation-exposed subjects in DOE-funded studies has once again focused public attention on the issue of human research subjects' rights, and here the government appears to be acting expeditiously in notifying subjects in the radiation experiments of their exposures. Workers in the NIOSH studies, often exposed to carcinogens and other hazards at massive levels, deserve the same kind of attention, rather than the unethical coverup that has characterized the federal reponse to date.

What You Can Do: To inquire about a specific plant contact NIOSH at 1-800-356-4674. To order Public Citizen's report send $10.00 to Public Citizen, 2000 P Street, NW, Suite 600, Dept. WH, Washington, DC 20036.

2 CENSORED

Powerful Group Of Ultra-Conservatives Has Secret Plans For Your Future

"RIGHT-WING CONFIDENTIAL,"
by Joel Bleifuss; *In These Times,* 8/8/94

On a spring night in May 1981, under a tent in the backyard of political strategist Richard Viguerie's suburban Virginia home, 160 new-right political leaders celebrated the change in their political fortunes. President Reagan had been elected that previous November.

And though a taste of power was the main entree, the new right's best and brightest also dined on cold lobster, Peking duck, sushi and a strawberry-festooned elephant.

As members of the press looked on, Interior Secretary James Watt, Office of Management and Budget Director David Stockman, Phyllis Schlafly, Joseph Coors, Sen. John East (R-NC), Sen. Orrin Hatch (R-UT) and new-right wunderkind Paul Weyrich, among others, quenched their thirst with drinks served in coconut shells by kimono-dressed waitresses. And with coconuts raised on high, this collection of administration officials, congressmen, industrialists and conservative Christians inaugurated a political federation that was to coordinate their political agenda, the Council for National Policy (CNP).

After this public kickoff, the CNP went underground. Consequently, we do not know much about the CNP's actions or agenda. What we do know is that the radical right is clearly ascendent within the Republican party. It has taken over state GOP organizations in Texas, California, Minnesota, Hawaii, Iowa, Nevada, Arizona, Idaho and Virginia. These coups give credence to CNP leader Weyrich's contention that "[we] are no longer working to preserve the status quo. We are radicals, working to overturn the present power structure in this country."

Russ Bellant believes Weyrich should be taken seriously. Bellant is one of the few researchers who has delved into the shadows of CNP operations, devoting one chapter of his book

The Coors Connection to the group. Bellant's latest examination of this organization is the cover story in the forthcoming issue of *Front Lines Research*, a new publication of Planned Parenthood. "When the leadership of the American radical right needs a strategy, chances are very good that the planning will occur in a meeting of the CNP," writes Bellant. "The meetings of this secretive and little-known organization are often a springboard for radical-right campaigns and long-term planning. But these efforts will seldom be traced to the CNP."

Bellant told *In These Times* that Paul Weyrich is "probably the single most important person of CNP." Weyrich is also the founding president of the Heritage Foundation, a right-wing think tank, and he's the man who suggested the term "moral majority" to Jerry Falwell. In addition, Weyrich proposed that the Republicans include a plank in their 1988 platform that AIDS be controlled by "reintroducing and enforcing anti-sodomy laws."

As a political strategist, Weyrich is second to none. He has spent the last 20-some years using his considerable political skills to bind together a coalition of America's diverse right-wing tendencies. As a result of his efforts, far-right secularists and authoritarian Christians have found common ground in the CNP.

Weyrich was able to revive the right by convincing funders that ultra-conservatives needed to build a national infrastructure that included think tanks, special interest organizations, publications and a computerized fundraising network. Currently, Weyrich is pioneering the frontier of electronic organizing with a closed-circuit satellite television network, National Empowerment Television, which allows far-right groups to organize and exchange information through teleconferences.

Fred Clarkson, editor of *Front Lines Research*, says: "There is no doubt in our mind that the CNP is the central leadership network of the far right in the United States. It's the organization in which the key strategies of the far right are formulated."

Bellant sees the CNP as serving multiple purposes. "It provides an organization for networking, for planning and for funding political projects," he told *In These Times*. "It brings a certain efficiency by avoiding duplication of effort. For example, if Lou Sheldon of the Traditional Values Coalition is the CNP point man for anti-gay and lesbian activity, funders know to give him the money and connect with him on that issue."

The CNP was originally created by two members of the John Birch Society, former Rep. Larry McDonald (D-GA) and California investor William Cies. They tapped the Rev. Tim LaHaye of San Diego to become the organization's first president. LaHaye had been a leader of the Moral Majority in California.

Addressing the CNP founding fathers and mothers who were gathered under the tent in Viguerie's backyard in 1981, LaHaye explained the political facts of life: "Liberals don't believe in moral absolutes. For us conservatives, adultery is adultery. But for liberals, adultery is just an affair. ... Liberalism comes from humanism, which is situational ethics. Liberals believe values are optional."

LaHaye has described day care as a "secular humanist plot to steal the hearts and minds of millions of little children." As LaHaye sees it, humanism dates back to the Renaissance, a period that gave birth to artists like Michelangelo, whose depiction of naked flesh was "the forerunner of the modern humanist's demand for pornography."

LaHaye was succeeded in the post of CNP president by Tom Ellis, a leader of Jesse Helms' political apparatus. Ellis was a one-time director of the Pioneer Fund, which promotes the view that blacks are genetically inferior to whites. Ellis, who has since disavowed his racist past, once warned that the goal of integrationists was "racial intermarriage and the disappearance of the negro race by fusing into the white."

Since Ellis, CNP presidents have included Nelson Bunker Hunt, the John Birch Society leader who once tried to corner the silver market; Pat Robertson, the televangelist and founder of the Christian Coalition; and Richard DeVos, the president of Amway.

Today, the CNP's president is Edwin Meese, the former attorney general. The group meets quarterly behind tightly closed doors. The CNP is so secretive, in fact, that the group's Washington office will neither confirm nor deny where, or even if, the group meets. It is known, however, that the council has quietly gathered in such far-flung places as Sinaia, Romania.

The roster of the 500 people who are members of this organization is also confidential. According to CNP material obtained by Bellant, CNP membership costs $2,000 in annual dues; to join the group, prospective members must secure the support of two council members. Once nominated the candidate must gain the unanimous approval of the 14 members of the CNP executive committee, which votes by secret ballot.

Members of the CNP are known to include Jerry Falwell, whose current organization is the Liberty Alliance; Oliver North, a longtime member who sits on the CNP executive committee; Sen Don Nickles (R-OK); Sen. Trent Lott (R-MS); Sen. Jesse Helms (R-NC); Rep. Bob Dornan (R-CA); Brent Bozell III, of the Media Research Center; Iran-contra figure Gen. John Singlaub; Richard Shoff, the former leader of the Ku Klux Klan in Indiana; Republican pollster Richard Wirthlin; Robert Weiner, head of Maranatha, a Christian cult; Howard Phillips of the Conservative Caucus; Linda Bean Folkers of the L.L. Bean Co.; televangelist John Ankerberg; and Bob Jones III, president of Bob Jones University.

Last year, CNP Executive Director Morton C. Blackwell wrote a memorandum to members attending a meeting in St. Louis. As Chip Berlet reported in *Covert Action Quarterly*, Blackwell instructed council members that all remarks made at the conference were to be strictly private. "The media should not know when or where we meet or who takes part in our programs, before or after a meeting," Blackwell wrote.

Despite Blackwell's call for secrecy, a lot of information on that St. Louis meeting has leaked out. People for the American Way, the Washington-based liberal watchdog group, obtained a copy of the agenda for that two-day meeting, as well as biographical sketches of some of the members in attendance.

The following are some of the speeches on the St. Louis conference's agenda:

■ "Update on the Supreme Court and the Justice Department," by Edwin Meese.

■ "How We Can Stay on the Winning Track," by Phyllis Schlafly.

■ "The Campaign Against *NYPD Blue*," by Donald Wildmon of the American Family Association. (Wildmon once described Universal Studios as "a company dominated by non-Christians.")

■ "Crisis in the Oil Patch and Excessive Environmental Regulation," by Don Hodel, former secretary of the Interior and Energy under Reagan.

■ "The Environmental Movement: Bad for the Environment," by David Ridenour, vice president of the National Center for Public Policy Research.

■ "Update on the Hatch Act and Striker Replacement Legislation," by Reed Larson, president of the National Right to Work Committee.

Perhaps the highlight of the conference was the presentation of the Winston Churchill Award, which is given in the spirit of Churchill's famous quote, "Victory at all costs, for without victory, there is no survival." The award went to David Brock, the *American Spectator*'s sexual-affairs correspondent who has tirelessly promoted tales of Clinton's alleged infidelities. A previous recipient of the award was CNP member Ralph Reed, the executive director of the Christian Coalition— whose 1 million members dominate many state Republican organizations.

One of the more colorful CNP members is retired Gen. Gordon Sumner, a far-right foreig policy expert, who claims that part of the problem with Latin America stems from the genetic mix of the Spaniards, who were behind the Inquisition, and the Aztecs, who practiced human sacrifice. "Somehow, this combination makes a very violent reaction," he has concluded.

But Sumner's ignorance pales in comparison to the CNP's R.J. Rushdoony, a leader of the Christian Reconstruction movement. Rushdoony argues that right-thinking Christians should take "dominion" over the United States and do away with the "heresy" that is democracy. *Christianity Today* reports that Rushdoony believes that in a Christian nation, "true to the letter of Old Testament law, homosexuals ... adulterers, blasphemers, astrologers and others will be executed."

It would be easy to dismiss CNP as a collection of right- wing nuts. But that would be a mistake.

"These are groups that move with unswerving determination," Bellant told *In These Times*. "Virtually all the people I see in the leadership of CNP are committed to either an anti-democratic or theocratic social system. Once they really gain the upper hand, they do not intend to ever let their enemies come back again."

The radical right does not now have the upper hand, but it is nonetheless a significant force in U.S. politics—as evidenced by the rightward shift in national politics in the past 15 years.

Bellant puts some of the blame on liberals. "The liberals are genuinely ignorant of who the right is and how they operate. They keep acting as if all that matters is the bottom line on voting day and they ignore all the base-building that goes on in the years preceding election day." he says. "Remember, it was the far right that used so called social issues—abortion, guns, taxes—to split the coalition of the Democratic Party. But the leadership of the constituency groups of the Democratic Party and of the party itself largely ignores the right wing. It beats me why people can't see where it is all coming from and go right to the heart of it. The Republican establishment is married to the Christian Right; it can't win an election without them. But the Democrats refuse to address the essential role of the Christian Right in the Republican Party, so the coalition is allowed to thrive and defeat them."

If Weyrich was a Democrat, he would advise the party to follow his lead and, as he has said, "go for the jugular." The Democrats could learn other things from Weyrich, such as the value of building a national political infrastructure to support grass-roots actions, the importance of forging political coalitions and the need to communicate ideas forcefully and effectively.

But in order to communicate ideas, the Democrats would first have to have some.

Secret Pentagon Plan Pays Defense Contractors Billions To Grow Larger

"FLAK FOR DEFENSE MERGER," by Patrick J. Sloyan; *Newsday*, 7/28/94

WASHINGTON—A secret Pentagon decision to pay military contractors billions of dollars to underwrite expenses connected with acquisitions and mergers was attacked in Congress yesterday as a Clinton administration program to play "fairy godmother" to major defense companies awash in profits.

Under fire for changing Pentagon policies designed to prevent taxpayers from subsidizing mergers were Defense Secretary William Perry and his deputy, John Deutch.

Republicans and Democrats alike on the House Armed Services Investigations Subcommittee challenged Deutch's repeated assertion that the unprecedented payment plan approved without any announcement last year was designed to save taxpayers money. According to Deutch, the mergers would help reduce overhead charges by defense contractors as the industry becomes smaller. Various members portrayed the policy change as a potential windfall for defense contractors and an incentive for hostile corporate takeovers, with taxpayers picking up the bill.

Perry, working on the Rwanda relief effort, canceled his appearance before the panel, leaving Deutch to explain the policy shift, first reported earlier this month. But Deutch did not answer crucial questions on what defense contractors would get paid for. "I'll get back to you," Deutch said repeatedly as he was peppered for details.

"The specifics of any savings are just not there," said David Cooper of the General Accounting Office after reviewing the policy change. Cooper told the panel that the GAO study concluded that the new policy could involve "several billions of dollars" in payments to defense contractors for postmerger restructuring costs that have yet to be defined.

In one heated exchange with Deutch, Representative Lynn Schenk, D-Calif., objected to secrecy surrounding a $60 million Pentagon payment to Martin Marietta Corp. in connection with its purchase of a General Dynamics subsidiary in her San Diego district, which is being reduced in size.

"I don't know how you explain this payment to laid-off workers in my district," said Schenk of Martin Marietta's plans to shift former General Dynamics operations to Colorado. She said her constituents viewed it "as the Big Guys going into what I hope was a smoke-free back-room and cutting a deal."

"It was a convention of the sugar daddies and their fairy godmother," Schenk said.

But the plan was supported by Norman Augustine, chairman of Martin Marietta. He argued that the federal government would reap lower costs from defense mergers over the long term.

Under the plan, Augustine's company would get $330 million from the Pentagon to cover expenses related to the purchase of the former subsidiary of General Dynamics and also a purchase of a General Electric subsidiary. The $60 million payment for the General Dynamics acquisition was previously reported, but yesterday's hearing mentioned for the first time that there was an additional $270 million payment planned for the GE deal.

It was Augustine who urged Perry and Deutch to reverse the ban on such payments last year. Both Perry and Deutch were on the Martin Marietta payroll before joining the Clinton administration.

But the administration's payment plan was challenged as illegal and unnecessary by a Brookings Institution expert, Lawrence Korb, who served as a senior Pentagon official during the Bush administration.

"Defense is still a profitable business and defense stocks are still quite high," Korb told the panel. "Taxpayer subsidization is not necessary to promote acquisitions and mergers." Korb and committee members noted that Augustine's company recently offered $2 billion in a failed attempt to acquire Grumman Corp.

Committee members appeared ready to demand that the Pentagon be able to prove actual savings from a merger before permitting payments to defense contractors. The hearing was called by Representative Norman

Sisisky, D-Va., who has won House approval of legislation to ban post-merger payments after last May 4.

4

Poisoning Ourselves: The Impact Of Incineration On Human Health

"POISONING OURSELVES: THE IMPACT OF INCINERATION ON FOOD AND HUMAN HEALTH, AN EXECUTIVE SUMMARY,"
Prepared by Mick G. Harrison Esq., Government Accountability Project, 9/29/94

By the later part of the 1980s the U.S. Environmental Protection Agency (EPA) understood two very important facts that should have fundamentally altered waste disposal policy. First, government officials knew that incineration produced dioxin as a byproduct. Dioxin is one of the most potent, toxic and carcinogenic chemicals known to science. Current scientific evidence indicates that dioxin produces serious health effects at extremely low doses. Some of the effects include cancer, immune deficiencies, and a variety of developmental impacts on unborn and young children.

Second, EPA scientists knew that dioxin accumulates through the food chain much like the banned pesticide DDT accumulates in the environment. Dioxin is a persistent substance that easily stores and remains in the tissues of plants and animals. A recent analysis by the EPA indicated that the health risks posed by consumption of dioxin through the food chain was 1,000 to 10,000 times greater than the risks posed by inhalation.

After close examination by GAP lawyers in the federal court case involving the Waste Technologies Industries (WTI) hazardous waste incinerator in East Liverpool, Ohio, EPA officials admitted that EPA had no standards to address the immense risks posed by food chain contamination from incinerators emitting dioxin. Further, an internal EPA memo leaked to Greenpeace and GAP during the case acknowledged that attention to the food chain risks could have major implications and require reevaluation of risks at many other sources of air emissions.[1]

Despite this information, incineration has rapidly proliferated throughout the country as the "profitable answer" for disposing of the nation's stockpile of toxic waste and garbage. In fact, incineration does not destroy the waste, it transforms it. Dioxin, lead, mercury, PCBs and other air emissions from

---

1. Among the significant statements from then-Acting Assistant Administrator Richard Guimond to new EPA Administrator Carol Browner is the following: "The analyses of the WTI situation show that many air emission sources could be affected if EPA were to adopt the indirect [food chain] exposure analysis procedures in the assessing exposure risks."

incinerator smokestacks cannot be adequately contained even with the most advanced equipment. These poisons are widely dispersed, and like acid rain, result in uncontrolled pollution of the surrounding water, soil, and farmland.

The dangers of these bio-cumulative chemicals multiply dramatically as they are absorbed up through the food chain from soil and water to plant and animal life to humans. In the case of dioxin, it takes seven years for your body to eliminate half of the dioxin in your system. And, it takes twelve years for half of the dioxin that accumulates in soil to be eliminated. Public health experts have stated that the amounts of dioxin currently contained in each of us, and the amounts we are exposed to daily, are enough to cause non-cancer adverse health effects. Consequently, experts urge immediate action to prevent any additional exposures to this highly toxic chemical. For example, the International Joint Commission on the Great Lakes has issued a resolution recommending the elimination of any further discharges of dioxin, PCBs, and related chemicals in the Great Lakes region.

Despite industry promises to local governments, incineration is *not* profitable. In fact, according to the *Wall Street Journal* (8/11/93), garbage incineration is on an economic "death spiral" with excess capacity far exceeding disposal needs. The substantial public health risks resulting from waste incineration cannot be justified by a cost/benefit analysis. Moreover, this capacity surplus would increase substantially if local governments implemented aggressive waste reduction, toxins reduction, and recycling programs. However, municipalities already financially strapped by waste incinerators are seeking to import garbage to make incineration more economical, rather than pursue the alternatives of reuse and source reduction.

Who is paying the highest price for the operation of incinerators? It is those most vulnerable to the adverse health effects of incinerator emissions: the young, the sick, and the elderly. But, no one is safe. Studies show that long range transport of air pollutants are hurting all of us. For example, remote lakes in the wilderness areas of Wisconsin have become so highly contaminated with mercury that the fish cannot be eaten. Research has shown that long range transport of mercury from incineration and other air pollution sources is the only possible source of contamination. In addition, food growing areas that are subject to incinerator fallout ship food all over the country and the world. The dioxin waste incinerator in Jacksonville, Arkansas, for example, is located on the border of two counties that are nationally ranked for their agricultural production.

When risk assessments are done for incinerator facilities the only fallout that is examined is that which allegedly occurs within a three to ten mile radius of the machine. Pollutants that cross this imaginary boundary are totally ignored. Moreover, government and industry risk analyses virtually never take into account the fallout from other incinerators, even when they are nearby. Like a fistful of stones thrown into water, concentric circles of emissions from hundreds of incinerators in operation across the country are now overlapping and interacting. Communities are exchanging poisons that can become even more lethal in combination. EPA has purposefully avoided documenting the cumulative effects of hazardous and solid waste incineration.

Simply stated, our national policy of promoting incineration and other combustion methods of waste disposal is poisoning us. In federal court testimony, EPA officials began their risk analysis of an incinerator by explaining that the cancer rate in this country is twenty-five percent. (Some health experts believe that one out of three of us will contract some form of cancer.) EPA assumes that the twenty-five percent rate is acceptable and attempts to explain how the proposed incinerator will only marginally increase the cancer rate.

On close analysis, it is clear that there are many flaws in the EPA-industry risk perspective including: 1) the failure to acknowledge that our current national cancer rate is largely the result of environmental exposures to industry pollutants, and 2) the use of risk assessment methods, that when corrected for error and non-conservative assumptions, warrant far higher projections of risk than those reported by EPA and industry.

The most recent so-called breakthrough on the hazardous waste incineration front has been the new draft EPA waste combustion strategy. Unfortunately, this policy has no teeth. For example,

■It is not being applied to incinerators that are used in Superfund cleanups. Over 1,000 communities have some sort of waste cleanup problem that may warrant Superfund action.

■The EPA policy has not been applied to the dioxin waste incinerator in Jacksonville, Arkansas, despite gross evidence of failures to meet standards and rulings in federal court that the Vertac Superfund site incinerator is a threat to the community.

■The policy is not being used to require timely and strict compliance with *current* standards. The WTI incinerator in East Liverpool, Ohio and LWD incinerator in Calvert City, Kentucky are prime examples of non-compliance problems.

■EPA policy is sporadically applied at commercial hazardous waste incinerators. Hazardous waste incinerators in Calvert City and Rock Hill, South Carolina, for example, are not required to stay within any specified dioxin emission limit. Implementation of a minimum dioxin emission limit has been undercut by agency interpretation allowing incinerator owners and operators to try to justify higher limits via site specific risk assessment.

■Finally, the policy is not being used in any significant manner to provide *maximum* protection for public health as touted by Carol Browner when the policy was first announced. This is evident by the refusal to take swift action to prevent communities from being unnecessarily exposed to dangerous pollutants in East Liverpool, Jacksonville, Rock Hill and Calvert City, among others.

President Clinton's health care policy directly, but only rhetorically, addresses the very problems faced by incinerator plagued communities. It espouses an intent to "Protect Americans against preventable ... exposure to toxic environmental pollutants ..." Nowhere is such preventative action more important than in the communities where unnecessary hazardous waste incinerators saturate the air and food supply with dioxin, lead, mercury, cadmium, and other persistent toxins.

GAP is playing an important role in challenging national policy on waste disposal. Our work in partnership with Greenpeace and community groups in East Liverpool and Jacksonville was instrumental in forcing the creation of the EPA's draft hazardous waste combustion strategy. In our experience, there is no more effective approach to compelling change in government than using inside information to push for accountablity. For the last fifteen years, GAP has pioneered the technique of providing concerned government and industry workers with a safe haven to provide information and dissent against illegal or improper practices. This approach has forced significant change in the handling of commercial nuclear power plants, Energy Department bomb factories, and our nation's meat inspection system.

Now, for the first time, GAP has obtained inside information from industry workers at an incinerator site. At the Vertac incinerator in Jacksonville where the dioxin waste from producing Agent Orange is being burned, concerned workers have complained that the incinerator is unsafe for them as well as the community. Their acts of courage have allowed

GAP to inform EPA, the media, and Congress about the outrageous conditions and repeated inability to meet federal regulatory standards that plagues the Vertac incinerator.

GAP expects that the example set by the Vertac workers will encourage other workers at incinerators around the country to expose the serious problems experienced by incinerators. With information from industry employees, EPA whistleblowers and other government workers, GAP will provide ongoing technical assistance to members of Congress as they consider incineration moratorium legislation and other reforms this year. Our goal is to ensure that the facts and public health standards prevail, rather than "business as usual."

For more information, please contact GAP attorneys Mick Harrison or Richard Condit at (202)408-0034.

Clinton Administration Retreats on Ozone Crisis

"FULL OF HOLES: CLINTON'S RETREAT ON THE OZONE CRISIS," by David Moberg; *In These Times*, 1/24/94

What ever happened to Ozone Man? Al Gore once earned that moniker from George Bush for his professed environmental passions. But during its first year in office, the Clinton administration has been moving backward on protecting the stratospheric ozone layer, which shields the earth from the sun's ultraviolet radiation. Ozone Man has been silent.

Many environmentalists feel betrayed by the administration on the ozone issue. The biggest knife in the back came in mid-December, when the Environmental Protection Agency (EPA) asked Du Pont to keep making chlorofluorocarbons (CFCs)—the most notorious ozone-depleting chemical—until 1996. The company had originally planned to halt CFC production at the end of this year.

The EPA defends its decision as a "consumer protection" measure that will make it easier for car owners to recharge their old air conditioners, which use CFCs as a cooling agent. But it is an environmental retreat—with harmful implications beyond the creation of another 75 tons of CFCs. It is also bad economic policy, retarding rather than encouraging emerging ozone-safe technologies that can tap vast new markets.

Bill Walsh, coordinator of Greenpeace's U.S. atmosphere and energy campaign, argues that the Clinton administration's "spineless" decision on car CFCs sets a "precedent about how they'll deal with any sensitive environmental problem." And that's not the only precedent it will set. The move opens the gates for other industrial countries to stall on their own CFC phase-outs. And it puts the administration in a far weaker position to argue for an accelerated phase-out of CFCs (and harmful CFC substitutes) in the developing countries, where CFC production is soaring.

It's been 20 years since scientists first figured out that chlorine compounds from CFCs deplete the ozone layer in the upper reaches of the atmosphere. That discovery came nearly a half century after a Du Pont chemist developed the first industrial CFC. Marketed as Freon, it became the leading cooling fluid for refrigerators, freezers and air conditioners. Later, CFCs were widely used as solvents (especially in electronics), as aerosol propellants and as a means of blowing bubbles into foam plastics.

The United States and a few other countries banned CFC aerosols in the late '70s, but it was not until 1987 that the Montreal Protocol was negotiated among most of the nations of the world to phase out production of CFCs. Hailed as a landmark environmental agreement, the Montreal Protocol and legislation in individual countries have cut CFC production by roughly half. Nonetheless, overall production of ozone-depleting halocarbons remains about the same as before the protocol, due to increases in the manufacture of other chemicals.

Evidence has mounted to indicate that both the destruction of the ozone layer and the resulting dangers to human health and the ecosystem are far more serious than scientists had first recognized. The ozone hole over Antarctica, whose emergence surprised atmospheric scientists, has continued to grow virtually every year since its discovery in 1985. Damage to the ozone layer over heavily populated areas of the Northern Hemisphere has also been increasing rapidly. Last year, scientists recorded all-time low levels of ozone over the United States.

Ultraviolet rays that penetrate a weakened ozone layer have been linked to increased cataracts, skin cancer, genetic damage and infectious diseases among humans—as well as reduced plant growth. New research, to be released in February, reportedly indicates that the health effects—especially supression of the immune system—are more serious than previously believed, and that sunscreens may be ineffective protection. Ultraviolet radiation from ozone depletion, argues former United Nations Environmental Program chairman Mostafa Tolba, may turn out to be "AIDS from the sky."

In response to the growing threat, there have been three revisions of the Protocol to speed up the phase-out of CFCs and to cover additional chemicals. Yet even if the current phase-out proceeds according to plan—which calls for most production of CFCs in industrial countries to halt by 1996—the peak destruction of the ozone layer is expected to occur between 2000 and 2010. After that, the ozone layer is supposed to regenerate—but scientists warn that there are often surprising, non-linear changes in the atmosphere (like the Antarctic ozone hole) and that any additional chlorine in the stratosphere is a gamble.

In light of these risks, the Clinton administration's actions are especially troubling. Auto air conditioning is in fact one of the least morally defensible uses of CFCs—especially when compared to cooling schools and hospitals in tropical countries. Furthermore, air-conditioning units in cars are extremely prone to leak CFCs. They also require big charges of CFCs to cool hot cars quickly (although that need could be drastically reduced by installing a small $25, solar-powered fan to cool off a parked car).

The EPA's decision came in response to only the slightest of pressure from the auto companies. But the administration may have also been worried about public opinion: the EPA concluded that angry motorists might face a cost of up to $1,000 to retrofit replacements for their old CFC auto air conditioners.

But the dilemma was due in large part to the agency's own botching of its program to recapture and recycle CFCs, according to Damian Durant, director of the Ozone Safe Cooling Association, a trade group. Durant points out that there are good, relatively untapped recycling technologies as well as a cheaper "drop-in" replacement process, both of which the EPA has failed to promote.

Clinton's policies "reward companies that drag their feet," such as the auto companies, Greenpeace's Walsh argues, and fail to encourage sound alternatives. The main alternatives to CFCs now are hydrochlorofluorocarbons (HCFCs) and hydrofluorocarbons (HFCs).

HFCs, which are used in new car air conditioners, do not contain chlorine and do not destroy the ozone, but they are extremely powerful global warming agents. Pound for pound, HFCs have 3,200 times the global warming effect of carbon dioxide. Within a few decades, they could account for as much as one-tenth of global warming. HCFCs do contain chlorine and destroy the ozone—but less quickly than CFCs. Their advocates in the chemical industry messed with the numbers to greatly play down HCFCs' likely impact on the ozone. But looking at its short-term effects, which would coincide with the expected peak of ozone destruction, HCFCs appear to be about one-sixth to one-fourth as bad as CFCs.

The chemical companies continue to argue for HCFCs as "transitional" chemicals, even though alternatives that do not destroy the ozone are available or on the brink of commercialization. In 1992, the industrialized nations agreed to slowly phase out HCFCs by 2030, which will give the chemical industries time to profit from their huge investments in HCFC facilities. (Du Pont has already invested $500 million in HCFCs and HFCs.)

Rather than search for a similar chemical replacement for CFCs, other companies have been developing quite different solutions. The U.S. electronics industry, for example, has quickly shifted from CFCs as solvents to water-soluble pine and citrus-based solvents, or to revamped clean-production systems that require no cleaning fluids. Alternatives for aerosols range from gas propellants to mechanical spray pumps. Vacuum panels and other insulation could easily replace plastic foam. Wherever foams are needed, blowing agents such as carbon dioxide can replace CFCs and HCFCs.

Moreover, there are dozens of alter-natives, especially for cooling, that have not been developed in the United States because the chemical companies have promoted HCFCs and HFCs. The EPA has thrown its support behind these chemical industry favorites, and done virtually nothing to support better alternatives.

For example, the EPA last year co-sponsored a conference with the chemical industry and provided subsidies to big companies like Du Pont. Yet the agency refused to co-sponsor a conference of ozone-safe manufacturers—and provided virtually no funds for these mainly smaller firms.

James Mattil is the 46-year-old owner of Colorado-based Climatran Corp., which has developed a promising, environmentally sound technology for air conditioning vehicles. Despite this, Mattil has been forced to the edge of bankruptcy by federal government policies.

Climatran's system relies on a simple principle: hot air from outside the vehicle passes over water in the air conditioning system and cools down as it evaporates water. Although this works best in dry climates, a two-stage system that relies on a preliminary device called a heat-exchanger makes this system widely applicable.

Mattil has already produced 400 of these completely ozone-safe cooling systems for city buses in Denver and Salt Lake City. The federal Department of Transportation, which provided Denver a grant to try the buses, found this system used 90 percent less energy than conventional air conditioners, cost one-eighth as much to maintain, had a 70 percent cost advantage over its entire life cycle and cost nearly the same or slightly more up front.

So why isn't everyone buying these systems? Although the federal government supplies most of the money for city transit buses and buys many buses and similar vehicles for its own fleet, it hasn't bought a single evaporation-cooled vehicle. Worse yet, federal policies and red tape have discouraged cities from using this technology.

For example, the Department of Transportation requires bus manufacturers to undergo extremely expensive testing of vehicles employing alternative air-conditioning technology. Although bus makers were ready to offer Climatran's systems, they couldn't afford the test costs. Mattil finally appears on the verge of being exempted from the tests—but only after two years of pleading.

Also, Mattil has been subjected to bewildering Catch-22 explanations for why the EPA will not underwrite research on heat exchangers. He's been told that the technology is too commercial to qualify for funds; he's also been told that it's not commercial enough.

The EPA was even suspiciously slow in certifying Climatran's system as environmentally acceptable. This approval, which by law must be completed within 30 days, helps companies to market their ideas, and to get funds for research and development. But when Mattil applied, the agency was busy approving HFCs. Two years later, under threat of a lawsuit, the EPA finally approved his technology last fall.

"We have felt blocked from the marketplace until after the chemical companies established themselves as viable substitutes," Mattil says. "Now we've got to dislodge them. They wanted a beachhead, and they got it."

Mattil's case is hardly unusual. Steven Garrett developed an innovative technology called thermoacoustics, which resonates sound waves through gases like helium and argon to create cooling effects. Although it has been used in the space program, Garrett can't get funding for commercialization, despite the fact that some Japanese firms have recently shown interest.

"This could be the next generation of cooling technology, entirely environmentally benign," Durant says. "Soundwave cooling is akin to the first transistor or silicon chip. Yet for an administration concerned with technology, it's left lying in the backwater."

Even in cases in which alternative technologies have been developed elsewhere, U.S. companies are often slow to act. In cooperation with Greenpeace, an East German refrigerator company that had been floundering after unification began manufacturing refrigerators using pentane and butane as cooling agents. This "Greenfreeze" mixture of basic hydrocarbons doesn't deplete the ozone and has minimal effects on the climate. The consumer response to an environmentally friendly refrigerator was so great that bigger companies began producing Greenfreeze models. But no U.S. company, including Whirlpool, which makes a European Greenfreeze refrigerator, offers this alternative.

Administration policies do nothing

to push manufacturers along the environmentally preferable route—which is also where the long-term market lies. This long-range market includes the rapidly growing sales of cooling and refrigeration equipment in developing countries, which will probably follow the West's technological lead, for good or ill.

The administration's failures on ozone policy are too consistent to reflect simply bureaucratic incompetence. Last spring, when it was clear there would be record levels of ozone loss over the United States, NASA scientists urged the federal government to issue public health warnings, much as Canada has done for a couple of years. But the government gave little publicity to the findings and issued no warnings.

Later, in the mad scramble to buy votes for NAFTA, U.S. Trade Representative Mickey Kantor promised Florida agribusiness concerns that the administration would violate the Montreal Protocol and delay the phase-out of methyl bromide, a fumigant and potent ozone depletor. Although the administration backtracked when the deal was revealed, growers are still demanding the regulatory retreat.

The old ways of doing business remain at the EPA. Robert Sussman, the deputy administrator who requested that Du Pont keep manufacturing CFCs, came from a law firm that represented the Chemical Manufacturers Association. Bush's head of EPA, William Reilly, is now on the board of Du Pont. If, as the title of Al Gore's book proposes, the earth is in

the balance, then the EPA is still tipping the scale to the chemical industry—despite the Ozone Man's presence in the halls of power.

1947 AEC Memo Reveals Why Human Radiation Experiments Were Censored

"PROTECTING GOVERNMENT AGAINST THE PUBLIC,"
by Steven Aftergood; *Secrecy & Government Bulletin*, March 1994

One of the more remarkable documents to emerge from the Energy Department's openness initiative is a 1947 Atomic Energy Commission memorandum on the classification of human radiation experiments. It states:

"It is desired that no document be released which refers to experiments with humans and might have adverse effect on public opinion or result in legal suits. Documents covering such work should be classified secret."

Thus the true enemy is identified: public opinion. And the means to defeat the enemy? Classification.

The practice of classifying information in order to prevent embarrassment to an agency has long been prohibited. And yet it is commonplace. The AEC memo itself was classified Secret (meaning it supposedly "could be expected to cause serious damage to the national security"), and was only declassified last month. A copy of the document, obtained by Rep. John Dingell's subcommittee on oversight, is available from S&GB.

"THE RADIATION STORY NO ONE WOULD TOUCH," by
Geoffrey Sea; *Columbia Journalism Review*, March/April 1994

Suddenly, at the close of 1993, the public was bombarded with "news" about the feeding of radioactive substances to pregnant women and mentally retarded students, about the unethical irradiation of workers, soldiers, medical patients, and prison inmates, and about the government's own internal fears that these experiments had "a little of the Buchenwald touch." But the story that appeared in *The Albuquerque Tribune* (circulation: 35,000) on November 15-17, and was then projected into the national headlines by the forthright admissions and initiatives of Secretary of Energy Hazel O'Leary, was hardly new.

By 1984, activists and researchers across the country were systematically investigating the human experimentation program and attempting to bring it to public attention. By 1986, documentation of the program was massive, solid, and publicly available.

I am among those who persistently tried to get national media coverage of this outrageous example of government wrongdoing. To say that the media were reluctant to listen would be an understatement. The fact is that, for more than a decade, documentation

was ignored and facts were misreported.

What follows is a chronology of significant events in the strange history of this important story—one that began to receive adequate coverage only after almost all the victims were dead and most of the perpetrators retired:

1971: *The Washington Post* reveals that a research team at the University of Cincinatti, under the leadership of Eugene Saenger, has been irradiating "mentally enfeebled" patients—all of them poor and most of them black—at dose rates known to have harmful effects. The aim of the research, funded by the Department of Defense: to discover whether and under what conditions soldiers on an atomic battlefield would be cognitively impaired.

A review panel is established at the University of Cincinatti. However, the ethical issues are subordinated to the relatively technical question of the mechanism for obtaining consent. The experiments continue. No one seems to consider the obvious ethical problem involved in extracting "informed consent" from patients selected because of their "low-educational level ... low-functioning intelligence quotient ... and strong evidence of cerebral organic deficit." The researchers claim that the patients "benefit" from the radiation exposure, despite the fact that the radiation far exceeds recommended therapeutic doses, that the treatments are not intended to have a therapeutic effect, and that, in Saenger's own estimation, eight patient deaths could possibly be attributed to the "treatments."

1972: The researchers quietly end

their experiments when evidence of harmful effects begins to mount. After a cursory review by the American College of Radiology, no one bothers to reopen the case for public scrutiny. No attempt is made to monitor the health of the surviving experimental subjects.

1975: Following revelations of army-sponsored LSD experiments, Senator Edward Kennedy chairs hearings on human experimentation funded by the Department of Defense and the Central Intelligence Agency. Radiation experiments, however, are not mentioned either in the hearings or in media coverage.

1976: *Science Trends*, a newsletter published in the National Press Building in Washington, D.C., reveals an experiment carried out in San Francisco, Chicago, and Rochester, New York, as part of the Manhattan Project, that "involved the injection of relatively massive quantities of bomb-grade plutonium into the veins of 18 men, women, and children." The article implies that the experiment was an isolated historical case, and concludes: "Whether injecting the key ingredient of the atomic bomb into unsuspecting patients can be equated with Nazi wartime experiments is a matter which is today considered moot."

1981: The case of Dwayne Sexton, irradiated as a child as part of NASA-sponsored research aimed at discovering the potential effects of radiation exposure on astronauts, gains fleeting attention when the mother of the child links the death of her son to the experiments. *Mother Jones* runs a cover story on the Sexton case. Albert Gore, then a young congressman from Tennessee, where the experiments had taken place, follows up with hearings on the Oak Ridge Total Body Irradiation Program. Neither the article nor the hearings links the Sexton case with the Saenger experiments or with the broader program of human experimentation with radiation.

Early-1980s: A network of activist-researchers starts to compile the full and extensive record of U.S. radiation experiments on humans.

In Cincinatti, Ohio, Dr. David Egilman of the Greater Cincinatti Occupational Health Center and I are investigating experiments conducted on nuclear workers and following the trail of the Saenger experiments. At the time, I am employed as a health consultant by the Oil, Chemical, and Atomic Workers Union and the Fernald Atomic Trades and Labor Council. The unions are concerned about the intentional radioactive contamination of workers' skin as a means of testing external cleansing agents and about the continuing use of workers as experimental subjects in the development of chelation drugs to treat internal exposure to radioactive heavy metals.

In the course of pressing claims for worker's compensation, we discover that the AEC/DOE has secretly contracted with local hospitals and coroners for the collection of fluid and tissue samples, surgically removed organs, and autopsy specimens—in some cases, whole cadavers of atomic workers. Some of these specimens are being taken and destroyed by the government, often without the knowledge or against the expressed wishes of the workers and/or their survivors.

We suspect that this "body-snatching" program serves a dual purpose: it helps the government accumulate data for military purposes, while at the same time it results in the destruction of physical evidence that could support compensation claims. Finally, we are concerned that Dr. Saenger has become the chief consultant and expert witness for the government in defending itself and its contractors against liability suits.

In California, Dorothy Legarreta, who had worked on the Manhattan Project as a laboratory technician, organizes the National Association of Radiation Survivors (NARS) and starts to write a book about human experimentation. In 1982, while examining the papers of Joseph Hamilton—the scientist in charge of radiation experiments at the University of California— at the library of University of California at Berkeley, she comes across a 1950 memo written to Shields Warren, then director of the Atomic Energy Commission's Division of Biology and Medicine. The memo advised that large primates—chimpanzees, for example—be substituted for humans in the planned studies on radiation's cognitive effects (the very same program of experimentation that Dr. Saenger was to execute). The use of humans, Hamilton wrote, might leave the AEC open "to considerable criticism," since the experiments as proposed had "a little of the Buchenwald touch."

After Legarreta finds the so-called Buchenwald memo, Hamilton's papers are removed from public access by University of California administrators. Soon after this, Legarreta files a Freedom of Information Act request with the Department of Energy, asking for all documents concerning experiments in which humans were intentionally exposed to radioactive materials through injection or ingestion. Later that year, NARS receives a two-foot-high carton of documents in response—documents that, for the first time, expose the widespread human experimentation program of the U.S. government.

In Missouri, Dotte Troxell is trying to document her own horrific experience and to demonstrate the bonds that unite all experiment survivors. In 1957, while working at the AEC's Kansas City plant, run by Bendix, she had been involved in a serious radiation accident. When the symptoms of acute radiation syndrome began appearing (hair loss, nausea, purpura, and hemorrhaging), she was sent to the Lovelace Clinic in New Mexico, a clinic established by the AEC for developing treatments for radiation injury. Because Troxell was thought to be near death, and presumably because she had been exposed to a Cobalt-60 calibration source that allowed the dose to her organs to be precisely determined, the doctors at Lovelace did exploratory surgery on her, probably to obtain tissue biopsies from her internal organs. When she awoke from surgery and asked what had been done to her, the doctors said they could not tell her for "national security" reasons. After suffering radiogenic cataracts in both eyes and giving birth to a son with congenital diabetes, Troxell founds VOTE: Victims and Veterans Opposed to Technological Experimentation.

In Knoxville, Tennessee, Clifford T. Honicker and Jacqueline Kittrell are investigating the human experimentation program at the DOE's nuclear complex at Oak Ridge. They locate and begin to analyze the papers of Stafford Warren, who had been medical director of the Manhattan Project and who subsequently directed the Oak Ridge medical program. Those of Warren's papers that are obtained, including classified documents and medico-legal files, provide a clear picture of the origins of the government's human experimentation program, as well as of the government's policy of denying compensation to radiation survivors. Honicker and Kittrell found the Radiation Research Project, which later becomes the American Environmental Health Studies Project.

Mid-1980s: Our network has accumulated enough documentation on the human experimentation program to go public. We do so at press conferences held in Cincinatti (November 1984), Knoxville (May 1985), Kansas City (May 1986), and Berkeley (July 1986). At each of the last three conferences, Hamilton's Buchenwald memo is released to the press, but no mainstream paper mentions it.

1985-86: In contract talks, the labor council representing workers at the DOE's Fernald, Ohio, uranium plant demands disclosure of all human studies involving uranium and plutonium, as well as information about toxic releases to the environment, use of atomic workers as experimental sub-jects, and the body-snatching program. Rather than release this information to the labor council, DOE officials contact the AFL-CIO leadership and threaten to close the plant if labor will not honor its "national security obligations." Frank Martino, president of the International Chemical Workers Union, writes to Paul Burnsky, president of the AFL-CIO Metal Trades Department, calling for an end to "continued efforts to represent the community"—a reference to the council's attempt to obtain information from the DOE through collective bargaining. The unions back off on their demand for information and abruptly terminate my employment. Dr. Egilman is instructed to stop all radiation-related work. He chooses instead to resign.

Dr. Egilman and I decide that now is the time to take everything we have and give it to *The New York Times*. Dr. Egilman gives the Buchenwald memo to *Times* reporter Matthew Wald, a college acquaintance. But no article appears in 1985, and there is no word from the *Times*. I contact *Times* reporter Stuart Diamond, describe the outlines of the story, arrange a meeting, assemble a stack of documents, and fly to New York. Diamond and I meet at a restaurant at La Guardia Airport. After reviewing the documents, including the Buchenwald memo, he says he will come to Ohio and look into the story.

On January 28, 1986, the date of Diamond's intended arrival, I am working at my desk with the television turned on but the sound off, as I often do. I am distracted at one point by a striking picture on the TV screen: a beautiful white plume of smoke unfurling against the azure sky. It is the explosion of the space shuttle Challenger. Within the hour, Diamond calls to say that he will be investigating the Challenger disaster—and thus won't be coming to Ohio anytime soon. He tells me to wait until he's done with the Challenger story. I wait for three months.

On April 26, the number three unit at the Chernobyl nuclear energy station explodes, and melts down. Diamond leaves to cover the accident. I leave Cincinatti and head for Kansas City, where, on May 5, Dotte Troxell and I hold a press conference. We say that U.S. criticism of Soviet secrecy is hypocritical and call on the U.S. government to release all data on human experimentation. In our press release we attack the credibility of Dr. Saenger—who has quickly been hired to advise the U.S. government on Chernobyl's impact on U.S. personnel stationed in Europe and has become the media's authority on Chernobyl's health effects. Our press release also details the U.S. human experimentation program "that has, at various times, included the exposure of prisoners, mental patients, terminal cancer patients, and paid volunteers to 'non-therapeutic' radiation doses...." Again, we show the Buchenwald memo to the press. The press responds with silence.

A number of us start working our congressional contacts. Cliff Honicker, Dorothy Legarreta, and I all had a close working relationship with the House Subcommittee on Energy Conservation and Power when it had been under the chairmanship of Representative Richard Ottinger of New York. Near the end of his tenure, Ottinger had authorized a full-scale staff investigation into the DOE's human experimentation program.

By 1986, chairmanship of the subcommittee has passed to Edward Markey of Massachusetts. Eager to see some result of the investigation, we press the subcommittee to go public in hearings and a report. No hearings are held—a curious fact given the magnitude of the issue—but in October the staff issues its report, "American Nuclear Guinea Pigs: Three Decades of Radiation Experiments on U.S. Citizens." Markey simultaneously issues a press release that states: "The purpose of several experiments was actually to cause injury to the subjects ... American citizens thus became nuclear calibration devices for experimenters run amok."

The Markey report, which contains all the relevant facts that would be treated as major revelations seven years later, results in minor and often misleading news stories in several papers. *The New York Times's* Matthew Wald extracts a single strand from the ninety-five-page report—news that some of the releases of radioactive iodine from the Hanford, Washington, nuclear facility had been intentional—and turns it into a story that runs on page A-20. The other ninety-plus pages of the report, which deal with unethical clinical experiments, are downplayed in a small, unbylined piece headed VOLUNTEERS AROUND U.S. SUBMITTED TO RADIATION. Contrary to the Markey report and to fact, the headline and article imply that all subjects had volunteered for the experiments and that they knew they were subjected to radiation. Neither article mentions the Buchenwald memo.

Of all the papers that come to our attention, only *The Daily Californian*, the student newspaper at the University of California at Berkeley, points up the Buchenwald memo. In a piece titled "At Buchenwald and Berkeley," editor-in-chief Howard Levine quotes from the November 28, 1950, memo by Dr. Hamilton and incisively criticizes reporting on the Markey report by the *San Francisco Chronicle* and *The New York Times*. Both papers, he writes, "minimized the gross inhumanity of these tests by downplaying their scope and ignoring the fact that most of the experiments were conducted without the 'informed consent' demanded by the Nuremburg protocols of 1946-47."

1987: Eileen Welsome of *The Albuquerque Tribune* starts looking into the plutonium-injection experiment, after coming across a footnote about it in a report on animal experimentation at the Air Force Weapons Laboratory at Kirtland Air Force Base in New Mexico.

1988: Dorothy Legarreta is killed in a mysterious car crash, reminiscent of the death of Karen Silkwood. Legarreta's briefcase—listed on the accident report as being found—is missing. The tow-truck driver says that the solid aluminum case was discarded because it was badly damaged, though such an action would be against the law. I was working with Legarreta just prior to her death and know that her briefcase contained a file titled "hot docs"—formerly secret documents that she and I had culled from government papers obtained through a class action lawsuit by veterans who had been intentionally exposed to atomic blasts and radiation while in the service.

1989: On November 19, *The New York Times Magazine* publishes an article by Cliff Honicker titled "The Hidden Files." The subtitle reads: "In 1946, a Nuclear Accident Killed One Scientist and Injured Several Others. The Government Response to That Tragedy Established a Pattern of Secrecy That Still Exists." Based in large part on the files Honicker had discovered five years earlier, the closely focused article does not deal with the government's years-long human experimentation program and its origins.

1991: *60 Minutes* airs a segment on the government's body-snatching program. In his introduction to the January 13 segment, Harry Reasoner says: "In the case of the men and women who have worked in this country's nuclear weapons industry, the government is apparently willing to go to any lengths to defeat workers' claims that they were injured or killed by exposure to radiation—any lengths, including falsifying records, concealing evidence, even trying to steal human remains ..." Oddly, according to the segment's producer, one of the most powerful interviews—with a courier who arranges for the shipment of body parts to Los Alamos and who was present at a secret autopsy at which body parts were removed without the knowledge or consent of the family—winds up on the cutting room floor.

Meanwhile, Jackie Kittrell and Cliff Honicker have been combing the hills of Tennessee, trying to track down women who, while pregnant, had been unwitting subjects in radioisotope ingestion studies decades earlier. Since some of the initial recruitment for the experiments had been through classified ads placed in newspapers in remote Appalachian towns, Jackie and Cliff try, repeatedly, to get the same papers to run articles describing the experiments and asking the women to come forward on a confidential basis. They try to persuade the Nashville *Tennessean* to run such articles because one of the largest experiments, involving more than 800 pregnant women, took place at Vanderbilt University, in Nashville. At least one reporter—Carolyn Shoulders at *The Tennessean*—proposes articles about the experimentation program to her editors, but no proposal meets with approval.

1992: In May, frustrated by the feeling that we are shouting in the wind, Dotte Troxell announces that she will begin a hunger strike in July, which she says she will continue until death unless the government releases all data on the experiments and provides care for all survivors. She says she prefers death "on her own terms" to a slow, quiet death preceded by the intensifying pains of her radiation injuries and she wants to use the hunger strike to help establish a union called IRIS: International Radiation Injury Survivors. But, fatigued and under the influence of pain-killing drugs, she dies in a tractor accident in late-May. She leaves behind the text of an intended final speech in which she asks to be cremated so that "the perpetrators of cruel and barbaric experimentation" will be denied "the knowledge they seek." She also forgives all those in the government, the public interest community, and the media who continue to "ignore our plight, for they know not—they were not on shipboard in the nuclear Pacific tests or in the trenches in Nevada, nor are they with the veterans in VA hospitals ..."

1993: In mid-November, *The Albuquerque Tribune* publishes Eileen Welsome's three-part series, "The Plutonium Experiment." In late-December, a decade after Kittrell and Honicker alerted the paper to the story—*The Tennessean* finally publishes an article about the Vanderbilt experiment and its medical follow-up study.

Emma Craft, who had never known that she had been fed radioactive iron in the 1940s, reads a detailed description of the 1958 death by cancer of an unnamed eleven-year-old girl whom she recognizes as her daughter.

1994: Craft, along with a handful of other women who have learned through *The Tennessean* that they had been experimental subjects, files a class action lawsuit against a long list of defendants, led by Vanderbilt University. (I sign on as a radiation expert with the law firm representing the women and surviving children.)

Acting as if the recent "revelations" are news to him, John Herrington, Secretary of Energy in the Reagan administration and now vice-chairman of the California Republican party, tells The Associated Press that during his tenure "there had not been enough work done to establish that there was a problem." This is reported without comment or correction.

Geoffrey Sea is an Oakland-based writer, radiological health physicist, and international activist on radiation issues. He is the founder and director of In Vivo: Radiation Response and the Atomic Reclamation and Conversion Project of the Tides Foundation, and a co-founder of IRIS: International Radiation Injury Survivors.

7 CENSORED

Industrial Fishing Fleets Waste 60 Billion Pounds of Fish Annually

"THE CRY OF THE OCEAN,"
by Peter Steinhart

"BATTLE FOR THE DEEP,"
by Hal Bernton
Mother Jones, July/August 1994

THE CRY OF THE OCEAN

"Unlike rhinos, tigers and bears, when you deplete fish populations, you're threatening the survival of humanity."

Life on earth began in the moonpull and seawind of the oceans. Human blood still has the salinity of seawater. We are, ourselves, miniature oceans, dressed in skin and gone exploring the arid world that rose out of ancient seas.

We haven't gone far: Half the world's population still lives within 50 miles of the coast.

Nonetheless, our acquaintance with the sea generally ends at the first slap of ocean wave; what happens beyond the surf is hidden. But what is happening out there is something we should be angry about.

The signs are ominous. On a good day in the 1960s, an Atlantic fisherman could harpoon 30 large swordfish. Today, such swordfish are hardly ever seen; commercial fishermen on the East Coast set out a 15-to-30-mile line baited with 1,000 hooks. Even then, many they catch are immature.

What has happened to swordfish has happened to hundreds of marine species. In the last 15 years, New England cod, haddock, and yellowtail flounder have declined 70 percent; South Atlantic grouper and snapper, 80 percent; Atlantic bluefin tuna, 90 percent. More than 200 separate salmon spawning runs have vanished from the Pacific Northwest.

We are mining the seas of life. The number of fish caught in 11 of the world's 15 major fishing areas has declined from peak years, and four areas are at or near peak catch.

The human cost of this crisis is considerable. For many it means hunger, since in some countries more than half of the population's animal protein comes from the sea. Says Michael Sutton of the World Wildlife Fund, "Unlike rhinos, tigers, and bears, when you deplete fish populations, you're threatening the survival of humanity."

For others, it means the end of a way of life. The collapse of the

Newfoundland cod fishery put 40,000 people out of work. In the Philippines, as traditional fishing by net and spear yields smaller and smaller returns, divers stay down 150 or 200 feet for hours, breathing air pumped through hoses, in hopes of spearing a profitable catch. In some villages, paralysis and brain damage caused by submersion at such depths is now a common affliction.

For centuries, people have gone to sea with heroic madness in their eyes. We went out to lift from the depths not just food but something mystical. We looked upon fish as castoffs from another world, as strange shapes and distant wills. We went to tempt the shimmering darkness and pull it into the light.

Even today, fish seem to us cold, silvery dreams to which we do not attribute a capacity for thought or feeling. We feel no remorse when the dazzle fades from their scales. We have never thought of fish as fellow creatures, and we do not—deep down—think of the sea as part of the living world.

In our technological age, such thinking has terrible consequences. Our ancient awe now floats in steel hulls, dragging multifilament net over miles of seabed to pull masses of life from the ocean. A modern North Pacific trawler can reportedly take in one million pounds of fish in a single day.

Since World War II, nation after nation has built fleets of such vessels, and as a result the world's finfish catch quadrupled between 1950 and 1990. It looked for a time as if the sea were an inexhaustible source of wealth.

But that was an illusion. Most of the increased catch came from a few distant water fisheries, whose limits were quickly reached. Meanwhile, coastal fishermen had to sail farther and farther from port to catch anything.

Large-scale fishing technologies have become less and less selective: Fish too small to be taken and species not legally fished are caught, and then thrown overboard to die. Lee Alverson of Seattle's Natural Resources Consultants estimates that in addition to the estimated 84 million metric tons of marine fish legally landed in the world each year, approximately 27 million metric tons are caught and dumped at sea. With an unreported catch that may be as high as 30 percent of the legal take, we are removing far more than the 100 million metric tons of marine fish that scientists estimate is the globe's maximum sustainable yearly harvest.

We like to think of the oceans as so vast and ancient as to be above greed or vanity. Byron wrote, "Man marks the earth with ruin—his control stops with the shore." But we now have the technological capacity to do to fish exactly what we did to the buffalo and the passenger pigeon.

We are reducing the oceans' productivity. We risk hunger, poverty, dislocation, and war. We destroy links to our evolutionary past and to the future. We turn our backs on the world and lose its kindness.

What can we do? Refusing to eat fish doesn't even begin to address the problem because others will assume our place. We must reduce the size of the world's fishing fleet, set new limits, and enforce them.

Government agencies are investigating restrictions on the gear fishermen may use, as one way to limit catch. More effective area limits and fishing quotas may also be required. For these or other controls to work, however, we need international agreements binding all nations to a common set of rules.

Unless we find new ways to care for the sea, we will be its darkest legacy. Cast up from its depths millions of years ago, we may now be the agents of its destruction.

Peter Steinhart, author of "Tracks in the Sky" and "California's Wild Heritage," writes about nature and environmental affairs.

BATTLE FOR THE DEEP

The Alaska fishery could be America's last great resource giveaway—and powerful companies are fighting for a piece of it.

Don Tyson has never fished aboard a Bering Sea trawler, risking his life against treacherous weather to bring home a catch of cod or pollock. He hasn't worked a midnight deck shift in 30-foot seas or used a baseball bat to pound at the ice that builds up on riggings and rails.

Tyson lives in the hill country of northwest Arkansas, more than 3,000 miles from Alaska. "I'm just a chicken farmer," he likes to say. But this chicken farmer has turned a modest family business into one of the nation's largest food conglomerates, grossing more than $4 billion a year.

Tyson Foods now wants to claim one of the biggest shares of the Alaska fishery. The harvest rights it seeks from

the federal government would be worth tens of millions of dollars each year. And unless federal law is amended, the government may hand over the fishery without Tyson—or anyone else—paying a dime in royalties.

Tyson has developed strong ties with President Bill Clinton, and those ties could help the company as it makes its case. The Alaska governor's office says Tyson representatives "definitely" led them to believe they have influence in Washington.

The privatization of the Alaska fishery could be the country's last great resource handout. The prairies were homesteaded in the past century; the railroads have claimed their vast land grants; many of the rich mining deposits on public lands have long since been staked out. The Alaska fishery is one of the richest in the world, with a treasure trove of pollock, cod, crab, and other species. It's a resource many Americans don't even know they own.

Tyson ventured into the fishing industry in June 1992, just about the time that Bill Clinton consolidated his hold on the Democratic presidential nomination. The corporation sought a seafood entree for its corporate dinner plate, and so spent $212 million to buy Arctic Alaska Fisheries Corp., the largest fishing company in the country.

Some industry observers questioned Tyson's purchase because Seattle-based Arctic Alaska had an aging fleet and a formidable array of legal problems. The worst of these problems were detailed last April, when a federal grand jury hit Arctic Alaska with a 44-count indictment. It charged the company with sending unsafe ships to sea, falsifying documents, and lying about crew qualifications, among other crimes. The grand jury said these acts were part of a conspiracy that had put profits ahead of people and led to the 1990 sinking of an Arctic Alaska fishing vessel, an accident that killed nine people.

But Arctic Alaska's single-minded pursuit of fish helped it to become one of the biggest seafood harvesters in the Bering Sea. And the quantity of fish Arctic Alaska caught, irrespective of how many laws it may have broken to catch them, has put the company—and its new owner Tyson—in a position to win a big share of the fishery.

Tyson Foods is wealthy and well-connected, but it isn't the only major player in the high-stakes fish lotto. Another is Christiania Bank of Norway, which bankrolled a big chunk of the Bering Sea fleet with more than $300 million in loans. Most of those loans are now in default, and the bank hopes to take the fishing shares of the boats that can't pay up. Other players include largely Japanese-owned shore processors; the catcher-boat fleet and hook-and-line fishermen who deliver to the processors; and native Eskimo and Aleut fishermen.

They all recognize that big changes are coming to the Bering Sea fishery. Too many fishermen, wielding awesome fishing technology, are going after too few fish. When the fleet shrinks there will be winners and losers. All the players are trying to make sure that whatever reform takes place will put them in the winners' circle.

So far, the federal government has tried to manage the catch by limiting the seasons for different species of fish. Seasons that once stretched out for most of the year have shrunk to a few months. This turns the harvests into frantic derbies in which boats grab as much as they can as fast as they can. The result is incredible waste, unsafe fishing practices, and economic chaos for the industry.

Scientists are also increasingly concerned about the effects of this intensive fishing on the broader Bering Sea ecosystem. The Steller sea lion, for instance, is now listed as a threatened species. Scientists have also tracked sharp population declines in fur seals and some sea birds. And while the stocks of pollock still appear relatively healthy, their total biomass has declined.

Meanwhile, the fishermen slug it out in ever-shorter seasons. Under the derby system, they lack the time and financial incentives to try to avoid catching fish that aren't worth processing or are not legally in season. Last year, the Alaska fleet caught 4.2 billion pounds of fish, then dumped a staggering 763 million pounds—seven times more fish than is retained by the entire New England fleet. As the competition intensifies, so do the pressures to keep fishing through the worst winter storms, increasing the risks in an occupation that has already killed more than 165 fishermen off Alaska in the past six years.

To top it all off, the harvests, despite their gargantuan scale, are too small to sustain the overcapitalized fleet. Some vessel owners have already filed for bankruptcy, and more filings are expected later this year.

As a solution to these problems, Tyson and some other players are politicking for a kind of 20th-century homestead act. The plan would divide the annual harvest into shares, which would be given to fishing companies in proportion to some part of their historic catch. The more fish and crab an operator caught in the past, the bigger its share. Companies could then leisurely fish their shares (called "individual transferable quotas," or ITQs), lease them to other operators, or sell them to the highest bidder. The total market value of all the shares could easily exceed $1 billion according to several industry officials.

By ending the race for fish, factory trawler operators say they could curtail the waste. Boats would target the species they want and would take the time to process whatever fish they caught. Skippers would avoid practices that endangered the lives of their crew members. And the fleet would shrink as marginal operators sold out their shares. "We are convinced that the future of the fishery up there is dependent on getting toward some sort of ITQ system," said Archie Schaffer, an Arkansas-based spokesperson for Tyson.

But not everyone agrees that privately held quotas are the best way to reform the harvest. Even if the government does turn to private quotas, critics say, the public should scrutinize the deals and gain fair payment. They fear quotas would prevent future generations of small boat fishermen from breaking into the harvest. And they question a system that would reward those companies with the biggest historic catches, since those companies may have been the ones that flooded the harvest grounds with too many boats, or broke safety and environmental regulations, or wasted the most fish.

"The people who overcapitalized the most, who showed very often the least business sense, are the ones who stand to gain the most," says Bob Storrs, a fisherman who helped organize the Alaska Marine Conservation Council. "No matter how they treated this resource, regardless of their attitude toward this publicly owned thing, we're going to give it to them forever. This is absolutely ridiculous."

The hub of the Bering Sea fishery is the remote island community of Unalaska, located some 800 miles southwest of Anchorage on the Aleutian chain. Unalaska moves to the rhythms of the fisheries, with great spasms of activity each winter as the factory trawler and crab fleets move north from Seattle to prepare for season openings. Hundreds of boisterous—sometimes brawling—fishermen and processing crews descend on the island bars as the vessels take on fuel, food, and other supplies. Then they take to the sea to work in mind-numbing shifts of six hours on, six hours off, for what may be weeks on end.

More than half of the Alaska bottom fish is taken by an at-sea factory fleet that harvests with trawl nets and lines dangling thousands of baited hooks. Tyson has a considerable stake in this fleet, but many of the biggest vessels are financed by Christiania and other foreign banks, and some are actually owned by foreign investors.

In addition to the factory ships, there are boats that deliver fish to shore plants for processing. One of the smallest of these is the 85-foot Lone Star, skippered by Chuck Burrece.

In the early days of the fishery, Burrece could find plenty of cod without venturing far from port. But this year, the season was short and the old fishing spot near town was closed to protect Steller sea lions. To find cod, Burrece had to push the Lone Star to its limits, journeying 60 to 70 miles out to the dangerous strait known as Unimak Pass.

He worked the fishing ground for three days with a trawl net that scooped up about 200,000 pounds of edible fish. But Burrece and his two crewmen dumped some 70,000 pounds of dead and dying pollock, sole, and halibut. They got rid of the halibut because federal regulations retain them for the hook-and-line fleet. The rest went over because the plant Burrece delivers to was only prepared to handle cod.

Burrece recognizes that such waste is a miserable way to do business. But so long as the processor doesn't want those fish, there's no sense bringing them ashore. "We're not wasteful people," Burrece said. "I think it's bullshit to just shovel it all over the side. It's stupid because there's only so much out there."

The shore processors (most of which are owned by Japanese conglomerates) are another group concerned with how the fishery is reformed. They have managed to win special federal protection that guarantees them 35 percent of the pollock harvest through 1995. After that date, they fear they will lose out altogether in a reform program that simply doles out catching rights. They have argued for a second tier of "processing rights" that would mandate that they handle a portion of the catch. "If there's some benefit that's going to be handed out, we want to belly up to the bar like everyone else," says Dennis Phelan, a vice president of the Pacific Seafood Processors Association.

Tyson's outpost in Unalaska is in a small two-story office building squeezed between the mountains and a long dock frequented by its fleet. A sign posted on the wall warns crew members that "fighting, public intoxication, and reporting to the vessels under the influence of alcohol" are cause for firing. Don Tyson's son, John, who helped to arrange the Arctic Alaska buyout, has tried several times to visit the company's Unalaska outpost, but each time his aircraft was unable to land due to foul weather. The senior Tyson has yet to make the journey.

From a single chicken processing plant in the 1950s, Tyson has grown into the world's largest poultry producer. During the past 25 years, the company, through more than 20 acquisitions, sought to dominate a major share of the American food industry by expanding its "center-of-the-plate" protein offerings to include pork, beef, and now fish.

So far that strategy has paid off for both Tyson and its investors. The company's stock ranked third in total returns during the 20-year period that ended in 1992, according to one financial analysis. Last year, Tyson reported sales of $4.7 billion.

Tyson has also cultivated political ties, most notably with Bill Clinton after he was elected Arkansas' governor. Tyson offered Clinton rides in the company's corporate jet and became an important fund-raiser during his presidential bid. Tyson Food executives and their families gave $20,750 to Clinton's campaign and another $22,000 to Democratic Party organizations. The company's chief legal counsel, James Blair, is a close personal friend of the Clintons and advised Hillary on her well-publicized cattle futures trading.

The week before Tyson announced its 1992 purchase of Arctic Alaska, word of the buyout apparently leaked, triggering a surge of Arkansas investment in the fishing company. The federal Securities and Exchange Commission is now investigating a group of Arkansas investors, including a firm then headed by White House Administration Director Patsy Thomasson, for possible insider trading. For those investors, short-term profits were spectacular. When Tyson announced the buyout price, Arctic Alaska's stock shot up 69 percent.

But Tyson's stock dipped at the news, foreshadowing later trouble. Tyson took over a company that would ultimately be saddled with a criminal indictment.

Arctic Alaska was founded in 1983 by fisherman Francis Miller. At the time of Tyson's buyout, the company owned more than 30 trawlers, hook-and-line boats, and crab vessels.

Many of the vessels had been converted from other uses and shipped north without meeting stability standards required by the Coast Guard. One of those vessels, the Aleutian Enterprise, sank in a 1990 accident that claimed nine lives and triggered April's grand jury indictment against the company, Miller, and other Arctic officials of that era.

Schaffer, the Tyson spokesperson, said the indictment makes no suggestion that anyone in current management was involved, and adds, "[Tyson] deeply regrets the loss of life. The only other thing that I can say is that the company will vigorously defend the case."

The indictment painted a chilling picture of unqualified officers leading green—sometimes teenage—crews out to sea in unsafe ships. Officers must submit sea time to gain certification, and an affidavit unsealed after the indictment charged that Arctic Alaska officials had falsified that sea time.

In addition, Tyson has found that Miller was lax in pollution controls. Last year, Arctic Alaska was hit with a $750,000 fine by the Environmental Protection Agency for failing to grind and properly dispose of fish wastes under the Miller regime. The company also faces a criminal lawsuit filed by the state of Alaska charging that the fleet repeatedly fished with illegal bottom gear in sensitive coastal waters. Tyson has hired Alaska Gov. Walter Hickel's personal attorney, Hal Horton, to help settle the still-pending charges against Arctic Alaska. According to state officials, Tyson also flew legal counsel and Clinton friend James Blair up from Little Rock to plead Arctic Alaska's case.

Some fishing industry insiders wondered why Tyson would invest in a North Pacific company when it was apparent that too many boats were already chasing the fish. In an interview a few months after the acquisition, John Tyson told a trade journal that the company took its cue, in part, from industry proposals to create the share system. Tyson hopes that Arctic Alaska's long catch history will ensure a large slice of the fish pie. As it lobbies for the new system, Tyson is positioning itself as an "all-American" company that has a more legitimate claim to the resource than the foreign investors and banks that stand behind many other fishery players.

For decades foreign fleets controlled many of the trawler harvests in U.S. coastal waters. The 1976 Magnuson Act, which put a 200-mile zone under U.S. control, was in large part an attempt to claim the harvest for Americans. That vision was reaffirmed in 1987 by legislation that banned most foreign vessels from reflagging as U.S. ships, and also restricted foreign ownership of U.S. fishing vessels.

But some in Congress had doubts about squeezing off foreign investment that might help finance the American fleet, and the legislation had plenty of loopholes. During the next five years, some boats came under the direct control of foreign investors, while others were beholden to foreign banks.

The single biggest financier was Christiania Bank of Norway, which loaned at least $315 million to factory trawlers and other vessels. These vessels stampeded into the Bering Sea in the late 1980s and early 1990s. Now,

with the short seasons and low prices, many ship operators can't make their payments. Christiania has foreclosed on at least four factory trawlers.

Along with the vessels, Christiania hopes to gain control of any fishing rights awarded to these companies. According to a Christiania loan document, the bank has asked its borrowers to sign covenants that pledge these rights as collateral. That means if the bank calls a loan, it will end up with both the vessel and a piece of the U.S. fishery.

Christiania officials say they don't plan to use the fishing rights. Instead, they want to sell them to recoup loan losses. But Tyson challenges Christiania's claim to the resource. "The whole idea of the Magnuson Act is to Americanize the fishery, and that just hasn't happened," says Tyson spokesperson Schaffer. "We believe that American ownership is important and that the companies that are American need to be rewarded."

The power to determine the fate of the Alaska fishery rests with the North Pacific Fishery Management Council, an 11-member group dominated by fishing industry representatives. They pass their plans on to the National Marine Fisheries Service, an agency in the Commerce Department, for final approval.

Most of the council members are from Alaska, and they have frequently aligned themselves with the shore plant operators out of concern that a share plan would give most of the harvest to out-of-state factory trawlers.

Nonetheless, the council has already approved a share plan for the $100 million-a-year hook-and-line harvest of halibut and black cod, and is now considering a share plan for the rest of the harvest. The hook-and-line plan set aside a small percentage of the catch for regional natives, and the new plan might do the same.

The council has been slow in developing the new share plan. In April, it voted to consider a two-step process that would first limit the size of the fleet, then eventually award rights. In a nod to conservation concerns, the plan also called for incentives that would give extra quotas to fishermen who reduced waste.

Tyson and other factory trawler owners have been lobbying to get the program on a faster track. For Tyson, that's also meant trying to improve the company's image in Alaska. Last March, Don Tyson flew to Alaska to meet with Gov. Hickel and other state officials. Tyson talked of investing in shore plants and using the corporation's power to push more fish into the American diet.

Alaska state officials claim that one Tyson representative said the company could talk to the White House about lifting a ban on the foreign export of Alaska oil, a congressional embargo that costs the state hundreds of millions of dollars in lost revenue. "They definitely left us with the impression that they had influence with the Clinton administration," says John Manly, Gov. Hickel's spokesperson. What Tyson wanted was fishery council members who would support a quota system.

Tyson spokesperson Schaffer says the Alaska officials were the ones who asked whether there was a way Tyson could influence Washington on the state's behalf. "What I told them is that I don't know whether there is or not but that I would look into it," says Schaffer. "That's about as far as it's gone." (If Tyson wanted to join forces with Alaska in fighting the oil embargo, they need look no further than the firm of Hal Horton, the lawyer they hired to defend Arctic Alaska—it is representing the state in a suit to overturn the federal government ban.)

Thus far, Tyson's success in shaping the council has been limited. For each vacant seat, the governor proposes three candidates, one of whom is selected to fill the post by U.S. Commerce Secretary Ron Brown. One of the nominees Tyson favored was pressured to withdraw by Alaska officials who feared a council tilt toward the Arkansas company. Another Tyson-backed candidate, Clem Tillion, is a controversial figure in Alaska, and the state Senate has asked Brown to pick someone else.

But Tyson is not ruling out further efforts. "We have not lobbied or talked to anyone in Washington about any candidate," Schaffer says, "but I think that Clem [Tillion] is someone who, if we decided to get involved in the process, we would be supportive of. . . . Fish regulation and fish politics are very different from what we'd been accustomed to, and we're still trying to find our way around the whole council system."

If the council fails to deliver on the quota plan, Tyson or other factory trawler operators could go over their heads by lobbying the Clinton administration and Congress. Some factory trawler representatives have already proposed an amendment to the Magnuson Act—now up for reauthorization—that would give the Commerce Department power to develop a plan on its own.

But Rollie Schmitten, the director of the National Marine Fisheries Service, says the regional council should decide whether to introduce share plans. Schmitten also proposes a new fishing industry fee to finance $82 million of his agency's $280 million annual budget, a cost currently picked up by taxpayers. And he thinks those fortunate enough to claim harvest shares bear a special burden to pay. "If you are going to bestow a public resource to certain individuals, then there ought to be some sort of equity to the public," Schmitten says.

The Magnuson Act generally prohibits the government from levying fees on the use of national fisheries, but many members of Congress are joining Schmitten in pushing for amendments to the act that would allow for fees to help pay the cost of managing the resource and enforcing regulations.

However, any move to make the industry pay substantial fees or royalties will probably face a chilly reception. "We're open to discussing [fees and royalties]," says Schaffer. "But we've not taken a formal position on it."

The battle over the future of this fishery is likely to play out over the next few years both in Washington, D.C., and at Alaska council meetings. And while fishermen fight over who gets to profit from the resource, it will be up to the council and fishery managers to keep the fishery healthy.

Many fishermen are convinced that Alaska fisheries will remain strong, avoiding the fate of New England, Newfoundland, and other great fisheries that have been fished out. But conservationists fear these harvests could be the last buffalo hunts of a dwindling resource.

Everyone from Tyson officials to small boat fishermen like Chuck Burrece now speaks the gospel of conservation. But there are no saints in the fishing industry, especially when jobs are at stake.

Burrece, for example, feels squeezed between factory trawlers who are hogging the resource and regulators who might make him pay royalties for fishing rights. "We put our lives on the line, that's how we're paying," Burrece says angrily. "I got a lot of friends laying out there dead from catching fish. That's how we pay. That's enough."

Burrece knows he risks the same fate if he keeps defying the weather to go cod fishing. But in the race for fish, he figures he can't afford to be idle too long. On a dank evening last March, Burrece fidgeted at the dock. The forecast for the next day was bad: northeast winds gusting more than 60 miles per hour. But Burrece kept thinking about those factory trawlers that would be sure to haul in cod right through the storm.

Late in the evening, Burrece made up his mind. He told his crewmen to untie the lines, and the Lone Star motored out into the blackness of the Bering Sea.

Hal Bernton is an Alaska-based journalist who has written extensively on fisheries.

WHERE THE FISH AREN'T: Most of what we know about fish populations comes from fishermen, not biologists, and fishermen report declining levels world-wide. Other factors may enter in, but few dispute that overfishing imperils all of the world's major fisheries. The United Nation's Food and Agriculture Organization determined in April 1994 that roughly 60 percent of fish populations they monitor are fully exploited or depleted. Of the 15 major fishing areas, four have declined 30 to 50 percent from estimated peak numbers, seven have declined 9 to 29 percent, and only four are at or near their estimated peak.

SOURCE: PETER WEBER, WORLDWATCH INSTITUTE, BASED ON FAO DATA.

THE FISH ARE CALLING: Something is terribly wrong in the ocean and the fish are dying to tell us about it. About 235 million years ago, however, the sea recovered from a mass extinction that killed 96 percent of all life, so it can probably outlast the current human demolition derby. We won't.

WASTING AWAY: Alaska's trawlers threw away 763 million pounds of fish last year. Under the reform backed by Tyson, some of the most wasteful companies would get the biggest shares of the fishery.

FAST FOOD, SLOW FISHING: When the world fished only with small nets, hooks, and lines, instead of trawls the size of small shopping malls, the ocean could make fish as fast as we killed and ate them. From 1988 to 1990, Americans ate a record 47 pounds of seafood each, much of it imported; the Japanese, 160 pounds; and Icelanders, 203 pounds. The Maldivians on the Indian Ocean were the champions at 293 pounds.

FISH FIGHTS: The politics of fish in America have clearly promoted development over sustainability. Modern industrial fishing is run by insiders, many of whose fortunes depend on the decisions they make. Foxes and henhouses come to mind.

8 | CENSORED

Why Haven't We Stopped Tuberculosis?

"WHY DON'T WE STOP TUBERCULOSIS?"
by Anne E. Platt; *World Watch*,
July/August 1994

Tuberculosis, a disease many people associate with sequestered sanatoriums that were long ago abandoned or razed, has now reemerged as the number one killer among the world's infectious or communicable diseases. In 1993 alone, tuberculosis, also known as TB, killed 2.7 million people and infected another 8.1 million. In 1993, an estimated one-third of the world's population, or 1.7 billion people, were infected but had not yet developed the disease.

The current TB epidemic is expected to grow worse, especially in the developing world, because of the evolution of multi-drug-resistant strains and the emergence of AIDS, which compromises human immune systems and makes them more susceptible to infectious diseases. Since the medical knowledge exists to treat and cure TB, "this tragedy is totally unnecessary," Dr. Hiroshi Nakajima, Director-General of the World Health Organization (WHO) said in January.

The resurgence of tuberculosis comes at a time when other infectious diseases that were thought to be well-controlled—malaria, cholera, and dengue fever among them—have increased and new diseases, notably AIDS, have emerged. Despite the advances in modern medicine, infectious diseases have persisted and continue to have a major effect on public health: in the 50 years following the discovery of antibiotics, efforts to control age-old epidemics have been overcome not by a lack of medical knowledge but by structural problems, including the lack of adequate health care in many parts of the world and increased rates of travel and migration.

Dengue fever, which causes hemorrhaging of the mucous membrane in the skin and abdomen, as well as aches, rash, vomiting, and fever, has been called "the epidemic waiting to happen." Dengue is endemic in Southeast Asia, Africa, and the Caribbean, while malaria is rampaging in sub-Saharan Africa, cholera is breaking out in South America, and the AIDS epidemic is sweeping through Africa, Asia, and the developing world. But the comeback of tuberculosis threatens more people than AIDS, cholera, dengue fever, and other infectious diseases *combined*. An estimated 2 to 3 million people were infected with HIV in 1993 worldwide, compared to WHO's estimate of 8 million people infected with TB.

By the year 2000, the global incidence of TB alone is expected to increase to 10.2 million cases per year—an increase of 36 percent over 1990's 7.5 million cases. Three-quarters of this increase can be traced to poor TB control programs, population growth, and the advancing age of the population; the remaining quarter is attributed to the interaction between the TB virus and the HIV virus. AIDS destroys the human cells that keep the TB virus dormant and accelerates the speed at which TB progresses from harmless infection to life-threatening disease. Overall, tuberculosis deaths are predicted to increase by one-sixth, to 3.5 million by the year 2000, killing 30 *million people* in this decade alone.

"The factors contributing to the increase in tuberculosis are multiple: it is not only HIV, it is not only the emergence of multi-drug-resistant strains, and it is not only because of the undermining and weakening of public health services worldwide," says Dr. Jonathan Mann of Harvard University's School of Public Health. "It is all of these things combined." The world is suffering from such a severe epidemic of tuberculosis that the World Health Organization declared a global state of emergency in April 1993.

To complicate matters, the United States and other countries are combatting drug-resistant TB strains. The U.S. National Academy of Sciences' Institute of Health reported in 1992 that *M. tuberculosis* strains that are virtually resistant to all effective drugs have emerged in cities in the United States and elsewhere, with mortality rates over 50 percent. The academy concluded that a successful control program requires "an arsenal of vaccines and drugs" alongside diagnosis and surveillance.

Tuberculosis has special characteristics that set it apart from other infectious diseases, most of which rely on mosquitos, rats, or water to transmit infection. Tubercle bacilli only live in human tissues, and tuberculosis can only be transmitted by close contact with an infected person. In a healthy individual, the immune system is normally able to wall off and isolate the bacilli in a nodule. This essentially neutralizes the tubercle bacillus, so the person has what is referred to as an *inert* infection. If the immune system remains strong, there is only a 5 to 10 percent chance of developing TB from an inert infection. But if the immune system is under severe stress—from HIV, diabetes, or chemotherapy for cancer, for example—the chances that the infection will develop into disease increase to as much as 10 percent in a single year.

A person who has active TB can spread the infection simply by coughing, sneezing, singing, or even talking. Another person has only to inhale the bacilli to become infected. If the infection is not detected and treated promptly, one person with active tuberculosis can infect an average of 10 to 14 people in one year and sometimes many more.

The estimated 1.7 billion people who have inert TB infections may show no symptoms at all. Only if those infections are activated will these people be at risk of developing the disease and transmitting it to others. Unfortunately, little is known about what activates a latent TB infection beyond the fact that people with healthy immune systems run a low risk of developing an active case of TB.

Because the already poor and disenfranchised populations of the world carry a disproportionate burden of tuberculosis, the disease has a certain stigma attached to it. But the unsanitary and crowded living conditions that are often connected to poverty do not *cause* TB to spread; they increase the *chances* that the infection will spread from person to person and the chances that a person's immune system may already be weak and therefore less able to fight the infection. Despite the misconceptions, tuberculosis is exacerbated only by the failure to detect and treat the infection properly and by close contact with infected individuals.

More than 95 percent of TB cases reported in 1990 were in the developing world, an estimated two-thirds of them in Asia. India accounted for 2.1 million cases. Developing countries are faced with a disproportionate number of cases because AIDS is spreading quickly, health services are inadequate, and little money is available for treatment. But tuberculosis is not limited to the developing world: Eastern Europe, France, Spain, and the former Soviet Union have also reported increases. In the United States, the U.S. Centers for Disease Control and Prevention reported 26,000 cases in 1992, up nearly 20 percent from 1985.

Global monitoring by the World Health Organization and regional health NGOs to identify and diagnose TB must be combined with sufficient infrastructure and resources, such as vaccines, medicines, trained health personnel, and clinics. As with other diseases, funding for research and prevention and treatment programs is essential.

Thanks to modern medicine, there is a low-cost, effective TB treatment with high cure rates among infected adults. It relies on four inexpensive drugs (rifampicin, isoniazid, pyrazinamide, and ethambutol) that have a 90 percent success rate if used *every day* for six to eight months. But if patients don't take the drugs consistently or don't complete treatment, TB strains develop that are more resistant to medicine, and sometimes even untreatable. If this drug regimen were used throughout the world, it would reduce the rate of transmission and cut the number of deaths by half over the next 10 years, according to WHO. In 1993, the World Bank identified short-term tuberculosis treatment as one of the most cost-effective ways to reduce the global burden of disease. In China, it costs only $13 for a supply of all the drugs needed to cure one person. In most developing countries, it costs less than $30 to save a life and prevent further transmission of the disease. In the United States, it costs up to $10,000 to treat an active case of TB compared to $200,000 to treat an active TB infection that has become drug-resistant. Worldwide, early treatment could prevent nearly 12 million deaths in the next decade, and save vast amounts of money.

The growing TB epidemic is a classic case of a public health crisis that could be headed off easily and inexpensively. Its fate will largely depend on the willingness of government and public health officials to invest up front in prevention and early intervention. If we ignore the extraordinary opportunity that exists now to fight the epidemic, we will pay a high price in lives and extensive health care costs later.

Anne E. Platt is a staff researcher at the Worldwatch Institute, where she studies environmental health and fisheries issues.

9  CENSORED

Project HAARP: The Military's Secret Plan to Alter the Ionosphere

"PROJECT HAARP: THE MILITARY'S SECRET PLAN TO ALTER THE IONOSPHERE,"
by Clare Zickuhr and Gar Smith;
Earth Island Journal, Fall 1994

The Pentagon's mysterious HAARP project, now under construction at an isolated Air Force facility near Gakona, Alaska, marks the first step toward creating the world's most powerful "ionospheric heater." Scientists, environmentalists and native peoples are concerned that HAARP's electronic transmitters—capable of beaming "in excess of 1 gigawatts" (one billion watts) of radiated power into the Earth's ionosphere—could harm people, endanger wildlife and trigger unforeseen environmental impacts.

The High Frequency Active Auroral Research Project (HAARP), a joint effort of the Air Force and the Navy, is the latest in a series of a little-known Department of Defense (DoD) "active ionospheric experiments" with code-names like EXCEDE, RED AIR and CHARGE IV.

"From a DoD point of view," internal HAARP documents state, "the most exciting and challenging" part of the experiment is "its potential to *control* ionospheric processes" for military objectives [emphasis in the original]. According to these documents, the scientists pulling HAARP's strings envision using the system's powerful 2.8-10 megahertz (MHz) beam to burn "holes" in the ionosphere and "create an artificial lens" in the sky that could focus large bursts of electromagnetic energy "to higher altitudes...than is presently possible." The minimum area to be heated would be 50 km (31 miles) in diameter.

The initial $26 million, 320 kW HAARP project will employ 360 72-foot-tall antennas spread over four acres to direct an intense beam of focused electromagnetic energy upwards to strike the ionosphere. The EarthÕs ionosphere is composed of a layer of negatively and positively charged particles (electrons and ions) lying between 35 and 500 miles above the planet's surface. The next stage of the project would expand HAARP's power to 1.7 gigawatts (1.7 billion watts), making it the most powerful such transmitter on Earth. While the project's acronym implies experimentation with the Earth's aurora, HAARP's public documents make no mention of this aspect. For a project whose backers hail it as a major scientific feat, HAARP has remained extremely low-profile—almost unknown to most Alaskans, and the rest of the country.

A November 1993 "HAARP Fact Sheet" released to the public by the Office of Naval Research (ONR) stated that the Department of Defense (DoD)-backed project would "enhance present civilian capabilities" in communications and "provide significant scientific advancements." However, while previous DoD experiments with smaller high frequency (HF) heaters in Puerto Rico, Norway and Alaska were conducted to "gain [a] better understanding" of the ionosphere, internal HAARP documents obtained through the Freedom of Information Act (FOIA) reveal that the project's goal is to "perturb" the ionosphere with extremely powerful beams of energy and study "how it responds to the disturbance and how it ultimately recovers..."

The public fact sheet describes HAARP as "purely a scientific research facility which represents no threat to potential adversaries and would therefore have no value as a military target." However, while ionospheric experiments at the government's Puerto Rico transmitter site are managed by the civilian National Science Foundation, the Journal has learned that proposals for experiments on HAARP are to be routed through the Pentagon's Office of Naval Research.

A February 1990 Air Force-Navy document acquired by the Journal lists only military experiments for the HAARP project, including: "Generation of ionospheric lenses to focus large amounts of HF energy at high altitudes...providing a means for triggering ionospheric processes that potentially could be exploited for DoD purposes...; Generation of ionization layers below 90 km [145 miles] to provide radio wave reflectors ("mirrors") which can be exploited for long range, over-the-horizon, HF/VHF/UHF surveillance purposes, including the detection of cruise missiles and other low observables." The document concluded that "the potential for significantly altering regions of the ionosphere at relatively great distances (1000 km or more) [1613 miles] from a heater is very desirable" from a military perspective.

One of HAARP's less-publicized goals is to find ways to disrupt the global communications capabilities of adversaries while preserving US defense communications. The Pentagon also wants to know if HAARP could bounce signals to deeply submerged nuclear subs by heating the ionosphere to trigger bursts of Extremely Long Frequency (ELF) radio waves.

Patents held by ARCO Power Technologies, Inc. (APTI), the ARCO subsidiary that was contracted to build HAARP, describe a similar ionospheric heater invented by Bernard Eastlund that claimed the ability to disrupt global communications, destroy enemy missiles and change weather (see sidebar). One of ARCO's patents identifies Alaska as a perfect site for a transmitter because "magnetic field lines...which extend to desirable altitudes for this invention, intersect the Earth in Alaska."

While HAARP officials deny any link to Eastlund's inventions, Eastlund has told National Public Radio that a secret military project was begun in the late-1980s to study and implement his work and, in the May/June 1994 issue of Microwave News, Eastlund claimed that "The HAARP project obviously looks a lot like the first step" toward his vision of surrounding the entire planet with a "full, global shield" of charged particles that could explode incoming enemy missiles.

The military implications of HAARP were further underscored in June, when ARCO sold APTI to E-Systems, a defense contractor noted for its work in counter-surveillance.

ELECTROMAGNETIC GUINEA PIGS

HAARP surfaced publicly in Alaska in the spring of 1993, when the Federal Aviation Administration (FAA) began advising commercial pilots on how to avoid the large amounts of intentional (and some unintentional) electromagnetic radiation that HAARP would generate. Despite the protests of FAA engineers and Alaska bush pilots (for whom reliable communications can be a matter of life or death) the Final Environmental Impact Statement (FEIS) gave HAARP the green light. Ironically, the FEIS also concluded that the project's radio interference would be too intense to allow HAARP to be located near any military facilities.

On November 11, 1993, Inupiat tribal advisor Charles Etok Edwardsen, Jr., wrote to the White House on behalf of the Inupiat Community of the Arctic Slope and the Kasigluk Elders Conference. "Many of us are not happy with the prospect of ARCO altering the Earth's neutral atmospheric properties," Edwardsen wrote. "We do not wish to be anyone's testing grounds, as the Bikini Islanders have been...." referring to Pacific Islanders subjected to radiation exposure from US atomic bomb testing. Edwardsen has appealed to President Clinton to deny further funding to HAARP.

In the past, the EPA has accused the USAF of "sidestepping" the non-thermal hazards of electromagnetic pollution from powerful radar transmitters. Over the past three decades, numerous US and European studies have linked electromagnetic exposure to a range of health problems including fatigue, irritability, sleepiness, memory loss, cataracts, leukemia, birth defects and cancer. Electromagnetic radiation can also alter blood sugar and cholesterol levels, heart-rate and blood pressure, brain waves and brain chemistry.

Wildlife advocates also have cause to be concerned. The HAARP site lies 140 miles north of the town of Cordova on Prince William Sound, on the northwest tip of Alaska's Wrangell-St. Elias National Park. Since ordinary radar is known to be deadly to low-flying birds, HAARP's powerful radiation beam could pose a problem for migratory birds because the transmitter stands in the path of the critical Pacific Flyway. In addition, HAARP's ability to generate strong magnetic fields could conceivably interfere with the migration of birds, marine life and Arctic animals that are now known to rely on the Earth's magnetic fields to navigate over long distances.

The HAARP fact sheet states that "most of the energy of the high-power beam would be emitted upward rather than toward the horizon." Later on, however, the fact sheet notes that care will have to be taken "to reduce the percentage of time large signal levels would be transmitted toward large cities." The closest large cities are Fairbanks and Anchorage.

Even if HAARP's beam were to be directed primarily at the ionosphere, people on the ground would still have reason to be concerned. According to DoD consultant Robert Windsor, clear damp nights, downdrafts and temperature inversions can cause "ducting" and "super-refracting" that can send energy beams streaming back to Earth with "a significant—up to tenfold—increase in field intensity."

In addition to their main beams, all electromagnetic transmitters produce large swaths of "sidelobe" radiation along their flanks. US-based PAVE PAWS over-the-horizon radars, for example, use approximately one megawatt of power to send a 420-430-megahertz (MHz) beam on a 3000-mile-long sweep. At the same time, the "incidental" sidelobe radiation from these Pentagon radars can disable TVs, radios, radar altimeters and satellite communications over a 250-mile range. PAVE PAWS radiation can also disrupt cardiac pacemakers seven miles away and cause the "inadvertent detonation" of electrically triggered flares and bombs in passing aircraft. At peak power, the energy driving HAARP could be more than a thousand times stronger than the most powerful PAVE PAWS transmitter.

HAARP'S HIGH-LEVEL HAZARDS

HAARP project manager John Heckscher, a scientist at the Department of the Air Force's Phillips Laboratory, has called concerns about the transmitter's impact "unfounded." "It's not unreasonable to expect that something three times more powerful than anything that's previously been built might have unforeseen effects," Heckscher told Microwave News. "But that's why we do environmental impact statements."

The July 1993 EIS does, in fact, admit that HAARP is expected to cause "measurable changes in the ionosphere's electron density, temperature and structure," but argues that these disruptions are insignificant "when compared to changes induced by naturally occurring processes."

Subjecting the ionosphere to HF bombardment can ionize the neutral particles in the upper atmosphere. The HAARP Fact Sheet notes that "ionospheric disturbances at high altitudes also can act to induce large currents in electric power grids" on the ground, causing massive power blackouts. According to the 1990 Air Force-Navy document, power levels of one gigawatt and above "can drastically alter [the ionosphere's] thermal, refractive, scattering and emission character." While the ionosphere over the government's smaller HF transmitter in Puerto Rico is relatively "stable," the document notes that the ionosphere above Alaska is "a dynamic entity" where added bursts of electromagnetic energy could trigger exaggerated effects.

Writing in Physics and Society (the quarterly newsletter of the American Physical Society), Dr. Richard Williams, a consultant to Princeton University's David Sarnoff Laboratory, denounced ionospheric heating tests as irresponsible and potentially dangerous.

"Trace [chemical] constituents in the upper atmosphere can have a profound effect" on the formation of ozone molecules, Williams stated. It is known that altering the temperature of the ionosphere can affect the chemical reactions that produce ozone. Referring to the Montreal Protocol (the international agreement to protect the ozone layer from ozone-depleting chemicals), Williams warned that activating HAARP's ionospheric heater "might undo all that we have accomplished with this treaty."

"Look at the power levels that will be used—10^9 to 10^{11} watts!" Williams told the Journal in a recent interview. "This is equivalent to the output of ten to 100 large power-generating stations. A ten-billion-watt generator, running continuously for one hour, would deliver a quantity of energy equal to that of a Hiroshima-sized atomic bomb."

"Of course," Williams added, "they will operate in a pulsed mode [producing a series of short, powerful bursts], rather than continuously." The HAARP fact sheet states that the HF beam, which operates in the 2.8-10 MHz band, will only be used 4-5 times a year for several weeks at a time over a 20-year period. Nonetheless, Williams argued, to proceed without a full public discussion of HAARP's potential impacts runs the risk of committing "an irresponsible act of global vandalism. With experiments on this scale," Williams concluded, "irreparable damage could be done in a short time. The immediate need is for open discussion."

Dr. Daniel N. Baker, director of the University of Colorado's Laboratory for Atmospheric and Space Physics, offered a less-alarming assessment. "The natural input of energy to the magnetosphere from the sun is very commonly 10^{11} - 10^{12} watts," Baker told the Journal. "Thus, HAARP may be a small fraction of the energy that flows into the region." Baker added that the ionosphere is, by nature, a "highly dynamic and fluctuating" environment that is able to "flush" away energy disturbances in a matter of hours or days.

Of course, in nature, one cannot simply "flush" something away without anticipating potential "downstream" consequences. Caroline L. Herzenberg, an environmental systems engineer at the Argonne National Laboratory, has suggested that, by "changing the chemical composition of the atmosphere; [and] transporting plumes of particulates or plasma within the atmosphere," HAARP may violate the 1977 Environmental Modification Convention, which bans all "military or any other hostile use of environmental modification techniques having widespread, long-lasting, or severe effects...." The US ratified the convention in 1979.

THE PENTAGON'S $90 MILLION CAT SCAN

On June 14, a Senate committee report noted that the Deputy Secretary of Defense had called for increasing HAARP funding from $5 million to $75 million in the 1996 defense budget. The sudden increase would be used to promote a disturbing new mission for HAARP.

Instead of just pouring its vast energy into the skies, the transmitter's power would be aimed back at the planet to "allow earth-penetrating tomography over most of the northern hemisphere"—in effect, turning HAARP into the world's most powerful "X-ray machine" capable of scanning regions hidden deep beneath the planet's surface. According to the Senate report, this would "permit the detection and precise location of tunnels...and other underground shelters. The absence of such a capability has been....a serious weakness for [DoD] plans for precision attacks on hardened targets...."

Meanwhile, construction on the larger HAARP facility—with a potential effective radiated power of 1.7 GW (1.7 billion watts)—is set to begin in 1995. This expanded version would require additional funding from Congress. According to the 1990 project document: "The desired world-class facility... will cost on the order of $25-30 million." The Senate Committee's April report, however, predicts that the cost "could be as much as $90 million."

What You Can Do: Write Congress to demand a review of HAARP's environmental impacts. Request that the National Telecommunications and Information Administration [NITA, c/o US Department of Commerce, Washington, DC 20230] reject the HAARP frequency/power request pending the outcome of a Congressional inquiry. Queries and contributions may be sent to NO HAARP c/o Jim Roderick, PO Box 916, Homer, AK 99603.

Clare Zickuhr, a former ARCO employee and ham radio operator based in Anchorage, is a founder of the NO HAARP campaign. Gar Smith is editor of the editor of Earth Island Journal.

10  CENSORED

News Media Mask Spousal Violence In The "Language Of Love"

"CRIMES AGAINST WOMEN: MEDIA PART OF PROBLEM FOR MASKING VIOLENCE IN THE LANGUAGE OF LOVE," by Ann Jones, *USA Today*, Op-Ed, 3/10/94

In New York City, a cop drags his ex-girlfriend out of police headquarters where she works, shoots her four times, killing her, then kills himself. The *New York Post* headlines: "Tragedy of a Lovesick Cop."

An unemployed man, rejected by the girlfriend who supported him, sets fire to a crowded social club, where she works, and 87 people die. *New York Newsday* reports: "Love Story Ends in Hate."

Heavyweight champ Mike Tyson beats up his wife—in the days before he went to prison for raping another woman—and reporters write zippy leads about "the Tyson-Givens love match."

These stories turn up all the time. And no wonder. Every 12 seconds in this country, some man batters his current or former wife or girlfriend.

And every day, four or five men track down and murder women who are trying to get away from them.

These stories are not about men who love too much. They are about men who use violence to forcibly deprive women of their freedom, their civil rights and their lives.

What happens is simple:

A man wants "his" woman to do what he wants. She won't. He uses force to get his way. That's assault. That's a crime. But read the papers or turn on TV, and you're lost in "love."

Battering is currently the leading cause of injury to American women, sending more than 1 million every year to doctors' offices or emergency rooms for treatment.

It drives women into the streets, too: 50% of homeless women and kids across America are fleeing from male violence.

It figures in one quarter of all suicide attempts by women, one half of all suicide attempts by black women.

According to the American Medical Association, it also injures fetuses in utero: 37% of all obstetric patients are battered during pregnancy.

Yet battering—the most frequently committed crime in America—is conspicuously missing from the current national debate on crime. That's where the press comes in. It could go a long way toward providing accurate information and setting a serious tone for public discussion of this issue. Instead it often fails to cover crimes against women at all.

Some papers that report every local traffic violation can't find space for "routine domestics." Or they cover this undeterred crime wave against women in the language of love. Crime becomes "crime of passion," as though Miss Lonelyhearts were working the police beat:

■A man guns down his former wife and her new boyfriend; reporters call it a "love triangle."

■A man shoots and kills several co-workers, among them a woman who refused to date him; the press reports a "tragedy of spurned love."

■A man kidnaps his estranged wife, rapes her, accuses her of an imaginary affair and chokes her to death (all in front of the children); a reporter writes that he "made love to his wife," then strangled her when "overcome with jealous passion."

This slipshod reporting has real consequences in the lives of real men and women. It affirms a batterer's most common excuse for assault: "I did it because I love you so much."

It supplants a woman's experience of fear and pain with a confusing "explanation" that may snare her in forgiveness: "He did it because he loves me so much."

And it provides all readers and listeners—all policymakers, voters, taxpayers, jurors—with an *understanding*: Things happen this way because of *love*.

Certainly, the press isn't solely to blame. In fact, there's plenty of blame to go around.

For one thing, the criminal justice system still wears a blindfold. As recently as 1991, only 17 states recorded incidents of male violence against women in the home, and most confined reporting to "serious" bodily injury, rape and murder.

For another, the "family violence" academic establishment applies innocuous labels like "spouse abuse" and "domestic violence"—presumably a tame version of the real thing—to obscure the facts of who's doing what to whom. And even some feminists invoke elaborate psychological syndromes to "explain" terror and self-defense.

When everybody runs shy of labeling male violence against women for what it is, it's understandable that the press would rather talk of love than crime. But journalists have a special responsibility to find facts and to call things by their right names. In the interest of journalistic standards, not to mention justice and equality, the press should clean up its act.

The media should understand that in reporting on battery, assault and homicide, they are reporting *crime*. They should stop abetting batterers by failing to report "routine" crimes; and, in the interest of public safety, they should print the names of men subject to restraining orders. They should stop sympathizing in print with the offender—the "spurned lover," the "rejected" husband.

Instead of relying solely on local cops and prosecutors as sources, they should add women's advocates and legal scholars to the Rolodex. They should read some books about rape and battering: *Battered Wives* by Del Martin, *Rape in Marriage* by Diana Russell, *Women and Male Violence* by Susan Schechter, *When Battered Women Kill* by Angela Browne. And they should read *Virgin or Vamp: How the Press Covers Sex Crimes* by Columbia journalism professor Helen Benedict.

Above all, they should investigate events, report facts, and eschew sexist cliches, ready-made romantic scenarios and the language of love.

Ann Jones, author of Next Time, She'll Be Dead: Battering and How to Stop It, *teaches journalism at Mount Holyoke College, South Hadley, Mass.*

THIS MODERN WORLD by TOM TOMORROW

Panel 1: THE NEWS MEDIA HAVE HAD A *FIELD DAY* LATELY... FROM TITILLATING RUMORS ABOUT BILL CLINTON'S *EXTRAMARITAL ACTIVITIES*--

...RUMORS WHICH HAVE RECEIVED MORE COVERAGE THAN THE *FACTS* CONCERNING THE PREVIOUS ADMINISTRATION'S COMPLICITY IN *ARMING IRAQ*...

Panel 2: --TO THE ONGOING SAGA OF THE *BOBBITTS*...NO ASPECT OF WHICH HAS GONE *UNEXAMINED*--

HONEY, LOOK--THIS FULL-COLOR DIAGRAM SHOWS WHY JOHN BOBBITT'S FIRST ATTEMPT TO HAVE SEX SINCE HIS OPERATION WAS *UNSUCCESSFUL*!

JUST A SECOND, DEAR--I'M READING THE FIRST-HAND ACCOUNT OF HIS WOULD-BE PARTNER'S *DISAPPOINTMENT*!

Panel 3: --AND WHICH, UNFORTUNATELY, ISN'T OVER *YET*, AS LORENA BOBBITT'S TRIAL *REKINDLES* THE MEDIA FRENZY...INCLUDING, ABSURDLY ENOUGH, *LIVE COVERAGE* ON *CNN*--

MR. BOBBITT, WOULD YOU DESCRIBE YOUR UNPLEASANT SEX LIFE IN *LURID DETAIL*?

WHY, I'D BE *HAPPY* TO!

NOW THIS IS WHAT I CALL *NEWS*!

Panel 4: --AND, OF COURSE, YET ANOTHER ROUND OF TIRESOME *SEVERED PENIS* JOKES ON LATE NIGHT TV...

--A NEW JOB AT *BENIHANA*!

--A SET OF *GINSU KNIVES*!

--A REAL *ENTITLEMENT* CUT!

--HAVING A *HALF-OFF SALE*!

ET CETERA!

ET CETERA!

SNICKER SNICKER SNICKER SNICKER SNICKER SNICKER CKER SNICKER SNICKE

How to Nominate a Censored Story

Some of the most interesting nominations Project Censored has received are from people who spot something in the back pages of their newspaper or in a small-circulation magazine they subscribe to and wonder why they haven't seen anything reported about it elsewhere. In the same way, you can help the public learn more about what is happening in its society by nominating stories that you feel should have received more coverage from the national news media. The story should be current and of national or international significance. It may have received no media attention at all, appeared in your local newspaper or some special interest trade magazine, or been the subject of a radio or television documentary which received little exposure or follow-up. Your nominations, input, and suggestions are important to the success of Project Censored and we appreciate them. To nominate a Censored story of the year, just send us a copy of the story, including the source and date. The annual deadline is October 15. Please send nominations to:

NOMINATION
PROJECT CENSORED
Sonoma State University
Rohnert Park, CA 94928

INDEX

About the Author

Dr. Carl Jensen is a professor of Communication Studies at Sonoma State University and Director of Project Censored, an internationally recognized media research project. Founded by Jensen in 1976, Project Censored is America's longest-running research project which annually explores news media censorship.

Jensen has been involved with the media for more than 40 years as a daily newspaper reporter, weekly newspaper publisher, public relations practitioner, advertising executive, and educator. He spent 15 years with Batten, Barton, Durstine, and Osborn, the international advertising agency, where he was an award-winning copywriter, account supervisor, and vice president.

Specializing in mass communications, Jensen received his B.A., M.A., and Ph.D. degrees in Sociology from the University of California, Santa Barbara, in 1971, 1972, and 1977, respectively.

Since 1973, he has teaching media, sociology, and journalism courses at Sonoma State University where he developed Sonoma State University's B.A. degree in Communication Studies and the University's Journalism Certificate Program.

Jensen founded the Lincoln Steffens Journalism Award for Investigative Reporting in Northern California in 1981. He also participated in the development of the Bay Area Censored awards program by the Media Alliance in San Francisco in 1989 and in the development of Project Censored Canada in 1993.

He has written and lectured extensively about press censorship, the First Amendment, and the mass media.

Jensen has been cited by the national Association for Education in

Journalism and Mass Communication for his "innovative approach to constructive media criticism and for providing a new model for media criticism." The Giraffe Project honored Jensen "for sticking his neck out for the common good" and for being a "role model for a caring society." The Media Alliance presented Jensen with the Media Alliance Meritorious Achievement Award in the "Unimpeachable Source" category. The Society of Professional Journalists in Los Angeles awarded him its 1990 Freedom of Information Award.

In 1992, Jensen was named the outstanding university professor of journalism in California by the California Newspaper Publishers Association and was awarded the 1992 Hugh M. Hefner First Amendment Award in education from the Playboy Foundation for his achievement in defending the First Amendment.

He has been a guest on many radio/television news and talk shows including a Bill Moyers PBS television documentary on Project Censored.

Jensen is married and has four children and three grandchildren. He, wife Sandra, and Danske, their great Great Dane, live in beautiful downtown Cotati, in Northern California.